A GATE OPENS

HERBERT VOLLMANN

A GATE OPENS

GRAIL FOUNDATION PRESS
GAMBIER, OHIO

This book contains the translation according to the sense of the original German text. In some cases the word-forms of the translation can only render the meaning and contents of the original approximately. Nevertheless the reader will come to a good understanding of it, if he strives to absorb the meaning of the contents inwardly.

Only authorized edition
Composite Volume, ISBN 3-87860-139-5
Licensed to Grail Foundation Press by
Verlag der Stiftung Gralsbotschaft ©2004

CONTENTS

Part I

The World, as it could be!

I.

II.

III.

Part II

Knowledge for the World of Tomorrow!

I.

II.

The Cosmic Turning-Point

Man and the Cosmic Turning-Point

Babylon, the Great City

The Reeling Earth

Ignorance does not Protect from Punishment!

Part III

What lies behind it . . . !

I.

II.

III.

Part IV

A Gate Opens!

I. Ways to Self-contemplation

II. Supra-earthly Happening

III. The Solution to Social Problems

IV. The Conflict between Light and Darkness

Appendix

FOREWORD

This book is intended to show how the building-blocks of the Knowledge of Creation, which the Work, *In the Light of Truth: The Grail Message* by Abd-ru-shin, gives to men, can be joined together like mosaic pieces, with the aim of a joyful spiritual experience, if in being put together the picture emerges complete.

May the essays worked out in this way stimulate a deeper reflection, above all about ourselves, without our falling at the same time into unhealthy pondering.

Then a gate may suddenly open that until now had remained closed, behind which emerges an ever brighter path that can lead unswervingly out of many oppressing errors, doubts and afflictions: Upwards to the Light!

For all human spirits who bear within them the firm volition for the good, there is only one way to the Light. Manifold are the human paths that lead there, whether they be marked by bitter suffering or filled with joyous longing.

But with serious seeking there will always come the day when all these paths converge on that path that leads into the Light of Truth, whether it be here on earth or in the beyond.

May the recognitions given in this volume be of help to seekers in finding and treading the path that leads upwards to God's Luminous Realms, and finally to Eternal Life!

Vomperberg, August 1983

Herbert Vollmann

Part I

THE WORLD, AS IT COULD BE!

The purpose of the various examples is to show how important is the new Knowledge of the Laws of Creation, and how these must be applied in earthly life in order to shape the world in which we live as it could be: a Kingdom of Peace and Joy!

In the application of the new Creation-Knowledge, may it be recognized how wonderful is the working in Creation, which arose through the Will of God.

1. THE LAW OF BALANCE

There is a Law that is decisive for the continuance of the entire Creation: The Law of the Necessary Balance between Giving and Taking.

Every happening in Creation is subject to this Law, whether it be the interaction between the forces of the celestial bodies or the sense of balance of the physical body. We follow it daily, though mostly unconsciously, when breathing in and breathing out. Or we endeavor to "get things to balance." On the other hand we come to grief when something "upsets our balance" in things big as well as small, for nonobservance of this Law causes obstruction and disturbance, and if it is persistently disregarded, even downfall and ruin. Let us think for a moment of the relation between work and rest. Unnecessary exaggeration in work is just as harmful as a comfortable life, a "retiring from work." Both bring disease and premature death. Only the right alternation between them has a balancing effect.

The constant balance between giving and taking makes for healthy movement, which alone brings upbuilding and maintenance, and invigorates and refreshes the spirit. Harmony and peace enter when giving and taking balance each other.

Giving ranks first here, for only in giving is taking implied; just as we must first give something through proper exhalation, in order to be able to receive the invigorating elements through the deep inhalation thus brought about.

Therefore Jesus also said: "It is more blessed to give than to receive" (Acts 20, 35). He who gives selflessly, whether of earthly or spiritual values, ultimately gives most to himself, because he may receive many times more than the good fruits arising from his good seeds!

Every act of giving must be balanced by a counter-value in some form. Even a person without means can thus bring about a balance by a kind look, heartfelt gratitude or some good advice.

The same meaning lies in Goethe's utterance: "What from your fathers' heritage is lent, earn it anew, to really possess it!" (Faust, Part 1). The act of earning expresses the exerting of oneself, the work that must first be given in order to receive and possess something.

As an illustration, the system of bookkeeping by double entry can also be quoted here, the purpose of which lies not in the double entry in debit and credit, but in the checking of the balance between output and return.

In his novel Wilhelm Meister's Apprenticeship, Goethe wrote about this type of bookkeeping: "What an advantage for the merchant is the system of bookkeeping by double entry; it is one of the sublimest inventions of human genius, and every good householder should introduce it into his establishment" (Book 1, Chapter 10).

Yet man could not invent it but only discover it, as a faint repetition of the Principle of Balance, which has been anchored in Creation from the very beginning.

Naturally this principle holds good equally for what takes place spiritually. The spirit of man also lives from the spiritual power that the Creator gives perpetually into His Creation for its maintenance and expansion. With this power he forms his intuitive perceptions, his thoughts and his deeds.

But the counter-value, which he owes to his Creator as a return for its use, is gratitude, joyful gratitude through the deed, that is through the right application of this power. Thus gratitude in the relationship between men is also an important balancing factor, if it is really heartfelt and not superficial.

Through the one-sided application of the spiritual power of Creation for what is base over thousands of years, the human spirit has lost the balance in every sphere of life. He has taken and taken from the rich gifts of Creation, and from what he has taken he has formed almost exclusively what is wrong and evil, and in so doing has forgotten the balancing factor of giving.

Is it then surprising to us when now the compensating justice of God redresses the balance? The happenings on the whole earth, which become more and more violent, certainly speak to us in plain language.

To maintain strictly and justly the constant balance between giving and taking in every sphere of earth life is a great future task for earthmen, who through a thorough knowledge of the Laws of Creation will then be in a position to do so.

Thus the Law of Balance between Giving and Taking will one day also form the basis for a true understanding between the peoples. That is the time when the peoples, standing *side-by-side*, respect, help and further each other in the recognition that every viable nation, every healthy race, possesses something that is absolutely essential for the completion of the whole, and which other nations and races do not have. These are the earthly and spiritual values that constitute the "wealth of the people."

To the spiritual values, for instance, belong the abilities, the gifts, the nature and strength of the connection with the Power of Creation, and its application; to the earthly values belong the capacity to work, the visible and invisible treasures of Nature, such as the forces of water, fire and air, the treasures of the earth, and also the beauty of the landscape.

All these values make an exchange *imperative*. Not without coming to grief can any people withhold the gifts and treasures particularly entrusted to them by the Creator from other peoples, who are in need of these for their own completion. For a people that does not continually pass on such values thereby cuts off the vitally necessary exchange. Yet the exchange is to be carried out in such a way that no people will take advantage of the other. Giving and taking must always counterbalance each other.

2. A SOUND MONETARY SYSTEM

Money has become such an important factor in men's commercial transactions that these can no longer be thought of without it.

All the greater are the reverses that result when a monetary system proves unsound. The consequences may assume catastrophic proportions, as they keep recurring when great devaluations (inflations) take place.

But it seems that the heavy material losses this causes ever again, the great psychic distress involved, the change in the conception of law and order, and the destruction of good faith, have hardly at all led to any reflection as to the cause of the error, which is still repeated even today.

It is no excuse when a war, a state of emergency or Providence is often given as reasons for all this distress. For man himself is to blame for every kind of misery. Yet in all probability it will hardly occur to anyone that man's failure might lie in an insufficient observance of the Laws of Nature or the Laws of Creation, which are also authoritative for human life on earth.

Only the heeding and recognizing of the lawfulness in Creation, and its application to earth life, bring about genuine progress, ensuring not only earthly benefit but also above all spiritual values.

One example of such lawfulness is the necessary balance between giving and taking, to which all processes in Creation are subject. It is self-evident that the financial and economic systems must also be based on this Law of Balance, so that a lasting sound balance can be achieved within them, all the more so since just here the symbol of this Law, the scales, reminds us of it.

This undoubtedly eliminates artificial measures. How little safe and natural these are has been demonstrated by past inflations, and is again demonstrated today by the complicated manipulations, as well as by the only temporarily effective pegging of the market, which are continually needed in order to support unsound currencies.

These do not put an end to the evil, which lies in the one-sidedness of a currency, where taking predominates and counter-values are not given in the right proportion. Nothing is more dangerous just here than one-sidedness, which always remains unnatural, and therefore cannot bring about anything viable.

Man must therefore find ways and means that correspond with the Laws of Creation and that are adapted to secure his financial system. The history of money, the ups and downs of the monetary systems during thousands of years, teach us that up till now this has not been achieved. Always the same road can be seen, which men must follow in all spheres of earth life when they place their pseudo-knowledge above the Creator's Will, Which manifests in the Laws of Creation: They lose their balance, and their works, which have arisen from this pseudo-knowledge, prove to be wrong.

This means that a secure monetary system can only be built up and maintained by inwardly secure human beings, whether leaders or citizens of a state. Everyone must contribute to this. The leadership of a state is also made up of individual human beings, each of whom must bear his personal responsibility according to the Laws of Creation.

But the inner security, that is the security of the soul, can only be attained by the human spirit's adjusting itself in all things to the Laws of Creation, to which the Laws of Nature also belong, and by completely translating into earth life the recognitions that it reaches when studying these Laws.

Thus man must above all adjust monetary matters and economic life to the Law of the Necessary Balance between Giving and Taking.

In this Law rests the long-sought firm basis upon which a sound monetary system can be built, as a secure foundation for the many-sided structure of the economic life of a people. The just balance thus made possible will permit confidence, contentment and harmony to develop steadily and come to fruition.

Such a thorough change can certainly not be carried out overnight, but it is worth thinking about, so that at the given time, after all the bitter experiences, a lasting earthly foundation can this time be laid for the spiritual ascent of mankind.

3. THE SECRET OF ATOMIC (NUCLEAR) ENERGY

It has been reserved to our time to penetrate the secret of the structure of atoms and atomic nuclei, and to register the unifying energy of the elementary particles of atomic nuclei-even to liberate this energy to a certain degree. This unifying energy that keeps protons and neutrons together within the atomic nucleus is termed atomic (nuclear) energy; and its existence is explained by the extremely powerful forces operating between the nuclear particles over very short distances (some ten billionths of a centimeter).

So much for the scientific explanation! The nature of these powers of attraction has not so far been recognized, and despite the abundant partial knowledge acquired, the question has remained unanswered: What is atomic (nuclear) energy, and where does the inconceivably great and mighty force concealed in matter come from? The power as such is known but its origin and nature remain a secret that cannot be solved nor explained in the earthly realm.

If we nevertheless attempt to find an answer to the question, an objective can be reached only by dealing with the connections whose origin and beginning must be sought in spiritual heights immeasurably far above the World of Matter. This has nothing to do with floating about in higher regions. On the contrary, if we wish to stand firmly as alert human spirits on the sod of reality, and if we strive to explore and to understand our nearest earthly environment, this can be done only with the knowledge of the supra-terrestrial connections in Creation.

This applies particularly to the useful research and investigation of science, which despite its untiring struggle for ultimate understanding, is again and again forced to a standstill when it trusts and relies solely on the instrument intended for the earth, namely the intellect, and has not the courage and confidence to penetrate into the extrasensory sphere of the other world-but with the spirit, which by virtue of its higher origin is directly in a position to do this. We need not on that account fear that this knowledge of the connections would alienate us from God; on the contrary, it brings us ever closer to His immutable Will as evidenced in the entire Creation, and thus also closer to humility, which we so much need before we can begin to sense His great Goodness and Grace.

In considering the connections relating to atomic nuclear power, we must fundamentally realize that between the Spiritual part of Creation, to which Paradise, man's spiritual home, belongs, and the Sphere of the Divine Kingdom, lies the Primordial Spiritual part of Creation, which comprises seven basic steps or spheres, in the same way as there are also steps or spheres in the Spiritual part of Creation. These spheres of the Spiritual, as of the Primordial Spiritual parts of Creation, are equivalent to the various "heavens." The common expression, "To be in the seventh heaven," still expresses the almost forgotten knowledge that there is not one but several heavens. The Son of God, Jesus, had to traverse all these Primordial Spiritual and Spiritual spheres on His way down to the earth, and once more on His ascension, on His return to God the Father. The Bible expresses this in the words: "He that descended is the same also that ascended up far above all heavens" (Ephesians 4, 10) and: ". . . that is passed into the heavens" (Hebrews 4, 14).

In the Primordial Spiritual part of Creation there are power centers of a spiritual nature, which are like gigantic magnets of inconceivable size, radiating downwards. Despite their quality of attraction, their magnetic power also sends forth radiations, which likewise have a magnetically attracting effect. As a secondary effect of the specific activity of these centers, spiritual currents develop that make their way downwards as a result of the Law of Gravitation into the other, lower-lying parts of Creation. In this process these currents split into innumerable tiny spirit-motes or spirit-particles. These particles, however, are of a different kind or gradation, and are also weaker in their power of attraction than the human-spiritual, for "spirit" has many gradations. Finally, these spirit-particles flow from the beyond into the earthly, the Gross Material World, as the last offshoot of Creation. Only here in the World of Gross Matter do they cause and bring about the formation of atoms, of which there are over one hundred kinds pertaining to the structure of the whole of earthly substance.

The animistic powers of Nature, which are subordinate to the spiritual power, help in this formation of atoms by fashioning "individual parts" such as protons and electrons, which are then united and held together by the magnetically operating spirit-particles. Nuclei then develop, around which electrons revolve, as do the planets around the sun.

In structure and behavior the atomic system manifests the same lawful regularity as the solar system. It is immaterial whether such processes as attraction, repulsion and the maintenance of the balance of forces occur on a large or on a small scale, visibly or invisibly. The lawfulness is always the same for similar processes throughout the entire Creation. Only the outer form of the effect is different, being dependent upon the environment, that is to say, on the species of Creation in which they operate.

Therefore matter is by no means a dead rigid mass, but is in unceasing motion, invisible to us, because its component parts, the elementary particles, move continuously. And the carriers of this power that set everything in motion and maintain everything in motion are the inconceivably tiny and yet in terms of energy so gigantic spirit-particles, which are so to speak "incarnated" in matter, and become free again upon its decay.

But what form do they take upon leaving matter? This can best be observed in the radioactive elements, which by nature decay gradually. In this process there above all appear three types of rays, which for example become free in the decomposition of radium. The Alpha rays or Alpha particles have been identified as helium ions, and the Beta rays are electrons, which are known as the carriers of electric power. But what are the Gamma rays? They differ particularly from the other two types of radiation in that they are electromagnetic waves of great velocity and with a marked power of penetration. Owing to their extremely fine substance, which is lighter by far than that of the Alpha and Beta rays, the Gamma rays penetrate even lead in relatively thick layers. In their quality the Gamma rays resemble the nature of the spiritual, and the conclusion is suggested that Gamma rays are nothing more than spirit-particles with an outer covering of very delicate matter!

Thus wherever we are permitted to gain deeper insight into the weaving of Creation, completely new connections and astonishing recognitions are disclosed to us, of which until now we have suspected or known but the smallest part.

One of these important recognitions is the fact that the mysterious energy in the atomic nucleus, the unifying agent or "atomic glue," which holds together the atomic structure, is spiritual living power! Spiritual power, which comes down to us on earth from remote far-off distances, from the Primordial Spiritual part of Creation, in the form of tiny, delicately covered spirit-particles, finally streaming uninterruptedly from the beyond into this world.

In this connection it must be noted that it is wrong to assert that the spiritual power, which with all its gradations operates in Creation, is God Himself, as for instance in the case of Pantheism, which states that God is *present* everywhere in Creation, in every flower, in every tree, etc. God is *outside* Creation. With the words, "Let there be Light," He sent only His *radiation* into the Universe that was void of Light. The entire Creation has come into being from the spiritual, creative power contained in this radiation, and the same power grants Creation continued existence and development.

An artist who has created a work does not merge with his work either; he stands *beside* his work. The relation between God and His Work, Creation, is exactly the same.

One of the many gradations of the spiritual, living power that streams through Creation is the tiny spirit-particles in the atomic nuclei.

Hence we now know that it is spiritual power that, to quote Goethe in Faust, "is the inmost force, which binds the world."

By "World" are meant the transient Worlds of Fine and Gross Matter lying below the Eternal Paradise, which would have to remain inactive in their various strata, if they were not warmed and animated by the spiritual power, in association with the elemental powers of Nature.

The well-known physicist Sir Isaac Newton (1643-1727) came fairly close to the fact of the existence of a spiritual power in matter when he wrote in his *Mathematical Principles of Natural Philosophy* (Section 5) of the "spiritual substance," which "penetrates all solid bodies and is contained in them!" And Jakob Lorber wrote in 1847 in his work *Earth and Moon*: "It has been all too often demonstrated to you that spiritual substance is always contained within the material, and that actual, visible matter is in itself basically nothing but imprisoned, enchained and fixed spiritual substance . . . ."

Man most vilely abuses this spiritual power when he makes improper use of atomic power! He thus demonstrates unmistakably that he does not fulfill the condition of spiritual maturity required for the safe and beneficial use of such enormous energy. He himself is to blame for this. His intellect, the product of his transient earthly brain, and consequently fully versed in the field of technology, has indeed made great strides in it, but this *earthly-technological* "flight" lacks the same *spiritual* flight that must control and direct, and which in accordance with the Laws of Creation, must naturally *lead the way*. It is this existing disproportion between the over-development of technology, which can gain a foothold only in the material world, and the under-development of the spirit, which alone is able to rise above the earthly, that makes the present situation so critical. Hence the great danger of playing with fire — which cannot yet be assessed in its entirety.

Therefore we have only one possibility: to make a fundamental change in our attitude towards matter, with the inevitable result that the human spirit, of its own accord, of its own volition, places itself above all matter, considering it and making use of it as it is meant to be — a God-given *instrument* for the period of his earthly sojourn, to be used only constructively. On the other hand, if the human spirit continues to bind itself to matter, and even misuses it, grief will inescapably follow, if not even ruin and annihilation. This is particularly true as regards the liberation and release of the spiritual energy bound in matter.

The question is really whether in order to obtain such enormous energies other procedures than nuclear fission cannot be found, which are easier and above all not dangerous.

It could be considered, for instance, whether it would not be easier and simpler to use the energy streaming from the Universe onto the earth before it has taken on the covering of coarse earthly matter. In this condition only the finer material coverings around the spirit-particle are present, which may offer less resistance to the liberation and use of the energy.

Be that as it may, man must always keep in mind that in his hands this liberated spiritual energy can have a constructive, furthering and beneficial effect only when from the knowledge of the Truth, as a mature human spirit, he learns to control and apply it. And to control means: pure humility before God!

4. SOME THOUGHTS ON THE PENAL LAW

"Eye for Eye, Tooth for Tooth"

Three basic Laws of Creation are especially important for the penal law: the Law of Gravitation, the Law of the Power of Attraction of Homogeneous Species, and the Law of Reciprocal Action. Like all the Laws of Creation, these three Laws are also uniform in all the visible and invisible parts or spheres of Creation. What is different in the various spheres of Creation is only the form of their effect.

We see the effect of the *Law of Gravitation* in the earthly sphere when, for example, we put a piece of iron and a piece of cork in water. The iron sinks immediately owing to its heaviness, the cork remains on the surface. If we press the cork to the bottom of the water and let go, it rises. The process in the world invisible to us is exactly the same when, for instance, man has laid aside his physical body. If we have made it heavy through base propensities, the ethereal body, which is separated from the physical body, sinks to that place in the beyond that is of the same heaviness. There it will also find its homogeneous species, for like heaviness implies like species. Or if through striving for higher and purer things we have made it lighter, the ethereal body floats upwards like a cork into more luminous realms.

The *Law of the Attraction of Homogeneous Species* is expressed very much to the point with the popular saying, "Birds of a feather flock together." We experience it every day when people of a like mind come together for some purpose, in the same way as it also operates with associations on a large scale, such as castes, social classes and political parties. But under its influence thoughts of a homogeneous nature also unite and thus become stronger.

After all, the iron and the cork, like all matter, also consist in each case of the same individual tiny particles (molecules), which have united through the effect of the Law of the Attraction of Similar Species.

The *Law of Reciprocal Action* operating in Creation exactly corresponds with the Biblical words, "Whatsoever a man soweth, that shall he also reap" (Gal. 6, 7). This applies not only to the seed we put into the earth. Our intuitive perceptions, thoughts and deeds are also seed, whose harvest will in fact one day have arrived for us as with the earthly harvest, many times over and above the seed. They are the works that follow us at death, and which we take over into the beyond.

We stand always amid the multiple harvests of our good and bad seeds, just in the final effect of the Law of Reciprocal Action. With this Law the effect changes. First it goes out into Creation from man, and then it changes into an effect returning to him.

If through an intentional evil volition, man has committed a wrong and thereby burdened himself with some guilt, he must one day count on an increased evil reciprocal action. Increased, because on its way the evil volition has been strengthened through the attraction of homogeneous species. This becoming stronger through uniting is expressed in the Biblical words, "They have sown wind, and they shall reap the whirlwind" (Hosea 8, 7). If the perpetrator has come to realize his wrong, the reciprocal action will bring him redemption, which is the severance from the evil, as a result of which his guilt has been atoned. Otherwise the reciprocal action can give rise to further evildoing. Besides there is also the possibility to redeem some guilt in advance, if man has seriously turned to the good, even before the reciprocal action sets in. The dark fate streaming back is then so weakened by the human being's surroundings having become lighter, that it is merely released symbolically in the earthly sphere. This premature redemption of guilt is one of God's mercies, which is interwoven with His Laws.

Thus the three basic Laws of Creation bring about reward as well as punishment for the human being, and now we shall also understand the real purport of the words of the Old Testament, "To me belongeth vengeance, and recompense" (Deut. 32, 35) and "Eye for eye, tooth for tooth" (Deut. 19, 21), whose deeper meaning has so far never been understood.

They are an expression of Divine justice. "Vengeance" and "recompense" are nothing but the reciprocal effect of a man's good or evil deeds, which take place strictly and justly according to the Laws of Creation, "Eye for eye, and tooth for tooth." In the words "Eye for eye, tooth for tooth," the same kind of effect and reciprocal effect of seed and harvest is expressed, hence kind for kind or suffering for suffering, and joy for joy. Just as always wheat grows only from the grain of wheat, so will an evil volition likewise bring only evil and a good volition only good.

Therefore these Biblical words are to be understood not in the earthly sense but in the spiritual sense. Man must leave "vengeance" and "recompense" to the Laws of God. He must not carry them out himself, perhaps out of personal revenge, by knocking out the evildoer's eye when the latter has done the same to him. For it is explicitly stated:

"Vengeance is *mine, I* will repay!" And this "vengeance" and "repayment" is absolutely just down to the very last detail, more just than man could ever be.

And it is in this way that Paul's words to the Romans must also be understood: "Dearly beloved, avenge not yourselves, but rather give place unto the wrath (the reciprocal action) of God; for it is written, 'Vengeance is mine, I will repay, saith the Lord!'" (Romans 12, 19).

What the earthly punishment, that is to say the punishment administered through men, should be like will be explained in a later section.

Personal Responsibility

But what releases the effect of these Laws of Creation, so significant for man? What is it that sets them in motion like an invisible lever? It is the activity of the spirit, the actual human being, whose home is in the Spiritual Realm, in "Paradise." This activity calls forth something that is known to everyone: the intuitive perception!

But to carry out his spiritual activity aright man needs in addition something very essential to enable him to decide what he wants to do: the free will!

The free will! A much-discussed concept! And how can it be explained?

To the spirit of man belongs, as a part of his spiritual nature, the ability to attract. This means that he would attract all that exists, if he had not been endowed as another part of his nature with a counter-balance, namely the free will to make decisions. Therefore he can attract only what he really wants. In this ability to make decisions lies at the same time his responsibility, no matter how he exercises the free decision, whether in thoughts, actions, choice, agreement or obedience. Yet only the decision is free, the consequences of the decision are no longer so! Man is unconditionally subject to them. They strike him through the Law of Reciprocal Action (the Law of Sowing and Reaping) according to the nature of his decisions.

Hence a man, who by earthly law is "not accountable" for a punishable offense has at some time or other, in a former life or in his present life, voluntarily laid the foundation for this state of "not being accountable," and therefore before the Laws of Creation he is also answerable for the consequences resulting from the free decision that has brought about a condition of "not being accountable."

To illustrate this, let us take the much-discussed subject of "alcohol and crime." A normally constituted human being has the free decision whether to become intoxicated.

If he does so, he is from the spiritual point of view also subject to the consequences of this decision, all the more so, if under the influence of alcohol he harms his fellowman. It is just the same as with the stone in one's hand. The decision to throw the stone is free. If it is thrown, the consequences of any material or physical damage must be accounted for by whoever has done it.

Infliction of Punishment

Furthermore let us now try to find out how a punishment on earth can be so adapted to the Laws of Creation that it will also be spiritually effective, and lead to the real atonement of some guilt. For guilt is not disposed of by serving a sentence laid down in earthly laws, which are established on a purely intellectual basis!

If in order to solve this question we apply *Creation's Law of the Attraction of Homogeneous Species*, we can obtain a usable basis. Though we stand constantly in the effect of this Law, we still have not as yet recognized the vast possibilities offered by its conscious application everywhere in earth life. In view of today's conditions these lie in the future.

The application of the Law of Homogeneous Species in the infliction of punishment necessitates firstly the classifying of all prisoners into larger homogeneous groups, and accommodating them in different places and in strict seclusion from the outer world, separating women from men. Hard and useful work and consistent just treatment everywhere are important for all. The classification can be made according to punishable offenses of a light nature, crimes committed on impulse, crimes perpetrated through propensity, etc. Homogeneous species should again be separated within these groups, beginning with those who remain obstinate and not open to improvement, right up to those who are willing to change inwardly for the good.

The motive for evil actions lies in men's faults and weaknesses. Above all it is his propensity from which man finds it most difficult to sever himself, and which is often the mainspring for his criminal acts. There are many propensities, such as covetousness and avarice, the urge to steal, to commit arson, to murder, careless negligence, sordid sensuality and fraud. For this reason special attention is to be given to those who commit crimes through propensity.

In cases where solitary confinement is not absolutely necessary, living together within the individual groups should be tried. Apart from the outer seclusion, this also contains a punishment of great educational value. For when people must be compulsorily together for a time, many of them will in one way or another experience their own wrong behavior through others, even if only the personal radiation can be mutually felt. This may produce a rising disgust or shame at one's own bad actions, and the desire to get away from the present place of punishment to a better one. If in addition there arises in some the volition unselfishly to help along others who are not yet so far advanced in the recognition of their evil conduct, then this may bring many a person more quickly to the longed-for goal of atonement.

The most important help, however, lies in *psycho-therapeutic care*. It is the task of those called for it gradually to lead the prisoners, according to their inner readiness, to the recognition of their guilt. This means occupying oneself painstakingly with the problems of life, so as to be able to explain to those who have been sentenced how some guilt is incurred, and how by observing the Laws of the Creator it can be redeemed; why man is on earth and what his task is in Creation, how much he obstructs his path upwards through the propensity for base things, and through not observing the Laws and Commandments of God.

In other words, knowledge of life must be offered, giving the condemned ones psychic support, and allowing the way to a complete inner change for the good to be recognized and found!

These are then consciously applied, valuable helps in making use of the knowledge of Creation, which really correspond with the principle that an earthly punishment should not retaliate in the same way but should give help! Through himself, through his cooperation and through extensive psychic care the guilty person is helped to a real experience, which may result in spiritual ascent for him even here on earth. The effect of these helps is more profound and speedy than is possible in a community confined together indiscriminately. At the same time the unwilling and the willing prisoners are thus also separated from each other, so that those who are willing cannot be disturbed or hampered in any way by others.

Infliction of punishment from the above points of view would correspond with the demand of advanced modern psychology that the punishment should awaken in the culprit the wish for atonement, and that in the infliction of punishment the opportunity should be given for psychotherapeutic counseling.

Only in a very few cases is deprivation of freedom alone enough as a stimulus towards real atonement. Something else must be added, which will touch the core of man, his spirit, and allow the evil that has led to the deed to be recognized. This is only guaranteed with individual types of punishment, where the emphasis of the punishment is on the person of the wrongdoer, as opposed to the principle of guilt for the deed, on which at present the penal law is often based; by which mainly the deed as such and the conduct of the wrongdoer are dealt with, thus rather the outward features. What is decisive, however, is the personal guilt (the guilt of the wrongdoer), because God has endowed man with personal responsibility.

But there is something else besides, something very important, namely the *infliction of punishment without a time limit!* In what takes place spiritually, the time for atonement cannot be determined in advance. Accordingly the judge must inflict punishments without a time limit, which will be effective until true atonement, equivalent to a complete inner change for the good, offers sufficient guarantee that such people will no longer disturb the peace and obstruct a healthy ascent. A further great aid to bestirring themselves spiritually would be given to many convicted persons through the mere fact that it is left to themselves to determine the time of their segregation.

As regards the real improvement of the prisoner, psychologists in the United States of America expect very much from imprisonment without time limit, and in some prisons such a progressive method of punishment is already practiced. In these cases the negative and positive qualities of the wrongdoer are first ascertained through a personality test; following this an attempt is made to bring about an improvement by educational, psychological and professional methods. Here also the view is held that prisoners who are not willing to change should remain in custody for the protection of the public.

It is generally the case today that a guilt according to the Laws of God may have been recognized long since, truly atoned for and thus redeemed, when according to earthly law the wrongdoer must still spend many years behind bars. On the other hand, how often is some wrongdoer released after serving the prescribed period of his sentence — even earlier, if his conduct has been good — without showing the least signs of an inward improvement, to say nothing of atonement!

But he who is released from a detention center of homogeneous species has truly redeemed his guilt. A truly redeemed guilt is forgiven and effaced in the spiritual and in the earthly sense, as if it had never been. Hence also the earthly conception of justice must no longer treat such a purified human being as one "previously convicted." He must be readmitted unconditionally to human society; contrary to the present time, when the outlawing by society often affects him far worse than the actual punishment.

From the above explanations there also follows automatically the solution to the problem of limitation. A punishable offense can naturally only "lapse," which means that it can no longer be punished on earth, if it is spiritually atoned. Here too the rigid earthly letter of the law does not agree with the actual happening. Therefore when an evildoer is found out only many years later, he should be examined as to his real atonement. If this has taken place he will be exempt from punishment. If it has not, he will remain in custody until he has changed for the better.

It must naturally not be overlooked that the realization of these progressive recognitions will only be possible when the necessary conditions for it are provided, which lie primarily within men themselves.

The Judge

The interpretation of earthly law, which is inherent in the Laws of Creation, demands great responsibility and spiritual maturity of the judge and all the parties concerned.
For the judge, too, a sentence is a free decision, for which both in the spiritual sense and in the earthly sense he is wholly responsible to the Laws of Creation. No earthly law can absolve him of the responsibility or protect him from any wrong judgment.

Now what help has the judge in his highly responsible task? The simplest help would probably be the one suggested years ago in the heading of a newspaper article: "Judges in Juvenile courts should be clairvoyants!" The subject dealt with was a juvenile court conference held in Germany, at which experts in jurisdiction demanded a personality test for every juvenile person in order to base a sentence on that. An absolutely justified demand, which however is also applicable equally to adults. The heading was probably to indicate that it would be much the simplest thing, if the judge, apart from any advice and tests, could himself "see through" those under judgment.

It is better, however, if the judge is not clairvoyant, because it would impede him in his work. But it is nevertheless possible for him to find the right verdict through the intuitive perception of his spirit!

Spirit must not be confused with intellect, which latter, like the thoughts, is produced by the activity of the frontal brain, and is intended to serve only as an instrument to facilitate life on earth, under the direction of the intuitive perception. The comprehending-capacity of the intellect only suffices for what is earthly; on the other hand the comprehending-capacity for what is beyond the earth lies with the intuitive perception.

The latter again must not be confused with feeling, which is dependent on physical instincts and the intellect.

It is already evident, which is the more valuable, the intuitive perception or the intellect, from the fact that after physical death the spirit retains its intuitive faculty, whereas the intellect perishes together with the physical body!

In our language the origin of thoughts and of intuitive perception is clearly distinguished. Thoughts are spoken of in connection with the head, which stands for "brain." For example: "There is no room in his head for any other thought."

The intuitive perception, on the other hand, is associated with the heart. By "heart" was originally meant the solar plexus. It is the place where the spirit within the soul has an effective connection with the physical body.

Through this close connection, any stirring of the spirit is communicated via the soul and solar plexus to the heart, so that very often there is a feeling that these stirrings are called forth in the heart itself, whereas in reality they are only the radiations of an experience of the spirit.

Hence expressions such as "To take heart," "To be sick at heart," "It goes to his heart," refer to the intuitive perceptions of the spirit.

And it is also the intuitive perception, the "inner voice," which is a part of the conscience, whose other part consists of the silent working of kind helpers in the beyond, thus of human spirits who are still near the earth, and who can therefore through his intuitive perception give effective advice and warning to the earthman who is open for it.

And so the first impression, that is to say, the first intuitive perception, is always right. It weighs with the speed of lightning, and instantly recognizes what is the nature of the other person. But care must always be taken to ensure that the stirrings of the spirit, thus of the intuitive perceptions, are not afterwards pushed aside by the intellect, and that the intellect does not gain the upper hand. This danger unfortunately exists through the deliberate over-development of the frontal intellectual brain (the cerebrum) for thousands of years, while the back brain (the cerebellum), as the spiritually receiving part, has been too much neglected. Therefore the intuitive perception must always be leading and the intellect carrying out.

Certainly the judge may still draw on other assistance to confirm or supplement his findings and judgments, which assistance may also include consultation with a clairvoyant who can be taken seriously.

But in the end it is the intuitive perception that must always remain authoritative and decisive. For the judge it is the best basis for the ability to form individual and fair judgments. The more alive the intuitive ability becomes, and the more vigorously it is developed, the less likelihood there is of errors. With such an intuitive perception, and equipped with the knowledge about the connections in Creation, the judge is truly a servant of the Divine Laws!

Conclusion

We can see from these problems how seriously we must regard the fact that the Laws of Creation are effective not only in the visible world, but also in the world that is invisible to us. The two worlds are closely connected with each other and form a complete whole, with a uniform system of Laws. The invisible world, then, is the primary factor, that which has existed first, only after which the visible world has developed.

Likewise earthman is also a complete whole, consisting of his physical body and, with the spirit as the core, of the finer invisible coverings needed for his development. When he lays aside his physical cloak, together with the so-called astral cloak, his spirit has still only the finer coverings, and in this state it is called "soul." Now if there were two different systems of laws for the visible and the invisible world, thus for the physical body and the soul, earthman could not exist.

All this means that the transcendental, the super-sensory, must quite naturally be included as an important factor in serious investigation, in order to arrive at a real solution. With a way of contemplation that is limited to this world alone, we must already come to a halt at physical death. Just the most important fact, namely what comes afterwards, is thus not taken into account.

Hence, bearing in mind the connections between this world and the beyond, there definitely are possibilities of adapting earthly justice to the Laws that apply in Creation. As already emphasized, however, the human and material conditions for this must first be brought about.

Therefore may these explanations in the present great conflict with man's hither-to-existing wrong thoughts and actions point the way towards a natural justice in the future, which will follow as closely as possible the Laws of Creation, to which the Laws of Nature also belong. Actually in so doing we only follow the Will of God, Which manifests in His Laws.

Bearing this in mind, an attempt has been made to show by a few examples how the earthly laws can be adapted to the Laws of Creation, especially with regard to the duration of punishment and its infliction.

With such a foundation for law there can no longer be either gaps or flaws, still less so when it also embraces the Ten Commandments of God, which will always be applicable as long as there are human beings on earth. If interpreted aright they are an invaluable pointer. But does present-day humanity really know what the correct interpretation of these Commandments means for them? Do they realize, for instance, that to the "other gods" in the First Commandment there may also belong a propensity to which man becomes enslaved, and which he puts foremost in his life, whether it is money, power or a woman; do they realize that in the Fifth Commandment not only physical killing is meant, but also a suppressing, which strikes the soul by preventing the development of gifts, smothering some hope or betraying another's trust? Concerning the Seventh Commandment, do they reflect that part of a man's property is also his reputation, which may, for instance, be stolen by undermining the confidence that a person enjoys; and with regard to the Tenth Commandment, have they ever become aware why man has no cause to desire anything of his neighbor's possessions, since everyone is born into the conditions, which of his own free will he has previously made for himself, as a result of what he has sown in his various earth lives?

God's Love has given men the Commandments to observe and obey, so that they may follow the way to the Luminous Kingdom of Eternal Life. This same Love is also anchored in the eternal and unchangeable Laws that operate in Creation. Eventually men must also interweave it with the earthly laws and with all earthly life in general. But it is necessary first to gain understanding of the Divine Love, because it is different from the present soft and all-forgiving human love.

Divine Love, the greater part of which is severity, only wills what is of benefit to man, what furthers him spiritually, and not what he likes and what pleases him.

During the great spiritual transformation in which we find ourselves, true Love will again arise, together with true Justice. "For Love cannot be separated from Justice; they are one!" (Abd-ru-shin)

5. THE ORIGIN OF MAN AND THE HUMAN RACES

If we wish to occupy ourselves with the human races we must not in a one-sided way merely think of the features of the physical body, but must also consider the non-material core of this body, the spirit, through which the physical cloak is first animated.

This calls for a widening of our contemplation to include the spiritual. Only through this shall we at the same time also obtain a general view of the connections between the necessary developments.

The origin of man lies far above time and space of the Worlds of Matter — it lies in the Spiritual Realm. This is the true home of the human spiritual.

Inconceivably long ago the human spirit as an unconscious spirit germ was, "expelled" from this Realm, from Paradise. This was no punishment for it, but one of the great mercies of the Creator, Who permitted fulfillment of the urge for development and becoming conscious, which is inherent in every unconscious spirit germ.

The development of an unconscious spirit germ, however, cannot take place in the Spiritual Realm, but only in the Worlds of Matter lying below it, to which the gross matter of our earth also belongs. Only the much coarser influences and impressions of this world can enable an unconscious spirit germ to come to an awakening and finally to become conscious of itself. Therefore spirit germs had to incarnate in physical bodies in order to receive the necessary instrument for their maturing in the World of Gross Matter.

But how did the spirit germ of man come to an instrument of flesh and blood, when as yet there were no *human* mothers on earth with whom it could have incarnated?

This process took place once only, and was not repeated; it came about in accordance with the Laws of Creation: Male and female spirit germs incarnated in the developing bodies of the then most highly evolved animals, thus using them as a bridge to earth life.

This species of animals, which resembled the present anthropoid apes, had concluded its development, and before becoming extinct it supplied the spirit germs with the physical body required for the transition. Only these may be described as "primeval human beings" of the earth. With these the human race began to exist on earth, and under the influence of the human-spiritual a great epoch of further development opened up, also for all that is gross material, for which otherwise, with the perfecting of the most noble species of animals, there would have been stand-still.

We have an illustration in the Bible of this decisive event: "And the Lord God formed man of the dust of the ground, and breathed into his nostrils the breath of life; and man became a living soul" (Genesis 2, 7).

The "making" or "forming" of the dust expresses the long chain of evolution of life in the material sphere, from the first cell right up to the most highly evolved animal, in which as "the breath of life" the spirit germ then incarnated.

Under varied impressions and experiences the spirit germs now existing on earth grew to maturity, thereby ennobling the animal body to the present form of the human body; and separated into races, which were endowed by nature with different physical features and colors, exactly according to the requirements of the region and the part of the earth to which they belonged.

By the hitherto discovered skeletons, implements, utensils, cave paintings, engravings, etc., from various periods of evolution, we can today clearly follow the change from animal to human behavior, and especially also the advancing ennoblement of the appropriated animal body by the human spirit. These periods of evolution span millions of years.

Thus came to pass the coming into existence of man, which until now has been an enigma. An enigma because in contemplating and reflecting on the earth life of men the knowledge of incarnation is not considered. For this reason no explanations, however cleverly thought out, reach any solution, because in the end incarnation, as an important link in the chain of deductions, is missing. It is the entrance of the soul, thus of the spirit with its various protective coverings, into the growing child's body about half way through pregnancy. This process is still the same today, and at that time it also formed the bridge to the earth for the first spirit germs, only these were noble animals, which belonged to the transition that was most important for the development of Creation.

Therefore it is quite right to say that the physical body of man derives from the animal, but not its animating content: the spirit. This distinction is clearly evident in the blood composition, which changed with the change of the content in the animal body. After this change the *spirit* is responsible for the forming of the blood, because it needs the blood as a bridge to its activity on earth. Previously the animal soul, which derives from the entirely different species of Creation of the animistic, determined the composition of the blood. Today we know that animal and human blood are fundamentally different.

From these connections and developments it follows that the cause of all these happenings is not arbitrary action, but a wise ordering in Creation, which works consistently and logically according to the Will of the Creator.

All the more is it therefore man's duty to become precisely acquainted with the Divine Order and to observe it.

But this he can only do when he is on indigenous ground, that is to say firmly rooted in the soil allotted to him by the Creator, when he seeks in everything to adapt himself to its inherent nature, as well as to the radiations of the stars and the earth. Only through being truly connected with their native soil can races, and the peoples that form from them, grow strong and advance in their development. Only thus is a healthy foundation provided for the upliftment of their particular culture.

And it is on such soil that genuine womanhood can blossom forth in purity. For in fact it is woman who is mainly responsible for her descendants, and who very often holds in her hand the destiny of entire races and peoples.

Yet it is not only the indigenous element that must be considered, but also the Law of Development, which implies progression in gradual stages; particularly when it is a question of uplifting and furthering races and peoples who have remained behind in their spiritual development, or who because of their spiritual indolence have retrogressed once more to a lower stage. Accordingly, an up building for the blessing of the peoples concerned can only take place from that stage, which has been fully experienced and grasped. The omitting of stages avenges itself bitterly and obstructs all progress. We experience this best in the upbringing and education of our children.

It is no different therefore with the lower races. The primitive belief in which they live and work is fully justified on their stage of existence, and must be taken into consideration and confirmed by educators. They must not suddenly be deprived of their belief and offered some ready-made religion in its place.

At a press conference many years ago Mrs. Emmy Bernatzik, wife of the late naturalist Dr. Hugo A. Bernatzik, made some interesting statements on this subject.

She pointed out, "that the primitive races should be divided into two groups, namely those loyal to their tribe who live in their villages according to old customs, and those already uprooted, who are engaged as workers and employees in European firms. The latter are exposed to the greatest harm that is caused by civilization. When European forms of society are forced upon them, when these people suddenly lose the belief in their gods, it leads to the moral collapse of primitive peoples, who have developed under totally different conditions. — What use is it when we teach the primitive peoples to read and write, when they study in Europe and wear European clothes, if on returning to their homeland they are not allowed for racial reasons to enter any hotel. — We have certainly taught the primitive peoples the tricks of civilization, but we have not imparted to them the spirit of it. Well, the white people are bad teachers".

So much for the statements made by Mrs. Bernatzik, who with her husband has over decades visited all kinds of primitive peoples.

Therefore the up building must begin with the belief of these peoples, with their characteristic habits and customs, in order to lead them stage-by-stage to an ever higher recognition, and finally to the highest, to the true recognition of God.

This recognition, which contains all part-recognitions, is the highest goal for all men, no matter to what race they belong. He who experiences this recognition himself will also acknowledge the Will of God, Which He has placed in His Laws, whether we call them Cosmic Laws, Laws of Nature or Laws of Creation. Such a person will also possess the necessary spiritual maturity to realize that the many-sided racial problems of the present time can only be solved justly and in a manner worthy of human beings by applying the incorruptible Laws of Creation.

Especially in the racial field, many errors have been committed at almost all times, and therefore many wrongs must be put right. But no fresh errors must be added to the old ones through biased and unjust treatment.

Therefore let us draw from the working of the Laws of Creation the corresponding practical application for our earth life:

The races are the expression of the Holy Will of the Creator. Hence they must be preserved in their individual kinds, and they must keep their indigenous character. The very variety of the human races and their peoples is like a great spring that dispenses continuous refreshment and invigoration.

For each race, each people, possesses intrinsic values that are peculiarly its own. Only through the mutual complementing of these values, whether spiritual abilities or the nature and strength of the connection with animistic and spiritual-radiation forces of Creation, can a complete whole (integration) come into being.

On the other hand the desire to reduce everything to the same level brings about standstill and retrogression. Therefore the process of amalgamating mankind on earth, which certain authorities today aspire to with the aim of establishing a far-reaching understanding through the intermingling of the various races, is wrong in the sense of the Laws of Creation.

Men of the individual races should become acquainted with each other, associate socially, exchange their spiritual and earthly values, as well as help and further one another. But this does not need the intermingling of alien races through physical procreation!

On the other hand, it is absolutely essential for men to create a sound foundation for mutual understanding and cooperation, and in this connection to become clear that the spiritual core of every human being on earth, no matter what the color of his skin, has the same origin: the Spiritual Realm or Paradise lying far above the material Creation, which all spirit germs leave in an unconscious state, with the aim of returning there as human spirits, who have become conscious of themselves and personal.

This is the great new recognition, that every human being has already been in Paradise before birth, but as an unconscious spirit germ, and that by returning to his spiritual home he completes the cycle that he has begun there.

Thus all earthmen are of the same spiritual origin. The only difference between them is to be sought in the spiritual development and maturity, which lies with each human spirit personally on account of its free will.

Only when looked at in this way does one arrive at the right "standpoint" for harmonious cooperation between all the races and peoples: They should not stand above and below one another, but *side-by-side*.

If men would only reflect deeply on this, prejudices, contempt, scorn and oppression would gradually subside, indeed enmity and hatred would disappear, and make room for the up building thoughts of a genuine understanding between the peoples.

For the time has come when races and peoples must at last enter the stage of true humanity at which, standing side-by-side, they will help and further each other in mutual respect, bearing in mind their common spiritual origin, and gratefully looking up to the Creator and Ruler of all the Worlds!

6. A GLIMPSE INTO THE FUTURE

Birds of a Feather Flock Together!

Let us imagine ourselves in the future. — Once more the earth circles on a course that has brought it nearer to the invigorating radiations from the Luminous Regions. A different human race has arisen upon it, for which a new and better epoch has begun. Men have so changed inwardly that their spirit can absorb the new knowledge of Creation.

Above all, they have recognized that without exception they must interweave with their earth life the Laws of their God, the Laws of Creation, to which also belong the Laws of Nature, if they are to succeed in ascending. Decisive for this are the three principal Laws: the Law of Reciprocal Action (the Law of Cause and Effect, or the Law of Sowing and Reaping), the Law of Gravitation, and the Law of Attraction of Homogeneous Species. The latter is of particular importance in regard to the new arrangement of social life.

The so-called "social instinct," that is, men's efforts to unite on the basis of common thought and volition, as also of the same habits and customs, is one effect of this Law. History shows that all the peoples have had such associations, which are known as castes, ranks or classes.

It displays the same effect in men's everyday life. Always such people come together that have some characteristic in common, be it in regard to work, sports or other occasions. From this observation arose the popular sayings: "Birds of a feather flock together," "Like father like son," "A man is known by the company he keeps."

In Nature this Law can be observed in the communities of plants and animals; and matter is formed through the union of identical individual parts, of molecules.

The same Law rules in the beyond. In connection with the Law of Gravitation the region in which its homogeneous species dwells attracts the human spirit, after physical death. Within these similar species there are gradations dependent upon the state of the actual maturity of development.

On the reverse path of the human spirits from the beyond to the earth, it is primarily also the Law of Attraction of Homogeneous Species that plays an important role. The human spirit striving towards an incarnation enters the developing child's body about half way through pregnancy. For this the power of attraction may issue from the parents, or from other persons who are often near the mother-to-be. The attraction here comes about through some similar quality of the spirit that is about to incarnate and of the human being already living on earth. The similarity may be in faults and weaknesses, as also in good qualities.

On this bridge the human being in the beyond comes to the earth, and under the protection of his physical cloak can further mature here through the experiencing that the earth offers him. —

Also on the new earth in the various physical bodies are anchored human souls with various homogeneous qualities, whose right union is of the utmost importance for their maturing.

At the beginning of the up building these did not directly unite according to their homogeneous species, as is the case in the beyond. There the human spirits are immediately separated into homogeneous species, whereas the physical body renders the very opposite possible — the close proximity of human beings in all stages of development.

Therefore on earth "called" leaders first had to make a separation through classification into definite groups; let us call them circles. Neither property nor money could be decisive for this, as has often happened in the past; nor had the classification anything to do with spiritual maturity, but it was necessary to use for this some outward earthly characteristic, which is inherent in all human beings, and which is decisive for their conduct in their everyday association with each other: the nature of man's bearing and culture as expressed in his behavior.

Also earlier peoples had already recognized this unconsciously when they divided their populations into social ranks and cultural classes.

The leaders now saw to it that according to this characteristic each came into his appropriate environment, because only there can a joint swinging arise, and can a man of a more delicate intuitive perception be protected from being harmed by the coarser nature of another.

After these first basic divisions there took place, by means of the attraction of homogeneous species through incarnations, a further classification into individual circles, where enough opportunities for ascent exist. Changing into other circles is also possible.

Meanwhile man had grasped that each prepares his own destiny, and thus also the place that he receives through birth. The classification, after all, was nothing other than assignment to the self-chosen place. They could not advance in a wrong place, any more than could a plant, which uprooted from its accustomed soil, is transplanted into an unfamiliar one. Only on soil homogeneous to himself is man in a position to unfold all his abilities and qualities in a healthy growth to full blossom; only there, standing on a sound foundation, is he able to cooperate with the true up building of his people.

He finds this fertile soil only within the circle of his own kind.

The circles are the foundation for the social development of every people, and the solution of all social problems is closely connected with them. —

This experience, and last but not least the prudent guidance of their leaders, made it easier for men of the new era to become accustomed to the natural order of society. Although to begin with they felt the guidance to be unusually severe, yet they soon saw in it the incorruptible justice with which everything was carried out. This was finally expressed in a genuine trust, which they unreservedly placed in their leadership, the need for which they perceived to be right. —

Without guidance there is no progress in the entire Creation. A long chain of guides and helpers, beginning with the spiritual Primordial Creation right down to the material Subsequent Creation, is unceasingly active in the Will of God. Where there is development there also must be leaders to guide and direct it. The earth is no exception. Great human leaders, such as Moses, the Prophets, Buddha, Lao-Tse, Zoroaster and Mohammed are a few examples of this.

One of the great evils of past eras was the lack of persons genuinely gifted with leadership, who above all possessed a comprehensive knowledge of the Laws of Creation. Very often those who were to be led themselves took the place of the missing or unsuccessful leaders, or they were given substantial right to participate in the leadership, which resulted in considerable wrong developments.

Seen in this way the desire for genuine leadership is understandable; whose first duty is always to fulfill the Will of God, Which He has anchored in His Laws of Creation. But the fulfillment lies in interweaving these Laws with everyday life on earth, and acting in accordance with them. —

The concept of equality had also changed. Equality exists when the unconscious spirit germs leave Paradise. In this state they are all equal as regards the gift of their still slumbering talents. Equal again are all human spirits who return fully conscious to Paradise, which implies equal spiritual maturity.

But between these lies the inequality of all the human spirits on their journey from Paradise into the World of Matter, and back to Paradise. The inequality is founded in the free will of man, by which each one himself determines the degree of maturity of his development, whereby an equal maturing of all human beings is impossible. As a consequence, unequal earthly conditions and lifelong habits also emerge. For this reason any attempt at equalization, wherever it may be, is doomed to failure from the beginning.

At the same time it should be noted that in spite of all the inequality men can yet have the most diverse *homogeneous species*.

The difference in spiritual maturity is confirmed by the different blood composition, because the spirit forms the blood. The blood groups A, B, AB and O did not remain the only ones; they were considerably extended. But during the investigations another step was eventually taken by establishing blood formulae of individuals. In doing so it was discovered that with the increasing number of personal formulae there were ever fewer persons with exactly the same formulae, thus with the same blood composition. With further improvement on the methods of investigation there would hardly be any human beings left with the same formulae.

The reason for this is that, in spite of possessing the same *basic* spiritual gifts, there will hardly be two people who, as a manifestation of the free will, are completely alike in their spiritual development and maturity.

But since the spirit forms the blood, a differing blood composition must also correspond with the varying spiritual maturity of men! Hence the diverging personal blood formulae.

The spirit influences the physical body through the blood. It is in this sense that the saying of Schiller must be taken: "It is the spirit that makes the body" (The Death of Wallenstein 3, 13); and W. v. Humboldt said: "It is unbelievable how much strength the soul can lend the body" (Letter to a friend, 1833). The lending of strength is again only possible through the mediator-the blood. It simply is, as Goethe said, "a very special liquid," because the spirit influences its formation. —

Thus man's knowledge of Creation expands ever more. It helps to make the cooperation of the circles, whether in social, cultural or business relations, a joyful and harmonious one, becoming ever more perfect.

Looking back, men will come to understand why the former classes had become involved in a power struggle, and had fought one another to extermination.

It was due to the wrong division into *upper*, *middle* and *lower* social classes. This was the fundamental evil right from the beginning. It bred arrogance in the upper classes and hate and envy in the lower, while the middle classes in their indolent comfort became ever more impassive.

Also the political parties stood on wrong soil. This showed itself in continual disagreements and quarrels, increasing to the point of hostility and preventing a lasting, fruitful cooperation for the welfare of the people.

In the new era these wrong divisions will no longer be possible, because instead of working below and above each other all circles will work *side-by-side*, through the recognition that in the God-Willed order of Creation each circle is an equally valuable and therefore indispensable member, and just as important as the other in the fulfillment of its earthly duties. For every circle that forms according to the Law of Attraction of Homogeneous Species has its earthly and spiritual values, which are complementary, and belong absolutely to the growth and prosperity of the whole people. Therefore no circle can look down upon any other. Gellert expresses this mutual complementing in a simple way: "You do not have what others have, and others lack your gifts; from this deficiency springs good fellowship" (Fables: *The Blind Man and the Lame Man*).

Men of the new earth have recognized all this to be right, and they eagerly strive now to make the Laws of Creation the basis of their entire earth life. After all, they know from conviction that the Will of God is expressed in His Laws of Creation, and that only obedience to these Laws is equivalent to fulfillment of the Divine Will. Out of this has grown mutual respect and consideration, with the firm intention no longer to harm one's fellow man.

With this recognition mankind have at last attained to the longed-for inward and outward peace. There is neither mass misery, nor class warfare or pride of place. For they know only the one goal: true humanity to the honor of God!

It lies with men of the present time to attain this goal. This picture of the future should help in this, and should stimulate reflection.

It introduces Creation's Law of the Attraction of Homogeneous Species, which is so important for men's association together, and the main outline demonstrates its application in the social field.

Perhaps through this it will also become easier to understand the affliction and confusion in present-day human society.

7. DEATH AND THE BEYOND

Birth and death are the beginning and the end of earthly life, and no human being who has within him even a faint longing for the Truth can disregard the two important questions — how does life enter the physical body and what becomes of it after death?

Most human beings are so fixed in their inferior views, which are focused only on earthly things, that they can no longer free themselves from them. Through the one-sided cultivation of the earthbound and therefore transient intellect, they have in their investigation into the enigmas of life lost a very important key, namely the ability to draw conclusions from that, which has its origin "above," down to that, which manifests "below" as the effect. In spite of this, many a higher recognition may yet be gained alone by studying the effects "below," if it is borne in mind that the same Laws operate in the visible world as well as in the physically invisible world.

These Laws of Creation form not only what is on earth but also what is in the "beyond," and furthermore it is through the effects of their working that nothing in the great Creation is lost. Hence also the life that has left the physical body at the time of death must have some form, and this form must have gone somewhere. And it is so indeed. The "formed life" that leaves the dead body is the soul, which after death passes over in human form into the so-called "beyond" — a collective term for a number of different regions.

The Law of Gravitation determines the place to which the soul comes there. Depending on how light or how heavy it has made itself on earth through its thoughts and deeds the soul, after leaving the body, either rises or sinks to the region that has the same gravity as itself, where it is then attracted by its homogeneous species.

Man holds far too narrow and one-sided conceptions about the living activity in Creation, thus also about the continued existence of the soul after death, supposing he really believes in it. He is often of the opinion that after death the soul goes to rest. Just the opposite is the case: If the soul wishes to remain alive after death, then it must not rest but has to move! For only movement is life! Phrases like: "He has gone to eternal rest" and "Rest in peace!" therefore give an entirely false conception of what takes place in the beyond.

The most lively activity prevails in the beyond, and experiencing there is much stronger and richer than here on earth. Man finds again in the beyond all that he thought and intuitively perceived on earth. These are his "works," which follow after or await him, the good as well as the evil. These alone would be sufficient to prevent him from coming to rest. Thus there is no question of a personal resting or repose of the dead up to the Last Judgment!

The "awakening for the Last Judgment," has a quite different meaning from what men imagine: Not all the dead, but all that is dead shall be awakened! By this is to be understood also all the evil qualities slumbering in the human souls as if they were dead, which will be roused through the Divine Power that is increased at the time of the Judgment; that is to say, they will be forced into the strongest movement, so that they may thereby pass judgment on themselves. He who as a result of his self-incurred failure does not stand the test of this great World Judgment sinks into the "other death," which is the "eternal one." With this he loses his laboriously acquired self-consciousness.

Therefore man should never forget the actual goal of his existence — Paradise! The road there leads through the beyond; earthly death is but a gateway on this road, which continues beyond the earthly sphere and offers to the upward-striving world wanderer a surprising vista into another physically invisible world, which is much vaster and more beautiful still than the earth.

Unfortunately earthman has almost completely closed himself to this world, which actually does exist. He can no longer understand it because he has voluntarily narrowed down his perceptions, and confronts the happenings in the beyond with disbelief and doubt. Yet at any moment he can establish the connection with the beyond in the simplest way; he need be gifted neither with mediumistic nor clairvoyant qualities for this.

We all know the "conscience," but without ever having rightly discovered its true meaning: It is closely connected with the working of those deceased human beings, who seriously strive with their greater experience to help their fellowmen still sojourning on earth, to guide them safely and to protect them — provided that through genuine longing or heartfelt prayer earthmen prepare the way for it. The quiet working of these helpers in the beyond is a part of our conscience, the other part being the voice of the spirit, thus our intuitive perception!

How often do those in the beyond try through an admonition or warning to restrain us from doing evil? How hard they strive again and again through a gentle urging to remove our hesitation, which still keeps us from a good deed. How many a time do they pass on good and useful advice to us? But of what use is their influence, however seriously meant, if we do not let them "appeal to our conscience," but instead try to lull it to sleep, only to realize later that this certain something, which suddenly crossed our minds to the contrary, was right after all but was suppressed by our intellectual cleverness! Naturally these helpers in the beyond can never force us, for they too must respect the free will.

Therefore blessed is he whose conscience is still alert, who by his own decision follows the voice of his conscience, and who willingly allows himself to be guided, led and protected by his helper in the beyond. In the helping and accepting of help there lies reciprocally a great blessing, which may bring an unsuspected spiritual upsurge for both parties.

But at times earthmen are given still other possibilities of a connection with the beyond, developing naturally and having nothing to do with artificial aids that are always potentially dangerous and seldom pass without damage to body and soul. Thus for example the English poet H. Dennis Bradley, who died in 1934, had promised to communicate after his death, if this were at all possible. And shortly afterwards he actually succeeded in giving a very good description of his experience in the beyond through a medium, which runs as follows:

"The landscape in which we live is a great deal different from that of the earth. It is of a blessed purity and clearness. There is a tremendous amount of light, and nothing is gray or even dark.

"There is soil here too, as well as an ocean, trees and flowers, but everything is more beautiful and more wonderful than on earth.

"Even the plumage of the birds is more radiant and more colorful. But strangest of all are the flowers. They not only exude fragrance, but also emit delightful sounds that the physical ear cannot hear, and which are different for each kind of flower.

"There is no weariness here and no need for rest, instead one feels oneself always overflowing with a wonderful strength. Time is of no importance. One is always busy, for there is a million times as much to be learned as on earth.

"There are millions and millions of departed souls to be found here. The spirits can communicate with one another, even though they spoke different languages during their earthly lives.

"The ability to move from one place to another is also wonderful. It is not the same as on earth, for there are no physical bodies here. Even though I do have a form that could be compared with a body, it does not bind me.

"Here it is enough simply to wish to be somewhere, and immediately you are there.

"In the future it will probably again be possible for human beings still on earth and souls in the beyond to communicate. But for this it is necessary for the human being in simple trust to open the gates of knowledge, which he has closed to himself by his lack of belief".

Physical death must lose its terror when we know that for the forward-striving human being it is simply a crossing from one sphere of Creation to the other. The soul, with the spirit as its core, only strips off the perishable earthly cloak; however, it retains the bodily form as a characteristic of the spirit, whose actual home is the Spiritual Realm, also called Paradise. The way there is long, but it is bordered by luminous gardens in which the upward-striving human spirit finds wonderful helps and refreshing strength. It is one of these luminous gardens that is described by the deceased poet from the beyond.

Not only once must a human soul be born and die again, until it has attained that lightness, and with it that purity, which completely detach it from the earthly. Then one day comes an earthly death, which for it will be the last. Freed from all earthly burdens, the spirit can jubilantly press on towards the Luminous Heights until at last the gates of Paradise will open for it. In stepping over the threshold to the Realm of the Spiritual, it has attained to the "other life," and above it forms a wondrous radiant halo, causing it to give an exultant cry of supreme happiness: the Crown of Eternal Life!

8. INCARNATION AND REBIRTH

By giving preference to his earth-bound intellect, man has deprived himself of the ability to consider with his spiritual intuitive perception Creation as a whole, of which he is also of course a tiny particle. Thus he prevents himself from obtaining undreamed-of glimpses into the other world, which would show him clearly and logically how he could master the problems and perplexities with which he struggles today.

Logic certainly is the doctrine of consistency — but of what use to us is logic, if in the quest for higher things it remains caught in earthly matters through purely intellectual activity, and is not pursued with the spirit, which after all, in comparison with what is earthly, is the original, and therefore must also govern any true logic. So also the question of how the human soul comes to earth in order to be active here in flesh and blood, and how often this happens, can only be considered and resolved from the spiritual point of view, bearing in mind the corresponding Laws of Creation.

When the soul comes to earth it is especially Creation's Law of Attraction of Homogeneous Species that takes effect. It causes the nature of the incarnating soul to be attracted through the similar nature of the parents or their environment. The threads, which form between the homogeneous species on earth and the coming soul, gradually become more and more firm, and finally bring about the incarnation, that is to say: the entry of the soul into the developing child's body about the middle of pregnancy.

By "soul" is to be understood the spirit with its non-physical coverings. It is completely independent, and is connected with its parents on earth only through a similar nature, but sometimes also through special threads of fate. It is therefore not the case that parents impart something of their spirit to their children at birth, as is often wrongly assumed.

Hence it follows that in no case can abilities and qualities of the soul be hereditary. They are therefore not subject to physical, gross-material transmission, but remain with the soul after earthly death as it separates itself from the body, and only return with the newly-incarnating soul into the new physical body. This indeed appears like heredity, but is actually a result of the attraction of homogeneous species. The popular sayings, "Birds of a feather flock together" and, "Like father like son" refer to this Law, which operates uniformly throughout the entire visible and invisible Creation, and which is also expressed in a saying of Goethe: "A noble man attracts his like."

Therefore it is also impossible to contribute to the improvement of the human spirit through artificially induced changes in the hereditary factors (genetic manipulation). Man's improvement can only issue from the spirit. And the spirit, with its abilities and qualities, cannot be reached by these earthly-gross-materially limited experiments.

How often a human soul that is reborn is incarnated on earth depends on its stage of spiritual development, on the strength of its spiritual consciousness. For in the beginning, at the start of its journey through Subsequent Creation, the human spirit is only a germ, which must develop from an unconscious state to being conscious of itself. To this end the spirit is helped by experience during its various earth lives. Once it has reached this goal, and freed itself from all guilt, the rebirths come to an end. It finally detaches itself from what is earthly, and can ascend unburdened as a personality, who has become fully conscious.

The knowledge about earthly incarnation and rebirth is very ancient. In the East the teaching about it is contained in the philosophies and religions. However, the Christian Church suppressed the belief in it, although the knowledge about reincarnation was not unknown even at the time of Jesus. The question as to whether Elijah had returned as John the Baptist, and the question of Nicodemus: "How can a man be born when he is old? Can he enter a second time into his mother's womb, and be born?" are indicative of this, although in the latter case the reference was to spiritual rebirth, which Nicodemus had misunderstood and applied to earthly matters.

From Jesus Himself no utterances about reincarnation are handed down in the Bible. But this is no proof of its non-existence. Many a happening in Creation was not explained or mentioned by Jesus to the people of His time, because they did not require it then for their spiritual progress, and would certainly not have understood it. Therefore He repeatedly pointed out that the coming Son of Man would impart this knowledge.

Later, too, especially in the utterances of poets, thinkers and other Western personalities, we find repeated allusions to the existence of an earthly rebirth. Goethe was convinced of it. He wrote to Wieland about Charlotte von Stein: "I cannot explain the significance, the impact, which this woman has upon me, in any other way than through the transmigration of souls. — Yes, we were once husband and wife!"

Richard Wagner wrote to Mathilde Wesendonk: "Only in the profound assumption of the transmigration of souls could I discover the consoling point towards which everything converges at the same high level of redemption . . ."

The Greco-German writer Constantin Christomanos, who was teacher and private secretary of Empress Elizabeth of Austria during the 1890's, mentions in his recollections of the Empress (*Diaries*, 1899) the following remarks of hers, which express her belief in repeated earth lives: "Every man has culture in himself, as an inheritance from all his previous existences . . ." And in reference to Dante and other personalities: "They are souls who have recently come to earth out of past eras . . ."

Henry Ford, founder of the Ford factories, said in a conversation with the philosopher Ralph Waldo Trine: "What some seem to consider a special gift or talent is, in my opinion, the fruit of lengthy experience gained in many lives. But I must first explain that I believe that we are born again. You and I, we are all reborn many times, live many lives and store up a wealth of experiences . . . "

This knowledge of incarnation and rebirth is confirmed by serious accounts of genuine recollections of former earth lives, although these must be considered exceptional. The accounts stand the test of objective examination completely and must not be dismissed as products of fantasy, as schizophrenia, telepathy or the like. The authenticity of such recollections is conditional upon their resulting from natural gifts and not from being artificially induced as through hypnosis, which is wrong because it binds the free will of the human spirit, and hinders its true ascent.

It is for his own benefit that man is generally prevented from surveying his previous existence. Otherwise he would occupy himself far too much with the past and so neglect the present. This can be clearly seen from the wrong practices carried out today. People investigate their former earth lives in a desire for sensation, out of curiosity, vanity and self-aggrandizement. Yet they do not even know whether the information supplied to them by others is really accurate; for just in this field the possibility of errors and delusions is very great. Besides, all this holds a great danger for man, because it is only the experiencing of the present, of the existing situation into which he has been born according to his own volition, which can have lasting value for his spiritual progress.

The poet Lessing, who occupied himself with this problem, wrote about it at the end of his work, *Education of the Human Race*: "Why should I not return as often as I am sent to acquire fresh knowledge and new skills? Do I achieve so much in one sojourning as to make it not worth my while to return? Is that why? Or is it that I forget my former sojourn? Well for me that I forget. The recollection of my former states would enable me to turn my present condition to but poor account. And have I forgotten forever what I must forget for the time being?"

But the knowledge of incarnation and reincarnation has been given to man for quite another reason, namely that through it he is meant to recognize the wonderful connections in the happening of Creation, and benefit accordingly for himself and his surroundings. Then he will also gratefully experience that there is actually no division between this world, the earth, and the beyond, the other world.

He himself journeys continually between the other world and this one, often changing his physical body, as Krishna already proclaimed in the over-two-thousand-year-old Bhagavad-Gita, the *Song of the Sublime*. "Just as a person casts off worn-out garments and puts on others that are new, even so does the embodied soul cast off worn-out bodies and take on others that are new . . . for to the one that is born death is certain and certain is birth for the one that has died . . . until man perfecting himself through many lives, then attains to the highest goal."

The "highest goal" is Paradise, Eternal Life, after the human spirit has developed during the transmigration of its soul from the state of spiritual unconsciousness to a personality conscious of itself.

To the European the expression "transmigration of souls" is charged with ideas that have streamed into western thinking from Indian teachings. According to these, the soul at its various rebirths is supposed to develop in an ascending line from a stone into a plant, from a plant into an animal, and from an animal into a human being. With this is connected the belief that after physical death the soul at its next rebirth can pass into a plant or an animal.

This is contradicted by the fact that the spirit, as the core of the soul, is spiritual already from its origin. Hence it can neither develop from the nature of a stone, a plant, nor from the nature of an animal, because these are of quite different species, and therefore the spirit can ever again incarnate only in a human body.

Therefore the transmigration of souls is really the journeying of the human spirit with its non-physical coverings through material Creation, during which it must also take on the physical body on earth. The purpose of the journeying is to obtain spiritual maturity by reaching the self-conscious state of an independent personality from the initially unconscious state of the spirit. Only spiritual maturity gives the human spirit the lightness that lets it ascend to Paradise.

Moreover, the transmigration of souls is limited by time, and is not, as some teachings state, without a definite end. The limitation is set by the Last Judgment, during which every human being must render account for the development of his spiritual abilities. He who has developed wrongly is in danger of being cast out as a "useless stone," because there is no use for him in Creation. He loses his claim to further opportunities of development and with it his painstakingly acquired self-consciousness.

Therefore man should earnestly strive to grasp the knowledge of Creation, of which the understanding of incarnation and physical rebirth forms a part. Only true knowledge frees us from a pressure, which we have indeed felt but until now have been unable to explain. It allows us to breathe more freely, and gives us the right basis for a useful and constructive activity on earth, bringing us at the right time nearer to the longed-for spiritual goal.

9. "IN THINE OWN BOSOM LIES THY DESTINY!"

How often does our own fate or that of others bewilder and puzzle us! How many a man, whom we know to be bent only upon doing good, is heavily oppressed with cares and troubles. How many a child comes to earth with a physical infirmity, a congenital disease, or with deficiencies of character, and thus is burdened with a fate that it has certainly not yet caused in this earth life. There are many such instances, where people have to endure the lot of finding more bitter fruits than sweet ones falling from the tree of fate upon their life's path, and this despite their best volition, the sincerity of their aspirations, and the integrity of their conduct.

Here the question confronts us: What can be the cause of this, if there is said to be only one life on earth? In very few of these cases can cause, reaction and recognition of this reaction be pressed together in one earth life. For where is the man who attracts to himself an evil fate or karma by trespassing against the Laws of Creation, and who is able completely to redeem his offenses in the same earth life? This would of course first require a thorough inner change in a man, which in the present long-standing spiritual indolence is extremely rare.

On the other hand, how differently is the question resolved when we know that through the great Grace of the Creator a human soul is permitted to return, and so in a further earth life to receive the opportunity of expiating its guilt. Otherwise it would have to suffer continuously from its unredeemed fate, and at last perish from it spiritually, if it would have no opportunity of redeeming this fate at the place where the soul has brought it into the world, namely on earth. According to the Law of Revolution, the cycle of an event must close at the point where it has been begun. Thus a visible evil deed on earth must also be expiated here, to which end the human soul must in most cases be born again on earth.

Yet the redemption of past failures is not the sole and primary purpose of rebirth. Rather it is for the spirit germ of man, which is at first unconscious, to learn through experiencing in its repeated lives on earth those lessons, which it needs for its development and maturity, until as a spirit conscious of itself it can ascend to its spiritual home, to Paradise.

Man, however, has disregarded the development provided for him through the Law of Creation, by arbitrarily setting out on wrong paths. So it comes about that today almost everyone has to deal only with his evil fate.

Fate is subject to the Law of Reciprocal Effect or Reaction, which is expressed so simply and appropriately in the words of the Bible: "Whatsoever a man soweth, that shall he also reap" (Galatians 6, 7). He will even reap it many times more! This holds well not only in Nature, but equally for the thoughts and deeds of man; for as a creature he is no exception to it.

Viewed spiritually, he is a sower scattering his fateful seed. Under the working of the incorruptible Laws of Creation it ripens into fruit that exactly correspond to what he has willed, and of which he alone must partake. Only he can take upon himself the sin he committed, and only he can atone for it; no one else can do this for him. Not even Jesus, the Son of God. Not for nothing is it said: "Whatsoever a man soweth, that shall he also reap" — he, the man himself!

Let us just consider in the light of the lawfulness of sowing and reaping, of effect and reciprocal effect, the stigmata generally known today. Naturally only genuine stigmata (wound marks) that appear spontaneously are meant, not those caused through religious ecstasy and fanaticism as the result of self-suggestion.

What have those persons on whom the stigmata appear more or less strongly sown? Since they have to suffer painfully from them, both physically and psychically, the cause cannot have been a good one. To reap suffering will never be the result of good seed, any more than thistles, for instance, would grow from grains of wheat. Moreover this would be an injustice, which according to the incorruptible Laws of Creation is impossible.

It is striking that the wound marks of the stigmatized are exactly like those that were painfully inflicted on Jesus, the Son of God, when He was crucified. From this fact a personal connection can be inferred: Between Jesus and these persons something incisive must have taken place, which has given rise to such a fate. Therefore we are perhaps not far wrong in seeking the cause in the enmity shown toward the Son of God by human souls on earth at that time, who of their own free will mocked or even reviled Him as He suffered and died on the cross.

Thus the stigmata can be explained as the result of a personal offense against Jesus, which finds visible expression in this way during the particular incarnations of these human souls! Moreover such souls are not then distinguished or "blessed" by their wound marks but on the contrary they must be regarded as branded by their self-incurred fate. Only recognition of their guilt and prayer for forgiveness can release them from it; then the stigmata will also cease to appear.

By thus applying the lawfulness of seed and harvest to the course of human life we arrive at quite different conclusions, which surely correspond far more nearly to reality and truth than do the generally prevailing and propagated human opinions. We are thus able to recognize that man is in no wise subject to an arbitrarily predestined fate, nor does he stand powerless before a predestined fate, as the fatalists contend.

Firstly, "predestination" lies always in his own hands; secondly, he is not powerless as regards his fate. For just as he can exercise his free will to do evil, so is it also possible for him at any moment, of his own accord, to bring an end to his wrong tendencies by simply and seriously striving to think and do only good. In this way he is able to diminish the reaction of dark threads of fate, which must have its effect upon him at some place and at some time. Through a persistent good volition he may even annul the reaction, which is equivalent to a symbolic redemption. On the other hand, it is impossible to mitigate or obviate the reaction of an existing guilt by imposing some form of penitence!

Accordingly, fate means the good and the evil that man voluntarily allows to arise in his soul, and which he then "sends" forth into the world. What he has sent out will inevitably come back to him one day, and then in the reciprocal action he will be afflicted by fate, will suffer heavy blows of fate, or else he will experience the smiles of fate as the harvest of good.

The origin of fate lies always in man himself and never elsewhere-as Schiller makes the Maid of Orleans say: "In thine own bosom lies thy destiny!" He who realizes this will first look within himself for the cause of all the misfortune and distress that befall him, and thereby open for himself the way to humble recognition of his guilt. Without this he cannot receive the Grace of God resting in the Laws of Creation, which alone can grant release from sin and therewith forgiveness.

10. THE SILVER CORD

We know from the Revelation of John that there are robes also in the beyond": And have washed their robes, and made them white" (Rev. 7, 14).

During the earthly phase of life, in addition to its physical body the human spirit also wears an ethereal body, which together with its physical-gross-material body is needed for the protection and maturing of its spirit on its journey through the World of Matter, also called the World or Subsequent Creation.

It is these ethereal bodies that may also be called raiments or coverings, which are meant by the robes in the Revelation. They must be made white and light, that is to say, cleansed of all the dirt of evil thoughts and actions, if men wish to enter Paradise.

Even Paul in his First Epistle to the Corinthians (15, 35-42) mentioned in addition to the physical body also a different one: the spiritual or celestial body.

At physical death the human spirit lays aside its physical cloak, and after separating from this cloak it stands in the Ethereal World, the so-called beyond. Here it now feels, hears and sees with its ethereal body that bears human form. In this state, that is without its physical body, but with its ethereal body and other delicate coverings as well, the human spirit is called "soul."

With its ethereal body the human spirit can penetrate all that is of a coarser nature, just as also when incarnating it has entered the coarser physical body. Or let us think of other processes. Invisible electric current runs through cable, invisible radio waves penetrate walls, and there is nothing to impede thoughts in their distant flight, when for example the person thinking is in a closed room. All this is the final effect of the lawfulness that enables the finer species always to penetrate the coarser species.

Thus after His physical death, Jesus too, with His ethereal body, could suddenly enter the room where His disciples had gathered, although the doors were shut (John 20, 19).

The ethereal-non-physical body and the gross-material-physical body are connected with each other as by a navel cord, which in its natural state is said to be of a silvery sheen. Hence this cord is also called "the silver cord."

Even the author of *Ecclesiastes; Or, The Preacher* in the Old Testament (12, 1-6) used this expression when in his figurative speech he described the last days of a dying man:

"Remember now thy Creator in the days of thy youth,
while the evil days come not,
nor the years draw nigh, when thou shalt say,
I have no pleasure in them;
While the sun, or the light, or the moon, or the stars
be not darkened, nor
the clouds return after the rain;
In the day when the keepers of the house shall tremble (the arms),
and the strong men shall bow themselves (the legs),
and the grinders cease,
because they are few (the teeth),
and those that look out of the windows be darkened (the eyes),
and the doors shall be shut in the streets (the ears),
when the sound of the grinding is low (the mouth),
and he shall rise up at the voice of the bird,
and all the daughters of music shall be brought low (the songs) . . .;
and the almond tree shall flourish (the white hair) . . .,
or ever the silver cord be loosed,
or the golden bowl be broken . . . ."

The Preacher exhorts man to think of the Creator in good time, before death comes, and the silver cord is taken away. The golden bowl has been interpreted as the aura, which radiates round the head of earthman, and which is extinguished at death.

Clairvoyants are able to observe the process of dying. In Shaw Desmond's book *How you Live when you Die* (Rider & Co., London), he says on pages 20/21:

To come more nearly to the consideration of what happens immediately after death, it should be stated that death does not ensue instantly upon the heart ceasing to beat From what we have been told by the astral physicians and, indeed, to a certain extent by actual observations in the sick room on this side of death, the silver cord is not severed for a day to four or five days after apparent death.

The actual separation takes *only a few seconds*. In that instant of severance, the 'dead' person finds himself or herself looking down upon his or her own body! It is an extraordinary moment. It is so, if only because for the first time the man or woman has found out *that the body was not himself or herself.* That it was no more than a suit of clothes or a dress with which one had finished and so was thrown aside."

The severing of the silver cord is not always easy.

Only man himself is responsible for its condition, thus for its density and detachability. The more he chains himself to earthly things the denser and heavier it becomes, and with it also the ethereal body; hence in certain cases such a man must feel not only the last earthly-physical pains, but also the disintegration of his physical cloak.

But in such a state also cremation will not pass by the soul without leaving some trace. The English poet H. Dennis Bradley asked a deceased person through a medium about this, and received the following answer, which he published in his book *Towards the Stars* (T. Werner Laurie, London), pages 264/265:

"In a sense you are wrong about the burning of bodies . . . On the other hand, you are not quite right in believing that this sudden and complete destruction does not wound. In a sense it does. Because, as you know, there is a fragile envelope that surrounds the soul as a tissue might, which fades away shortly after death. It is a membrane, as it were, and this is very sensitive immediately after death, for what you would call a few days or a week. If the body is entirely destroyed, this membrane, which in a sense is still attached to the body, is severely hurt. It suffers, and this is imparted also to the discarnate part. So you must not smile completely at those whom you call fools, who believe that the body is entirely severed from the other parts at death. It is so after a very short time, but not immediately. Before the soul and spirit leave the darkness in which they are brought after they sever from the body, this membrane has withered away from them, but not at once."

The "membrane" that is still attached to the body, and which only later withers away, is the so-called astral body, which after severance of the soul from the physical body disintegrates with the physical body. The astral body, which is dependent on the soul, is a mediator to the physical body. The so-called "phantom pains" point to the existence of the astral body. People who have had a limb removed still suffer pains from time to time in the same place where the limb used to be. This is because the corresponding limb of the astral body cannot be removed along with it; the astral body remains as it is.

It should be mentioned here that there are people who even in their earth lives can leave their physical body temporarily with their ethereal body. This may occur for instance during sleep. Also in such cases a connection between the two bodies always remains through the silver cord, which according to earthly concepts has an inconceivable capacity to stretch.

The Bible describes the awakening of the dead through Jesus, which He did as long as the silver cord was not yet severed. Only in this way could the souls already severing from their physical bodies return to them.

60

From these explanations it appears that the process of dying is not yet ended with "clinical" death. There is also an astral body, which in certain circumstances dies only much later than the physical body. As long as this astral body is still connected with the physical body and the ethereal body, that is, as long as the connecting cord is not yet broken, any interference with the dead physical body can be painfully felt by the soul.

Let us read what, according to an account by a doctor, C. A. Wickland, M. D., in the book Thirty Years Among the Dead (National Psychological Institute, Los Angeles, California, 1924), pages 155/156, a departed soul, in this case a girl who died through her craving for drugs, communicated about it through a medium:

"I died in that terrible condition. My physical body was gone. I had worn it out, just worn it out. Then I was operated on (post mortem) but I still lived. I wanted to get to my body.

"They operated on me, and after a while I felt that something was picking me to small pieces (dissection). I cried and I fought, because I wanted that body so I could satisfy my very soul. I was burning up.

"They picked at every nerve; they looked at my heart, my shoulder, and down to the eg — pick, pick, pick, all the time!

"I got so desperate I fought with all my power, and I scared some away from my body. They never touched it again. There were five or six men, with knives, all wanting to do something with my body — pick, pick, pick!

"But there came another; he looked and looked at me, and picked and picked, and he drove me wild. I thought, if I could only get hold of him, I would fix him. He paid no attention to me. I tried to scare him, as I had scared the others, but I could not budge him. He would not move one inch from that body of mine.

"I followed him and thought I would haunt him, but all at once I got well, (controlled the psychic) and began to fight him with all the strength and power I had for picking me to pieces.

"To my great surprise, after this gentleman (Dr. W.) talked to me, I found I was dead. I did not know I had lost my body, for I had not been dead at all. This gentleman told me that the people working on my body were students and that it was necessary for them to work on a dead body before they were able to pass their examinations. I scared five of them and they never touched me again, but I could not scare this one.

"(To Dr. W.) Now I come to thank you. You were the one who enlightened me and gave me an understanding of the real life beyond. I found I could not throw my sins on

Christ. He was our teacher, but we must live our own lives, as He taught us to live, and not throw our sins and troubles on Him."

This human soul was so interested in its physical body that only much later, through the enlightenment of Dr. Wickland, did it become aware of the change into the non-physical. Surely there can be no doubt that in order to obtain a clear picture, physical death must be regarded not only from this world but also from the beyond.

But contemplation of this other, invisible side cannot be done with the intellect,which itself is transient, thus of this world, because it is produced by the frontal brain that perishes at death.

As little as it is possible to drive in a nail with a goose-feather, so is no one in a position to recognize or to grasp what is in the beyond, that is, ethereal matter, with the gross-material brain, because the two are of an entirely different species.

Hence the only course open is to use the intuitive perception of the spirit, which has a higher origin than have the Worlds of Matter, and which can therefore view and understand all the visible and invisible connections in the entire World of Matter.

And only from *this* point of view must the increasing transplantations of physical organs from the just deceased into living persons be regarded. This is really a question of interference in man's personal sphere, to which he is defenselessly relinquished, because he can no longer attract attention physically to himself. But respect for one's neighbor, which also includes his physical body, and the commandment to do no harm to him whatsoever, applies not only to the earthly phase of life but also beyond death.

What use then is the consent given in ignorance of conditions in the beyond? The reality of the Ethereal World, into which a small glimpse was given here, will soon and painfully enlighten the departed soul.

Therefore such experiments on the human being must cease, simply because hardly anyone, not even the doctor concerned, can answer for the consequences of his interference in the beyond; for he is ignorant of them and thus cannot assess them. Moreover, Nature itself usually sets a limit through the diversity and incompatibility of the tissue groups, although attempts are made even to break through this natural barrier.

Interference with the dead physical body, which also includes dissection and cremation, should, in the temperate zones, definitely not be undertaken within the well-known three days, for it is to be assumed that in normal cases the soul will only have severed itself from its physical body by the end of that period. This would then in any case rule out the removal of parts of the body for the purpose of transplantation, because such removal would have to be carried out immediately after clinical death in order to be at all clinically possible.

Nevertheless, not only the doctors concerned but also those persons who wish to give physical organs after their death, and equally the relatives of suddenly deceased persons who must consent in their place, and last but not least the recipients of such organs, must also consider what takes place in the beyond, and base their decisions on that.

It is a different matter, of course, when considering the widespread view of which the basic idea is that after death it is "all over." With this kind of thinking there can be no room for the reflection that at physical death something that is living and not visible also severs from the physical body, which through intervention in the physical body just laid aside might be injured. Here the physical body is simply material from which individual replacement parts are taken when needed.

Yet also with this opinion the responsibility of those who think in this way is not annulled before the Laws of Creation, either here or "there." For ignorance of the Laws of Creation is no protection from its consequences.

But for those who bear within them the conviction of survival after death, physical death is birth into the Ethereal Realm. Just as at birth into the gross-material, the earthly, the navel cord is severed, so the silver cord is severed at birth into the ethereal, the beyond. Death need not be feared by anyone who bears within him the living firm volition for good, even if the resolution for it has arisen only just before his physical death. It will help him safely over the threshold, and on the other side helping hands will carefully guide him on to that recognition, which is still needed in order to ascend towards the Light.

11. GOD IS NOT SILENT

When man on earth dies his soul leaves his physical body and enters the world beyond in complete form.

The physical body perishes, and with it one of the most important organs that serves the human spirit in this world here on earth as a necessary instrument: the brain!

In one part of the brain, the cerebrum or frontal brain, thoughts are produced, out of which the intellect is finally made up. At death this also dies. It is perishable because the place of its origin — the brain — is perishable. Nothing in this Creation, whether in the earthly or non-earthly, can go beyond its species; neither in its being nor in its activity. Thus man, for example, cannot suddenly change into an animal, nor can an animal think and act as a human being, because the two species of Creation are fundamentally different. Hence there follows the extremely important conclusion that the intellect can grasp only that, which is perishable like itself. It cannot understand anything beyond this, anything, which is eternal — it simply has not the nature for it. The intellect cannot work beyond the material substance of its brain.

But we have within us something else that enables us to recognize the imperishable, the eternal, and even God, and that also remains intact for us after our physical death: the human spirit, which expresses itself in the intuitive perception, also called the inner voice.

The intuitive perception is part of our conscience. It knows exactly what is good and what is evil. Its warning or assenting voice cannot be missed, if man wishes to hear it. Wilhelm von Humboldt (1767-1835) had this to say about it: "Everyone must be a judge unto himself, and indeed is so. For whenever anything deserves disapproval, the inner voice states this more loudly and hurtfully than outside criticism could ever do."

Therefore a man who suppresses his intuitive perception, and relies only on his intellect, is without a conscience, and acts and thinks without principle.

According to the order in Creation the spirit rules and the intellect carries out. We may describe the natural cooperation between spirit and intellect, each in its appointed place, as *reason*.

In the course of his development man has voluntarily disturbed this natural relationship; he has become "lacking in reason." *That* is the *hereditary sin*: the over-cultivation of the intellect and the suppression of the spirit.

This in time has resulted in the failure of mankind. The suppressed spirit and the one-sidedly cultivated intellect, which is bound to what is perishable, are mankind's real problem, around which everything revolves. All other problems are only consequences of this one main problem. And here too is the only weak point, where Lucifer, the Antichrist, succeeds in making men subservient to him.

On the plane of that which is perishable, namely in the World of Matter, he is able to harness for his hostile dealings against God those human beings who through their excessive intellectual activity bind themselves to matter.

The over-cultivated frontal brain continues to be handed down, and with it the tendency (not the compulsion!) to go on suppressing the living spirit of man, and to prefer the volition of the intellect to that of the spirit, as Paul has already stated: "For I delight in the law of God after the inward man (spirit): But I see another law in my members (intellect), bringing me into captivity to the law of sin" (Rom. 7, 22-23).

In this disparity between spirit and intellect also lies the cause of the estrangement from God, and it is not surprising when people say and write that the fundamental problem of religion today is no longer Martin Luther's question, "How do I find a merciful God," but "Is there a God at all?"

And men further ask: "If there be a God, how can all the dreadful and horrifying things which we see, hear or experience every day come to pass?" Those who ask this doubt the justice of God. They should reflect that the authors of these terrible end-effects are men themselves. In separating themselves from God they have disregarded His Laws, among them also the simple Law of Sowing and Reaping, from which human thoughts and actions are not excluded. Man stands always in the harvest of what he has sown in past and present earth lives through his intuitive perceptions, thoughts and actions.

Certainly on many occasions the words "Thy Will be done!" are uttered. But who makes it clear to himself how and where this Will of God is expressed, in order really to absorb It inwardly out of conviction, and not just let It be done out of blind or acquired faith?

For man the Will of God can only be recognized in Creation, with its inflexible Laws. Even the sciences acknowledge the fact of these Laws and their immutability, although they deny, refuse to know or exclude from their thinking the origin of these Laws. No one can deny that we harm ourselves by acting against the Laws of Nature. But these Laws are part of the Language of God. To obey these Laws means nothing other than to fulfill the Will of God and to understand His Language.

God is not silent. But there are men — and very many of them — who say that God is silent, that God is a long time in coming, that humanity at the present time is in a state of remoteness from God. They write books and produce films about it; they establish complete scientific or instructional systems on the subject.

What is supposed to be the purpose of all these statements? Is it uneasiness or fear that after all it could be different? Or are they meant to lull the conscience to sleep? Yet it is just the conscience that gives many people no peace. For there is in fact a genuine distress of conscience that arises from man's preference for enslavement to matter, to which the brain as origin of the intellect also belongs, and from the not yet entirely suppressed inner voice. This enables man to sense that it must be *otherwise* with the remoteness from God, that it is man who has withdrawn from God by voluntarily raising a barrier between himself and his Creator, a barrier that separates him from God. He closes himself to God's Spiritual Power, which from the beginning of Creation unceasingly flows through Creation, and without which man simply cannot live.

Yet still other forces have a share in forming our conscience: the helpers in the beyond who quietly urge, advise, exhort and warn us. If we would listen to their voices, our weak sensing would be more and more strengthened, until we became certain that it is really man who is silent to God's perpetual call. God speaks constantly to men through His Creation. The entire visible and invisible Creation is His Language.

The very people who believe neither in the words of the Bible nor in God, and who say: "We believe only in what we see, we keep to the facts, because these are what we understand," are just those who no longer even notice that daily and hourly they have these facts before their eyes.

The entire Creation, and with it the earth and Nature, are facts that speak of God. As Paul wrote to the Romans: "For the invisible things of him from the creation of the world are clearly seen, being understood by the things that are made, even his eternal power and Godhead . . ." (Rom. 1, 20).

The reality and perfection of God, for which theology is today asking and seeking, are revealed in Creation.

When contemplating the wonders of Nature, from the minute structure of an atom to the huge celestial spheres moving in rhythm, an eternal order, which is perfect because it issues from the Perfection of the Divine Will, is revealed to the alert human spirit.

Such order cannot have formed from primeval substance that was disorder (chaos) before the Creation of the world, or from nothingness. Then the question would still remain as to who or what caused the chaos to arise and formed it, or who or what created order from nothingness.

No teaching about the beginning of the world can prove or make clear that the world could have begun "of itself." The question as to the ultimate reason, as to the cause, remains. It is equivalent to the question about God.

The order of Creation is a forming, a shaping, that logically depends on a power through which the order has been accomplished. For the origin of this power there is only one Name: God. — And that which works out of God is His Holy Will, the Divine Will. This Will permeates all parts of Creation, whether they were created immediately or have developed over long periods of time, or are still in the process of development.

The question often asked today in connection with a conception of God and His Creation — "Evolution" (development) *or* "God's Creation" — is wrong. For Creation contains *both*: Primordial Creation and developed Creation. But all parts of Creation, the created and the developed, have the same origin out of God, because there is only *one* Divine Power out of which everything was formed and has developed, and all this is subject to the *same* Laws of God.

Spiritual Primordial Creation came into being as first Creation with the Words "Let there be Light." It is below the Divine Sphere. The history of Creation as contained in the Bible in Genesis, concerning the seven Days of Creation, refers to this first Creation and not to the earth. This account of Creation is not of a symbolic character, but gives explanations about actual spiritual events that took place at immeasurable heights.

It is logical that the Creation that God made *in the beginning* (Genesis 1, 1), thus first, cannot refer to the earth, which is furthest removed from God, and hence has undergone a long process of evolution to its present state.

If we recall the words that Paul wrote to the Ephesians about Jesus (Ephesians 4, 1 0), "He that descended is the same also that ascended up far above all heavens . . . ," they plainly state that between the earth and the Divine, from which Jesus came, there are still other Spiritual Realms (heavens). This also indicates that the earth cannot be the first Creation.

Nor did God make His Creation from "nothingness," as is generally assumed; but it was His Creative Power, His Radiation, which with the Creative Words "Let there be Light" streamed forth into the unlit Universe. And everything formed and developed from this Living Power. In some old Creation-myths the Act of Creating is depicted as if the Supreme Being made Creation from Himself, that is from His heart or other parts of

His body. This figurative symbolic account plainly illustrates that some "substance for creating" existed, and still exists today, and hence that Creation has by no means arisen from "nothingness."

For this reason both the Genesis of the Bible and the scientific recognition of the development of the World are right. Hence no one need become unsettled in his belief. For development also is willed by God. A good example of this is the human spirit himself. Although he is eternal, yet he has not been created fully conscious. He must first work his way up from an unconscious "spirit-seed-grain," which through a natural process was "expelled" from the Spiritual Sphere (Paradise), to a fully conscious personality in a world that is likewise subject to development. In the struggle with its alien influences he is meant to gather his experiences, and thus at the same time ennoble his surroundings through his spirit, until he gradually becomes so mature that he can return to Paradise. He is like the prodigal son who finds his way back again to his spiritual home.

But even there he is still infinitely far away from God. Never can a human spirit come face-to-face with his God personally, because He is enthroned in unapproachable distances. God is not so "near" as men imagine Him to be, for "as the heavens are higher than the earth, so are my ways higher than your ways, and my thoughts than your thoughts" (Isaiah 55, 9). God is near to men only when a Part of Him (a Son) sojourns in Subsequent Creation (the World).

But man has the ability to *recognize* God by His Works. He is in the position to draw references from these Works about their Creator, about His Perfection and Sublimity. In this way he can gradually attain to the right belief in God, to the true recognition of God, and to the divining of the Greatness of God.

Since man as a creature is part of this Work, it is only natural that he should ask about his Creator and His Works. With normal spiritual development man will also strive and long to establish a connection with the Creator. Then he will experience that the Work is absolutely dependent on the Creator, which makes it impossible for man ever to be or to become creator or master himself.

Ever since man sojourned in the World he bore this longing within. He has brought it with him as a heritage from his eternal Homeland, this longing for the Light. It is implanted in him, and guides him safely to his goal, if he remains alert. Through discoveries and excavations more and more indications and proofs are being found that even in remote antiquity, long before the recording of the Old Testament, men of that time adored and worshipped a Supreme Being. For God was and ever is.

Today this God-seeking and God-experiencing is buried through the increasingly earth-bound state of man. The intellect that has been raised to the position of ruler bars the way to the possibilities of recognition. In fact it is the intellect that makes the assertion that God is dead. Yet it is not God Who is dead, but through the propensity for transient things the spirit of man has allowed itself to be so walled in that it is as though dead. In this gloomy state it cannot help looking upon God as dead.

Already today many Christians all over the earth are saying, "God is dead." Even Christian theologians assert this because they say that the existence of God cannot be verified. It is no longer surprising, therefore, when today there is more and more talk about "Christian atheism," contradictory as these words are. Or it comes to the grotesque demand that the creature "man" requires *proofs* of the actual existence of the Creator.

All these absurdities are fallacies on the part of man, who cannot see the forest for the trees. He stands amidst God's wonderful Creation, is himself a part of this Creation, and does not recognize it as such because, through firmly clinging to material substance, he allows his view of great and essential things to become obscured, although they literally force themselves upon him in the Work of the Creator.

Psychic shocks will make it possible for the firm embrace through material substance, to which the intellect also belongs, to be gradually loosened, so that the human spirit will once more be able to understand the Language of his God.

For: *God is not silent*! It is the fault of man alone, if he cannot hear and recognize Him!

12. THE GUILT OF GOLGOTHA

The Crucifixion

When Pilate asked Jesus during His trial: "Art thou a king then?" Jesus answered: "Thou sayest that I am a king. To this end was I born, and for this cause came I into the world, that I should bear witness unto the truth. Every one that is of the truth heareth my voice." And Pilate said to Him: "What is truth?" (John 18, 37 and 38). The four Gospels of the New Testament do not answer this question. But we read the answer in the Gospel of Nicodemus (III, 2)*: "Jesus answered him: Truth is from heaven. Pilate said: Is there not truth upon earth? Jesus said to Pilate. You see how those who speak the truth are judged by those who have authority on earth."

It was an inevitable consequence that in the course of His earthly work Jesus, Who came from the Truth, simply had to unmask the enemies of the Truth, who were to be found mainly in the ruling priesthood, with Caiaphas, the High Priest, as their leader. They would not tolerate Jesus filling the Mosaic Law with a new spirit, and gaining ever-greater influence over the people. He thereby threatened their power and authority. The distrust and scorn with which they met the Bringer of the Truth soon changed to open hostility and deadly hatred.

After they had first tried to make Him appear untrustworthy through asking insidious and subtle questions, they soon demanded His earthly destruction. Caiaphas pronounced the death sentence on Jesus with the words. "It is expedient for us, that one man should die for the people, and that the whole nation perish not" (John 11, 50). For "from that day forth they took counsel together for to put him to death" (John 11, 53). But some lawful reason had yet to be found, which soon presented itself. Through his betrayal Judas made the intended arrest of Jesus easier. When before the High Council Jesus acknowledged Himself to be the Son of God they sentenced Him to death as a blasphemer, according to the letter of their law. They delivered Him up to the Governor (Procurator) of the Roman occupation forces, Pontius Pilate, who was in authority at that time, because they were not allowed to carry out death sentences (John 18, 31).

---

* New Testament Apocrypha, Vol. 1, E. Hermecke, Lutterworth Press, London.

The High Council, however, could not make use of its own verdict that Jesus was a blasphemer, because Pilate attached no importance to their religious disputes. Hence they had to continue proceedings on the political level, in order to enforce a conviction under the Roman law, which among other things stated that crimes against the emperor were punishable with death. Thus Jesus was represented to Pilate as an agitator and insurgent who rebelled against the emperor, although they knew perfectly well that Jesus was the very One Who had taught: "Render unto Caesar the things which be Caesar's, and unto God the things which be God's" (Luke 20, 25).

Pilate found no guilt in Jesus, particularly because He had answered him: "My kingdom is not of this world" (John 18, 36). He considered Him harmless, and tried several times to have Him released. Yet the leaders of the Jews threatened: "If thou let this man go, thou art not Caesar's friend: whosoever maketh himself a king speaketh against Caesar" (John 19, 12). This settled the matter, for Pilate did not wish to lose the friendship of the emperor. He thereby risked his whole professional career; for "friend of the emperor" was a title of honor, and its loss had serious consequences.

Pilate yielded to the threats, although his wife had warned him at the last minute: "Have thou nothing to do with that just man: for I have suffered many things this day in a dream because of him" (Matthew 27, 19). Thus he sentenced Jesus to die on the cross, and washed his hands before the people to demonstrate that he did not consider Jesus to be guilty. His words, "I am innocent of the blood of this just person," were answered by the shouting of the crowd and their deluded leaders: "His blood be on us, and on our children," a dreadful self-cursing, by which even future generations were cursed as well (Matthew 27, 24 and 25).

Thus the "Hosanna" with which the crowd hailed Jesus when He entered Jerusalem was soon afterwards changed to abuse, scoffing, and finally to the demand: "Crucify Him!" Who among the evildoers at that time would have thought that forty years later Jerusalem and its temple would be completely destroyed by Titus, the Roman commander-in-chief! According to tradition thousands of Jews are said to have been crucified then.

When on His last journey to Jerusalem Jesus beheld the city, according to the Gospel of Luke He said concerning its destruction: "And (thine enemies) shall lay thee even with the ground, and thy children within thee; and they shall not leave in thee one stone upon another; because thou knewest not the time of thy visitation" (Luke 19, 44), that is to say, the time when the Son of God dwelt within thy walls.

"Thou Shalt not Kill!"

In those days Jesus could only fulfill His Mission to proclaim the Truth among the Jewish people, because in their midst were human beings, who through their spiritual maturity, offered the support that was needed for an embodiment of the Divine Word. But among this selfsame people the Darkness too found in the ranks of the religious and worldly leaders men whom it needed for its plan of destruction, and who moreover held the power in their hands. It was especially reprehensible that among those were also priests who called themselves servants of God, and then had His Son put to death.

But all this conduct on the part of the chief offenders would immediately appear in a different light, if the death of Jesus, according to the opinion of many, had been provided for in God's plan of salvation or redemption. For the guilty ones themselves this of course results in a very paradoxical situation. On the one hand they are made responsible for the murder of Jesus; on the other hand, by the assumption of a death provided for in the plan of redemption, they are forced into the role of executive instruments that have to cooperate as traitors, judges, and executioners of the death sentence.

With regard to such a plan of redemption, how is it possible for God to demand that men should murder His own Son, whereby He would transgress His own Commandment? And where in this connection is the free will of man, which was laid with him in the cradle of his spirit?

All this would be possible, only if the plan of redemption were based on Divine arbitrary actions, which however God's Perfection would never allow. Hence only men can have conceived this plan, with its complete lack of logic. God did not send His Son to earth in order to let Him die for the sins of others.

When from the very beginning God has interwoven with His Creation the Law of Sowing and Reaping, then it is for all eternity an immutable Law that nothing can overthrow, not even a Son of God. In the very fact that the Laws of this Creation also apply to Parts of God, Who descend to Creation, lies the Greatness and Perfection of God. Jesus Himself confirmed this with the words: "Think not that I am come to destroy the law, or the prophets; I am not come to destroy, but to fulfill" (Matthew 5, 17).

Hence Jesus, being innocent, cannot take upon Himself the guilt of others, because He has not sown the seed for it. When the death of Jesus was foreseen by the Prophets, and later His own death was also foreseen by Jesus Himself, it was for an entirely different reason from that of the propitiatory sacrifice of His Son allegedly laid down in God's plan of redemption.

The true reason for these predictions lies in the depravity of men, the majority of whom had sunk so deeply at the time of the prophets' predictions that, unless they were to change, the end of their wrongly adopted course could be accurately foreseen. Added to this was the knowledge that they would remove every Truth Bringer who faced men on this course of hostility to the Light unless they were prepared to accept his message.

Therefore the entire greatness and grace of the sacrifice made by the Son of God, Who in spite of the greatest dangers already discernible in the beginning took His Mission upon Himself, can hardly ever be divined. For without this Mission even the few still carrying within them a spark of longing for the Light would have been lost.

For Jesus Himself death on the cross had only the one meaning: confirmation of the Truth of the Word brought by Him, Its continuation and the spreading of It. Had He yielded in the face of His enemies, and renounced His Origin and Teaching, His entire Mission would have failed.

Physical Resurrection

Yet another interpretation of the death of Jesus should be mentioned here. It states that Jesus did not die on the cross; that He was still alive when He was taken from the cross. The Turin Shroud, which is considered to be Jesus' winding-sheet, is said to furnish proof of this. Jesus is then supposed to have regained His strength in the tomb, and to have arisen in the physical body, which He had hitherto worn. For this reason the Jewish people were not guilty of the murder of Jesus. Also, in order to cross the earthly boundary when ascending to Heaven He had not changed His physical body into His ascension body before He arose from the tomb, but just shortly before He ascended.

With the help of the Shroud, other scientific sources have established that Jesus died on the cross from suffocation as a result of the crucifixion.

To this it must be said: What was decisive for the guilt was the resolve of the priesthood to kill Jesus, which was certainly not made with the intention that He should not die on the cross.

Even if Jesus had still been alive after being taken from the cross, it could only have been for a short time; but this cannot be assumed because, through maltreatment and suffering on the cross, His physical body was no longer capable of living.

The resurrection of Jesus after His physical death is a matter of the beyond and not of this world. Jesus could not ascend to Heaven in His physical body, because this is impossible according to the Laws of Nature, which express nothing other than the Will of God.

There is only one solution to the empty tomb, namely that the physical cloak of Jesus was secretly buried in an unknown place by His disciples or friends in order to protect it from being arbitrarily seized.

When after His physical death Jesus was seen by His disciples and other people, it was not His transfigured physical body but His ethereal or non-physical body, which like every human being He bore already on earth, and which enveloped His Divine Core. Nevertheless it can be said that Jesus arose in full bodily form, but with His ethereal body, which also has a human form. Hence Jesus could say to His frightened disciples: "Behold my hands and my feet, that it is myself" (Luke 24, 39). This non-physical body also bore the wound marks.

But this seeing was possible only with men's ethereal eyes, after their eyes had been opened for it, as is explicitly stated (Luke 24, 31); that is to say they had first to be made clairvoyant. Likewise Jesus was able to pass through closed doors with His ethereal body (John 20, 19 and 26), because the finer species can always penetrate the coarser, just as for example radio waves pass through walls.

Collective Guilt

In all these considerations as to the chief offenders we must not forget one thing. Jesus came because of the sins of *mankind*. They were sins against the Holy Spirit, thus against the Will of God, Which is expressed in the Laws of Creation. Yet not only the Jews were involved in the sins of mankind, but also all other men, through continually trespassing against the Divine Laws, Commandments and Teachings during many earth lives.

The sins, or rather the products of the sins, which have forms and bear within them a certain life, were even at that time so great that a huge city could form from them in the non-physical (ethereal) planes: Babylon, the wicked city, under the dominion of Lucifer (Rev. 17, 5; 18, 2). From it comes the Darkness that holds the earth in its grip. From the outset this hate-filled Darkness sought to render the Mission of Jesus impossible. For this every means, however reprehensible, were suitable. But as it could find no fault with Jesus Himself, it sought and found willing helpers and underlings among men.

That ugly thing came to pass on a big scale, which takes place every day on a small scale.

Let us assume that for some reason men harbor envy. This envy shapes itself into invisible, very active forms, which in accordance with the Law of Attraction of Homogeneous Species merge into a center, within which threads again connect all the envious ones.

If at some time and at some place a member of this "envy-community" commits a crime on earth, all the others are involved in it and partly responsible through their envy-filled volition, even if their day-consciousness experiences nothing of it. A common guilt, the collective guilt, then links them all.

Thus the roots of a collective guilt lie in the similar thoughts and intuitive perceptions of men. Generally on earth only the person who committed the deed will be caught. All other "accomplices" will remain concealed, because no one can follow the threads in the beyond, unless there be a special clairvoyant gift for it, which however is rarely to be found. Yet the accomplices must also in some way atone for their guilt in accordance with the Divine Laws, from which nothing escapes.

It is in this light that the problem of the guilt of Golgotha is also to be regarded. The earthly barriers must be crossed, in order to gain the necessary comprehensive view. For sin does not stop at national borders. Therefore the idea of a collective guilt on the part of the Jews alone cannot be upheld, precisely because the whole of mankind is involved in the murder of Golgotha, through their combined sinful conduct.

Repeated Earth Lives

Many will now ask: Can a man who is living today be personally implicated in the crucifixion of Jesus that took place two thousand years ago? If his sin only arises now, it cannot have contributed to the burden of sin at the time of Jesus.

This question leads us to take a wider view of the activity in Creation, and to seek the solution in repeated earth lives. The knowledge of this gives us above all an insight into the connections of the great weaving in Creation, and helps to close many a gap in our questions and problems, which without this knowledge would always have to remain open.

Almost all the great ones among many peoples have believed in the reincarnation of the soul, and still do. It is not the case that again and again a soul is newly formed at procreation or birth. The soul exists even before birth, and halfway through pregnancy is incarnated into the physical body, which it leaves again at death.

The Law of Attraction of Homogeneous Species, as expressed in the popular saying, "Birds of a feather flock together," and in some cases also the Law of Reciprocal Action (the Law of Sowing and Reaping), are decisive for an incarnation. Thus each soul comes to the place where it belongs, and no one need fear that he might be mistaken in the choice of his parents. Often man only thinks so when, for instance, the similar species that contributed towards the attraction is also founded in evil qualities. Then faults, weaknesses and propensities form a mutual source of irritation, often to the point of becoming unbearable; but at the same time this provides the opportunity to experience and lay aside one's wrong conduct.

This is especially important for the present time. For we are in the final happening, equivalent to a final judgment, in which all the threads of fate from former earth lives must be experienced and redeemed through an inner change towards the good and beautiful, so that men become free from every burden for the new up building on earth, in peace and harmony, as promised by God.

Hence the reactions and releases of individual and mass destinies increase in an uncanny way, because over thousands of years almost nothing has been sown but evil volition, which must now bear fruit.

The return of mankind's heavy karma of Golgotha also falls due at this final time. This means that those who were present then are again on earth, whether as Jews or as embodiments in other peoples. For reincarnations do not stop at nations and peoples either. Here only the state of spiritual maturity and the qualities acquired count.

For this reason stigmata need not appear among Jews. Stigmata, that is the wound marks of Christ, are borne by people as the consequence of a grave personal offense against Jesus during His sojourn on earth. Let us recall, for instance, the thief on the cross who mocked Jesus. They must naturally be stigmata that appear spontaneously, and are not caused through religious ecstasy.

The spirit of man is therefore much older than is supposed, much older than past physical bodies and the present one. Although in most cases he knows nothing of this, he has nevertheless absorbed the lessons and experiences of many earth lives, and makes use of them unconsciously.

But the knowledge of repeated earth lives should make one thing absolutely clear to him with regard to the problem of the guilt of Golgotha: How petty and base are the hatred and persecution of Jews, or even reprisals against them! Who among those who do such things knows whether he himself has not burdened himself with some guilt as a Jew at that time, be it only through indifference towards the Message of Jesus.

"To me Belongeth Vengeance"

Even in the Old Testament men were urgently warned of such wrongdoing with the Words of God: "To me belongeth vengeance, and recompense" (Deut. 32, 35). These words, together with the saying "Eye for eye, tooth for tooth" (Deut. 19, 21), give testimony to the immutable Justice of God that manifests in the Law of Sowing and Reaping, of Effect and Reaction, or we can also say: in the Law of Reciprocal Action, which permeates the entire Creation. The spiritual seed of men is just as much subject to this Law as the seed that we entrust to the soil.

Eye for eye, tooth for tooth. These expressions in the language of the Old Testament illustrate to us how the Law of Reciprocal Action, which is closely connected with the Law of Attraction of Homogeneous Species, works. Always wheat can arise only from the wheat grain that we put into the earth; from the good we bring into the world only good can come, and the evil we produce returns to us again as evil, each many times over, just as the seed bears manifold fruit. Hence that is what is meant by the words "Eye for eye, tooth for tooth": Like brings forth like, joy causes joy and affliction causes affliction.

It was never meant to demand that we should knock another person's eye out, if he has done that to us. It is to prevent this that the words, To me belongeth vengeance, and recompense, are given; namely, man must leave vengeance, recompense or harvest to the Laws of God, thus to His Will, Which down to the most minute detail will ensure such a just harvest, exactly corresponding to the seed, as man could never succeed in doing.

It is also in this way that the words of Paul to the Romans are to be understood: "Dearly beloved, avenge not yourselves, but rather give place unto wrath (the reciprocal action); for it is written, Vengeance is mine; I will repay, saith the Lord" (Rom. 12, 19).

These Biblical words, which were given to the people of Israel thousands of years ago, and which until now have hardly been understood in their deeper significance, are to warn us all against acts of retaliation out of personal vengefulness, even in connection with those human beings whose fate is closely linked with the dark deed of Golgotha.

"Hear, O Israel: The Lord our God is one Lord" (Deut. 6, 4). This has been the wording of the Jewish creed for thousands of years. And in the Jewish Prayer Book it says, "I believe with perfect faith that the Creator, blessed be his name, is a Unity, and that there is no unity in any manner like unto his, and that he alone is our God, who was, is, and will be."*

To the Jews this "unity" means "sole," "unique," and to them it admits of no Son of God or Divine Mediator. For this reason, too, Jesus is rejected as the Son of God. Hence the Messiah still awaited by many Jews even today can be no Son of God, but at the most one chosen at birth, a high spirit especially empowered by God, who has no part in Divinity.

But it should be borne in mind that the Unity of God was especially emphasized in view of the polytheism prevalent in those days. And then it must not be forgotten that the earthly relationship of father and son, which is of two completely different persons, cannot be applied here. A Son of God can only be a Part of God, Which God severs from Himself and sends into His Creation, but Which always is and remains one with Him, and only outwardly appears as two in Its *working*, by which the Unity of God is not annulled. It is as Jesus said: "I and my Father are one" (John 10, 30).

Therefore the references by the Prophets Daniel and Isaiah to the second Son of God, the Son of Man, should be considered and examined, because here lies the solution to the question of the Messiah, Who has for long been ardently awaited.

Isaiah proclaims of God: "Before me there was no God formed, neither shall there be after me. I, even I, am the Lord; and beside me there is no savior" (Isaiah 43, 10 and 11). But God has also let the same prophet proclaim Imanuel, Who in Daniel (7, 13 and 14) is still called by the name Son of Man: "Therefore the Lord himself shall give you a sign; Behold, a virgin shall conceive, and bear a son, and shall call his name Imanuel" (Isaiah 7, 14). Also the time is given when Imanuel will appear, a time when it becomes physically manifest that nothing that is not resolved and carried out according to the Will of God can last; all else must perish, "it will come to nought." It is the great time of perplexity, in

---

* Authorised Daily Prayer Book of the United Hebrew Congregations (Eyre and Spottiswoode Ltd., London).

which one conference follows another, when distrust is everywhere, unrest and great uneasiness, when hopeless confusion spreads ever more. Already thousands of years ago this time was foretold by the Prophet Isaiah with the words: "Take counsel together, and it shall come to nought; speak the word, and it shall not stand: for God is with us" (Isaiah 8, 10).

The Biblical passages were mistakenly related to Jesus. So, for instance, the Evangelist Matthew confused Imanuel with Jesus (Matthew 1, 22 and 23), Whom Micah prophesied (Micah 5, 2). Jesus never called Himself Imanuel, nor did others ever call Him so.

The expectation of a Messiah, the establishing of a Messianic World Kingdom, thus of an earthly Kingdom of Peace, as foretold by the Prophets, concerns all men, because it is only the spirit of man that counts before God, and not races, nations and religions.

Finally, leaving aside all dogmas, every human being must in his own interest recognize a Son of God as such. For this, however, he needs an alert spiritual intuitive perception, which alone can help him to recognition. He must be like the wise virgins in the parable that Jesus ends with the words: "Watch therefore, for ye know neither the day nor the hour wherein the Son of Man cometh" (Matthew 25, 13).

The Cross of Truth

The basis of Christianity is Judaism, which takes a firm place in the spiritual history of the development of mankind. Just let us think of the Ten Commandments, of the Sermon on the Mount, of the Lord's Prayer, all of them Divine Words that have been given to the people of Israel, to the Jews.

They too have the selfsame spiritual origin and the selfsame common road through material Creation as have all men.

For at one time all men came as "spirit-seed-grains" from their spiritual home, from Paradise, into the material, transient world of Creation, in order to return thence to their spiritual home as fully conscious personalities after the completion of their development.

But most of them strayed from the road and no longer found the goal. For that reason the immeasurable Love of God inclined to the earth, in order to speak directly to the almost lost human beings, and to tell them that the Truth can come only from God.

Therefore let us take to heart the words that Jesus spoke to men: "If any man Will come after me, let him deny himself, and take up his cross *daily*, and follow me" (Luke 9, 23), or ". . . take up the cross, and follow me" (Mark 10, 21).

By the Cross Jesus meant the sign of Divine Truth, the equal-armed Cross. From discoveries and excavations it transpires that this Cross is an ancient symbol that was known on earth before Christ, and which can also be seen in many churches, sometimes encircled with a ring, sometimes without the ring. It must not be confused with the form of the Golgotha cross of suffering.

He who takes up this Cross takes up the *Truth*, but *not a burden*, as it is wrongly interpreted.

Jesus has never intended with His words to call upon men to take up a daily burden. On the contrary, He wanted to make their life easier by exhorting them to live up to the Truth *every day*, to look for and recognize It in the Laws of Creation, and to adjust their daily life to these Laws.

He who does so frees himself from all burden and guilt, likewise from the guilt of Golgotha, which according to the Eternal Laws now returns at this time in order to be redeemed. For him the Golgotha cross of suffering will be changed into the redeeming Cross of Truth, which victoriously conquers all Darkness!

13. "BEHOLD THE LAMB OF GOD, WHICH BEARETH THE SIN OF THE WORLD"
(John 1, 29)

To understand these words aright we must first of all deal with the *concept of sin*. Its cause lies in the wrongful use of the flesh. As Paul says in the Epistle to the Romans, there is a "carnal way of thinking," which sells men under sin (Rom. 7, 14 and 18). But where is the point in the flesh that makes man into the slave of sin? It is the brain, that is the cerebrum, which produces the thoughts and the intellect, and which like all flesh is perishable.

This *intellectual brain* is absolutely needed as an instrument on earth. Out of vanity and pretended knowledge man has simply made the mistake of over-cultivating it, and of eventually allowing it to rule his spirit, thus yielding to the intellect a place that according to the order of Creation belongs only to the spirit, which manifests in the intuitive perception.

This is the reason for the Fall of man and for hereditary sin. Hereditary sin, however, is not equivalent to an irrevocable compulsion of having to sin! What is hereditary is only the physical tendency that is due to the intellectual brain, which has been over-cultivated through one-sided use. Hence the tendency is not compulsive, but it contains a danger that man can avert by keeping his intuitive perception alert. That which is spiritual cannot be handed down.

Only through the over-cultivated intellect, which on account of its origin can only understand what is perishable, is Lucifer the Antichrist in a position to carry out in the World his activities, which are hostile to the Light. As soon as man does not listen to his spirit, to his inner voice, and gives preference to the intellect, there is already the danger of sinning, which consists of man's wrongful use of the spiritual power streaming through Creation.

Since "in the beginning" God made Creation, this power, like the pulse beat of the heart, streams through all parts of Creation sustaining and renewing them. This pure creative power is the "river of water of life," proceeding out of the Throne of God (Rev. 22, 1). Yet this power is not God Himself, but His radiation.

At the time when they were gathered together in memory of Jesus, the disciples of Christ were overcome by this power. It was the very time when the power — as happens every year — was poured out anew into Creation.

All human spirits stand in this spiritual stream and live from it. Only rarely do they become conscious of it; usually when for once their souls are shaken by deep suffering or pure joy. From this stream men draw the power to form their good and evil works. For man has the ability by his own free choice to use and to direct this power, just as he is able to use the power of a machine for destructive or constructive purposes.

The works are the good and evil intuitive perceptions, thoughts and deeds. They are referred to in the Revelation when it says, "their works do follow them" (Rev. 14, 13). They follow the soul of man into the beyond at its physical death.

These works naturally represent something. They have invisible forms, with an invisible content of a finer nature than coarse earthly matter. If they were nothing they could have no effect, they could not follow.

In the use of the creative power continually streaming through Creation lies also the solution to the often asked question: "How could God bring forth evil that is so contrary to His Being," or "Has evil also come into Creation through the Act of Creating?" The concept expressed in these questions is wrong. *It is not God Who brings forth wickedness or evil, but man, by taking the pure, neutral power of Creation and forming evil with it.* To that extent the Biblical words, "I am the Lord . . . and create darkness," have not been rightly handed down (Isaiah 45, 6 and 7).

It is not hard to understand that these forms are dirty and ugly. For in fact they represent the sin and guilt of men. From them, through the union of homogeneous species, such as envy, hatred, avarice, hypocrisy, a craving for pleasure, etc., there are gradually formed centers, which in turn have a harmful influence on people of a similar nature. Hell itself is a product of men's evil works, and has arisen through thousands of years of "activity." In exactly the same way, there are naturally also concentrations of good forms, which spread joy, peace and harmony.

Thus man not only pollutes the earth, water and air with his earthly wastes. Far worse still are the "psychic wastes" in the shape of his impure thoughts, which have turned his ethereal surroundings into a disgusting swamp, out of which he no longer finds the way by his own strength. We find the visible deposits of these psychic wastes everywhere, in the spoken and written word and in pictures.

Can we imagine that we bring Christ, Who after all Is Divine Purity personified, in contact with our dirty forms of sin by saying: "Cast all guilt upon Him?" For the guilt of sin is indeed a reality, and has forms. It makes no difference that we cannot normally see them.

According to the view generally held Christ is supposed, through His alleged expiatory death, to have vicariously taken upon Himself the burden of sins for men, to bring about a reconciliation thereby between God and men.

It is striking that in the Revelation of John, which after all came into being and was proclaimed only *after* the death of Christ, and which contains all the important spiritual events, not a word is said about this taking over of sins. On the contrary, it is clearly stated that it is men who have washed their robes clean, and not Christ, which means that men had to wash off their sins themselves with the help of the *Word*, Whose Truth Christ sealed with His blood (Rev. 7, 14).

Indeed the Lamb of God, Which was "slain," is accusingly spoken of several times in the Revelation. And even from the promised Judgment of God alone, with the pouring out of the vials of Wrath, anything but reconciliation between the Godhead and mankind is to be inferred.

But if Christ had taken upon Himself or taken away the evil works of men, what works are then referred to in God's Judgment, which Christ Himself proclaimed? "For the Son of Man shall come in the glory of his Father with his angels; and then he shall reward every man according to his works" (Matthew 16, 27); and in the Revelation of John the Son of Man promised: "I come quickly; and my reward is with me, to give every man according as his work shall be" (Rev. 22, 12).

The words "every man" refer to *every* human being, whether Christian or non-Christian. Creeds are of no importance in regard to this spiritual happening. Here it is only a question of the human spirit, how it stands at the time of the Judgment, that is to say, in the Judgment it must reap what it has sown during its repeated earth lives, good and bad (Gal. 6, 7). The harvesting and sowing naturally applies equally to the seeds of the human works, namely to man's thoughts and actions, as to the seeds of Nature. This is a fact that only very few people make clear to themselves. And these repeated earth lives, in which many among the best of all peoples have believed and still believe today, give man the opportunity to make good the mistakes and sins of past lives in the newly given earth life. Of what use would this making good be in the various earth lives, if Christ had taken over the sins of men?

For this reason *Christ* cannot harvest what *men* sow. If this were possible, God would have to alter His Laws. But His Perfection does not allow this. Not even earthly jurisdiction permits a man to shoulder the guilt of another.

Christ certainly bears the sin of the world (John 1, 29). But He bears it in His wound marks, on Himself, as a visible sign of the sins committed against Him by men, *but not in the sense of taking over their sins.*

In many Bibles Martin Luther's correct translation, "Behold the Lamb of God, which beareth the sin of the world" has been changed to "Behold the Lamb of God, which *taketh away* or *taketh upon itself* the sin of the world." This does not correspond, however, to the real happening.

For there is something else besides, which makes the taking away of the sin impossible. The works of sin are firmly linked by threads with the author. Only *he himself* can redeem himself from them by inwardly turning to the good and recognizing his faults. Then these threads of fate will gradually dry up and fall away. Man is redeemed from his sin; his sins are forgiven him.

But he does not find this forgiveness and redemption from his misdeeds, faults and weaknesses in the taking-over of sins by Christ, but in the fulfillment of the Laws of God. Christ points out the way to it in His Word. He did not come to let Himself be put to death by men, and thereby, as it were, demand of them to transgress His Father's Commandment: "Thou shalt not kill!"

That this death was not in the Will of His Father plainly follows from the *Parable of the wicked husbandman* given by Christ (Matthew 21, 33-39). After the servants (teachers, prophets) whom the householder (God) sent to help the husbandman (human beings) had been received by them with enmity and had even been killed, God sent His Son to men, assuming that they would reverence Him (Chapter 21, 37). But Him they also killed.

In this parable, which shows in pictures that are to be spiritually understood how hostile is men's attitude towards the Love of God, Jesus forebodingly described His own violent death. But He also expresses in the parable that His death was *not intended* by His Father, otherwise God would not have said that men would reverence His Son. Surely the meaning here is that they would not dare to harm Him! Nevertheless they did. And the intercession of Jesus on the cross, "Father, forgive them, for they know not what they do," showed emphatically enough that men's actions were wrong.

Thus to their already existing sins they added a fresh heavy burden of sin, which must now be redeemed in the Final Judgment proclaimed by Jesus (Matthew 16, 27), so that at last the wounds, which the Lamb of God bears as a visible sign of the sin of the entire mankind, can close!

14. THE EMPTY TOMB

"Spirit" is the core; the true ego of man-"soul" is the spirit with its fine coverings, without the physical body. All these various coverings of finer nature are present in the physical body of man.

The astral body is part of the physical cloak itself, and is an important link between it and the soul. That this astral body does in fact exist is quite clearly demonstrated in persons who have lost a limb. Though it is no longer there, they often experience pain long afterwards in the place where it was. The medical profession has concerned itself for some time with these so-called "phantom pains," without finding their true cause. The cause lies in the astral body, whose limbs are not simultaneously severed, because they are of a finer earthly species than the coarse earthly body. Therefore the pains are not due to imagination, but are real.

We must bear in mind at this point that the spirit and all its coverings have human form. For the physical body has only been shaped in accordance with the spiritual prototype. The human form is a characteristic of the spirit. Hence when we see the soul of man represented in old pictures as a complete human figure, this corresponds to the actual form.

At his death man leaves behind his physical cloak, with the astral body, and enters the beyond in his ethereal body, which is now his outer covering. When it is said in the Revelation of John that the human spirits have washed their robes white, what is meant is not the earthly garments but the ethereal coverings of the human spirit in the beyond, which each can make light or heavy, bright or dark, according to his good or his evil volition.

With this ethereal body, the human spirit has the ability to penetrate all that is more dense and coarse. Therefore it happens not infrequently that deceased persons can suddenly appear in a locked room. This is the effect of a lawfulness existing in all Creation, whereby the finer species, in this case the soul, can always penetrate the coarser species, here physical matter, quite easily, as happens for instance every time a soul is incarnated in a physical body.

On the physical plane, these processes are quite familiar to us: We need only think of the radio waves passing through walls, or of the electric current running through cable. Exactly the same lawfulness holds true for the sphere that lies beyond the earth, and when the Bible relates of the resurrected Son of God, Christ Jesus: ". . . when the doors were shut where the disciples were assembled for fear of the Jews, came Jesus and stood in the midst . . ." (John 20, 19), the event described has also the same natural reason.

Only with His ethereal body was Jesus able to enter the locked room, after having to leave His physical body, which was broken on the cross. He could neither take this physical body with Him, even in a "transfigured" state, nor was it possible for His soul to be reunited after death with the perishable earthly cloak.

Although the core of Jesus' body was Divine and not spiritual, through becoming man He was subject to the Laws working in Creation in exactly the same way as the human spirit. Jesus clearly emphasized this when He pointed out that He had come to fulfill the Laws of God. All that happens in Creation takes place according to the Holy Will of God in unyielding, strict order and adamantine perfection, and it admits of no exception or arbitrary acts, even for a Divine Envoy when He has left the Divine Kingdom and enters the Spheres of Creation.

Nonetheless Jesus arose from the grave in *full possession of His body*: It was His ethereal body, whereas in exact accordance with the Laws of Creation He had to leave His physical body behind. It was this ethereal body of Jesus that the disciples and other blessed persons could see — being able to recognize it, however, only with their ethereal eyes. Therefore, as the Bible clearly states, their eyes had first to be opened for this; according to earthly conceptions therefore they became clairvoyant. All these are processes in accordance with the Laws of Creation, which would have developed in exactly the same way had the physical body of Jesus remained in the tomb.

However, all four Evangelists report unanimously that the physical body of Christ had disappeared from the tomb, and this they associate with the "resurrection" of the Son of God. But the empty tomb by no means proves the resurrection of the physical body of Jesus Christ, since according to the immutable Laws of Nature an earthly body cannot rise from the earth into a higher sphere of Creation. It stays behind when man dies, and goes the way of all perishable things — even in the case of a Divine Envoy! Hence for the empty tomb there remains only the assumption that Christ's earthly vessel was taken from the tomb and buried elsewhere.

In this case, however, the traditional accounts of that time, according to which the disciples were accused by the Jewish authorities of "stealing" the body of Jesus, would have to be considered and assessed from a different standpoint than hitherto; yet with the unqualified reservation that if the disciples removed the physical body of Jesus from the tomb, no evil intent must be imputed to them. Presumably it was only a few of the disciples who took this precautionary measure, without the knowledge of the others, in order to preserve the earthly body of Christ from outside interference.

Thus considered, the secret of the empty tomb is clearly and openly revealed before our eyes, and the event of the resurrection of Jesus Christ, just in its simple and natural greatness, bears impressive witness to the immutable and perfect Will of God — firmly anchored and eternally active in the Laws of the entire Creation!

15. "BY FAITH ALONE"
(Rom. 3, 28)

In hours of inner affliction Martin Luther had often pondered over how he could pass before God, how he could obtain His Grace.

In his distress of conscience he resolved in 1505 to enter the Augustine Monastery at Erfurt.

But here also he did not find his peace. Neither did much practicing of good works, nor pilgrimages and prayers, bring him any nearer to God. He called out in despair: "What are the good works that we do, they will not make a merciful God for us . . . ."

So an old friar drew his attention to the teaching of Paul, that a man is justified by faith without the deeds of the law (Rom. 3, 28). In these words of the Apostle, Luther finally found support; for applied to his position they meant: "Justification before God comes from faith, not from the works of the church."

By the words "without the deeds of the law" Paul meant quite definite works that were done only according to the letter, in order to obtain some entitlement before God. The words did not say that man gets by without any works. For Paul also supplements his teaching of justification when he writes in his Epistle to the Galatians: "For in Christ availeth only faith, *which worketh by love*" (Gal. 5, 6). Hence faith must be transformed into deed, and this deed must be filled with love.

But Luther wished to admit only faith as a basis and prerequisite of his justification. The good works would then have to come of themselves. In his pamphlet, On the Freedom of a Christian Man, he wrote: "Thus we see that in faith a Christian man has enough; he does not need to do any works in order to be pious," or, "that faith alone, without any works, makes pious, free and blest."

James had already held a different view. In his Epistle in the New Testament — as if to amend and clarify Paul's view — he wrote: "By works was faith made perfect" (2, 22); "Ye see then how that by works a man is justified, and not by faith only" (2, 24); "For as the body without the spirit is dead, so faith without works is dead also" (2, 26).

The dogma laid down by Martin Luther, "By faith alone", has given rise to much misunderstanding, and in all these centuries it could never be satisfactorily explained. Thus Lutherans are now reproached with being no longer capable even of making Luther's basic idea of justification through faith understandable to men. At the Plenary

Session of the Lutheran International Union in Helsinki in 1963, vain attempts were made to interpret Luther's teaching of justification anew, for the present time.

Yet the solution is not difficult, if we free the conception of man's works from the intellectual limitation of the merely external.

For the works result from the whole nature of a man's activities in everyday life on earth, whether they are visible deeds, or invisible intuitive perceptions and thoughts, which man in his free volition can produce every minute, whether these works are good or evil. They all cling to him, and are severed only when he severs himself from them. If he has not yet done this by the time of his physical death they will follow him into the beyond. With these works man is given a great power *and* a great responsibility! Therefore man will be judged according to these works in the great Divine Judgment (Matthew 16, 27; Rev. 22, 12).

To these works naturally belong also those mentioned by Paul and Luther, which are done out of habit, or only according to the letter, or calculatingly, in order to achieve something either here on earth or in the beyond. It is self-evident that with such works a justification before God cannot be realized, and hence both condemn works of this kind, because they lack the right faith.

Thus neither faith alone nor the works alone are enough for justification before God. What are needed for this are the right faith as well as the right works. A right faith is a living faith, not a blind faith. It is founded on conviction, which is gained through strict, unbiased investigation.

Right works are good works, which do not spend themselves in outward activities, but come from the inner being, from the soul of man, and are always in harmony with the Laws of Creation. This requires unceasing vigilance, because man continually produces works, that is, intuitive perceptions, thoughts and deeds. Then he must simply take care, and adapt these works to the Laws of God by a decision of his will. This is helped by a deep inner faith, a faith that comes from conviction! That is the connection between the faith and the works of men.

A man thus vigilant is what is meant in the parable of the wise virgins (Matthew 25, 1-13). He keeps his spirit alive in the constant striving for this vigilance, and in the liveliness of his spirit he will then become a "righteous man" in the Biblical sense, a human being who places himself aright in the Will of the Creator, and who does what the Creator wills. He becomes a doer of the Word and not a hearer only (James 1, 22). *In this lies his justification, by which at the same time he attests to being fully aware of his* responsibility towards God. Hence through his faith and through his works he will eventually partake of the Grace of God.

16. A NEW REFORMATION?

At a time when there was a striving after new spiritual recognitions in the German lands, Martin Luther again recalled to the conscience of his fellowmen the Gospel of Christ, that man could find his way into the Kingdom of God by himself, without the church. He demanded the abolition of all human mediation between God and those who were seeking God.

Thus he showed his fellowmen the lost way to spiritual freedom, whereby the opportunity was given for an undreamed-of spiritual up-swinging, which could have changed the destiny of the German people for the better.

Yet many did not follow the way shown, and wrangling, strife, dissensions, discord and even religious wars were the unhappy consequences of these spiritual calls for an awakening.

The Christian people soon forgot their freedom of conscience by constricting their spirits through rigid thinking.

The laboriously acquired freedom was once more so pressed into letters, teachings and formulae that two hundred years later Lessing sorrowfully wrote: "Luther! Great, misunderstood man. — You have freed us from the yoke of tradition: who will free us from the unbearable yoke of the letter! Who will at last bring us Christianity — as Christ Himself would teach it!" (A Parable, 1778).

Today the limitation of the spirit, its enchainment to matter, is so great that without the help of God a separation from matter is no longer possible. The decline of mankind has progressed to such an extent that once again, as before the flood, the ominous words, "And it repented the Lord that he had made man on the earth, and it grieved him at his heart," (Genesis 6, 6) could be uttered.

The question about God has become a question about the predominance of the intellect, which was only intended to be an instrument for what is perishable, but which men have raised by a free decision to the throne of the spirit. It is the intellect that is meant by the dreadful beast in the Revelation (13, 1), which John saw rise up from the sea of matter.

When a new reformation, a twentieth-century reformation, is spoken of today, the very first concern should be a renewal of the eternal spirit, thus of the inner man: He must be freed from the fetters of the perishable, so that his intuitive perception and his conscience will also become free again from the domination of the intellect.

It is not a question this time of establishing new dogmas, which in accordance with the thorough German nature would then be used for fresh schisms and controversies. Today, at a time of enormous revolutionary changes in all spheres of life, it is as never before in human history a question of "to be or not to be" for the whole of humanity. The struggle in the 20th century is determined by the longing for Truth, for the whole Truth of human existence in this Creation, with the final goal of a true recognition of God. Hence this struggle is above all creeds.

Only in humility can the human spirit find a merciful God in this hard struggle!

17. THE LINGUISTIC WORK OF MARTIN LUTHER

"Unless I am convinced and conquered by the testimony of the Holy Scriptures, or by clear rational arguments, I shall continue to be conquered by the Scriptural passages quoted by me, and my conscience will remain captive in the Word of God; and I cannot and will not recant, for it is hard, harmful and dangerous to act against one's conscience. So help me God, Amen!" (Propyläen World History, Vol. 7).

This was the reply given by Martin Luther on the 18th of April 1521 at the Imperial Diet in Worms, before the Emperor Charles V and all the eminent men of the Empire gathered there, when he was called upon to recant his writings.

The Emperor made a counter-declaration in which among other things it was stated: "Thus I am determined to adhere to all that has been achieved since the Council of Constance. For it is certain that a single monk is mistaken when he opposes the opinion of the whole of Christendom, since otherwise Christendom would necessarily have erred for a thousand years or more" (Propyläen World History, Vol. 7).

After his justification before the Diet in Worms Luther was indeed given the promised safe conduct, but his earthly life was forfeit. The imperial ban was pronounced upon him, and it was stated that "anyone was permitted to slay him like a mad dog, wherever he were found"; in other words he was outlawed.

Elector Frederick of Saxony pretended to have the banned and outlawed man taken prisoner on his way home, and brought him to the safety of the Wartburg.

Thus through higher guidance Luther was saved from death, and through these events he was at the same time compelled to devote himself to a task whose fulfillment was yet awaiting him: the forming of a new German language.

At the Wartburg — Luther called this place of refuge his "Patmos" — he was able in peace and seclusion to develop his linguistic activities fully, for which his efforts to make the translation of the Bible understandable to everyone was of definite help to him. For in those days there were still great differences between individual dialects. This made an understanding very difficult, especially through the spoken word.

In his Table Talk Luther himself gives his views on this: "But there are many dialects in the German language, different ways of speaking, so that often one does not fully understand the other, as Bavarians do not properly understand Saxons, especially those who have not journeyed."

The language too has its Laws of Development. In view of this, dialects should only be stages on the way to the perfection of a language, and there must be no standing still thereon.

Hence the time was ripe to form the basis for a common German language from the German dialects. That was the task to which Martin Luther was called. The language area in which he lived offered favorable conditions for his linguistic work, which he based primarily on the "Saxon official language" ("Sächsische Canzeley-Sprache"), the "Misnian" language. For the new formation of the language he strove in addition to use as simple and popular a mode of expression as possible. This was made easier for him since he came into contact with many strata of the population, and he was also able to observe the linguistic habits of simple people.

How conscientiously Martin Luther and his co-workers strove for linguistic expression is shown by his own words: "In translating I have tried diligently to be able to give a pure and clear German. And indeed it has often happened to us that for two, three and four weeks we have searched and asked for a single word, and still sometimes have not found it . . ." (An Open Letter on Translating).

A comparison between the first translation of the Bible, 1522, and subsequent editions, clearly shows Luther's untiring creative activity in the use of language, which last but not least also had an influence on the national unification that was to follow only later. The last edition revised by Luther appeared in 1545. On this final edition he put, as though for a legacy to the Germans, the words:

"While ye have light,
believe in the light,
that ye may be children of light"
(John 12, 36).

The new German language created by Luther was spread in almost all German lands mainly through his Bible translation. It was a memorable event when in September 1522 "Das Neue Testament Deutsch," which he had translated within a few months at the Wartburg, was published in Wittenberg. Hardly three months after the first edition the second edition, already linguistically improved, was printed. — It was providential that a few decades previously the art of book printing had been discovered, which up to the time of Luther's Bible translation had already been noticeably improved, and had spread surprisingly quickly in the German lands.

Martin Luther has decisively influenced the development of the German language. From the existing linguistic building-bricks, which he worked on and polished and to which he added new ones, he formed the basis for a uniform German literary language, on which other Called ones were then able to go on working. Thus a language was formed that was intended for the fulfillment of great tasks!

18. DISTORTED CONCEPTS

When men turned more and more to perishable earthly things, when they fettered themselves to them and thereby neglected their spirit, their spiritual capacity to comprehend diminished. The forming of right concepts became increasingly difficult, as they could no longer be grasped spiritually.

The fettering to what is earthly was done by the intellect, which arises from the earthly, because it is formed from the thoughts of the perishable brain. It gradually pushed itself into the foreground, suppressed the spirit, and eventually took over the forming of concepts in place of the spirit. They became distorted concepts that no longer fitted the word-designation concerned. The word in fact continued to exist but the idea, which should have been awakened through the word, and from which the spirit then formed the concept, was wrong.

For the intellectual power of imagination ends where the origin of the intellect is — in the World of Gross Matter, to which also belongs that which is earthly. This limit is given by Nature. Man cannot set or extend it himself. Any strengthening and refining of the intellect, however great and noteworthy, must halt at this gross-material-earthly boundary, which can only be crossed by the spiritual intuitive perception.

The effect of this was particularly damaging concerning those concepts that are of the greatest importance to spiritual development.

Let us first take as an example the word *cross*. The right picture for this word is the rectangular Cross with arms of equal length. It is the sign of Divine Truth. From discoveries and excavations it becomes clear that this Cross is an ancient symbol that was known on earth before Christ, and which can still be seen today in many churches, sometimes encircled with a ring, sometimes without the ring.

It is the selfsame Cross that appeared to Constantine I on the night before the decisive battle at Saxa Rubra (312). At the same time he intuitively perceived the words: "In this sign you will be victorious!" This was a challenge to establish under this heavenly sign an empire that would serve the Truth as Christ had brought It to men. But they did not understand the sign and founded an empire, which prepared the way not for the Heavenly Power, but for earthly power and glory.

A painting in an old manuscript of the 11th century shows how Constantine, under the sign of the equal-armed Cross, leads his troops into the battle of Saxa Rubra at the Mulvian Bridge near Rome.

This Cross must not be confused with the form of the Golgotha cross of suffering.

Jesus, Who came from out of the Truth, knew the Cross of Truth, and therefore He exhorted men to take up the Cross, that is, to live every day according to the Truth, and to look for It in the Laws of the Creator, to which the Laws of Nature also belong (Luke 9, 23; Mark 10, 21).

But what did men make of this concept? Let us first take the saying (in German): "He has the cross with him." As the meaning imputed to it is, "He is a trouble to us," or in other words, "Someone disturbs us, is burdensome to us," it shows how the sublime meaning of the Cross has been distorted into the very opposite. But there is also profound truth in the distorted meaning of the Cross. There is certainly a reason when the Cross is compared to a burden. For the Truth does in fact weigh like a pressure on all who do not take it seriously or even deny it.

Concerning the saying (in German): "Since he has a wife in his house, the cross has moved in" — in other words, "trouble has moved in with her" — we also find the conception of the Cross distorted. What is meant here is that with the man's marriage suffering caused by his wife has entered his house.

And yet, if we take heed of its true meaning, there is in this saying something exalting and pure, something filled with promise and blessing. It is just through woman that marriage and home should become a source of power and joy, a place of natural recuperation for body and spirit, because through her naturally finer intuitive susceptibility to the rays from the Truth she is more receptive than man.

Thus where there is a woman in the house, who opens herself in purity to the rays of the Divine Power, the blessing from the Cross of Truth cannot fail to come, if the man intuitively perceives and supports this lofty aspiration.

A further concept of special significance for spiritual life and for the way to Luminous Heights is the *longing* (literal translation from German — longing-seeking). It is implanted in the human spirit to enable it to find its way safely back to its spiritual home, to Paradise, which it left a long, long time ago. The true conception of the word should awaken in the human spirit the longing seeking for the Truth, for the meaning of life, so that on its journey through Subsequent Creation it will not lose its way in the lowlands of the World of Matter. But what has man made of it? Longings of all kinds which are directed at persons and all manner of earthly things, and finally degenerate into a longing craving for earthly pleasures, for material goals that drag him down rather than lead him upwards!

Let us look at another conception, whose wrong application has already caused much suffering and unhappiness: *freedom.*

True freedom must not be interpreted as earthly freedom; it cannot be compared with an *outward* liberty and independence. How easily does this give rise to the desire to become free from all ties, and to follow selfish ways at the expense of one's fellowmen, which finally end in lack of consideration, licentiousness and tyranny? Just let us think of living a completely unrestrained life, of letting oneself go completely, of freeing oneself from any outer and inner feeling of shame.

True freedom lies in the *spiritual* field. It is *here* that the endeavor to free oneself from all fetters of spiritual enslavement must begin, whether they be some propensity, some craving, some impure desire, or any outside views or wrong traditions that have been taken over.

This can only be done when man gets to know and acts in accordance with the Will of God, Which is interwoven with His Laws.

He who swims against the stream soon tires, is driven back and is endangered. He who swims with the stream makes it easy for himself and advances. This is a lawfulness that also applies to what is spiritual.

He who *opposes* the Laws of Creation, who disregards them by his unjust actions and thoughts, binds his spirit to threads of fate that win, obstruct and impede him, and may eventually ruin him — he will no longer be spiritually free. The selfsame Laws that return good for good will bring him bad fruit as harvest, if he has scattered the seed for it in the form of evil thoughts and deeds.

But he who lives *with* the Laws, who adapts himself to them, heeds and fulfils them, becomes free of *inner* ties and entanglements, and this means inner freedom, spiritual freedom. With this inner freedom, if it is really genuine, man has all the helps he needs. He will then also cope more easily with any *outer* constraint that oppresses him.

The conception of *Love* also is today but a caricature of that ideal Love, which Christ taught men, that Love, which helps and supports, and does only what is of *spiritual bene-fit* to the other, even if it be with just severity. This ideal Love has become a love of weakness, softness and indulgence, which out of sheer wrong consideration no longer pays attention to the real goal, spiritual advancement, and does only what *pleases* the other. It is just in the relationship between men that genuine love is of fundamental importance.

Also man has formed a conception of the *punishment of God* that does not correspond with reality. How often is it said: "That is the punishment of God!" But God does not punish personally! It is always left to the free decision of *man* to determine the punishment, which is then carried out by the *Laws* of God, the Laws of Creation.

How the carrying out of a punishment proceeds is clearly shown by the Law of Sowing and Reaping, of Cause and Effect (Reciprocal Action). Man only needs to give purity to his thoughts, in order not to have to harvest bad fruit. But if he thinks or does evil, the Laws of Creation will mete out to him a multiple of the same.

But since he is often struck by hard blows of fate, which he cannot explain, because he has perhaps given the cause for them in former earth lives, he is easily tempted to make God responsible for the punishment, that is for the consequences of *his* behavior, without considering that he is thereby committing a blasphemy and an injustice.

Reward and punishment for man lie always in the weaving of Creation, whose Laws incorruptibly mediate the fruit, which in his free volition he wants to have.

In conclusion, let us turn to the most sacred of all concepts: GOD!

A concept that allows us to divine the inconceivable Greatness, the immeasurable Power, the Perfection and Omniscience of the Creator, and which should awaken within us reverential love and humble adoration!

How have men of the earth over and over again for hundreds of years disregarded, abused, defiled and often enough debased to an empty everyday expression and a thoughtless form of salutation just this most sublime of all concepts. In the debasing of the concept of God the spiritual decline of mankind manifests most clearly.

May these few examples of distorted concepts stand for many another, and provide the incentive to strive and form the concepts as are right according to the Laws of Creation, so that the great decline, which already prevails in the world of concepts, is brought to a halt.

We shall thereby gradually bring about a healthy and harmonious basis for the up building of spiritual and earthly values, whereas the distortion and falsification of concepts produce disharmony and confusion, which in time will make themselves felt, in both psychic and earthly respects, to be hindering and damaging in all fields.

Here too the words of Christ are to serve us as the guiding principle, namely to take up the Cross, that is to say, to serve the Truth. We must try to become familiar with the Laws and Commandments coming from the Truth, thus from God, and to find and follow His Will in them.

19. THE RETURN OF THE STAR OF BETHLEHEM

The Star of Bethlehem has at all times exercised a special influence on men.

Time and again they have sought to penetrate its mystery, and to offer interpretations and explanations of it. Yet to this day its true origin and nature have remained unrecognized.

One of the most common explanations of the Star of Bethlehem is the so-called constellation theory, referring to a conjunction between the planets Saturn and Jupiter. If this were really so, the traditional writings would certainly have referred to the subject of the encounter between two planets. As it is, however, they give an account of only one star, and of the unusual qualities that distinguished it from the fixed stars and planets.

Surely there were significant constellations among the then familiar planets at the time of Christ's birth, regardless of the year in which human calculation places it, and the three Wise Men from the East, who were masters of astronomy, were aware of their significance. But in addition they observed for a short time an especially striking heavenly phenomenon, the Star of Bethlehem, which they followed.

The Evangelist Matthew vividly depicts it in simple words: "And lo, the star, which they saw in the east, went before them, till it came and stood over where the young child was" (Matthew 2, 9).

In the Book of James, another traditional writing, which however has not been incorporated in the Bible, the three Wise Men report: "We saw how an indescribably greater star shone among these stars, and dimmed them, so that they no longer shone; and so we knew that a king was born for Israel." In this Book of James, also called the Proto-Gospel of James, we have a script (circa 100 to 300 A.D.) in which the birth and childhood of Mary, the earthly mother of Jesus, as well as the birth of Jesus, are described.

Other religious persuasions likewise turned their attention to the appearance of this Star. Chalcidius, a philosopher living in the first half of the fourth century, in his commentary on Plato's Timaeus, mentions a story according to which "a star was seen, not to threaten man with sickness and death, but to proclaim the descent from Heaven of a sacred deity for the salvation and joy of mankind." When the Chaldeans, who were learned men and well versed in astronomy, observed this star during their nocturnal journeying, they are said to have sought out the newborn god immediately, and on finding the kingly child to have paid him the homage befitting only a deity.

One of the church fathers, John Chrysostom (344-407) devotes himself in great detail to the Star of the Wise Men in the 6th Homily (Sermon) of his Commentary on the Gospel of Matthew: "That this was no ordinary star, indeed as it appears to me not a star at all, but rather an invisible power, which had taken on this form, seems obvious to me first of all from the course it took."

Chrysostom then explained that the Star followed a different course from that of the familiar stars; moreover it shone also by day, and through the intensity of its own brilliance outshone the very rays of the sun. It appeared and then disappeared, finally sinking down. "It did not remain on high," Chrysostom continues, "in order to indicate the place from there, for then the Magi would not have been able to see it; no, it came down into the depths for this purpose." — "Thus how would our star have been able to point out the narrow space occupied by the manger and the hut, if it had not stood still above the head of the child? And this is what the Evangelist wished to suggest when he said: 'Lo, the star, which they saw in the east, went before them, till it came and stood over where the young child was.' "

Thus through the Star of Bethlehem the Three Kings from the Orient found the Son of God. This was an extraordinary guidance, which was not given just for a single act of adoration. Therefore the objection is rightly raised, here and there, as to why the Three Kings concerned themselves no further about the Son of God after worshiping Him. To protect Jesus during His life on earth was actually part of their mission. The necessity for this protection, ordained from the Luminous Heights, was demonstrated by the events that transpired shortly after the birth of Jesus: the flight of His parents with Jesus into Egypt, Herod's Massacre of the Innocents, then later on the attacks and persecutions instigated by the priests, and finally the arrest and violent death of Jesus. From those holding positions of power in His native land Jesus found no protection; and His earthly life would perhaps have taken a quite different course, in all events a better one, had the Three Kings been true to their mission and not deserted Him.

It is already evident from the few accounts quoted here that the Star of Bethlehem was an entirely different phenomenon, much more striking and impressive than the conjunction of Saturn and Jupiter, even if one or the other planet had lent itself to the encounter as well.

The Star of Bethlehem does actually exist. Only it is not part of our solar system, or of other celestial galaxies of Subsequent Creation, that is, of the World of Matter. Its origin lies far above the Paradise of the human beings, in the Primordial Spiritual Realm below the Divine Sphere, and the consistency of Its core is of a highly spiritual nature, radiating an immense magnetic Power. When it is said that this Star is to return at the time of the present Cosmic Turning Point, neither Its course nor the time of Its appearance can be determined, because these factors lie beyond any possibility of astronomical calculation.

The only indication of Its return, that is of Its entering the World of Matter before it is possible to see It, would be the perceptible release of Its enormous radiating pressure.

It is therefore natural to associate with this release the catastrophic events that we have already experienced for decades.

Earthquakes, volcanic eruptions, tidal waves and floods, unusual weather, all these are events that must have a cause, all the more so as they take place with a frequency that could correspond to the releasing pressure through Its coming nearer.

In any case, a "source of disturbances" that has not previously existed must be sending powerful rays into the Universe, which also penetrate all physical matter, and thus cause important changes.

Already for years modern science has been seeking an explanation for all these unusual and often surprising changes and disturbances on earth and in the Universe, and has raised the question as to whether their cause might lie in a remote, as yet undiscovered star.

That such powerful radiations from the Universe also affect the human body, often causing inexplicable cases of disease and death, can be assumed with certainty! And the brain cells will probably be particularly susceptible.

In this connection reference should be made to yet another prophecy. It is contained in one of the "Sibylline Books". These are prophecies made partly by Jews and partly by Christians in the period between the second and fifth centuries after Christ. In one of these fourteen books the following passage appears in the description of the World Judgment: "And then will God accomplish a great sign. For a star will burst forth like unto a radiant cross, shining and giving light from the brilliant heavens for many days."

We find a further allusion in the Revelation of John: "And the third angel sounded, and there fell a great star from heaven, burning as it were a lamp . . ." (Rev. 8, 10). "And the fifth angel sounded, and I saw a star fall from heaven unto the earth; and to him was given the key of the bottomless pit" (Rev. 9, 1).

Accordingly the Star, which "falls unto the earth," is the key for the release of the judgment on earth. Its radiations strike and destroy all Darkness, which has gathered in "the bottomless pit."

This time the Star of Bethlehem sends no salutation of peace, as It did at Jesus' birth, but comes to help in the fulfillment of the World Judgment, and only after that will It make Its constructive radiating power felt.

Such reflections on the return of the Star of Bethlehem are therefore by no means beside the point, and it is quite possible that God, through the appearance of the Star at the right moment, will give to all truly seeking people a renewed sign of His Eternal Love!

20. MEETING POINT EARTH

Genesis

"And God said, Let there be light: and there was light" (Genesis 1, 3). Upon this great Word the rays shot over the boundary of the Divine Sphere into the unlit Universe. That was the beginning of Creation.

These rays certainly contained everything needed for the making of Creation, but they were not God Himself.

God remained *outside* His Creation and did not merge with it as, for instance, Pantheism states. According to that teaching God is supposed to be *present* in every flower, every tree, etc.

An artist who has created a work does not merge with his work either. He stands *beside* his work. The relation between God and His Work, Creation, which has only arisen through His Radiation, is exactly the same.

Moreover it must not be assumed that the First Creation made by God was instantly the Paradise of the human spirits, or the earth. The Genesis of the first seven days, as described in the First Book of Moses, concerns the Primordial Creation. It is of a spiritual nature and lies below the Divine Sphere. The account of Creation is not of a symbolic character, but gives explanations about actual spiritual happenings, at immeasurable heights and distances.

Nor must we let ourselves be confused by the word *earth* used in the account of Creation. It is not to be related "locally" to our planet, but as a concept of Creation it applies to "the dry land": "And God called the dry land 'Earth,' and the gathering together of the waters called he 'Seas'" (Genesis 1, 10). This explains the conditions in Primordial Creation, which are also to be found there, but in character different and lighter than on earth. Hence even in Primordial Creation there are also mountains, forests, meadows, seas, animals and men of inconceivable beauty and perfection as prototypes for all further Spiritual Creations, which came into being after this first Creation, of which only the lowest is the Spiritual Realm of the human spirits, Paradise.

And when verse 27 of the First Book of Moses reads: "So God created man in his own image," this refers to the *first* men in Primordial Creation, thus to the "Primordial

104

Beings." They are spiritual ideals, who were never on earth; they are prototypes for all that has further come into being and developed, and for what will yet develop.

These immediately fully conscious first human beings, the *Primordial Beings*, are not as one might think, Divine, but are of a spiritual nature, for God created them in His own *image*, not according to His Being.

But the *human spirits* have their cradle only in the lower-lying Spiritual Realm, in Paradise. They are not primordially created, but are subject to development. Exactly as in Nature there are seeds and germs, so there also exist spirit germs, which can be found at the lowest boundary of Paradise. As germs they are not yet conscious, but they have the urge for it, and indeed it is this urge that "drives" them out of Paradise. In other words they are "expelled" from Paradise to the lower-lying Subsequent Creation or World, which consists of the Ethereal and Gross Material Worlds. The earth only belongs to the latter.

Subsequent Creation is not an immediate Creation, but the product of an evolution in accordance with the Laws of Creation, lasting millions of years, as science has correctly recorded, and in exactly the same sequence as quoted in the Biblical account of the first Creation: grasses, plants, aquatic animals, birds, land animals and men. Here in Subsequent Creation these are no longer created instantly, but formed in the course of a long-lasting evolution according to the original images of Creation. Therefore it is logical that the Creation, which God made *in the beginning* (Genesis 1, 1), cannot mean the earth, which is furthest removed from God, and hence has undergone a long process of evolution to its present state.

How Did the First Human Beings Come to Earth?

It is only in the World of Matter that human spirit germs coming from Paradise can mature into personalities through learning lessons and experiencing, and it is above all the earth that offers the opportunity for this because here they can find that experiencing and maturing through one another that is able to awaken and further the consciousness-of-self. In Paradise this is not possible.

But how did the first spirit germs of men come to an instrument of flesh and blood, when as yet there were no human *mothers* on earth in whom they could have incarnated?

As already explained (I, 5), this process took place only once, and was not repeated; it came about in accordance with the Laws of Creation in the further progressive development of the World of Matter: Male and female spirit germs incarnated in the developing bodies of the then most highly evolved animals, thus using them as a bridge to earth life.

Thus came to pass the coming into existence of man on earth, which has been an enigma. The enigma immediately disappears with the knowledge about incarnation. Incarnation is the entrance of the soul into the growing child's body about half way through pregnancy. This process is still the same today as it was then. Only at that time these were noble animals that served as a bridge to the earth for the first spirit germs.

On account of his spiritual origin man is the highest creature in *Subsequent* Creation, in the World, and may therefore be described as the crown of this Creation. It is only this part of Creation, to which the earth also belongs, which he can make "subject" to himself and control, by strict obedience to the Laws of Creation.

Any attempt to impugn man's dignity because of a relationship, according to natural history, with the animal world is misplaced. The relationship only concerns the appropriated animal body and not the content; for spirit and animal-soul are fundamentally different species.

The zoologist Thomas Henry Huxley (1825 — 1895) expresses this relationship as follows: "Thus whatever system of apes be studied the comparison of their modification in the ape series leads to one and the same result - - - that the structural differences, which separate Man from the Gorilla and the Chimpanzee, are not so great as those, which separate the Gorilla from the lower apes" (*Man's Place in Nature and other Essays*, Every Man's Library). It is the self-same T. H. Huxley who expresses himself on reincarnation as follows: "Only the teaching on reincarnation could mediate a picture of life that would be a just one."

We see from the above explanations that besides the immediate Creation (Primordial Creation) there is also a development. It is willed and provided for by the Creator. The Genesis of the First Book of Moses must not be so narrowly interpreted, as if there were only one immediate Creation; on the other hand it must not be one-sidedly inferred from Darwin's teaching that there is only development. There are *both*.

Even man is not exempted from development. It begins after he has left Paradise as a spirit germ, with the awakening of the noble and pure abilities slumbering in him, and finds its climax in the consciousness-of-self of a personality with free will, which implies full responsibility.

As a connecting link between the Spiritual Realm and the World lying below, he is in a position to mediate radiations of a spiritual nature, and thereby to ennoble everything.

And when one day he is allowed to return to his spiritual home — to Paradise — as a spiritually fully developed thus matured personality, his field of activity will continue to be Subsequent Creation. Then from Paradise he will be able to cooperate with the extension of Subsequent Creation lying below him, with which he has become thoroughly familiar from his own observation. In this activity really lies the meaning of life. The previous sojourn in Subsequent Creation serves only for the necessary development, in order to attain to the full maturity of his personality, which alone makes possible for him the conscious return to Paradise, to be eternally allowed to cooperate in Creation.

The Seven Universes of the World

Subsequent Creation is the World of Matter, which has been made after the prototype of Primordial Creation. To the World of Matter belong seven huge and in themselves complete Universes, which have formed over long periods of time at different points of radiation, and which follow an enormous cycle.

Each Universe has a Creation-name. In the Revelation of John these Universes are described as Churches, thus as World Churches with the following names: Ephesus, Smyrna, Pergamos, Thyatira, Sardis, Philadelphia, Laodicea (Rev. 1, 1). Each World Church has an Angel as a Guardian.

We cannot imagine the size of the Universes, any more than we can the distances that lie between them. We need only look into our universe. All that we are in a position to discover with the aid of the biggest and strongest instruments, the milliards of stars of inconceivable size and at inconceivable distances can be considered as belonging to the Universe Ephesus. As a tiny dot in that Universe moves our earth, as a satellite of the sun.

Never can earthman with his physical body get into another Universe. This is only possible for the spirit, if it incarnates in a body of the substance existing there, whose consistency is either of greater or lesser density in comparison with our coarse World of Matter.

Although we cannot gather from the messages to the Universes (Rev. 1, 20-3, 22) that in our Universe there are still other inhabited planets besides the earth, we can nevertheless infer from them that there are likewise celestial bodies in the *other Universes*, on which live human beings who have sinned just as much as earthmen. It is self-evident that these men have no fantastic shapes, but the self-same body-forms as earthmen. For the human form is a characteristic of the human spiritual in all Creation, and the particular coverings form accordingly.

The Messages to the Guardians of the Seven Universes

Although it is often assumed that the Churches named in the Revelation refer to *earthly* communities in Asia Minor with the same names, this is not actually so. Just as little can we in the historical sense relate the contents of the messages to the Churches to events that took place at the time of the Roman Empire.

Moreover, John did not receive the Revelation on the small Island of Patmos in the Aegean Sea, but on the Isle of Patmos that lies above the Paradise of men. What he was allowed to behold and to hear in the Spiritual Realm on Patmos after his physical death is intended for *all* mankind. So also the content of the messages to the Guardians of the Seven Universes, which must not be compared to relatively small earthly affairs. It is equally inconceivable that *earthly* communities should be represented in the Spiritual Realm (Heaven) by golden candlesticks, or that heads of such communities should be compared to angels.

The words, which John conveyed by decree of the Divine Will to the Guardians of the Universes, have an important spiritual content, which relates to the End Time of the World Judgment. As Guardians, the Angels receive indications above all of the dangers that threaten, if the failures, faults and weaknesses in their Universes are not redeemed. They are exhortations and warnings that of course apply equally to the human spirits of these Universes as help for their spiritual awakening. Men of this earth, which belongs to the Universe of Ephesus, are no exception to this.

The words of the World Judge directed to them are extremely grave: "Nevertheless I have somewhat against thee, because thou hast left thy first love. Remember therefore from whence thou art fallen, and repent, and do the first works; or else I will come unto thee quickly, and will remove thy candlestick out of his place, except thou repent" (Rev. 2, 4 and 5).

The "first love" is the love that comes first; it is clear, severe and impartial, and does to its neighbor what is of spiritual benefit to him. Its fulfillment demands that no one must inflict harm upon another. Man has forsaken this love, by putting in its place a love of weakness and soft indulgence that does not swing in the sense of Divine Love.

"Remember therefore from whence thou art fallen" refers to the intellect, which is a product of the earthly brain, and to which man has enslaved himself, instead of controlling it with his spirit and using it as a good *instrument* in life on earth. The binding to the intellect means binding to matter, because the brain also belongs to perishable matter, and ceases to exist after physical death. It is to matter that technology also belongs. Hence it is a field in which the fully developed intellect can bring about great works. But man must not become intoxicated by the perfection of technology, and he must not forget that technical works are dead works, which have no spiritual value, and which he must leave behind when he passes over into the beyond. They are useful only as an expedient for advancement on earth. What is decisive for the development of mankind is not the "flight" of technology, but the ascent of the spirit.

Attempts to reach in the physical body other planets within our solar system are meaningless for the spiritual development of mankind. The Creator allotted the earth to men for their spiritual progress. Here is the place where he can unfold and practice all the virtues of his spirit. But today he is so firmly bound to matter that without hesitation he uses the works of technology to the detriment and even to the destruction of mankind.

The concept "materialist" is taken far too narrowly. Being a product of the brain the intellect belongs to matter. Everyone who submits to his intellect, thereby cutting off his connection with the Source of Life, is thus a materialist, whatever view he may hold.

Hence it is high time for man once more to do the "first works," which are the works of the spirit. Man must now awaken and "strengthen the things that are ready to die" (Rev. 3, 2), which refers to his spirit. Only with the spirit-with the intuitive perception of the spirit-can he accomplish works for eternity and re-establish the connection with God.

Heavily weighs upon the mankind of our Universe the warning of the World Judge: "Or else I will come unto thee quickly, and will remove thy candlestick out of his place - - -," and enormous efforts are needed by men to work themselves up from being the slave of matter to becoming its ruler, so that the End Time will not be an end for man and the earth, but will change into a new time of up building and peace.

The Regions of the Beyond

During its sojourn in Subsequent Creation the human spirit must often change its physical covering. It is born, dies and is born again.

When it dies it lays aside its perishable earthly covering each time, and continues to exist beyond the earthly world. For it is not the case that all is over after physical death. After leaving its physical body the spirit, which with its nonphysical coverings forms the soul, remains intact in human form as an independent personality.

Just as little does it correspond with reality that those who have passed on will find eternal rest in the beyond. In all Creation there is no absolute rest. Everything is in continual movement, and especially in the beyond a much more active life prevails than here on earth, because there the considerably more ponderous characteristic of the earthly-material drops away.

Because of this livelier movement the experiencing of the soul there is also much more direct and quicker than on earth. But above all, through lack of the earthly covering as a protective mantle, a continual and exact classification of the spirits takes place in the beyond, for which the Law of the Attraction of Homogeneous Species and the Law of Gravitation are especially effective.

Even as on earth time and again "birds of a feather flock together," in small as well as in great matters, this applies all the more so in the planes beyond, where the attraction of similar species is even compulsory, and where each homogeneous group has its definite place. Whether it is envy, hatred, lying, passion or whatever other faults and weaknesses man is capable of producing, he is constantly forming for himself the corresponding places, which are always populated by similar souls. Thus hell too is not as one might think a place of punishment created by God, but it is the work of men alone. To bring about this work he misuses the spiritual power streaming through Creation, by shaping very active evil forms with it, by means of his intuitive perceptions, thoughts and deeds.

In the places of Darkness the souls can give vent to every passion and live out all faults and weaknesses without causing harm, because here only the like-minded are concerned, who through mutual suffering provide the opportunity for recognition of their guilt and thereby for gradual improvement.

But also the human spirits aspiring for what is higher find themselves in various places of the lighter regions.

In reality the so-called beyond comprises many divisions and gradations, beginning with the Regions of Light, which are the first steps to Paradise, as far as the Land of Twilight, and still further down to the Regions of Darkness that form hell.

The belief in various abodes for the departed in the beyond is an old one. The Gospel of Luke (16, 22-26), for instance, describes a place of punishment and one of the luminous spheres, and points to the unbridgeable gulf between them. Lorber in his Great Gospel of John mentions a place in the beyond for the arrogant: "An arrogant, tyrannical man is not judged by the Lord, but in the beyond he is placed in the same condition and the same life as on earth, but with the difference that there his fellow creatures far and wide have, are and want the same as he." From this description it follows that the real punishment lies in the togetherness of these homogeneous human beings!

Over-Population, Its Cause and Solution

It is frightening to read the figures of the swift increase in the earth's population, and the calculations for the years to come, should the growth continue at the present rate. There has long been talk of a population explosion that cannot be arrested by technical-mechanical means or birth control. In spite of all efforts to change things, in many countries with a very excessive birth rate it will be impossible to prevent further impoverishment and starvation.

Such an extraordinary happening moves every serious thinker. He asks himself: Where do these many human beings come from, why are they here, what is the deeper cause of these frightening events?

It lies in men's wrong volition! In accordance with the order of Creation only human souls from the more luminous regions of the beyond should incarnate on earth, in order to continue their development towards spiritual maturity. That is how it was in the beginning of mankind on earth, when they still drew unconsciously from the stream of life, and opened themselves in childlike trust to the Mercies of the Creator.

But the ever-increasing propensity for material things, the striving for earthly pleasures, and last but not least the lack of earnestness in regard to procreation, opened the gates through which souls were able to come to the earth-plane, who if the development had been a normal one, would have had to mature in regions far below the earth.

It is to them that, through their wrong behavior, men on earth gave the support needed for incarnations, thereby releasing a happening, which in the course of thousands of years has grown into an enormous catastrophe.

These intruders, who do not belong on earth, increased and together with failing earth-inhabitants they attracted further similar species in ever-quicker succession, so that soon vast numbers of inferior souls flooded the entire earth, afflicting and oppressing lighter human souls and preventing their spiritual ascent.

From the spiritual point of view this is the main cause of the enormous increase in the earth's population, apart from the more physical causes such as longer life spans through medical help, and prevention of epidemics through the systematic destruction of insects and bacteria with chemicals. But at the same time this also means that conditions prevalent in lower regions are transferred to the earth, and thus there is hell on earth.

In the first place it is woman who has a share in these evil conditions. In contrast to man, she has the finer and therewith also the stronger intuitive life, and therefore it is she who is mainly decisive with regard to the attraction of souls. Hence what kind of souls incarnate depends largely on the spiritual maturity of woman. Thus she holds in her hand not only the destiny of the family but of entire peoples, and has a decisive and deeply incisive influence on their decline or ascent.

The solution to the problem of over-population is to be found in the Revelation of John (the Apocalypse). From the descriptions of the plagues and the effects of the Wrath of God in the Final Judgment, it can be inferred that a great number of men on this earth must die. An idea of the numerical proportion is given among other things in the following passages: "And power was given unto them over the fourth part of the earth, to kill with sword, and with hunger, and with death, and with the beasts of the earth" (Rev. 6, 8). "And many men died of the waters, because they were made bitter" (Rev. 8, 11). "By these three was the third part of men killed" (Rev. 9, 18).

All the affliction that strikes men in this Judgment is nothing but the carrying out of their own sentences, which they have passed upon themselves in the course of thousands of years through their evil volition. To some extent they themselves even help in this carrying out of sentences. This begins with the pollution of water and air, the contamination of the environment with substances that are injurious to health, and that are breathed in or eaten without control every day, and ends with the technique of war with its dreadful biological, chemical and atomic weapons.

However, the most important and the last word concerning this far-reaching world happening of the Final Time will be spoken by the elements, compared with which all the atom bombs are as nothing.

For men have not only defiled their visible environment; there are also psychic wastes in the shape of evil intuition- and thought-forms that have defiled the ethereal environment. Thereby something that is not known to men has taken place: They have misused power-currents, putting them into a great confusion, which in the end will straighten itself out forcibly at a definite time. It is in this that the four elements of earth, water, fire and air are also involved, which in accordance with statements in the Revelation will cause enormous changes and upheavals on earth.

This happening is like a great purification, in the course of which all those who have "destroyed it" are first of all taken from the earth (Rev. 11, 18), exactly corresponding to the Law of Creation, "What a man soweth, that shall he also reap!" According to the Law of Development they do not belong on the earth, which the Creator has only provided for those human souls, who have kept awake their longing for what is pure and good. This depopulation of the earth would then be the solution to the problem of over-population, which does not lie in the hands of men, but which in a just way is carried out through the Laws of Creation.

Improvement of Mankind on Earth

In the Universe Ephesus a tiny star has been rotating for millions of years: the earth, the blue planet. It has been chosen and prepared to be a home for the human spirits during their various earth lives.

Thus it has become the most important meeting-point of men on their common journey through Subsequent Creation, but at the same time also the turning point on the way back to Paradise.

They were to be guests of the Creator, Who has graciously made over the earth to them for their development. But man wickedly abused the hospitality granted him, and the "crown of Creation" has become an arrogant world-ruler who knows nothing but his own will, and who has made the earth a playground for degenerate spirits.

If men had always fulfilled the Will of God, Which is expressed in His Laws, conditions on earth today would be like Paradise. From the hopeless conditions now prevailing it can be estimated how far men have distanced themselves from God, and in what way the happenings revealed have already come to pass.

Let us hope that the time is no longer too far off when the abused earth can follow its course, rejuvenated and invigorated, after it has shaken off all Darkness. Then a new and inwardly purified human race will arise on it, which will honor God because they will live only according to the Divine Will.

Earthmen can begin with this *even now* by helping to determine the selection of souls who are waiting in the beyond for an incarnation, provided they earnestly wish for a child.

The help towards a determination, which must be given at the right time, thus already before procreation, is based on influencing the attraction of homogeneous species. When earthmen through their increasing recognition eagerly strive to further within themselves the good and the pure, letting it become deed, they will also attract similar souls from the beyond for incarnation. They will offer them the opportunity for a new earthly existence, and support them during their spiritual maturing. Thereby they offer help that will reciprocally spread great blessing for all concerned.

This would then be a genuine contribution to the upliftment and improvement of humanity on earth, embracing a healthy family planning that is assured of success. At the same time it is an example of how during his earthly activity earthman can *consciously* apply the Law of Creation of the Attraction of Homogeneous Species, which is equivalent to fulfilling the Divine Will.

Part II

KNOWLEDGE FOR THE WORLD OF TOMORROW!

The world of tomorrow is not a world molded, as hitherto by human self-will, but a world that must adjust to the Will of God, if it does not wish to perish.

God has anchored His Will in His Laws, which permeate Creation, to which also belongs the World of Matter in which we live.

Every man of goodwill has the ability to learn to understand Creation and its Laws.

For this understanding of Creation a new, comprehensive and complete knowledge is necessary, for how little does man yet know of the working of these Laws of Creation, although he is dependent on them and must accept their effects at every moment.

In this Part important happenings and processes, hitherto partly concealed from men, are explained in the sense of this Knowledge of Creation, in order to show how the new knowledge is to be applied for the world of tomorrow.

The explanations contain repeated references to the Revelation of John, because we are in the midst of the fulfillment of one of its most important phases. In this connection keys to the interpretation of his metaphorical language are given.

I hope many earnestly seeking people will find in this book that which will induce them to reflect, and be of help to them in their search for the Truth.

1. SPIRIT, LOGIC AND INTELLECT

In Creation there are only two kinds of life: that which is conscious of itself and that which is unconscious. But it is not the case that the unconscious must always remain in that state. There is a *development* from the unconscious to the conscious. The best example of this is man.

At first he is in the Spiritual Realm, in Paradise, as an unconscious spirit germ. One of the new recognitions from the Grail Message, "In the Light of Truth", is that the origin of man is in Paradise. *Here* is his existence, before becoming man on earth. But he does not know this at the beginning of his development; he is still unconscious of it. Yet there is a longing within him to become conscious. God acceded to this gentle urging, and let it come to pass that the spirit germs were allowed to leave Paradise in order to become conscious. In Biblical language this means: they were "driven out" of Paradise, yet certainly not as a punishment, but because they are unable to awaken in Paradise to conscious life.

This is only possible through the coarser radiations of the World of Matter (Subsequent Creation), in which the spirit germs became immersed as if in fertile soil, in order to incarnate there in physical bodies so as to develop consciousness of themselves.

The number of those is not small, who in referring to his origin, regard man as a higher-thinking animal, but this does not touch the core. Certainly the *physical body* of man is descended from the animal, for at some time there must have been a beginning on earth. The first spirit germs incarnated in highly developed animal bodies, which then became extinct. They resembled the present anthropoid apes. The human spirits could not come onto this earth in any other way than over the bridge of these animal bodies. Hence the brains of men and anthropoid apes, especially of the chimpanzee, are still similar even today.

It could be assumed that human thinking does not greatly differ from the thinking of these animals. But this is not the case, because a fundamental difference does exist.

The reason for this is the core in the physical bodies. In the case of man it is the spirit that animates the body, and in the animal it is an animistic core, the animal soul, which comes from a plane that lies below Paradise. These are two fundamentally different species of Creation, which cannot be reconciled.

The human spirit in its physical body obtains the connection with the external world of material substance through the radiation-bridge: solar plexus — small brain — large brain.

The impressions from the earthly follow the reverse way to the large brain and the sense organs connected with it, via the small brain to the solar plexus, which transmits them to the spirit.

The solar plexus is a ganglion of the sympathetic nervous system, which lies beneath the diaphragm. Activities that are carried out without our will, thus involuntarily, such as respiration, digestion, the activity of the heart and the glands, are subject to this nervous system. It is connected with the brain through special nerve-paths. It is also called the connecting-link between body and soul, for the spirit is connected with the physical body in the solar plexus.

The brain exercises important functions, not only in earthly but also in spiritual matters. In itself it is a miraculous work: a magnificent central control, with innumerable nerve cells and an incalculable abundance of the finest electrical currents. Equally inconceivable is the potential of these cells for connection by means of minute receiving antennae and transmitters.

The large brain, thus the frontal brain, is the controlling factor not only for the sense organs, but also for the coming into being of *thoughts*, out of which is formed the *intellect*, which is necessary for the *earthly* faculty of comprehension.

The other part of the brain, the small brain, also called the back brain, is the *spiritually* receiving part, with the help of which *spiritual* comprehending is possible. For the large brain is not able directly to absorb the fine vibrations of the spirit. For this the small brain is needed as a transformation-point, which is connected with the large brain by plentiful nerve-lines, and which has the task of transforming the spiritual volition into coarser vibrations adapted to the large brain.

Thus the large brain, which produces the thoughts and the intellect, serves what is earthly transient. To this also belongs the feeling, which is dependent on the physical instincts and the intellect.

The small brain, on the other hand, is as a bridge at the disposal of the imperishable spirit, which manifests in the intuitive perception, called the inner voice.

A clear distinction between the origin of thoughts and the origin of the intuitive perceptions can also be found in our language.

We relate thoughts to the head, thus to the brain, when "something comes into our head," thus when we ponder over it, or when "we have a lot in our head," which means we must do a lot of brainwork.

On the other hand, we make use of the word heart in connection with the intuitive perceptions of the spirit. Originally the heart referred to the solar plexus. The radiation of the spirit is communicated to the heart by way of the solar plexus, whereby the impression often arises that its manifestations are caused in the heart. So for instance when we "take something to heart," "do something from the bottom of our heart" or when "something cuts us to the heart," that is to say, when we have a painful intuitive perception.

Thus there can be found many, and in part hidden, references in our language that point to the original.

For the small brain, too, there is yet another designation, which draws attention to its deeper meaning, to its mediating activity for the spirit. It is called the "tree of life," because a longitudinal section of the small brain shows a tree-like branching.

Now it would have been right, if in the course of his development man had made *equal* use of the two brain-parts, the large brain and the small brain, but this he has not done. Contrary to the established order in Creation, he has disproportionately trained and over-strained the large brain (intellectual brain) for thousands of years, and has thus forced its growth far beyond the normal size, to the detriment of the present-day "small" brain.

So it has come about that today, already from the third month of pregnancy, the large brain overgrows all the other parts of the brain, finally covering them up altogether. It is the small brain, which above all suffers from this. It has been suppressed, which has resulted in its gradual weakening.

Man has thereby prevented the God-willed, harmonious cooperation between the two brain-parts, and through voluntarily favoring the large brain he has subjected himself to the materially adjusted predominance of the intellect, which is just as transient as the brain that produces it. He has raised it to the place that is due only to the spirit. Thus he has cut himself off from the luminous helps, and has lost his way to Paradise.

That was the *Fall of Man*, which set in after the spirit germs' coming to consciousness of themselves, and which grew into the *hereditary sin*.

Hence Jesus said: "The spirit indeed is willing, but the flesh is weak" (Matthew 26, 41). That is to say, the spirit would like, and is meant to work in the earthly, but it is prevented from doing so by the weakness and deficiencies of its physical instruments, particularly by the over-cultivated intellect.

This unnatural interference with the Divine order has made not only the soul (that is the spirit with its various fine coverings) ill, but also the physical body, which has resulted in a diminished lifespan and in many illnesses, which would not otherwise have occurred.

But it is not the case that since the Fall of Man sinfulness is inborn in man; that he is thus compelled to live continually in a *hereditary state of sinfulness*, as is generally assumed.

The Fall of Man has become the hereditary sin because the over-cultivated large brain and the weakened small brain continue to be perpetuated as a *physical tendency*. Through this there certainly is the *danger* of, but not the *compulsion* to, an ever-continuing enchainment to the earthly, making the spiritual awakening very difficult.

Jesus showed the way to severance from hereditary sin in the *Word* that He brought to men. The purpose of His coming was to show men how they can free themselves from their sins, and how they have to behave in the future in order not to become sinful again. For Jesus, too, had to consider the free will of man.

The voluntary decision to sin must be cancelled again by an equally voluntary decision, and men themselves must bring about severance from sin. It is one of the great mercies of God that makes it possible, within the Laws working in Creation, for man to sever himself from all guilt, so that with the right recognition he need not bear it forever with him.

Man cannot leave the World of Matter (Subsequent Creation), to which the earth also belongs, and reach Paradise, until he has severed the last particle of sin. That is what Jesus meant by the words: "Thou shalt by no means come out thence, till thou hast paid the uttermost farthing" (Matthew 5, 26).

Hence man cannot commit a sin and then let another take it from him. Such onesidedness is contrary to the Law of Creation: "What a man soweth, that shall he reap."

The harvest is the logical consequence of his voluntarily made decisions. No learnedness is needed to understand this logic.

There are certainly many learned treatises on logic, of both ancient and modern times, but these are mostly so complicated and obscure that they must remain unintelligible to the plain thinking.

And yet logic can be easily understood, if it is based on the Laws of Creation, to which the Laws of Nature also belong.

Let us think of the sowing, growing, blossoming, and the bearing of fruit and passing away in Nature. Here we find a logical sequence according to natural laws, resulting from the Laws of Creation, which no man can change, and to which he simply must submit.

The Law of Sowing and Reaping, of Cause and Effect, is also expressed in it. If he sows a grain of wheat, after a certain time many similar grains will appear as fruit at the *same place*. The seed has multiplied.

Now if a man produces an evil thought, a multiple of this thought will return at a certain time to the same place where the thought arose, namely to the *originator*. For like the seed grain the thought has multiplied, and attracted other similar thoughts on its way. Hence the originator must harvest a multiple of the "thought-grain" sent out.

In this lies an incorruptible logic and justice. He, the originator, must harvest his seed, no one else can do it *vicariously* for him, not even a Son of God; this would be against all logic. Besides, man can only reap the *same* as he has scattered. Evildoing brings no joy in return, and noble deeds result in no "blows of fate."

All this is forcibly intermeshed, but the intellect can grasp it only in its limited sphere of the *earthly* seed and harvest. Above and beyond this the spirit must seek further, and recognize the *spiritual* seed and harvest.

Accordingly, logic means consistency. The consistent is everything that develops through the effect of the already-existing Laws of Creation. It is in no way connected with some *teaching* or other *thought out* by men. Therefore man must get to know the *Laws of Creation* in order to understand logic.

In the logic of the Laws of Creation, from which Nature has issued, is also found the answer to the question often asked today: "*Can Nature be inconsistent?*"

We can observe many processes in the earthly sphere, which have their beginning in unseen, supra-earthly places, and which are visible in the earthly only in their *ramifications*. Sometimes this misleads us into expecting arbitrariness from Nature, by describing it as "inconsistent."

But the fault lies with man, with his lack of logic; it is *he* who is inconsistent, because he has lost the ability to divine, to perceive intuitively, thus to grasp spiritually, supra-earthly happenings and connections, and to link them with what takes place on earth.

Therefore he is not in a position to infer and to develop one from the other. He lacks the perspective over the connections of the whole, for which recognitions *on this side* are *coarse* parts only; the *fine* parts matching the others must be sought with his *spirit*, beyond the earthly comprehension, thus beyond the earthly intellect.

Nature cannot be inconsistent. The Laws of Creation, which *uniformly* permeate Creation, thus also Nature, will not allow this. One step must be logically based on the previous one, even if in the course of this some steps may not be visible to earth-men.

The distribution of the physical organs, too, their task and their cooperation, has been determined in accordance with these Laws. Man cannot at his discretion suddenly change something of it by over-cultivating the one organ and weakening the other, as he has done with the large and the small brain. He thereby severely disturbs the cooperation between the two brains.

Hence it is important for us to make clear to ourselves for once how a *normal* cooperation between the two brain parts then takes place. Let us take as an example the *movement of the body*.

Here it is interesting to know how hard scientific brain research has tried in recent times to investigate the working of the small brain, and its relation to the large brain.

According to newspaper reports, neurologists in the U.S.A. are said to have succeeded in drawing up a complete circuit diagram for the small brain, the central organ for all orderly movements of the transverse muscular system, and for maintaining the tension of the muscles and the balance of the body. They regard the small brain as a center, which receives information from all parts of the body, makes instant decisions, and thereby controls and improves the movements of the body.

Professor Georges Schaltenbrand, of Würzburg, comes to the conclusion that in spite of outstanding investigations we are still far removed from a comprehensive understanding of the activity of the small brain. Nevertheless, the investigations have progressed so far that it can be said about the completion of a movement that the large brain already roughly regulates the nerve stimuli to the physical organs. But the fine adjustment is linked to the small brain, that is to say, it corrects the actual general posture of the body, thus for instance the position of the limbs, the speed of movement, the influences of the force of gravity. (G. Schaltenbrand: Allgemeine Neurologie, Thieme Verlag.)

These are important statements, which refer to the normal cooperation between the large brain and the small brain.

For it is normal for the *coarse* movements of the different body muscles to take place through the large brain; the small brain, however, effects the *refinement* of these movements. This means that by way of the small brain the spirit exerts an influence on the shaping of the movements.

Only through the cooperation of the spirit by way of the small brain are the coarse impulses for movement, which come from the large brain, so rounded off that the natural grace of the spirit is expressed in the movements, as the result of a combined harmonious cooperation between the large and the small brain.

124

The spirit is thus in a position by way of its instruments, the small brain and the large brain, to control every muscle of its body in perfect beauty *continually* in daily life. But this *real* control of his body is very difficult today, and mainly limited to definite performances. Let us think of the grace of the movements in gymnastics and dancing.

Thus it becomes clear that, through the weakening of the small brain, faults and deficiencies result in the posture of the body in walking, standing and sitting, and that the movements are often unnatural and one-sided, if not even tense and stiff in their effect.

How much the refining and regulating activity falls to the small brain can be observed in illnesses affecting the small brain. Disorders of balance will then result, and often the sick can make only uncontrolled or aimless movements, so-called pendulum movements.

Not for nothing is the small brain associated with the function of balance, in which the Law of Creation of the necessary equilibrium between giving and taking becomes effective. In the physical body the spirit through the small brain exercises the sense of balance.

Also the so-called short-reflex actions are closely connected with the small and the large brain. These are completely unpremeditated actions, occurring on the spur of the moment, such as come from great excitement and violent emotion. In this condition man is more or less robbed of his senses, he is "beside himself," loses his self-control and can be held responsible only to a limited extent for his deeds. This is also taken into account in the administration of justice.

Now there are two kinds of short-reflex actions. The one kind, called *impulses*, proceed directly from the spirit by way of the small brain to the physical organs, thus without the mediation of the large brain. The second kind is *emotional disturbances* or *stimuli*, which originate in the large or frontal brain, and from there influence the activity of the body.

Finally reference should be made to the obvious fact that today ever more thought is being given to the great failure of mankind, and its causes.

In pursuing the history of the human race, one is driven to conclude that something is wrong with man. For thousands of years men have killed, murdered and tortured each other; in wars, in revolutions, through shameful and wanton actions, men have destroyed what in turn men have built up and achieved. This degenerate behavior of men, the tendency to self-destruction, reaches its climax at the present time.

But where does the cause of this lie? Biologists speak of a wrong development, of a biological deformation of man. In the evolution of mankind something had gone wrong, which calls forth a senseless instinct of destructiveness. It was a question of a "fault in the construction" of man. And this fault is suspected to be in . . . the brain of man, in the disruptive growth of the human brain, which had slipped out of control. The growth had proceeded so quickly that it must be described as pathological, and that it was having a detrimental effect on psychic realms.

Here we are precisely at the point that is the origin of all evil, and which has already been explained in detail previously: the cultivation of the frontal brain beyond its normal size, and arising from this, the predominance of the earthly intellect; only with the difference that this unnatural growth is not a fault of the lawful development, but was enforced *by man himself* through his unnatural intervention in the order of Creation.

Hence the intellect must be referred back to its original place. Its strength lies solely in the earthly. As an example let us look at technology, which through the intellect has attained a great height, but only an *earthly* height that can never replace the soaring to *spiritual* heights. Because of its earthly origin the intellect is not capable of solving spiritual problems, however clever it may be.

Hence by nature the intellect must always remain under the domination of the spirit, as its executive *instrument* on earth, which here on earth has to realize the spiritual volition of man that is transmitted to it through the small brain.

For mark well, the intellect only becomes the enemy of the spirit when the decisions are left to it alone, without the spirit.

All these recognitions should make us take care in the future that even in the upbringing of children, and later on in the education of the young, the *right* activity of the large brain (intellectual brain) and the small brain (intuitive brain) is taken into account, so that in the time to come this grave interference with the order of Creation will cease, and the cooperation between the two brains will blossom again to full harmony.

2. THE COMING-INTO-BEING OF MAN ON EARTH

The coming of the human spirit to the earthly world, thus the coming-into-being of man, comprises three events, two of which are known to us: *procreation* and *birth*. But this is not yet enough, because in order to be born on this earth a third event is necessary: *incarnation*. It is the entrance of the soul — that is the human spirit with its finer coverings — into the developing child's body. This entrance takes place about midway through pregnancy, at a definite stage of maturity. Around this time the mother senses the nearness of the second spirit, and the first movements of the child make themselves felt.

Up to its incarnation the soul lives consciously near the mother-to-be. In the womb, that is during the time between incarnation and birth, the soul is asleep, it is not conscious of this state.

Until now the view has often prevailed that the soul of man comes into being at the time of procreation, or that it is formed in the womb. The view is also expressed that incarnation takes place only during the final stage of birth.

What is essential for incarnation is the choice of parents by the incarnating human spirit. In normal cases the Law of Attraction of Homogeneous Species is decisive here. Homogeneity can lie in good qualities, but also in faults and weaknesses, which is to be specially considered. Through this, strong tensions between parents and children may arise later on.

In many cases the *generation gap*, the great lack of understanding between young and old of the present time, can be better estimated when the attraction of homogeneous species at incarnations and in daily life is also taken into account.

The saying "like father, like son" renders the attraction of similar species between parents and children very well, because it clearly expresses that the children take after their parents!

Besides father and mother, persons who are often near the mother-to-be may also be instrumental in the attraction of homogeneous species. Hence it is not immaterial whom the mother allows around her during this time.

Thus bad souls can incarnate with good parents, and conversely more luminous souls are able to incarnate with bad parents. In neither case is it the parents, who cause the attraction, but some person or other in the surroundings of the parents.

In this way it is possible for a so-called "black sheep" to come into a good family.

Through carelessness with regard to the surroundings of the mother-to-be, a wrong incarnation was permitted, which can cause much trouble and worry. To a child that has not been attracted by the nature of the parents the phrase, "he is cast in a different mold," then applies.

Especially fateful ties are likewise able to contribute decisively towards an incarnation. But this cannot be so easily established because, for good reasons, recollection of former earth lives remains closed to us in most cases. Here only an inner sensing or divining that there must already have been a connection once in bygone times is able to give us an indication of this, without the need to ponder any more about it.

In any case no one need reproach himself at all with having been careless in the choice of his parents. In accordance with the Laws of Creation everything comes together in such a way that no injustice is done to him. Through birth each one receives the place that he deserves, that is to say, which is ordained for him through his good or bad karma, which on his own responsibility, he has formed for himself in former earth lives.

This lawful happening shows why there is no spiritual heredity. What appears as such is really the effect of the Law of the Attraction of Homogeneous Species, aptly expressed by the popular saying: "Birds of a feather flock together," or "Like attracts like." This takes effect everywhere and at all times in earthly life, and also holds good for incarnations.

Parents do not impart anything of their spirit to their children, as is often assumed, but only pass on physical hereditary characteristics; these, incidentally, also include the temperament, which is partly hereditary, because it is connected with the blood-radiation of the physical body (light blood, heavy blood, etc.). But the *human spirit* is indivisible, a complete personality in itself, with its more or less matured abilities and the qualities it has acquired in the course of its earth lives, which help to define its nature.

For example, let us take a family of musicians. Here great-grandparents, grandparents and parents successively attract similar kinds of musically gifted human spirits, so that the great-grandchild may also take after a deceased member of the family, who at the time of incarnation was no longer on earth.

In incarnation also lies the answer to the question of *when* earthman has his beginning, a moment, which in discussing possible times for abortions, could not be established until now.

In this connection, the view occasionally adopted that the human individual begins with the completed development of the brain in the growing child's body is not enough.

For this important moment, the final union of the incarnating human spirit with the developing infant's body about midway through pregnancy is decisive, so that it can be said that *only from incarnation onwards does earthman have his beginning*, and therewith he enters upon earthly existence.

However, there is not just *one* incarnation; but many reincarnations (re-embodiments), thus repeated earth lives, are needed for the growing and maturing of the human spirit, until finally it is able to enter Luminous Fields.

In any case, that is the *original* purpose of the reincarnations. When in addition the mistakes of past earth lives are allowed to be redeemed, this is a further grace of God bestowed upon men with repeated earth lives.

Even if men had remained inwardly good, they would still have had to come to earth repeatedly in order to mature; but certainly not so often as became necessary after their Fall.

Reincarnation in human bodies, which in the West is often described as an invasion of Eastern thought, is a lawful happening in Creation that takes place day-in and day-out all over the earth.

But a great many people know nothing of it, or they refuse to know, because nothing about it has ever been passed on to them. It is the Christian teachings above all that reject reincarnation, or the existence of the soul before incarnation.

If we enquire into how this rejection has come about, we find that at the Council of Constantinople in A.D. 553 it was decided to annul the doctrine of reincarnation. But already in 543 the "divine emperor," Justinian, under the influence of the early fathers, had issued an edict (Canones adversus Originem) against the Christian theologian Origen, who believed in reincarnation; which edict stated among other things that anyone who said or thought that the souls of men had had an earlier life (pre-existence) . . . and were now incarnated in bodies . . . would be anathematized!

The knowledge of reincarnation was thus withheld from many people, who *with* this knowledge could have given a deeper meaning and greater significance to their lives on earth and in the beyond. Today, at the time of the Cosmic Turning Point, this knowledge is also part of the subject matter that must be made up for in the "school of life."

Opponents of the doctrine of reincarnation always maintain that Jesus had never spoken about it. But who can prove that Jesus did not speak about it and that His words, as perhaps many another thing, were simply not recorded in the Gospels?

Something else should be mentioned concerning reincarnation. In one of the larger Western countries a public survey was carried out recently. The question asked was: "If you were to come into the world once more, would you rather be a man or a woman?"

It is particularly striking that repeated earth lives were taken for granted, a correct but nevertheless unusual assumption, if one considers that on the whole reincarnation is rejected, especially in the West.

The answers to the question asked above are remarkable-61 percent of the women acknowledged their sex, 25 percent declared they would rather have been men, and 13 percent were undecided. Of the men questioned, 88 percent were content to be males, and only 8 percent had the wish to change their sex.

Many may smile at the way the question was asked, and describe the change of sex as misleading, because they cannot imagine that in their next earth life men could be women and women men.

The deeper reasons for this lie in the psychic sphere. Namely, a woman, who tries to behave in every respect as a man, must in fact count on being incarnated in a male physical body in her next earth life, while on the other hand a weakly man's soul naturally has to expect a female incarnation, for which they will be attracted by similar types living on earth.

It is only from these unnatural psychic conditions that in many cases those wishes can form. Related to the present life on earth, the following possibilities thus emerge. On the one hand a *female* soul living in the present *female* physical body, who has taken on masculine qualities, can have the wish to become a man; or it is possible that a *male* soul dwelling in the present *female* physical body has recognized its faults through various experiences, and now wishes again to be a man in the next earth life.

With men it is the reverse. A masculine *woman* in a *male* body wishes, as the result of recognizing her weaknesses, to be a woman again in the next earth life, and a weakly, effeminate *man* in a *male* body would like to become a woman.

These types of human beings have distorted souls, because through a wrong volition they have suppressed, thus distorted, the natural and original in them. For a genuine man will always remain completely so, and will never get into the position of incarnating in a female body, and conversely it will be exactly the same with a genuine woman.

For spiritual development and maturity, it is not necessary to be born alternately in a female and a male body.

But here too there are enough opportunities to realize past errors, to learn and to draw practical applications from them for further life. With an inner conversion to the good and natural, however, the more ponderous earthly cloak is no longer able to change in the present earth life, so that the outward change of sex, apart from a few exceptions, will only take effect in the next earth life, as a new female or male child's body comes into being.

In this connection the aforementioned question, and the answer to it, gain deeper meaning.

Having considered the less pleasant aspect of becoming man on earth, the pleasant shall also be mentioned, namely that kind of attraction of homogeneous species that is based on the longing for what is nobler and higher, where parents and the incarnating soul are glowingly permeated by good intuitive perceptions, so that a secure foundation is provided for a harmonious life on earth together, and a mutual spiritual furthering.

The sojourn of the human spirit on earth, made possible through becoming man, is only a small but a very incisive part of its long journey through Subsequent Creation, which starts from Paradise and leads back to it.

Only for a time on this journey does it receive an earthly cloak, the physical body, which supports the necessary spiritual development, the aim of which is the conscious-ness of oneself, which the human spirit needs in order eventually to be able to return to Paradise as a fully conscious personality.

Thereby the physical body becomes an important instrument that must be carefully tended, as property entrusted by the Creator, for which man is fully responsible, and which he must neither cast away by committing suicide, nor wantonly damage or render unfit.

It is from *this* viewpoint that the coming-into-being of man on earth must be regarded, in order to give it the right place in the whole development process of the human spirit.

An important phase in the coming-into-being of man is *pregnancy*. At present it is at the center of many controversies dealing with the termination of pregnancy. According to the prevailing view of law and life, a termination of pregnancy, that is the deliberate induction of an abortion, is a crime to be correspondingly punished. For some time there has been strong opposition to this view in many countries; heated discussions about the retention, mitigation or abolition of the punishment for abortion of the fetus are in full swing, in the course of which legal, social, biological, as well as religious, moral and philo-sophical arguments for and against abortion are put forward. Experiences of the women concerned are also made use of.

Here the problem is to be discussed from the *spiritual* standpoint, by taking the Laws of Creation into consideration.

Advocates of abortion declare that the New Testament does not explicitly forbid abortion. This of course cannot be taken as consent. In those days surely there were hardly any such cases among the Jewish people, who were known for their great love of children; hence Jesus had no need to speak about it specifically.

Only later, at the beginning of the second century after Christ, do we find definite statements about it in the oldest surviving Christian Church ordinance, the Teaching of the Twelve Apostles, called in Greek the Didache. This takes the form of a guide to Christian customs and Christian community life. Among other things it enjoins: "Do not kill a fetus by abortion, or commit infanticide." Basil the Great (329-379), Bishop of Caesarea and one of the early church fathers, in a letter to Amphilochius expresses it even more clearly: "The woman who purposely destroys her unborn child is guilty of murder. With us there is no nice enquiry as to its being formed or unformed."

But Jesus says it much more comprehensively: "Love thy neighbor as thyself." In this lies the commandment so to conduct oneself towards one's neighbor that no injury is done to his body or soul. An abortion, however, is such an injury, and *the concept of the neighbor also includes here the soul in the beyond, who is preparing to incarnate in a physical body, or has already incarnated.*

Moreover there is the Fifth Commandment: "Thou shalt not kill!" That means not only murder, thus the deliberate killing of a human being already *born*, but also a killing is already committed against the *unborn* if the fetus is aborted once procreation has taken place.

For *at no time during pregnancy* has man the right to interfere with a process of development, which takes place according to Divine Laws, and the beginning of which he himself can determine by a free decision through procreation.

Hence there is neither any "permissible time," nor is birth control through abortion allowable.

Even if by earthly concepts it could be said that actual killing would begin only with the removal of the fetus *after* the incarnation of the human spirit, because it is from this moment that earthman has his beginning, this does not turn out to be so.

For even during the time *before incarnation* the fetus cannot be removed without something being destroyed thereby. What is destroyed is the already more or less firmly knotted fine radiation-threads between the human spirit awaiting incarnation and the developing child's body; also destroyed is the astral model for this body, which is prepared by the little nature-beings from the time of procreation onwards.

In ancient times the view was held that the whole human organism, fully formed in all its minute details, is already present in the germ from the very beginning, and that it gradually increases in size. This presumably expresses the lost knowledge that for every child's body developing in the womb there is an astral model, that is to say a model in a finer material, invisible to the physical eye, on which the gross-material-earthly body is then formed. This astral body, which man carries within him during his whole earth life, has an important mediator function between his soul and his physical body. Sometimes the little nature-beings are compelled to weave a dark karma (fate), brought about by the soul itself, into this astral model-body, which in the subsequent forming may manifest in the physical body as a defect. Thus for example a man, who in those days reviled and blasphemed the Savior on the cross, as an outward sign of his evildoing bears on his physical body in his various earth lives stigmata (wound-marks) of the Savior, which will disappear only with the recognition of his guilt.

But the killing mentioned in the Fifth Commandment refers not only to the earthly plane. There is a killing also in the psychic sphere, such as the smothering of a noble intuitive perception, the stifling of some hope, the suppressing of a talent, the feigning of friendship or of confidence. Here something that bears real life in it is also killed.

In the case of abortion under consideration, the hope of a soul in the beyond for speedier progress, or for the redemption of some karma, is perhaps smothered. Maybe through this unnatural action the earthly mother herself prevents the possibility of her own spiritual advancement, of her own necessary karma redemption, towards which the growing up and the rearing of a child, with all the worries and joys, could have helped her.

But there is yet another important connection that must not be disregarded: the close link between the coming-into-being of man and the maternal working in Creation.

The concept of the maternal must be taken in the widest sense, because it holds good throughout Creation. It comprises the activity of forming and growing, of tending and nourishing, of caring and nursing. The maternal has its origin in Divine Love, which far from the unhealthy softness and damaging indulgence of human love, works and creates in severity and justice for the benefit and well being of all creatures in Creation.

This sphere of activity of the maternal also includes motherhood on earth, to which in turn belongs the coming-into-being of man.

The prevention of this coming-into-being of man by the removal of growing life in the womb, is contrary to the maternal principle, which with a joyful heart tends, protects and allows to develop that for which the Will of God has intended it.

An exception should only be considered when an intervention, for grave medical reasons, would support it.

Where rape is concerned the individual case should always be examined; and at the same time it should be borne in mind that through good intuitive perceptions, and a trusting and confident attitude on the part of the mother, even in such a case a soul of good volition might be given the opportunity of incarnation, which as well as cares will certainly also bring joy with it, so that finally everything will be brought to a good ending.

Let it also be said here that the unnatural experiments to develop a living human being in a test tube must prove unavailing from the very outset, because they lack just that radiation-bridge, which only the woman with her more delicate intuitive faculty, is in a position to offer, whereby her blood-radiation also plays a decisive part in the earthly attraction.

It is also this finer sensitiveness, peculiar to woman alone, that awakens in man the respect for womanhood, and the longing for the Luminous Height. This is expressed in the words of Goethe: "That which is forever womanly draws us upward" (Faust, Part II).

In certain circumstances a deficient radiation-bridge alone can often be the main cause of miscarriages or childlessness. When a woman departs from her womanly nature, and takes on masculine qualities and characteristics, these delicate radiations, which signify the truly womanly, and which man does not possess, are weakened or even suppressed. The harmful consequences manifest in the most varying forms.

To sum up, it must be said that a *final* solution to all the problems associated with the coming-into-being of man is only possible when the *connections beyond the earth* as shown are also taken into account. Only these give a comprehensive insight, showing the right way out of distress and affliction, but also increasing the responsibility. Therefore man must all the more seriously examine whether he is not harming his neighbor with his thoughts and actions, whether they are pure or governed by desire and lust. The very knowledge that a human soul awaiting incarnation in the beyond is also involved should arouse a greater sense of responsibility. In this connection, procreation becomes a matter that cannot be taken seriously enough, in so far as it is desired by the married partners, and is not merely a question of a mutual exchange of fluids during their union. After all, the whole process of becoming man on earth is a Grace of God; offering to all concerned the most diverse opportunities to redeem all kinds of threads of fate, and to advance spiritually.

All the more, of course, must there be clarity with regard to the consequences, if the coming-into-being of man is prevented through termination of pregnancy.

Even if the completed abortion should be no longer punishable according to earthly laws, the Divine Laws are not influenced by this; before them neither the wrong committed nor the sense of guilt can be effaced thereby. Just as the opinion, "My body belongs to me," does not alter anything of the consequences, nor silence the warning of the conscience. An abortion during the time before incarnation can certainly mitigate the consequences, but not annul them.

The *personal responsibility* remains in every case. It is founded in the free will of man, who is at liberty to commit any deed, either good or evil. But he is then irrevocably subject to the *consequences* of his deed. It is an adamantine Law of Creation, which Nature always keeps before our eyes: What a man sows, he must reap!

Nevertheless there is no cause for despair if those concerned, on becoming conscious of their guilt, honestly strive for what is good and pure. Then sufficient opportunities will be offered to help their fellowman with caring and dedicated love, and thereby gradually to sever all the dark threads of fate.

All these problems and conflicting situations will cease to oppress and afflict men as soon as woman turns once more to her *true* task, namely, with her finer intuitive ability, and solely through her quiet working, to mediate to mankind those luminous radiations of spiritual power that help to keep awake and ever more strongly set aglow the longing for Paradise. Then true respect for developing motherhood and for the dignity of woman will once again come to life.

3. THE VIRTUES

The virtues come from God. They are most noble gifts with which the Creator invested the human spirit. Hence the virtues are eternal, and do not change. They belong to the abilities of the spirit that are the "talent" entrusted to it, which it is to "make the most of," that is to say, it is to make use of its abilities so that they will bring blessing (interest).

But man was not immediately equipped with ready-made virtues; he himself must see to it that they awaken and blossom. For this purpose he again needs corresponding radiations from the Universe, which help him to do so.

The starting-points of these radiations are to be found in the highest heights of the Primordial Spiritual Realm. They are female and male ideal figures, prototypes for all humanity, each of whom personifies one virtue. They send their radiations to the parts of Creation that lie below them, where they are received by many mediators and passed on all the way down to Subsequent Creation, which is described as the World, and which consists of various kinds of matter. Our earth is also a part of this.

For every virtue, for all noble qualities, indeed for absolutely everything that moves a human being inwardly, if only it is pure, these "radiating helps" give stimulus, animation and strengthening, whether they be, for example: faithfulness, truthfulness, grace, modesty, diligence, heroism, courage, skill, fulfillment of duty, wisdom, humility or compassion.

The ancient peoples knew the mediators, who come last in the luminous chain of helpers from above, because they were still able to see them with their inner eyes. They called them "gods and goddesses," because they appeared to them as mighty personalities, superior to themselves in strength and vigor.

The "gods and goddesses" are still there even today, although men have banished them to the realm of the unreal, the legendary. They are, of course, not "gods," but servants of the Most High, personalities, who in noblest perfection, immortal, young and eternally beautiful, live at the summit of Olympus (Valhalla) that lies below the human Paradise. From thence they work in manifold ways downwards to the material Subsequent Creation, controlling and guiding the forces and elements active in Nature, and thereby having a connecting, driving and forming influence.

These servants of the Most High, and with them many others besides, stand steadfast in the Laws of Creation, knowing only one task: fulfillment of the Will of God. That rules out the arbitrary actions imputed to them by men.

According to their language, the ancient peoples gave them different names. Thus the Zeus of the Greeks is identical with the Jupiter of the Romans and the Odin (Woden or Wotan) of the ancient Germanic peoples.

Gradually belief in the gods was lost, because the connection with them was disrupted through the ever more prominent material-intellectual thinking. The exalted figures faded, and in the course of time they were humanized and pushed aside by images produced by human fantasy.

The "pagan" belief in gods is really nothing other than an *intermediate stage* in the natural evolution of mankind to the highest stage of the recognition of God. In the struggle for religious recognition, the peoples of olden times had reached this stage, which corresponded to a genuine inner desire for higher development. It brought the highest recognition for the evolution of that time.

The often-enforced abolition of this belief in gods, which occurred in the course of Christian conversions, was a great mistake, costing much bloodshed and suffering. Moreover it gave proof of ignorance about the Divine Laws of Evolution. In the earthly school, which is nothing other than a coarse imitation of the great school of life, the intermediate grades are not suddenly offered the knowledge of the highest grades either, nor is the hitherto-acquired knowledge put aside as useless. For one step must be built on another, not a single one can be missed; otherwise empty faith without inner conviction will result.

Among the various myths and legends that have been handed down, it is not easy to discover the essence of the true working of the gods in Creation, especially in regard to the human spirit, because the many human additions, amplifications and embellishments hardly allow the essential factor to be discerned.

Hence the following portrayals of some of the gods and goddesses are to be regarded only as approximate accounts.

Thus for example in Zeus (Jupiter), the father of the gods and ruler of the world, we find the ideal image of the kingly ruler, awe-inspiring and majestic, severe and just in the conduct of his high office. In him was seen the personification of the principle of unchangeable order and harmony. The wisdom of his counsel and the depth of his knowledge were held in special esteem.

In Hera (Juno), the female counterpart of Zeus, we recognize the ideal of faithfulness. The high nobility of exalted womanhood finds expression in her. To the female sex in particular she is a faithful and motherly protector. She was revered as the guardian of marriage and protector of women in childbirth, who instilled respect for motherhood in human beings.

Pallas Athene (Minerva) is portrayed as a valiant goddess, with helmet, shield and spear. Her working is unflinching and unshakeable, distinguished by sharp-eyed vigilance, reliability and conscientiousness. She defends, protects and sustains the motherland, and as "goddess of war" she accompanies the army when it has to set out to defend the motherland.

Apollon (Apollo) is the victorious fighter against all that is impure and evil, against the powers of Darkness; the gift of prophecy is one of his characteristics. For their spiritual upward striving he is said to counsel men with: "Give thyself up."

In her chaste dignity, Artemis (Diana) shines as an example of purity and propriety. She takes part in enchanting dances with her nymphs in flowery meadows. Young girls especially revered her.

Ares (Mars) mediates strength, courage and the joy of battle. The planet "Mars," which is in his care, also has a stimulating and inspiring influence, corresponding to its similar nature. Through its radiating forces, as well as through the radiations of the other planets, metals, plants and stones were formed on earth.

Aphrodite (Astarte, Venus) is the goddess of beauty and fertility. She was sacred to all peoples, who strove for the purity of woman. They also called her goddess of the moon, because its light resembled the light of her sphere. Her radiations dispense grace and loveliness. The myrtle as the symbol of pure love is dedicated to her. Also Venus, her planet, swings in purity and beauty. In its radiations, colors and tones of wondrous beauty are formed in the Sphere of Matter.

Hermes (Mercury), the swift messenger of the gods, delivers the commands and instructions of Zeus. He escorts, protects and negotiates. The skill, with which he carries out his instructions, and his humility in serving, are examples of true virtues. In his physical and spiritual skill he was portrayed as a living example to the youth of Greece.

Hestia (Vesta) was honored as tutelary goddess of home and family. The hearth fire is her symbol. The nature of this goddess is also pure and clear as the flame. Colonists, who left their native land to found a new settlement, took with them fire from the altar of Vesta, on which burned an everlasting fire, as a symbol of the spiritual link between their homeland and the new colony. In accordance with the pure nature of this goddess, only chaste virgins were allowed to serve in her temple.

What people thought about the gods more than two thousand years ago, thus at a time when belief in them had not yet died out, is worthy of notice.

Cicero (106-43 B.C.), one of the most important orators and writers of ancient Rome, left behind an almost completely preserved work, Vom Wesen der Götter (*On the Nature of the Gods* Goldmann, Munich), in which representatives of Greek schools of philosophy speak about the gods in the form of a dialogue. A few sentences are given here:

". . . there are also other philosophers, important and famous ones at that, who hold it true that the entire world is kept in order and ruled by divine insight and reason. At the same time-so they believe-the gods also look after the life of men in a counseling and helping way. In their opinion fruits and other products of the soil, changes in the weather, the seasons and the firmament, through which everything the earth produces is made to grow and ripen, are gifts of the immortal gods for mankind." —

". . . Since this belief in gods has not arisen through teaching, old custom or law, and since the universal agreement of all is firmly established, there must needs also be the firm conviction that there are gods, because we have an implanted, or rather inborn, conception of them. Everything that harmonizes with the natural ability of all men will of course also be true. Hence the existence of the gods must be admitted. As this point is almost invariably given unlimited recognition, not only by all philosophers but also by the uneducated, we must certainly admit that there is in us the pre-comprehension of the gods, as I have called it before; or should I call it pre-knowledge?" —

Thus the often reviled and denied "gods and goddesses" are actually men's best helpers. Their radiations also awaken, further and strengthen the virtues, which man urgently needs in order again to be worthy of true humanity. —

Above all virtues is the virtue of Divine Purity, which manifests in the human spiritual as true faithfulness. Only in Its ray can the other virtues unfold.

Cultivation of the female virtues, in the first place faithfulness, is the best protection for woman against becoming masculine, as likewise in man the cultivation of male virtues prevents a sliding down into the weakly and effeminate.

Schiller quite rightly said: "And virtue, it is no empty sound; man can practice it in life." This means that he must acquire it through continuous striving for what is beautiful, noble and pure. Then he himself, in his human nature, is able to become an ideal figure.

What virtues man will choose is left entirely to him. Whether they be the general virtues that apply equally to womanhood and manhood, as for example humility, modesty and compassion, or the particular virtues of either sex, such as grace, or else courage, heroism and skill, among others.

Just as with a noble stringed instrument it is left to the player, which notes to strike, so the spirit of man is able in each case to call forth special vibrations, which borne by true longing, move out into the Universe. There they make contact with a similar vibration, which works in a strengthening and stimulating, invigorating and happy-making way, and gradually, according to the prototype of the heavenly virtues, allows the same human prototype to arise on earth.

How far-reaching is the conception of a virtue, and how manifold its effect in earth life, shall be shown by a few examples.

Simplicity and clarity in the intuitive perception and thought will surely lead to the virtue of *humility*, which is linked with serving, but which has nothing whatever to do with servility. To serve means "giving oneself up," which does not require withdrawal into solitude or seclusion.

Man gives up many an outward thing, his profession, his position, his dwelling-place, and takes in its stead something new, something different. But he is also capable of giving himself up, which means nothing more than placing his deeds and thoughts in the Will of God, adjusting his own volition to the higher Will of God, without making demands and without presumption. Thereby he gives himself up. Nothing else then is meant by the words that Apollo once gave to men: "Give thyself up!"

Man can easily observe the Will of the Creator, for he has the Ten Commandments, the Messages of God, and he lives in the midst of the Work that the Creator has created. From this alone he is able to read everything that is contained in the Laws of Creation. These Laws shape and guide the whole happening in Creation; any arbitrary deviation from them is impossible, because such would be contrary to Divine Perfection.

Thus man comes ever nearer to the consciousness of his own smallness before the power and greatness of his Creator. He sees himself as a tiny particle in the vast, mighty Creation, which is dependent on God. After all, he is only a developed spirit, which bears within it nothing of Divinity, and which can continue to exist only through the Grace of God.

If he has thus found the courage for true serving while maintaining his full personality, the gate to humility will open for him, and with humility another virtue enters his soul: *modesty*.

He who is modest never presumptuously overreaches himself, and always takes only *in due proportion* of that which Creation offers him.

In the present age of remoteness from God it is especially hard for people to awaken within them the virtue of humility, because in the end this also requires the recognition of God, the sensing of Divine Greatness and Power.

The virtue of *compassion* particularly affects the relationship between men. For this also has man long since found a substitute: pity, as product of the earth-bound intellect, born of vanity and self-love or earthly scheming. Personal benefit and advantage mostly take first place; the desire really to help others is nearly always lacking.

On the other hand compassion, in its spiritual greatness, is different. It arises from the pure spiritual intuitive perception of man, from kindheartedness, and not from selfish striving as in the case of pity. It helps for the sake of helping, and has no thought of personal advantage, because its aim is of a spiritual nature.

Therefore it also observes the Law of Balance between giving and taking. The giving that is done out of scheming or vanity transgresses this Law as much as the taking, which originates in an expectation that takes things for granted, in a demanding and asking, or in an "entitlement to be helped."

But there is something else inherent in compassion: the just severity that sees only the spiritual benefit of the other, which includes also earthly and spiritual activity; whereas letting oneself be helped from pity is much more pleasant and convenient, but also promotes spiritual indolence.

How important it is to be active is indicated by a Chinese saying: "If you give a man a fish he has food for a day. If you teach a man to catch fish he has food for life."

These simple words strike precisely at the core of a genuine help that is really beneficial to men. They could even be taken as the genuine foundation of help for the developing nations, which today is often offered only out of pity. How much is given here solely from a desire to dominate, for external matters, for a comfortable life, for the moment. But how little is done to awaken, to encourage and to further the natural self-help, the inner and outer activity, which only then brings blessing!

Through the fatal consequences of pity, the harmony of the mutual relationship between men has already been severely disrupted for a long time, because the giver as well as the taker act wrongly in this matter and seek only after earthly gain.

Compassion, however, swings in the Laws of Creation, and can therefore only release joy and gratitude.

It is often assumed that *gratitude* is a virtue, or a duty. It is neither; but like joy, with which it is closely linked, it is a compensating value that must be in the right proportion to what has been received. Hence gratitude towards men is *limited*, and it is wrong to speak of a duty to be grateful, and to expect far more than the gift is worth.

Gratitude should be *unlimited* only towards God, because for all that man receives from Him there is nothing he can do except give thanks.

In conclusion, let us just deal briefly with *diligence*, which is of special importance in the life of man, irrespective of whether it is to be counted among the virtues or among the good qualities of the human spirit.

Here too the original concept has been dragged down to the earthly. One person strives with persistent diligence for a carefree and comfortable earth life, another with pertinacious diligence for power and respect, and with laborious diligence a third does his everyday work without joy.

But who knows the right concept of *spiritual* diligence, which is closely linked with the Law of Continuous Movement in Creation: that diligence, which unremittingly tries with quiet confidence to strive for a high, luminous goal, to ennoble itself and its fellowmen and thereby to advance spiritually, without unnecessary extremes, without restraint and without haste?

In accordance with the Law of Movement, a harmonious spiritual swinging thus arises, which is subsequently transferred to the earthly working, and which allows neither love of comfort and indolence nor an unwholesome excess of zeal to emerge. Such diligent striving comes to an end during the necessary periods of rest, and thus at the same time again draws new stimulus for fresh activity.

Diligence, which is rooted in the spiritual, produces fruits for eternity, imperishable works that also help other people.

But with this diligence there arises on earth a joyful, blessed working, in honor and gratitude to the Creator!

So should it be, if man had kept to the path of virtue. But this path has become a lonely one. Man makes a "virtue of necessity," which means that he makes the best of an unpleasant circumstance, rather than occupying himself with the virtues as such.

And yet with this word a far-off chord should touch his soul, if it still carries within it a spark of longing. A chord that breaks through dark veils, giving way to luminous rays, refreshing, invigorating rays from eternal, inexhaustible springs that will once again endow man with the impetus for what is ideal and pure, noble and beautiful.

But in the present time of the great, spiritual impasse, of the ceaseless rushing in of bad impressions, of inner dissension of the soul and deadening of the individual personality, mankind is farther away than ever from this ideal of striving.

It weighs heavily upon them that they have so completely closed themselves to the radiant helps from the Height, and yield instead to the enticing currents of the Darkness, making a vice out of every virtue, and changing all good qualities to the contrary: thus courage to cowardice, compassion to pity, truthfulness to falsehood, grace to vanity, humility to arrogance, wisdom to sham knowledge, and faithfulness to unfaithfulness.

Difficult and hard therefore is the struggle for a new human image; so difficult because it is to become a clear and pure image, which must this time remain valid for all time.

This image cannot be molded without the virtues, for it is just these that bestow on the image an eternal splendor.

4. SPIRIT AND LANGUAGE

Incarnation is the entrance of the human spirit into the growing child's body about midway through pregnancy.

If men would concern themselves more with this fact, a process that takes place dayin and day-out all over the earth, many a problem now causing a great headache would be solved at once.

So also the question: how did the first men come to earth? Since in those primeval times there were as yet no earthly human mothers, they incarnated *first of all* in the most highly-evolved animals, prepared for it, which were already on earth before them, and which now formed the bridge to the earth life of men.

Male spirit germs incarnated in animal bodies of the male sex, and female spirit germs in those of the female sex.*

The most highly evolved animals became extinct at that time. They were similar in type to the present anthropoid apes.

After the spiritual had received the animal bodies as earthly coverings, it brought about something else in addition to the transformation of the animal blood into human blood: the development of human language. The urge of the human spirit to give outward expression to its intuitive perceiving, thinking and volition, and the better to be able to communicate with one another, gave rise in the natural course of development to the forming of the vocal organs necessary for it. This forming required a further important change in the physical body, which likewise emphasizes the difference between man and animal, and which has only been discovered at the present time: the gradual sinking downwards of the larynx; whereas in the case of animals, above all with the apes, there was no change in the position of the larynx!

Only this sinking of the larynx, and the simultaneous forming of the human shape of mouth and nose, made possible the complete voice and vowel production that is characteristic of man alone.

When today man begins his earth life with a cry, and through imitation learns to speak within a few years, he thereby passes once more within a short time through all the stages of development that he has undergone over long periods of time. Thus there is repeated in the child each time the sinking of the larynx, of which Adolf Portmann in his

---

* See: *The Origin of Man and the Human Races* in Part I.

144

book "Wir sind unterwegs" (We are on the Way) (Walter Publishing House), page 136, writes the following: "For in the adult the larynx in the course of time shifts a few centimeters further downwards. And this 'descent of the larynx' — already established by embryologists about 1905 — begins at the end of the first year of life and lasts up to the eighth or ninth year. This is quite a remarkable story, for a space is thereby formed at the back of the throat, which the anthropoid apes (and all other apes) do not have. It is the space in which also our so freely movable tongue can make very fine movements. And this space is particularly important for the formation of the different vowels: it is a true vowel-space. That is the position, which Liebermann and his colleagues have newly investigated. The formation of our own human language, especially of the different vowels, has been studied with all the facilities of modern research. Through the most careful study of the anthropoid apes and of the other apes, thus also of the macaques, it has been proved that they are denied the true, correct vocalization: simply because they do not experience the descent of the larynx. That is the newly examined position with regard to anatomy and the history of evolution. Therefore we must definitely assume that our ancestral form, which after all has evolved from some basic shape close to that of the apes, was similarly constituted to the vast majority of mammals; hence that the epiglottis reached right up to the palate."

At the end of his discourse we read: "Do let us seek to grasp what man can one day be, as now he marches towards the third millennium of our Western chronology. And for this it would certainly be very desirable to know whence this man comes, and what the first signs and manifestations of a spiritual world attitude may have been. The conception of spirit and language being such a close unit as to be inseparable has seriously become a new question today. And we await further explanations with close interest.

How then did the forming of the language proceed? Remaining at first bent like animals as they walked, men gradually adopted an upright posture. The initially hoarse sounds became more vocal as the larynx sank down, and the present shape of the human mouth developed.

To begin with men communicated with gestures and sounds, which they picked up from Nature; then they joined individual sounds and formed groups of sounds, which became words. Finally they assembled the words into sentences.

Thus they extended their language more and more, and therewith the ability to express themselves.

It must be mentioned here that in the natural course of his development man was provided with an aid, which was to realize the up-building aspiration of his spirit in the earthly: the intellect, which is composed of thoughts produced in the frontal brain.

With this the human spirit received an *instrument* that was useful to him also in the forming of the language.

Forming is the *right* expression, for there was nothing more for man to create. Every kind of building brick already exists in Creation. As with a jigsaw puzzle, man must merely put them together until the right picture appears. Even this way of working is in itself invigorating, and brings happiness.

But neither could the language have been formed so readily if there had not been teachers to instruct men. They were beings in the beyond, with whom men had undimmed connection in those days; they advised them on how they should form the language.

According to the radiations, which beings and things have, and which man sensed with his intuitive perception, he joined sound with sound until the tone of the word confirmed to him that his forming was right. In the same way he gave to abstract, thus non-material concepts the word-coverings in which they could swing.

Here it is clearly evident: the mystery of the language is founded in the spirit of man; only he has the ability to form and to speak the language. Even Genesis gives an account of how man made use of the gracious gift of word forming, and gave names to the animals (Genesis 2, 19-20).

Last but not least he was also helped in this by human spirits of higher origin, who incarnated here and there in maturing races of men in order to lead them another step upwards in their development.

The evolution of the human language, starting from the sounds of expression to the forming of words and sentences, proceeded normally as long as men understood and put into practice in their earth lives the *Language of God*, which is to be found in His Creation and in His Commandments.

This changed fundamentally when through the over-cultivation of the earthly intellect, and its boundless over-rating, they came ever more under the power of materialistic thinking.

The consequent decline, the turning away from God, is depicted in the Bible in the *allegories* of the building of the tower of Babel and the Babylonian confusion of tongues, as an incisive happening in the human history of evolution (Genesis 11, 1-9).

Men severed the connections with the Luminous Spheres and moved into the land of Darkness, into the lowlands of human vanity. There they built for themselves a tower of arrogance and presumption, which in their great pretension they wanted to build unto heaven, so that "they would make a name for themselves!"

146

With the disregarding of the Laws of God there simultaneously began a confusion of the language, which spread over the whole earth. But this is to be understood otherwise than is generally assumed. It did not consist of the development of many languages of the individual peoples, differing one from another, which made mutual communication difficult.

It was a spiritual happening! Men no longer understood each other because each had his own language, which means: each stressed his own selfish volition, was intent only on his own advantage, and hardly troubled any longer to understand his fellow man.

That Language, which everyone is able to read in the Book of Creation, the Language of God, was no longer understood by them. Therefore a wrong swinging also entered their earthly languages. Words appeared, which until then had never existed, because they were alien to the pure volition of the human spirits. They were dark and evil words, formed after the evil deeds and thoughts of men. Like a great discord they permeated the languages of the peoples.

All the evil that can possibly occur in this world was inflicted by men on one another over thousands of years, and in accordance with the Law of Creation they had to give a name to each evil, because it arose within them alive, corresponding to their free will.

Today the climax of all misdeeds has been reached, and the crime that men commit against the language is not the least.

The language is ever more misused through meaningless babble, empty talk and evil thinking. Ever more carelessly the meaning of the words is distorted.

What is there still left of the high concepts as they are described, for example, in the words justice, love, purity, truth, humanity, freedom, peace and faith? Each person imputed to them a meaning thought out by himself, corresponding with his selfish earthly aims, but far removed from the pure swinging of these concepts in the Creation-happening.*

Such misuse has grave consequences, because the language is alive, and may not be altered with impunity.

Here the oft-expressed intention to introduce small initial letters into the German language has also to be mentioned. On whatever ground it is demanded — it is in any case retrogression.

The use of capital and small letters in writing is not pedantry, but a *peculiarity* of the German language, and as such unique. The other West European languages have an

---

* See: "The Origin of Man and the Human Races" in Part I.

essentially different structure, a different sentence construction, which does not require the capitalization of nouns.

Capitalization, which was worked out over centuries, gives the nouns a special position in the structure of the sentence, and makes it possible to grasp the meaning of the sentences better through the prominence of the capitals.

Until the thirteenth century the development was such that only the beginning of the sentence was written with a capital, proper names (countries, towns, villages, etc.) being added later. Then gradually capitals came to be given also to nouns, in order to emphasize them. The capital letter at the beginning of a word — so it was said at the time — was to be the head, to which the other letters were joined like limbs.

Before capitalization was introduced in the beginning of the eighteenth century, and rules established for it, there was much groping and searching for the final form.

Not infrequently in manuscripts the same noun was spelled at one time with a capital and at another with a small letter, or there were capitalized prepositions and adjectives side-by-side with nouns written with small letters. And in the first editions of the Bible we still find the irregular use of small and capital letters for one and the same noun.

Even in those days, when capitalization was introduced there was no lack of dissenting voices declaring that it was very difficult for the simple person, and that it would be enough to capitalize the beginnings of sentences, or possibly also the names of people and places.

Although capitalization has been attacked ever again in the course of centuries, it belongs to the genuine form of the language that has been developed by the German spirit.

The *spirit* therefore intuitively senses the German language in its present form to be correct. If however its instrument the intellect interferes, then the language is all of a sudden antiquated, ponderous and in need of reform, and the demand to "write more sensibly," i.e., "with small letters," is urgently voiced. But what is the meaning of sensible, which is derived from sense? It is the natural cooperation between the intuitive perception of the spirit and the earthly intellect. "Natural" in turn means that in accordance with the order of Creation the spirit as the primary, thus the original, takes the lead, and the intellect is subordinate to it. This arises from the very fact that after physical death the human spirit continues to exist, while the intellect, which issues from the brain, ceases to be after death, thus is perishable.

A sensible manner of writing is therefore adjusted to the volition of the spirit and not to the intellect, for which such questionable changes aim only at easy usage at the expense of spiritual mobility. For the spirit demands more: a living language, swinging in the rhythm of the Laws of Creation!

But this cannot arise, if it is constantly being tampered with.

The introduction of small letters, or even spelling by sound (phonetic spelling), the already widespread craze for abbreviations and foreign words, as well as the great indifference and superficiality in anything to do with language, indicate the danger of the German literary language becoming shallow and rigid; this language, which was formed by many Called Ones in the course of centuries, often in the face of considerable opposition.

After all a word is no arbitrary combination of letters, but something that has grown naturally, that has a sound. If letters are removed from it there will be a dissonance. The harmonious swinging will be disturbed. A strange word-form arises, which no longer fits the concept it is to embody. Also a lengthened -h or -e, for example, like every letter, has its significance as a means of catching the eye, and as a "note" in the sound of the word, which helps to form the tone of the pronunciation. —

But not only the German language is the product of a lengthy evolution. The other languages also arose in accordance with the same laws of development.

While at the beginning of man's existence there were linguistic prototypes, with the spreading of men over the earth, above all through the separation into races, linguistic groups with differing linguistic abilities arose, who formed their own languages.

The degree of maturity of these groups in their spiritual development varied. It was even bound to vary because of the free will. Hence the forming of the language manifested differently in the sounds of expression, words and sentences. The fact that up to the present time linguistic prototypes have been preserved, and that there are affinities of language between individual peoples, is shown by the findings of philology.

In view of these separate linguistic developments, a uniform earth-language was not possible.

Today, however, the Creation-happening has advanced so far as to open the way to a *leading* living language. But the leadership is not to be judged from earthly aspects; it lies in the spiritual, and is dependent on the Will of God.

Members of all peoples can use this language for communication, above all for transmitting genuine spiritual knowledge, without detriment to the languages developed for their particular surroundings. —

The linguistic evolution lasting millions of years, which began with the first sounds and original forms, can only be completed when it adapts itself ever more thoroughly to the rhythm of the Laws of Creation.

All the sadder is it when man tries to restrain this development, and simply ignores the high gift, which he has received from his Creator, with the ability to form words, by continuously abusing it in a wanton manner.

He should consider: a faint reflection of the Living Word of God, from which Creation arose, still lies in the human word. Although it no longer has any creative power, it nevertheless has a formative influence on the environment, thereby setting in motion unseen forces, which when wrongly applied over a long time have devastating consequences.

Therefore man should always give thanks to his Creator for the faculty of being able to speak by using his earthly language in the right sense. In this connection, however, something very important has to be observed: besides the words themselves, the manner of speaking also has a strong effect. But since the *manner of speaking* forms man, it is not immaterial what words he chooses, how he assembles, pronounces and emphasizes them. Any neglect in this has a harmful, if not even a disastrous effect on man and his surroundings.

Only by using a manner of speaking that is controlled by the spirit can man work constructively through the language, and develop its inherent life to full blossom. How strongly the language can be filled with its own life is shown by the inspiring words of the poet Rudolf Binding, *Vom Wunder der Sprache* (*On the Miracle of the Language*), with which these explanations may come to an end.

". . . It (the language) allows thousands to sin against it, and does not restrain them. Centuries use it up, and millions of tongues seem to talk it away and wear it to shreds in the drift of everyday life, in general behavior, heedless and impious.

"Until one day it arises anew in one who masters the language, one with a special ardor — in a Luther, a Goethe, in one who is now alive or who is to come — and sinks into the breast of the people whose soul it serves, with greater purity, strength, might, depth, youth than ever.

"Not to the timid language-reformers, language-preservers and word-discoverers does it entrust itself, but to the great and unique.

"Then it becomes clear that the language is a whole. Though it works unceasingly on itself, just as it unceasingly wears itself away, yet still it arises to renew itself for the expression of its people as a whole . . ."

150

5. THE POOR IN SPIRIT

"Blessed are the poor in spirit: for theirs is the kingdom of heaven," states the authorized version of the Bible (Matthew 5, 3). In other translations it says, "Blessed are those who feel poor in spirit!" Elsewhere it is also said: "Blessed are the simple, for theirs is the kingdom of heaven."

Already many a seeker has seriously pondered as to what meaning really underlies the expression "the poor in spirit," and why it is just they who are to attain to the Kingdom of Heaven. There is a lack of clarity here that should not be, because Jesus always expressed His teaching in clear and simple terms.

If we wish to find the right interpretation, we must be clear about the concepts of *spirit* and *intellect*. Spirit is the eternal in man, which still exists even after his physical death. It manifests in the intuitive perception, which is also called the inner voice. But the intellect arises in the brain, which perishes at physical death. Hence it clearly follows, which has to take first place: the spirit of man. It must use the intellect rightly, as a useful instrument on earth. But the position today is that the intellect has developed into a distorted instrument, which in desperate domination and haughty arrogance suppresses the spirit.

If we regard the spirit from this aspect as what it really is, as the inner eternal core of man, as his real ego, then we ask ourselves: Can one who is spiritually *poor* attain to the Kingdom of Heaven? Surely the opposite would have to be the case. Only such a human spirit as has made the most of the talents entrusted to him, thus fully developed the slumbering abilities of his spirit and thereby become *rich in spirit*, should be able to attain eternal bliss.

But if we wrongly put spirit on a level with intellect, as is generally done today, then we have a man poor in intellect, who is described as "simple." But in today's ordinary speech simple means "good-natured," "limited" or "dimwitted." Those simple and thickheaded ones are now to be awarded eternal bliss as consolation and compensation, so to speak, for their intellectual poverty.

Jesus, of course, never intended these narrowly defined and wrong interpretations. When He spoke to men His words were meant above all for the *spirit*, not for the intellect of man; so also with the Beatitudes. Here it was a matter of spiritual and not of intellectual qualities or deficiencies. Men were to receive the Truth proclaimed by Jesus in the simplicity of their hearts, free from any complicated and subtle reasoning of the intellect. But simplicity here is not to be interpreted in the disparaging sense of limitation, ascribed to the word today, but rather in the sense of humbleness. Perhaps it becomes even clearer to us when we think of the word "unassumingness."

Here again we have yet another example of a distorted concept — through the increasing limitation of spiritual comprehension mankind have formed so many for themselves.

Originally the term "simple" held the meaning "humble," which was then gradually changed to "limited!"

Jesus knew the great value of humbleness (simplicity) in human nature. It is expressed in a clear intuitive perception, which certainly employs the intellect, a product of the brain, which is bound to time and space, as a necessary and useful instrument for earthly life, but which will not let itself be suppressed and thus controlled by it.

Therefore He also chose His disciples from so-called humble circles, which were not burdened by a complicated and wrongly trained way of thinking. He impressed on His hearers: "Except ye be converted, and become as little children, ye shall not enter into the kingdom of heaven" (Matthew 18, 3). This means that men are to think as simply as children, thus unassumingly and naturally.

It is also in this sense that Schiller's words are to be understood: "And what no intellectual mind perceives, is done in simplicity by a childlike heart" (Poem: Words of Faith).

Only simple thinking and intuitive perceiving brings clarity. Men have no idea of the true greatness of this simplicity. They value it too little, and therefore they do not recognize it, either, in the Laws of Creation, which express the Will of God.

The intellect cannot grasp this. It is of earthly origin, and hence is subject to the earthly limitation of time and space, whereas the spirit can make its way unrestrained to the spiritual height. The undimmed clarity of its intuitive perception opens this way for it, and mediates to it the connection with those radiations of Creation from which it can gradually form for itself a Jacob's ladder reaching right up to the Spiritual Realm (Paradise).

Therefore we have good reason to assume that the first of the Beatitudes is meant for those who tread their path through life in simplicity of heart and humble purity of mind, until they reach the fulfillment of their heavenly longing.

So the "poor in spirit" become the simple, who absorb what is true *in a simple way*, thus who approach the Truth in an unassuming and humble manner, without prejudice and free from preconceived ideas.

It is to *them* that Jesus promised: "Blessed are the simple: for theirs is the kingdom of heaven."

6. THE REVELATION OF JOHN

The Revelation of John must not be interpreted according to earthly concepts, and this also applies to time. It is to be taken in a much greater and wider, and above all in a spiritual sense.

When in verse one it is stated: "which must shortly come to pass," this is meant spiritually. It takes considerably longer on the earth-plane, for a thousand earth years are as one day in the Spiritual (Psalms 90, 4).

Only one was found worthy to receive the great Revelation of past and future happenings: John the Baptist, of whom Jesus said: "Verily I say unto you, among them that are born of women there hath not risen a greater than John the Baptist" (Matthew 11, 11).

Moreover, John received the Revelation not on the Island of Patmos in the Aegean Sea during his earth life, but after his earthly death — on the Isle of Patmos that lies in the Spiritual Realm, even above the Paradise of the human spirits. He passed it on to a human being on earth who was spiritually open for it, and who translated it into earthly words. Thus the Book with Seven Seals, the Revelation of John, was handed down to us.

The Revelation presents a vast survey of actual events that have taken place, and that will yet take place, in the Divine Kingdom and down to the lowest depths of the Darkness. It gives matters not only of the future but also of the past, in order to show the connections for the sake of a better understanding of what is to come. The language of the Revelation is a language of metaphor. Each picture corresponds to a definite happening. But its interpretation can only be a spiritual one, because it has been given out of the spirit. The source of the Revelation lies in a manifestation of the Divine Will, thus far above human opinions and views.

In this connection the question arises as to why it is possible to foretell future happenings that concern mankind a long time in advance, when after all man possesses free will. It is just because man has free will that this is possible.

Free will is founded in the freedom to make decisions. Once man has made a decision and transformed it into a deed, the consequences of this decision, which in accordance with the decision may be either good or bad, can indeed be foreseen. He is absolutely subject *to the consequences* of this decision.

It is exactly the same with the great world events. At the time of the Revelation of John, after the death of Christ, it could be perceived from the Spiritual Sphere that in spite of the Message of the Son of God a large part of mankind was refusing to forsake the already-chosen road to decline, thus that a change of decision was no longer to be expected.

This laid the foundation for the Revelation of those catastrophic events that will strike a great number of men on their self-chosen steep course to perdition. Out of the same knowledge Jesus, even before the Revelation of John, proclaimed to mankind the happening of the End Time (Matthew 24, Mark 13, Luke 21).

Therefore man should take the words of the Revelation to heart, and not meet them with indifference.

What John the Baptist was permitted to see and to experience in pictures on the Isle of Patmos in the Spiritual Realm is meant for all mankind, to warn and to help them in their spiritual ascent.

May the words at the beginning of the Revelation (1, 3) be fulfilled for many human beings: *"Blessed is he that readeth, and they that hear the words of this prophecy, and keep those things which are written therein: for the time is at hand."*

7. THE END TIME

In His prophecy, which has been handed down to us in the Bible, Jesus spoke of the End Time, and of the Last Judgment (Matthew 24, Mark 13, Luke 21).

End Time, however, does not mean the end of the world, as is often assumed, but the end of a great epoch. Thereafter begins the New Time, in which the Kingdom of God is to be established on earth: The Thousand-year Kingdom of Peace.

The Cosmic Turning Point linked with the World Judgment, also called the Last or Final Judgment, forms the transition from the Old to the New Time.

Without the World Judgment the New Time cannot begin, because there must first be a thorough cleansing from all evil, so that the foundation for the new Kingdom will be pure and clear.

For mankind the World Judgment signifies the time of the great harvest, bringing them the fruits, which in the course of thousands of years they have cultivated through their volition. That the bad fruits far outweigh the others is borne out by the hostile attitude of most men, often of unsurpassable intensity, towards God and His Laws.

The cause of this lies in the happening that has hitherto been designated as the "Fall of Man," and accepted without understanding. The Fall of Man brought about incisive changes in the development of the whole of mankind. How it really took place has remained a mystery until now, and without the knowledge of it the World Judgment cannot be understood.

Therefore it is worth considering the Fall of Man more closely, at the same time also taking into account the Biblical statement.

The human beings who lived on earth in the childhood days of mankind were still simple and natural in their being. They willingly bowed to the Laws of Nature, and gratefully accepted every help offered them from the Luminous Regions.

The spirit in them awakened more and more, and with its awakening there also grew the longing for the Light.

Beauty and wisdom blossomed forth. The earth had become a great, flowering and fertile garden, like an image of the Gardens of the heavenly Paradise.

But then shadow upon shadow began gradually to descend upon the splendor of this earthly Paradise, and to darken the earth.

Lucifer, the Archangel from the Divine Kingdom, who was sent into Creation to bring men the enlightenment of the earthly intellect, out of self-will introduced the principle of temptation in place of the principle of helping and supporting love. Instead of teaching the right use of the intellect, necessary as an instrument on earth, he seduced men into cultivating the intellect one-sidedly, and thereby into placing it above the spirit. And men succumbed to the temptation.

This was the beginning of the Fall of Man. It was the decisive moment when man pondered about himself, when he began to become conscious of his own personality, not however with the humility and unassumingness of the spirit, but with the calculating, arrogant cleverness of the earthly intellect. *This* was now made the measure of all things.

Lucifer could never compel man to do this, because he too had to heed the free will of men, which is anchored in the spiritual nature. They had freedom of choice to turn aside the temptation with the help of God, or to succumb to it.

Through men's failure the links with the Luminous Heights were loosened. Deep grief over the increasing darkness of the human spirit filled the many helpers in the beyond, who are always concerned with the upward striving of their charges on earth.

Man thereby shut himself out of his true home, the heavenly Paradise itself, from which he had once set out as an unconscious seed grain.

The further he distanced himself from God, the more desperately he sought to bring to the fore his perishable brain, as the producer of thoughts and intellect, in place of his spirit.

The spiritual intuitive perception was replaced by imagination, which in turn is called forth by the intellect in conjunction with physical feeling. The sense of beauty had to give way to the craving for pomp and vanity.

Finally men became slaves of their instrument, the distorted intellect. Fraud and deception, slavery and force, sensuality and lust, discontent, envy, hatred and murder are some of the evil consequences.

But above all is the lure of the great Tempter, *"And ye shall be as God!"* (Genesis 3, 5). That is to say, the human spirits, who as the uttermost precipitation of the spiritual species are furthest away from the Divine Kingdom, did not shrink even from the ultimate: "to be as God," in their boundless presumption and arrogant self-glorification *to regard themselves as Divine,* or at least able eventually to become so.

The Fall of Man is impressively described in the Bible. Let us read some extracts about it: "And the LORD God commanded the man, saying, Of every tree of the garden thou mayest freely eat: But of the tree of the knowledge of good and evil, thou shalt not eat of it: for in the day that thou eatest thereof thou shalt surely die" (Genesis 2, 16 and 17). "And the serpent said unto the woman, Ye shall not surely die: For God doth know that in the day ye eat thereof, then your eyes shall be opened, and ye shall be as God, knowing good and evil. And when the woman saw that the tree was good for food, and that it was pleasant to the eyes, and a tree to be desired to make one wise, she took of the fruit thereof, and did eat, and gave also unto her husband with her; and he did eat" (Genesis 3, 4-6).

The happening of the first Fall of Man, so incisive for all mankind, is described in the Bible in simple and striking words. If we reconcile this description with the present-day ability to comprehend, then we must not forget that here it is a matter of the allegorical rendering of a *spiritual* happening. Moreover the temptation did not take place in the heavenly Paradise, but on earth, where men had already been living for some time.

The Biblical words about the offering and taking of the apple were meant to convey that woman became conscious of the effects of her charms upon man, and also made use of them. He responded to them, and for his part sought to draw the attention of the woman to himself by accumulating treasures.

Thus man, with his awakening intellect, for the first time consciously and deliberately did something that was wrong: he opposed the Laws of God.

This was all the worse because he did it voluntarily. For even at that time, at the beginning of his development towards consciousness of himself, he was free to obey the Will of God alone, *without first having to know and experience evil at all.*

But he allowed himself to be led astray to such an extent by the serpent, by which is meant intellectual cleverness, that a threat of death had to be pronounced against him. The death threatened in the allegory, however, refers not to the earthly but to the spiritual, the eternal death, the effacing of the personality that has become conscious of itself. It occurs when man must be rejected as a useless stone in Creation.

Lucifer enticed men to cultivate their intellect one-sidedly, and thereby awakened the recognition of their vanity and the desire to enjoy more of it. Men could not resist the temptation to eat of the fruit of the "tree of knowledge."

In the slow development towards consciousness of themselves they came to know the concept of good and evil, but they used the ability of free decision to turn to evil, and out of vanity and presumption they enjoyed the wrong recognition.

For thousands of years now mankind of their own free will have placed themselves under the domination of the intellect, as a consequence of the Fall of Man and of the hereditary sin. Yet sins as such are not handed down, but as there is only physical heredity, only the physical cause of hereditary sin is passed on: the over-cultivated frontal brain (intellectual brain), which ever again harbors the danger of suppressing the spirit through its exaggerated, unnatural use.

In time this brought about an *unhealthy over-ripeness of the intellect* and an *immaturity of the spirit*. The consequences of surreptitiously eating from the tree of knowledge reveal themselves in the most disastrous way. They grew into a severe, very often a fatal craving, which applies to all the evil that can possibly be formed by men.

Jesus knew the true cause of the Fall of Man, and the full gravity of its consequences; He knew that also in the future men would hardly alter their wrong standpoint. Out of this knowledge He spoke of the final time, and of the manifestations of the Last Judgment.

Today we stand in the midst of the Judgment proclaimed by Jesus, and all the signs, whose frequency can no longer be ignored, point to the fact that it is nearing its climax.

At this point attention should be drawn once more to one of these signs of the time: the general *perplexity* that is spreading ever more in all fields. When Isaiah prophesied the Judgment of God, he spoke of it as an indication of the End Time: "Take counsel together, and it shall come to naught, speak the word, and it shall not stand: for God is with us" (Isaiah 8, 10).*

Imanuel is the Will of God! And all that men think and do in the present Judgment Time, and also later, will come to naught and cease to be, *unless they adapt it to the Will of God*, Which is expressed in His Laws of Creation.

Another sign important for the present time, which until now hardly anyone would have held to be a sign of the World Judgment, is *distrust*! It is deeply rooted in the souls of men, and spreads over the whole earth as a self-produced plague. Men torment themselves with it in the worst possible way, finally running the risk of despairing because of it. If we wish to understand the happening of the End Time better, we must regard the development of the human spirits in Subsequent Creation below Paradise as a *school of life*.

---

* In the Lutheran version it is "for here is Imanuel," which means "God with us" (Matthew 1, 23).

To this school belongs the sojourn of men on earth, of which Wilhelm von Humboldt wrote: "The earth is a place of testing and training, a step to what is higher and better; here we must gain the strength to grasp the supra-earthly" (Letters, 1832).

Mankind are now in that last phase of their development that is equivalent to a spiritual school-leaving examination. For this school of life, to which human spirits are admitted for development, also comes to an end some time. Here too there is a final date by which the "school certificate examinations" must be finished. And this final date, which is linked with the end of the World Judgment, has now arrived.

The main thing for all souls then is to make up for much that has been neglected; on the way to spiritual maturity they have "failed to make the grade" in the World of Matter in the fullest sense of the word, because they did not take the trouble to become familiar with the knowledge of Creation, and to adjust their life accordingly. They have thereby prepared many an evil destiny for themselves, from which they must now break away. The causes for this often lie far back in past earth lives. Much of it cannot be made good again in the beyond but only during life on earth, because it has arisen in the earthly-gross-material, and according to the Law of the Cycle it must also be ended here. Yet another incarnation is necessary.

Hence many souls who have recognized this in the beyond are pressing for incarnation on earth in order to sever as quickly as possible the dark threads of fate, with which they are still connected, so as to let their longing for the Light become once again a bright flame.

That too is a sign of the End Time, though visible only in its effect.

A sign in the sky has now also joined the many signs visible on earth: the comet Kohoutek, which came to us from an unknown distance of the Universe, and has again returned there. People are talking a great deal about it, asking whether this comet is the Star of Bethlehem, or the great Comet expected for this time.

According to the present opinion of astronomers, the core of a comet consists of ice, hydrogen, dust, rock and gases. It is made to shine forth by the sun. Hence it can be assumed that such a comet has its origin in the material world of Subsequent Creation.

But there are yet other kinds of comets, which have their origin in spiritual regions lying above Subsequent Creation. They are sent into Subsequent Creation in support of special missions. Generally speaking, therefore, a comet coming from a spiritual region, as opposed to a comet issuing from the material regions of the Universe must have a core of quite a different kind, with a considerably more powerful radiation.

The Star of Bethlehem was such a Comet.* It was sent from the Primordial Spiritual Realm, existing far above the human Paradise of men, as a witness for the Son of God Jesus. Its core was of a high spiritual consistency, and became visible to men through taking on various fine, and lastly material, coverings.

This would mean that it must have had an unusually strong radiation, and a high luminosity of its own.

Thus the church father Chrysostom (344-407) relates "that the Bethlehem Star followed a different course from that of the familiar stars; moreover it shone also by day, and through the intensity of its own brilliance outshone the very rays of the sun."

The great Comet expected at the present Turning Point will be of equal primordial spiritual consistency, thus it will have a core glowing and highly active in itself. But it will bring men no Message of Peace, as in the case of the Bethlehem Star. Its mighty radiation-pressure that reaches the earth even before the Star, as the source of this radiation, becomes visible, first has an accelerating, releasing and purifying effect on the World of Gross Matter, and only afterwards an up-building one.

It is also the radiations of the great Comet that help to accelerate the effect of all kinds of human fate, which man has made for himself, with evil greatly predominating.

Hence the startling and at the same time alarming accumulation of all kinds of severe, sorrowful individual and mass destinies.

No human power is able to stay or to prevent this effect of the Star. Under its powerful influence all that is evil, all that is wrong comes to light, is awakened and uncovered, however well it has been concealed and glossed over by the keenness and cleverness of the intellect.

It must reveal itself, visible to all men, in every detail, and then perish as a barren fruit, whose seed had been of evil from the very beginning. For as the seed, so shall the harvest be.

This mighty happening of fate, which embraces thousands of years, and whose driving force is the great Comet, is a sign of the time that in its clarity leaves nothing to be desired.

It is also called the "Radiant Star," and is the glowing seal under the New Covenant, which God makes with men for the last time.

In an old Sibylline prophecy concerning the End Time, reference is made to a manifestation, which may apply to the great Comet in the following words: "And then will

---

* See: "The Return of the Star of Bethlehem" in Part I.

God accomplish a great sign. For a star will burst forth like unto a radiant cross, shining and giving light from the brilliant heavens for many days."

Jesus also referred to a special sign in the sky, when He spoke about the End Time: "And then shall appear the sign of the Son of Man in heaven: and then shall all the tribes of the earth mourn, and they shall see the Son of Man coming in the clouds of heaven with power and great glory" (Matthew 24, 30).

We do not know when this will come to pass, what will be the nature of the sign of the Son of Man; whether the great Comet or some other heavenly revelation is meant by it.

Be that as it may: the sign of the Son of Man, as a powerful and majestic symbol of Divine Love, will far outshine in brilliance and strength all other heavenly manifestations, and shake the human spirits to the very depths of their souls.

Thus the comet Kohoutek is not the great Comet, because it does not display the latter's characteristics. But we must not on that account think that it had nothing to tell us.

Let us regard it as a forerunner of the great Comet, as a warning and as a sign of the Cosmic Turning Point in which we are living at the present time, with all its revolutionary events and fundamental changes, which very often take place in an incredibly short time!

Even though its radiation was of a weaker nature, it will not have been without effect in the cosmos, and will have influenced man and the earth. —

Thus the signs of the End Time appear ever more clearly and frequently. *In those days* Jesus exhorted men to be alert and to be prepared to heed these signs. *Today* these signs admonish and warn through their very presence.

They point in preparation to the coming great happening, and at the same time make us reflect how close the hand of the Cosmic Clock stands to the hour of twelve. Hence it is high time *to awaken spiritually*, and once more to find the right way, whose direction is indicated to us by the Comet: upwards, towards the Luminous Heights!

Men must now at last free themselves from all earthly ties and entanglements by recognizing their faults and abstaining from them in the future. They are left with no alternative but to put the *intuitive perception of the spirit*, which is also called the inner voice, in the first place again, and once more to pay close heed to their conscience, to which belong their own inner voice and the voices of the helpers in the beyond. One great help in this connection is the knowledge of the true cause of the Fall of Man.

Then perhaps the earth will, as in times long past, once more become an image of those heavenly Gardens, the attainment of which shall forever remain the object of our unquenchable longing.

8. EVENTS IN CREATION

The Cosmic Turning Point

The poet Friedrich Hebbel wrote in his Diaries (1837): "We must not complain that all things be fleeting. That which is most transient, if it really touches us, awakens within us something that is lasting."

These words touch upon the very essence of our contemplations. Transient and lasting (or perishable and imperishable) are two of the most important concepts for the development of the human spirit.

To discover what is transient, we only need to look around in Nature. Again and again we experience the same development everywhere. If a seed grain is planted in fertile ground it begins to grow; this is followed by blossoming and ripening, which is succeeded by over-ripeness and finally by decay. So is it also in all other spheres of Nature, be it those of animals or of minerals, which develop and become weathered. The physical body of man is also subject to this Law of Nature.

Coming into existence and passing away is the characteristic of what is transient. The entire Material Creation, including the Ethereal World, the so-called beyond, is transient. It is what we understand by "the World." Hence the words of Jesus: "My kingdom is not of this world . . ." (John 18, 36).

We can also call the World, which is finite, Subsequent Creation, because it has actually developed only *subsequent* to the real, the Spiritual Creation. The Spiritual Creation is the model or pattern for the subsequently created Material World. And so, "all that is transient is but an allegory" (Goethe, Faust, Part II, End). We could also add "of that which is lasting (imperishable)," thus a figurative reproduction, an image of the imperishable Spiritual Creation. *In this lies the solution to the question about the origin of the World.*

The Material Creation lies below the eternal Spiritual Creation. In contrast to this, in the World it is only the cycle of coming into existence and passing away that is eternal. This means an eternal forming, a joining together of basic materials, which after a certain time again dissolve into their original substance, in order thereafter, purified and refreshed, to unite anew in other forms, an eternal "dying and coming into existence" (Goethe).

The passing away and being renewed can be observed on a small scale, for instance, with the compost in the garden, which consists of all kinds of waste matter, that is, of substances where over-ripeness has already set in. After a certain time these residues have been completely decomposed and transformed into fresh humus.

The process is the same on a large scale as it is on a small one. Even the greatest unions in the World of Matter, the Universes, must perish one day. They are enormous parts, complete in themselves, with countless solar systems, following a gigantic cycle.

In the Revelation of John the seven existing Universes are described as Communities, thus World Communities, and are named as follows: Ephesus, Smyrna, Pergamos, Thyatira, Sardis, Philadelphia and Laodicea (Revelation 1, 11). Each World Community has an Angel as Guardian.

This has nothing to do with the earthly communities in Asia, which merely have the same name. The earth belongs to the Universe Ephesus, which is the most important for mankind on earth.

Just as in a small way, in the case of plants, animals and human beings, there are transitions in the process of maturing, during which a certain phase of development is concluded and a new one prepared, so is it again with the Universes. These too have transitions from one stage of maturity to the next, and each time a Universe turns from its previous state of development-maturity towards a new state of maturity, this is a *Cosmic Turning Point*!

But at some time in the cycle, comprising many millions of years, there comes for every Universe a *last* Turning Point, after which it enters the state of over-ripeness. This is followed by decomposition and dissolution into the original substance, from which new, fresh Universes with new celestial bodies are then again formed.

Such a last Turning Point, which has been ordained ever since the beginning of Creation, has now come for our Universe, because its cycle is coming to the end and thus to dissolution. Naturally this does not come to pass overnight, nor does it happen simultaneously for all the celestial bodies.

But this Turning Point, which brings the last phase of a long period of development, has already tangibly set in for the earth, manifesting in the ever-increasing revolutionary events of all kinds.

But what has man to do with this Cosmic Turning Point? Why is he, whose essence by virtue of his origin is imperishable, in this perishable World at all? What has caused him to expose himself to the dangers and temptations in the World?

The reason for this is to be found in the gentle urging towards becoming conscious, which begins at a definite stage of maturity, and releases a completely natural process — the expulsion from Paradise. For the cradle of the human spirit is Paradise, the Spiritual Realm. But there it is an unconscious spirit germ, unable to awaken of its own accord.

Therefore it must plunge into the World of Matter lying below it, in order to grow and to mature there, like a grain of seed in the earth.

Only the much coarser impressions and influences of this World, with which the human spirit must come to terms, are able to awaken the unconscious spirit germ to self-consciousness. Therefore the human spirit germ striving towards consciousness must make contact with what is transient. The more "genuinely" and effectively this takes place, in a natural way, the sooner it can rise from the World of Matter and return to the Spiritual Realm as a fully conscious, pure human spirit, as the "prodigal son," in order to enjoy the bliss of a conscious existence there eternally. "It is sown in corruption; it is raised in incorruption!" writes Paul in his First Epistle to the Corinthians (I Corinthians 15, 42). From the corruptible World of Matter in which the spirit germ incarnated, there rises one day the incorruptible, the perfected spirit, as a conscious personality to the Luminous Heights of its homeland!

Many will now ask, why does the origin of man lie just in Paradise? It could after all be in another, a lower-lying plane outside Paradise, and he could develop upwards from there, or he could only come into being with the developing child's body.

The solution to this question lies in the Law of the Cycle, according to which everything must in the end return to its *origin*. Only then is it perfected. In our World of Matter we see a graphic example of this lawfulness concerning the necessary return to the origin, to the starting point, in the circulation of the blood and of water. Ever again the blood must return to the heart; while the water, which as vapor rises from the ocean into the atmosphere, returns from there in liquid or solid form to the dry land, and thence again back into the ocean. The human spirit is subject to the same Law. It could never enter Paradise if as a spirit germ it had not already been in Paradise, as its place of origin.

The impetus to the cycle of the spirit germ lies in the urge towards becoming conscious, which must take place within a limited period in the World of Matter.

If man neglects the time allotted for his maturing, and uses his free will to follow wrong paths, he will eventually run the great risk of not finding his way back in time to the Spiritual Realm, and of remaining caught in the World of Matter. His ethereal body will then be drawn along into the disintegration of the World of Matter. It is a similar process on a small scale, for example, if an insect slips into a blossom, is unable to find the way out, and must perish with the blossom.

Then in the greatest torment the spirit of man loses its self-consciousness, its personal "ego" and therewith also the human form it has acquired along with consciousness. It must then return to Paradise as an unconscious spirit seed grain.

The Bible warns of this eternal, spiritual death, also called the other or second death (Revelation 20, 6). It is equivalent to eternal damnation and to the erasing of the name from the "Book of Life," or rather of conscious life. The effacing of the "spiritual" name is expressed in the words: "The memory of the just is blessed: but the name of the wicked shall rot" (Proverbs 10, 7). Even Sirach warns: "He that followeth destruction shall himself have his fill of it" (Ecclesiasticus 31, 5, The Apocrypha). He, who allows himself to be caught by the perishable and loses his control over it, pushing aside the spiritual, remains caught in what is perishable and must be lost in it. Or in other words: He who binds himself to the World of Matter, to the material, and who is unable to acknowledge anything but the material, unquestioningly accepting it as the only thing that exists, will perish with it, because he cannot detach himself from it when the World of Matter is dissolved, and changed back into the Primeval Seed of Subsequent Creation.

Thus this Cosmic Turning Point also becomes a Turning Point for mankind, a Turning Point in the whole existence of man, not merely of his earth life. It brings the closing of the development for the human spirit, which once left its homeland and entered the World of Matter as a germ, as unconscious as a child, who goes to school and only gradually becomes aware of the purpose and aim of the school.

According to the wise Plan of the Creator, the developing human spirits were given the best of teachers. Many a high spirit was incarnated on earth for this purpose, especially at the times of the Turning Points, in order to lead the human spirits faithfully and conscientiously onwards to the next stage of recognition, with new knowledge from the Book of Creation.

We know some of these teachers: Moses and the Prophets, Krishna, Zoroaster, Lao-Tse, Buddha, Mohammed. But long before them there were yet other leaders for mankind.

Their teachings were always adapted to the particular reasoning power and perceptive capacity of the individual peoples and races, and their goal was always the same: careful guidance from one stage to the next higher, right to the last stage, the stage of the recognition of God and worship of God through the deed!

Many matured human spirits were also allowed to cooperate in the earthly and spiritual perfecting, in all spheres of life.

Yet men gave little thanks to their Creator for all these helps. Almost invariably the teachings were already distorted soon after the death of the bringer, to suit their selfish wishes. False teachers and prophets also came, who took advantage of the spiritual indolence of many and offered them their own easy teachings, in order to attain earthly power and fame.

And then when Jesus came bringing the Word, and referred warningly to the coming of the Last Judgment, which is reserved to the Son of Man as World Judge and World Teacher, it was only here and there that He found fertile soil. Most people did not concern themselves with His Message from God. They did what they wished, and considered right, and withdrew ever further from God.

Men's attitude towards the messengers and teachers whom God had sent to help them and to further their development, even before Jesus' life on earth, was appropriately described by Jesus in the parable of the husbandman, which like all His parables must be understood not in the earthly but in the spiritual sense (Matthew 21, 33-43).

God, the Householder, created a vineyard (the World of Matter) and let it out to the husbandman (to men). His servants (messengers) whom He sent to them were treated with scorn and mockery, indeed even killed.

And when the Householder sent His Son they did not shrink from killing Him also!

Here Jesus forebodingly describes His own violent earthly death! —

But finally even men's hostile attitude towards the Creator will come to an end. And the Cosmic Turning Point is now bringing about this end with the World Judgment!

It demands of man the final decision, whether he wishes to tread the path to eternal Darkness or to eternal Life! During this Judgment man will retain his full freedom to make decisions. Thus he must pass judgment on himself! It will be carried out by way of radiation, through the Son of Man proclaimed by Jesus!

The development of man cannot last indefinitely, nor can it be interrupted as often as he likes and then continued again. A plant does not interrupt its growth for certain periods either, only to continue growing later, but steadily develops towards ripeness during the period of time *allotted to it for the purpose*. This Law of Nature also holds good without exception for the spiritual growing and maturing of man.

With the present stage of ripeness of Creation, he too should have been mature for the beginning of his ascent. Since he is not, he must make up for what he has neglected. But this he can do only if once and for all he abandons what is evil and wrong, and resolves only to will and to do good. How to achieve this is shown to him in the knowledge of Creation.

The period of time for making good and for the last maturing, looked at from the earthly point of view, may comprise many thousands of years or more to the beginning of the dissolution of the World of Matter. Yet it is only of short duration in comparison to the time spent on development up till now.

In connection with the development of the human spirit, something very important has to be considered in addition. The process of becoming conscious through many stages by the human spirit, and the absorbing in its many aspects of the knowledge comprising the whole of Creation, cannot be achieved in one earth life! A repeated existence on earth is needed for this, and human beings often meet again in their different earth lives. Sometimes a fleeting suspicion of this comes to us when we meet some person or other, who is unknown to us, and sense inwardly that we have known him for a long time. We experience a similar sensation when visiting certain places or regions.

All these processes of development are not subject to any arbitrariness, but are regulated strictly in accordance with the Laws of God, and when they are heeded they bring nothing but benefit and progress. They become dangerous to man only if he chains himself too firmly to what is perishable. He must never forget that he is only a traveler in this World, whose goal and home lie in the height, and not in the depth!

Babylon, the Great City

Unfortunately a great many human beings choose the depth, and therewith remoteness from God!

We find the reason for this in the Fall of Man already described, which brought in its train everything evil.

In the Revelation, John described this evil, which has grown up over thousands of years, as the dreadful beast, which he saw rising up out of the sea, that is, out of the World of Matter (Revelation 13, 1). It is the personification of the unlimited dominion of the intellect on earth, and owes its power to the dragon, which is Lucifer, the Antichrist, the Archangel, who fell through his own guilt (Revelation 13, 2). He enticed the human spirits to cultivate their intellect, and thus to chain themselves to the perishable. This resulted in the development of all evil, such as egotism, vanity, an insistence on knowing better, the desire for importance, pleasure-seeking, sensuality, etc., into the great sin against the Holy Spirit, that is to say, against the Laws of God! In the Revelation this sin is represented by the other (the second) beast (Revelation 13, 11).

It is only on the soil of what is transient that Lucifer, with the help of the earthbound intellect, can extend his power through those human beings, who voluntarily surrender to him. Thus the over-cultivated intellect has developed into a monster, which man can finally no longer restrain.

The end of this absolute dominion of the intellect, and the sin (Babylon) that has arisen in the World through it, comes in the World Judgment, which is linked with the Cosmic Turning Point (Revelation 14, 6-12).

"Babylon, that great city," mentioned in verse 8 of chapter 14 must be regarded as a conception of all the sins produced by man out of his wrong volition. There are so many that huge areas have arisen from them in the beyond, which together form a great city.

The *earthly pollution of the environment* is only a faint reflection of these places, a *consequence*, the cause of which lies with man himself, in his wrong and evil thinking. This pollution, which has already existed all over the earth for a long time, is now suddenly discovered in its full extent, because in its tremendous accumulation it can no longer be ignored — in other words, because the mire is already up to the neck. Warnings and alarm-calls point to this everywhere. Deeply disturbed scientists quite openly admit that the planet Earth is in danger, for it really does resemble a huge refuse dump.

But mankind are already too deeply embedded in the self-created morass to be able still to find the way out with their own strength. On the whole, where attempts are made, they are only a drop in the ocean.

The great purification from all filth and all wrong can only be carried out through the Power of God in the World Judgment, during which all the upward-striving good is preserved, refreshed and strengthened through the rays of Divine Purity.

While this takes place the "great city of Babylon" will also be destroyed, but not the entire World, as is often assumed, otherwise the same Revelation would not have promised the Kingdom of Peace of a Thousand Years on earth.

Not until then can the up building on earth begin with those who know that *purity of soul* is one of the most important foundations for it. It also includes the keeping of the earth pure of all filth in the future.

The World Judgment, as the name already indicates, is intended for the whole World, not only for the earth. Chapters 2 and 3 of the Revelation describe the judgments of the Son of Man as the World Judge, which John conveys to the various Guardians (Angels) of the World Communities.

From these judgments it is to be inferred that also in the other Universes there dwell human beings, who have sinned against the Laws of God, and who are now, like the human beings of our Universe, Ephesus, subject to the same World Judgment.

We may even take it for granted that in the other Universes there are also celestial bodies like our earth, where human beings are incarnated in the same form as we have. For the human form is a characteristic of the human-spiritual in Creation, and wherever a human spirit in Subsequent Creation incarnates in a material body this has the human form that we know.

Even though the judgments of the World Judge are always directed to the Guardians of the various World Communities, they are nevertheless primarily intended for the human spirits in their care.

Hence the admonishing words of the Son of Man, which He addresses to the Guardian of our Universe, are of the utmost importance to earthmen: "Remember therefore from whence thou art fallen, and repent, and do the first works: or else I will come unto thee quickly, and will remove thy candlestick out of his place, except thou repent" (Revelation 2, 5). "From whence thou art fallen" refers to the over-cultivated intellect, which has pushed aside the spirit and caused it to fall, so that it can no longer, as before the Fall of Man, do "the first works," namely, keep awake the spiritual intuitive perception, and thus maintain the connection with God.

The Reeling Earth

How disastrously men's failure has also affected the earth itself was foreseen by Isaiah, in his prophecy concerning the Judgment of God: "The earth shall reel to and fro like a drunkard, and shall be removed like a cottage; and the transgression thereof shall be heavy upon it; and it shall fall, and not rise again" (Isaiah 24, 20).

Man has brought not only himself but also the earth to ruin. The misdoing that is heavy on the earth comes from men, and consists in their using the Power of God mainly for evil actions, due to their one-sided intellectual volition. Of his own choice man can use the spiritual power flowing through Creation for good or evil intuitive perceptions, thoughts and deeds. The "works" arising in this way possess something, which has hitherto not been generally known to men, namely form, content and weight, but of a finer material nature. According to the Law of Gravitation, the light, thus luminous works, rise upwards, and the dim, dark and hence heavy works sink downwards.

Thus it has come to pass that through their mainly wrong intellectual volition over thousands of years, men have made the ethereal surroundings of the earth so dense and heavy that it could not continue in its originally luminous course, but had to "fall" into lower regions. Thereby it has reached the stage of over-ripeness *prematurely*, and is thus threatened with a premature dissolution! As the earth sank lower, rigidity has gradually come into everything.

Earth-humanity, together with the earth, would have to continue irresistibly and irretrievably on their self-chosen course into the depth, if the Love of God, for the sake of the few, who strive to follow His Laws and Commandments, did not at the last moment hold the earth back from being sucked into disintegration!

Thereby a further promise is fulfilled: "For, behold, I create new heavens and a new earth: and the former shall not be remembered, nor come into mind" (Isaiah 65, 17).

The new earth and the new heavens, which John was also allowed to behold (Revelation 21, 1), will come into being through the earth's gradual return from the dark regions to the luminous spheres, which through men's evil volition it once had to leave.

This upward course will bring in its wake many changes on earth and new discoveries in the Universe.

When it has completed this course it is purified and freed from all Darkness, which must remain behind, rid of those "who have destroyed the earth" (Revelation 11, 18). With a humanity purified through suffering and affliction, it will again rotate in luminous spheres, until at some far-distant time the earth too, like all that is perishable, must be dissolved. Only on this *new* earth, thus after the World Judgment, can the Millennium be built up.

We do not know the exact time of this climax. For "but of that day and hour knoweth no man, no, not the angels of heaven, but my Father only" (Matthew 24, 36).

Therefore all we can do is to heed the repeated exhortations of the Son of God Jesus to be inwardly alert and ready, so that we shall recognize the signs of the Cosmic Turning Point and the World Judgment. It is the Last Judgment, that is the Final Judgment. Help and redemption will come through suffering. That it must be suffering, and not joy and bliss, is the fault of men!

Ignorance does not Protect from Punishment!

"Remember therefore from whence thou art fallen" (Revelation 2, 5) — so read the admonishing words of the Son of Man to the World Community Ephesus! Through the Fall of Man! Following on this, man separated the gross-material-earthly world from the ethereal world, the beyond, thereby hampering the refreshing invigorating cycle of spiritual power.

Today the Fall of Man is manifesting to its full extent. On the one hand there are the excrescences of materialism, which are bound to space and time, and on the other a frightening decline in spiritual life, paralyzing all further development and thus all ascent. Over the thousands of years since it began, the sad effects of this disharmony have always been the same, steadily rising to the climax in the present time of the great reckoning, when everything wrong that has come into being through men must fall!

We certainly realize that we have reached the limit of our intellectual comprehension, and that at this boundary of the earthly we must now at last dare to take the vital step of objectively including, on the basis of the Laws of Creation, the beyond-earthly happening in our earnest seeking and investigating!

This actually means a spiritual revolution, a great inner Turning Point, a changing of places between intellect and spirit. But how are we to set about this?

Faith alone is of little use to us here. With the present way of thinking, faith in supra-earthly, in higher things, must be replaced by *conviction*, which is attained only through an inflexible weighing and examining. For man has so trained his intellectual thinking, so sharpened his instruments for thinking, that the child-like-simple faith that Jesus demanded at that time is no longer suitable, no longer sufficient for this today.

But examining and weighing does not mean judging solely with the intellect, which can always only reach the boundary of what is earthly. For anything further it is the intuitive perception that must set to work, called forth by the activity of the imperishable spirit, and able to grasp and divine all that is supra-earthly.

In the first place, to balance the sharpened intellect, the conscience should be made keener. It is part of the intuitive perception, also called the inner voice. In the future we must again pay heed to what our friends and helpers in the beyond allow us to perceive intuitively through their gentle urging and admonishing. We must again let them appeal to our conscience, and really carry out what is inwardly perceived by them or by our own spirit, and must not allow it afterwards to be pushed aside or pulled to pieces by the earthly intellect. The intellect understands nothing of what is spiritual, and cannot therefore form an opinion of it.

Then we ought to become better acquainted with the Laws of Creation, especially with their effect in the Spiritual Sphere. The principle of "ignorance does not protect from punishment," which has been established for the earthly laws, applies much more severely to the Laws of Creation! Let us take an example. When we sow wheat, the harvest will also consist of wheat, of the same kind as what has been sown, in fact many times more. We are able to grasp this intellectually, that is, with the earthly brain. If we further conclude that the same Law of Sowing and Reaping also holds good for our unseen intuitive perceptions and thoughts, which we sow spiritually, and that good thoughts retroactively always produce as their harvest only a multiple of good, and evil thoughts a multiple of evil, then in order to understand these processes we must pass beyond the limit of the intellect and make use of the intuitive perception, continuing to seek and investigate with it.

And finally we must strive to get to know the Will of God in the Laws He has placed in Creation. Only then shall we be able to obey them, and abstain from doing what is harmful and dangerous.

Never shall we be able to stand before God personally — we would surely perish before Him — but we are in a position to learn to understand and to recognize Him through His Will, Which is anchored in Nature, thus in Creation! For the recognition and worship of God through the deed and at any time, not only on Sundays, is urgently necessary, all the more so since the Cosmic Turning Point signifies the beginning of the Dominion of God and the end of the dominion of men on earth. What has hitherto been prevented through the wrong volition of men — "Thy Kingdom come! Thy Will be done on earth, as it is in Heaven!" — will now be fulfilled through the Omnipotence of God at the time of the Cosmic Turning Point!

9. THE QUEEN OF HEAVEN

In the Revelation granted to him, John beholds a "woman clothed with the sun" (Chap. 12). For many centuries men have reflected upon this mysterious woman, and the profusion of interpretations about her is bewildering. Thus it is said that the woman must be regarded as the personification of the Church, or else of the Christian Community; yet it could also be a symbol for Israel, for the Congregation of the Lord of the Old Testament. The Marian interpretation to the effect that this is the mother of the Messiah, that is, the earthly mother of Jesus, and that the child mentioned with her is Jesus, is widespread.

In his *Schriften des Neuen Testamentes* (*Texts of the New Testament*) 1908, Professor D. Johannes Weiss, the theologian, has this to say about it: "Firstly, let us consider the figure of the mother of the Messiah. The Christian interpretation has naturally linked the image with the Heavenly Mary; Dürer, Murillo and others have depicted the Heavenly Queen according to this image - as she stands on the crescent moon, bathed in the light of the sun, and wearing on her head the crown of stars. But it is certain that the Christian Apocalyptist was not thinking of Mary at all. Ancient Christianity knows nothing of a heavenly origin or ascension for the mother of Jesus. The Mary of the Gospels is still portrayed in quite a human way. All the more pressing for us is the question: What then could the Christian mediator of the Revelation, what could his readers, imagine by the figure? Let it be stated right away here: It has not been created by Christian imagination at all; no Christian would of himself have had the idea of depicting the mother of the Messiah in such a totally different way from the Gospels . . ."

Thus there are yet other interpretations and combinations of individual interpretations. With each one there are still contradictions to the text, because the descriptions and pictures in chapter 12, as throughout the entire Revelation, are taken in far too human-earthly a sense.

As already stated, the Revelation of John contains a metaphorical language. Each picture corresponds to a definite happening. But it can only be interpreted in the spiritual sense, because it has been given from the spiritual. Therefore speculations as to whether the 12th chapter of the Revelation is of Jewish or Christian origin are out of place. The origin lies in a manifestation of the Divine Will, thus far above human views and opinions.

It is equally wrong to believe that the author of the Revelation would borrow the material for his pictures from some Persian, Egyptian or Greek myth. The opposite would have been the case, namely that the tidings of what took place in the Highest Heights were handed down to men and thus portrayed, more or less changed and made earthly, in the various myths of ancient peoples. For in these narratives and folklore there appear again and again as the basic theme the birth of a male child, his persecution by an evil beast, as also the flight of his mother, and finally the victory over the evil beast.

In reality the woman whom John beholds is the Heavenly Queen or the Primordial Queen, Who bears the name Elizabeth. Her home in the Divine Realm lies immeasurably far above the Spiritual Realm (Paradise), which is the cradle of the human spirits. Thus the symbolical meaning of the woman is neither the Church, nor Mary, the earthly mother of Jesus. The latter, being a human spirit, has her origin in the Spiritual Realm, and can never cross the boundary upwards into the Divine Realm, to the place of origin of the Heavenly Queen, Who may also be called Primordial Mother, although She is virgin. She works in the severe Love of God, and is the prototype of all womanhood in Creation, the origin of all womanly virtues, the highest of which is purity. Within the Primordial Mother lies the maternal principle of cherishing and sustaining, of growing and tending.

Now and then it happens that, in fulfillment of his unshakable faith in the Heavenly Queen, or from a deep inner shock, a human being is permitted to see a radiated picture of the Primordial Queen Elizabeth, which is not to be confused with Mary of Nazareth. Man cannot see the Primordial Queen Herself, because he is unable to perceive and to grasp what is Divine with his spiritual nature. Only as an Act of Grace can he receive tidings of it. The power of such a radiated picture can bring unexpected helps of miraculous effect, if the soil of the soul has been prepared for it.

Sometimes blessed ones are shown the radiated picture of the Primordial Queen with a male child, just as John beheld it. This male child is Parsifal. He was shown as a child because He was only at the beginning of His Mission in the course of which He still had to mature into a man.

For His Mission, which comprises the salvation and redemption of the fallen, erring human race of Subsequent Creation, needed a long time of preparation, during which He had to journey through all the Parts of the World in order to gather from man's spiritual decline the experiences needed for His great Work of Redemption.

His World-wide Mission also includes the chaining of Lucifer, the fallen Archangel, for a thousand years, as depicted in chapter 20 of the Revelation, verses 1 to 3. The "angel" mentioned, who "comes down from heaven," is Parsifal. Lucifer, who had his origin in the Divine Realm (he is described in chapter 12 as a "great red dragon"), knew that the Child would one day be his conqueror, and hence he attacked Him. Even from the very beginning he sought to destroy in Him the great Work of Redemption. But Lucifer, together with his dark hosts, was cast out from all the heavens by the Archangel Michael and his vassals, and now turned his attention to Subsequent Creation (Chapter 12, 7-9).

In chapter 12 we read these words of warning: "Woe to the inhabiters of the earth and of the sea (in the World of Matter), for the devil is come down unto you, having great wrath, because he knoweth that he hath but a short time," that is to say, a short time before being chained by Parsifal.

When it is further said: "And the serpent (Lucifer) cast out of his mouth water as a flood after the woman, that he might cause her to be carried away of the flood," this indicates the dark currents of hatred and slander directed by Lucifer against the Primordial Queen. They rebounded from the Purity of the Light and returned to Subsequent Creation, where the "earth swallowed them up," which means that womanhood on earth received these currents. She voluntarily succumbed to the attacks and temptations of Lucifer, the Antichrist. Having failed to reach the Primordial Queen, he now "went to make war with the remnant of her seed," that is, with the human womanhood of Subsequent Creation, who also belong to the spiritual descendants of the Primordial Mother.

Through his activities, which were directed away from God, Lucifer gradually stifled the virtues of earthly woman, and extinguished the knowledge of the Primordial Queen.

Hence it is only in ancient writings that we still find some few traces of the existence of an ideal womanly figure in the Highest Heights, who stands in direct connection with God.

In an ancient Coptic text (the Gospel of Mary), mention is made of a female figure, who is found immediately next to the invisible God. There are similar references also in other traditions. In "The Acts of Thomas", for example, we read: "We glorify and praise thee (Jesus) and thine invisible Father and thy Holy Spirit, and the Mother of all Creation" (Act 4, Section 39). Besides the Divine Trinity, mention is also made here of the Primordial Mother!

There was once a time when belief in the Queen of Heaven was still alive, and when earthly womanhood occupied a high spiritual position, because through this belief they were still connected with the female prototypes in the Spiritual and the Divine Realms. Through the influence of Lucifer this belief began to waver, became distorted and was finally lost altogether.

But now comes a new era. Through the help of the Son of Man, womanhood is once more given the opportunity to take up anew the connection with the Primordial Queen and all Her attendant female helpers in the Luminous Realms. The foundation for this is a genuine longing for what is sublime and pure. The woman of today needs this radiation-connection so that, faithful to the task allotted to her by the Creator, she can lead mankind on earth in the now necessary ascent.

Thus the mystery surrounding the exalted Female Figure of the Revelation, Whom John once beheld in the radiance of flowing Light, as though the sun were Her raiment, is solved!

10. THE PHILOSOPHERS' STONE

The Philosophers' Stone became known mainly through the alchemists of the Middle Ages. They engaged in alchemy, which goes back to the ancient Egyptians, from whom the Arabs received it. From them is derived the word elixir, which means "Philosophers' Stone." Alchemy also included the art of making gold.

According to the belief of the alchemists, the Philosophers' Stone was a magic stone, containing the original substance of all things. It was said to transmute base metals into gold, but it was also held to be a means of prolonging life.

The alchemists investigated those processes in Nature that brought about the natural growth of minerals, in order then by imitation to reproduce this slow development in a faster way in the laboratory. For this purpose they sought the Philosophers' Stone, as the agent (catalyst) through whose presence the decomposition and transmutation of substances was to take place, which also included the transmutation of base materials into gold. Although the results of these attempts have hitherto been veiled in obscurity, the tests with the various substances nevertheless brought many a useful side-product, one of which is porcelain.

For alchemists who penetrated more deeply, the actual goal was more on the metaphysical plane. Through certain processes they tried to gain access to fields that are otherwise concealed from earthly eyes. In view of this, the obtaining of artificial gold was only of secondary importance.

The many efforts made to unveil the secret of the Philosophers' Stone have hitherto been fruitless; in any case it is not known whether the flood of alchemistic books and writings — there are said to be more than 100,000 of them now-have contributed towards any enlightenment.

In reality this Stone, which is said to work miracles, contains ancient knowledge that perhaps long, long ago was in the possession of blessed human beings.

If we wish to fathom the secret of this legendary Stone, we must seek the *connections* that have their beginning far above the Spiritual Realm, the Paradise of men.

We receive a hint about this in the Revelation of John. In the second chapter, verse 17, it is said: "To him that overcometh will I give to eat of the hidden manna, and will give him a white stone, and in the stone a new name written, which no man knoweth saving he that receiveth it." And in chapter 3, verse 12: "Him that overcometh will I make a pillar in the temple of my God . . . and I will write upon him the name of my God . . . and . . . my new name."

The Hidden *Manna* is the Heavenly Bread, the Word of God. The *White Stone* points to the Laws of God, through which Creation has come into being. The White Stone is used here figuratively for the *recognition of God.*

The recognition of God becomes possible for man by absorbing the Word of God as it has been brought to us through the Messages of God, and by recognizing in Creation the Laws that these Messages proclaim.

Both the *Word* and *Creation* are thus for man the *way to the recognition of God,* which must not be taken in a personal sense. For never can a man see God, he would have to perish before His immeasurable Power. "Thou canst not see my face: for there shall no man see me, and live," is written in Exodus (33, 20). But the human spirit has the ability to recognize God in His Word and in His Work, in Creation.

Whoever awakens this ability within him — and every human spirit seeking for the Truth is capable of doing so — receives the *grace of the recognition of God.* In the Revelation the "White Stone" is metaphorically promised for this.

But only "he that overcometh" can partake of this grace, that is to say, he who overcomes his own faults and weaknesses; he who becomes new within and gives purity to his thoughts.

With the recognition of God there is simultaneously linked the knowledge of the *New Name* that is written on the stone, because the stone is closely linked with the Name of Him Who has woven the Laws of God into Creation. The New Name, however, is: *Imanuel, the Son of Man,* Who like Jesus comes from out of God; He is a Part of God and the Alpha and the Omega, the Beginning and the End of Creation, the Living Word of God.

His Name is indeed new to men, because up till now the Son of Man, Imanuel, has been known only as the Holy Spirit." But the New Name changes nothing of the Trinity of God. Except that the Holy Spirit is to be thought of as Person. On ancient ecclesiastical works of art, the Trinity of God was symbolically depicted as *three* Persons.

Already in olden times Isaiah (7, 14), Daniel (7, 13-14), Solomon in Proverbs (8, 22-31), and others gave tidings of the Son of Man Imanuel, Who is not to be confused with Jesus. During His earth life Jesus Himself foretold the coming of the Son of Man for the Judgment (Matthew 25, 31; John 16, 7-15).

Imanuel means "God with us." Under this Name He is also mentioned in the Revelation of John: "And I heard a great voice from the throne saying, Behold, the tabernacle (temple) of God is with men, and he will dwell with them, and they shall be his people, and *He, Himself, God with them,* shall be their God" (21, 3).* This passage, correctly translated by Luther, was changed in later editions to "and He, Himself, God, will be with them," through which the original meaning "God with us" (= Imanuel) was lost!

In the 19th chapter of the Revelation of John, verses 11 to 16, Imanuel "The Word of God," the "King of Kings," is described in His Divine Majesty. His Name that "no man knew, but he himself" (Chapter 19, 12), is now revealed to men: Imanuel, the Son of Man, the bridge from God to man.

Thus there is an indissoluble link between the "New Name Imanuel" and the "White Stone."

The long-sought-for *"Philosophers' Stone"* is "The White Stone," not only as a symbol, but actually existing in Creation.

As wonderfully shining and radiating crystal, it is to be found in the highest Heights of Creation. The basic Laws of Creation lie hidden in it. Highest Wisdom and Power radiate from it, for it is closely linked with the Living Power from out of God.

A spiritual radiation-connection with this "Heavenly" Stone gives to the one called for it a special knowledge, which provides him with the key to the working and weaving in Creation. With purest humility and intuitive perception he is then able to find happenings and solutions on beyond-earthly planes, and with the help of his earthly intellect to transfer them to the spheres of earth life. *Thereby he has found the Philosophers' Stone:* the solution to *every* happening in the World of Matter on the basis of the eternal Laws of Creation. Chemistry (alchemy) is but a small part thereof.

What man does is really only a *finding.* For he can only form by imitation something that already exists as a "model" on other planes.

Up till now man has raised only a corner of the invisible working of Creation surrounding him. Most of it still awaits discovery.

But neither the electron microscope nor the powerful astronomical instruments directed into the universe will help him to achieve this. Just as little can he cross the invisible boundary with them, as with the intellect that works these instruments, which as the product of the earthly brain is perishable, and hence can have no understanding for beyond-earthly happenings.

---

* This is translated into English from the German of Luther.

The science of this world is certainly good for what can be seen, grasped, measured, weighed, but it is senseless for it to try to think with the brain, or rather the intellect, beyond the earthly boundary, because according to its nature the intellect exists only for gross material understanding.

With these earthly instruments man will not reach the reality of the beyond, which in comparison with the earthly-gross-material was the primary, thus the *first* to exist. It lies outside the earthly ability to comprehend. To reach it the intuitive perception of the spirit dwelling within us must become active. Therefore the research must now be continued with the *spirit*, if complete spiritual atrophy is to be avoided. The spirit alone is able to cross the threshold to the other world, that world, which is also open to the radiations of the White Stone. Only there will the spirit find the great connections, a picture of the actual happening, and finally the true knowledge that makes man humble and wise.

Yet there is still a very great lack of wise men today. Or to quote Goethe: "And even if they had the Philosophers' Stone! They would only have the Stone, and not the Philosopher." (Faust, Part II, Act 1). This is to imply that even if the Philosophers' Stone did exist, there would still be missing that wise man, who would be in a position to make conscious use of the mysterious powers of this stone in the sense of the Laws of Creation.

But apart from the human-spiritual connection with the radiations of the White Stone, it is within the realm of possibility that here and there — far away from the source — offshoots of the radiation of this stone may condense in Nature to form a most beautiful image.

For the beings of Nature, who in the service of their Creator bring forth the ice- flowers in delicate beauty as if by magic, are certainly also capable of forming a crystal of perfect form and radiation, containing powers that will unfold special effects.

Today, in the age of atoms and rays, this thought is no longer so farfetched. Perhaps such a treasure will be found later at a given time.

11. THE MYSTERY OF THE SPHINX

It is from the cycle of Greek legends that the Sphinx of Thebes is known — a female being with the body of a lioness, who stood before the city of Thebes.

To every traveler she could waylay she set a riddle. If he could not solve it, she killed him and threw him over the precipice. Until Oedipus solved the riddle, and the Sphinx, thrown into confusion as a result, cast herself into the depths.

Hence the expression "as enigmatic as a sphinx" describes something incomprehensible, inscrutable or impenetrable.

The origin of the sphinx-myth is veiled in obscurity. Presumably the sphinx was a symbol taken over by the Egyptians, but its original meaning was altered for reasons that are no longer discernible.

The Greek sphinxes were depicted as female beings, whereas with the Egyptians the sphinxes were male. Later, western art used the sphinx-figures as ornaments for entrances to castles and palaces, in gardens, etc.

If we wish to find the original meaning of the Egyptian sphinx we must concern ourselves with the animals.

There are animals not only on earth, but also in all beyond-earthly planes of Creation. From the story of Creation about the first seven days, as described in chapter one of Genesis, we learn that there are Animals even in the First Creation, Primordial Creation. Primordial Creation is of a spiritual nature and lies far above the Paradise of men, at the summit of the entire Creation. Its making must not be confused with the making of the earth.*

There are Animals even in the Divine Kingdom, which lies above the spiritual Primordial Creation.

In the Revelation of John they are mentioned by name (4, 6-8). ". . . and in the midst of the throne, and round about the throne, were four beasts full of eyes before and behind. And the first beast was like a lion, and the second beast like a calf, and the third beast had a face as a man, and the fourth beast was like a flying eagle. And the four beasts had each of them six wings about him; and they were full of eyes within: and they rest not day and night, saying, Holy, holy, holy, Lord God Almighty, which was, and is, and is to come."

---

* See: "God is not silent!" and "Meeting-Point Earth" in Part I.

Even in pre-Christian times tidings of the existence of these Four Animals must have penetrated into Creation, right down to the earth. Egyptian sages, who lived at a time of a high culture long since lost, possessed the knowledge of the four Animals, and formed them into a single figure, which expressed one part of each of the four Animals, and was later called by the name of "sphinx." In so doing they concealed a great mystery from succeeding generations.

Only a few sphinx-figures correspond to the original form. Thus the Sphinx of Giza, for example, is very similar to the combined figure of the four Animals. It is a human head with the body of a bull, the claws of a lion and the folded wings of an eagle. This enormous stone image, 73.5 meters long and 20 meters high, was carved out of the rock on the spot. It is supposed to have been made about 2,650 B.C., but is probably older than that.

Here and there some faint recollections as to the significance of the four Animals are to be found. It has been said that they are supposed to be representatives of the whole of Creation. In the Annotations of the New Testament, published by Otto von Gerlach (Berlin, 1863), it says of the four Animals: ". . . a symbolical representation of the highest powers that rule in Creation . . . It is a deficiency in our language that they must be called Animals . . . Their name designates living beings." Also there are repeated references in folk mythology, as for example the forming of the Universe from the Primordial Bull (Mithras-Cult in Iran).

In reality the Four Winged Animals around the Throne of God — a Lion, a Bull, a Ram with a human countenance and an Eagle — are Divine entities, which hitherto have been known only symbolically and by name.

The Ram bears a human countenance because it bears within it the spiritual of Creation, from which men are formed. The many eyes and the six wings or pinions indicate that they are knowing Animals, who swing in incorruptible loyalty and devotion — "resting not day and night," thus eternally — in the Will of God. Their whole being is filled with Divine Light.

The *six* wings, too, have a meaning, because the six is an important figure for the formation and structure in Creation. We find it, for instance, in the six days of creating, and in the description of the heavenly city of Jerusalem in the Revelation of John (21, 16): "The length and the breadth and the height of it are equal" (= six sides). But in the earthly also we encounter the six; thus in the structure of crystals, in the hexagonal honeycombs of the bees, and in the division of time and of the circle.

We human beings are not capable of understanding the nature of these knowing Animals, because they live infinitely far above our plane of origin, Paradise, and therefore cannot be compared with the animals of the earth either. But it is important to know what is their *relationship* with Creation.

The Four Powerful Animals that guard the Throne of God are the Square of Creation, because they bear concentrated within them the basic species of the radiation for the creations, thus the "substance" for the structure and content of the entire Creation!

That is the mystery of the stone image called "sphinx," incomprehensible to succeeding generations. In it are symbolically expressed the Four Entities at the Throne of God, which are so important for the whole Creation, which bear within them all the radiations necessary for Creation, and hence, which are firmly linked with it.

For radiation is *everything*. It is the key to the understanding of Creation, and therewith the World. In it is founded the ultimate mystery of the Creation-Happening!

12. THE QUADRATURE OF THE CIRCLE

Quadrature of the circle means converting a circle into a square that has the same area.

If we consider the old saying "as above, so below," the earthly form of the circle and the square must also correspond to a prototype, which is to be found "above."

This "above" is the Divine and the Primordial Spiritual Realm. In the explanations about the Mystery of the Sphinx, the winged Animals in the Divine Kingdom, which are on the steps of the Throne of God, were spoken of. They receive from God all the radiations that are necessary for the coming into existence of Creation.

The four Animals are on the steps of the Throne at an equal distance from one another, and form a square, the Square of Creation.

In the Primordial Spiritual Realm, which follows after the Divine Kingdom, the four Primordial Beings receive these radiations of the four Animals. These form there the Square of the Creation-radiations, and can be designated as "main pillars of the structure of Creation," because all the radiations necessary for the building of Creation are gathered in them.

From these radiations arose also the Material World, Subsequent Creation, which has the form of a mighty light-irradiated cube. The cube is a body with six equal square surfaces.

Hence the *square* has always been known as the image of this material world, as represented in its highest perfection.

The entire Creation, thus also Subsequent Creation, is kept in motion through the circulating of the spiritual power, which from the radiation-center in the Primordial Spiritual Realm below the Divine Kingdom, streams pulsatingly into Creation and floods back thence again, as with the blood-circulation in the human body. Here again we have the accordance between "below" and "above"!

Everything swings and lives in this circulating, spiritual power. Hence the *circle* is the symbol of God-willed life, whose beginning must return to the origin.

Now if the area of the circle equals the area of the square, this symbolically indicates that the spiritual power streams through and fills up Creation, thus also the material Creation-cube of Subsequent Creation, in a harmonious cycle.

In reality this harmony has not existed in Subsequent Creation for a long time, because the Creation-circling is disrupted through the human spirits developing in the

World of Matter. They use the spiritual power mainly for evil doing and thinking; thereby it remains caught in the World of Matter, and cannot flow back harmoniously. Thus through self-will man cuts off the harmonious, God-willed Creation-circling in this part of Creation, as a result of which the whole Creation must suffer.

He no longer heeds his task in the World of Matter. It consists in the highest unfolding of humanity through fitting in with the eternal Laws of God, which means to work in this part of Creation in an up-building and ennobling way, in the swinging of the spiritual power permeating Creation.

The wise men of ancient peoples have known of the deep meaning of the two symbols, the circle and the square. Traces of their knowledge can be found even today in their buildings. Let us think, for example, of the square base and the four triangular surfaces of the Pyramid of Cheops in Egypt.

It was certainly also known to these wise men that Subsequent Creation, which lies below the Spiritual Realm (Paradise), has the form of a cube; hence probably the peculiar shape of this building. If we imagine the corners of this cube of Subsequent Creation connected with its center, six equal cosmic pyramids result. One of these could have been their inspiration to create a testimony in stone of mysterious, cosmic wisdom in the form of a pyramid: the Pyramid of Cheops, which even in ancient times was considered one of the seven wonders of the world, and was the only one of them to be preserved.

Its special form and its measurements show that the builders had a comprehensive knowledge of the structure of the Universe, including the knowledge of the harmony-law of the Golden Section, and of the quadrature of the circle.

So, for instance, the circumference of the square base of this pyramid, divided by twice its height, results in the figure pi, which is important for calculating the area of a circle.

Moreover it is perhaps also conceivable that the builders pictured the pyramid as the form for the gathering of radiations, thus that they considered radiations in pyramid form especially effective.

Not for nothing does the Greek geographer Strabo say that the Pyramid was, "like an edifice let down from heaven, it was not the work of human hands."

There is also a reference to the square and cube in the Revelation of John. "And the city lieth foursquare, and the length is as large as the breadth . . . The length and the breadth and the height of it are equal" (21, 16). Here John describes the heavenly Jerusalem, the Holy City, as model for everything that developed in imitation of it.

Thus the origin and meaning of the symbols of square and circle become discernible to us. The two are closely connected with each other in the quadrature of the circle, just as the square of Creation, which dispenses all rays for the up building, eternally forms a complete whole with the necessary all-invigorating Creation-circling of the spiritual power.

13. THE NEW COVENANT

Already for a long time the Darkness, which men had made for themselves, had been weighing heavily upon the earth. They were no longer able to open themselves to the luminous streams from On High, and had so entangled themselves in the nets of vanity and of liking to know better, cleverly cast abroad by Lucifer, that it was hardly possible for them to escape any more by their own strength.

And so the immeasurable Grace of God inclined towards the ever more deeply sinking humanity. A Ray of Divine justice descended into Creation, also reaching the earth. The Darkness encircling the earth could be driven back.

The people of Israel, who had inwardly matured through affliction and oppression in the Egyptian captivity, absorbed the vibration from the Divine Justice and opened themselves to the helping rays. Gradually there grew in them a divining of the existence of the *One* God.

Thus it could come to pass that the God of the *Fathers of Israel* made a Covenant with the *people* of Israel. Already before that, God had entered into a Covenant with Noah and with Abraham; the token of the Covenant with Noah was the rainbow. But now it was a whole people who were to belong to the Holy Covenant that was intended as the foundation for God's Kingdom on earth.

Through His chosen servant, Moses, God proclaimed in a promise to the people of Israel: "Now therefore, if ye will obey my voice indeed, and keep my covenant, then ye shall be a peculiar treasure unto me above all people: for all the earth is mine: And ye shall be unto me a kingdom of priests, and an holy nation" (Exodus 19, 5-6). On Mount Sinai (Horeb) the people received the charter of this Covenant: the Ten Commandments. Guided by luminous hands, Moses engraved the words on tablets of stone.

After this great happening Moses received another task from God: "And let them make me a sanctuary; that I may dwell among them" (Exodus 25, 8).

And the Tabernacle was built, with the Holy of Holies separated by a curtain. In it was set the Ark of the Covenant containing the Tables of the Law. Above the Ark was the Mercy Seat with the two angels (cherubims). Here God "dwelt" and from here He declared to Moses all that he was to proclaim to the "children of Israel" (Exodus 25, 21 and 22).

But the "dwelling" is not to be taken literally, for God cannot come personally into Creation, upon the earth; it would perish in His direct Power. But He could anchor in the Holy of Holies a Radiation from His Power, through Which Moses was able in his purest serving to take up the connection with the Will of God, in order to receive every help for his people.

This radiation-connection must have been visible to human beings with a deeper insight. For the Jewish tradition speaks of a radiance, the so-called Shekinah-Light, which filled the Holy of Holies in the Tabernacle, and later in the Temple of Solomon. Shekinah means the Light of the Divine Presence among men. Solomon also sensed that God could not dwell on earth in the Tabernacle. At the solemn consecration of the Temple he expressed it thus: "But will God in very deed dwell with men on the earth? Behold, heaven and the heaven of heavens cannot contain thee; how much less this house (Temple), which I have built!" (II Chronicles 6, 18).

Thus the people of the Israelites were showered with blessings from the Love of God. The greatest Grace was given to them in the Ten Commandments, which contained all that they had to do in order to mature spiritually, and to complete their journey through the World in peace and harmony. Yet they were only Commandments, for they read "Thou shalt" and not "Thou must." Men were not forced to keep the Commandments. This they had to decide for themselves. For they possessed the free will peculiar to their spiritual nature.

But how often this free will of the spirit failed because it was darkened through the wrong volition of the earthbound intellect that worshipped the golden calf of earthly transience. How often men, who ever again rebelled against the Will of God, against His Laws, broke the Covenant one-sidedly! It was just because of this that very soon after the making of the Covenant, Moses shattered the stone Tables of Laws, and prayed to God to forgive the wanton behavior of his people, so that God showed compassion, and Moses was allowed to write down the Commandments once more.

What pains the prophets took ever again to call the people to order, to the Divine order, although this had been given to them clearly enough in the Ten Commandments in the most simple way.

When even the prophets could no longer penetrate, God sent His inborn Son Jesus for their help and salvation.

People often ask themselves why it was just among the Jewish people that Jesus had to be born, why not among the Roman people, who were then at the height of their power, whereas the Jewish people were torn and unstable within, groaning under the power of the Roman occupation.

It was done for the sake of the few, who had preserved for themselves the belief in God in a purity such as could be found nowhere else on earth. Thereby they offered the necessary earthly support for the Truth-Bringer from the Light. Thus the incarnation of Jesus on earth took place in order to bring the Light of Truth to the human beings, who were going astray in the Darkness.

He wished neither to give a new dogma nor to found a new religion. He showed men the lost path to the Kingdom of Heaven in quite a simple way, by calling upon them to do the Will of His Father (Matthew 7, 21). But to do the Will means to observe and to obey the immutable Laws working in Creation.

He thereby opposed the religious leaders, whom He reproached with: "But woe unto you! For ye shut up the kingdom of heaven against men" (Matthew 23, 13). They could not bear the Light of Truth that Jesus brought, and only a few years after the beginning of His mission on earth they had Him crucified as a troublesome Truth-Bringer. Thus the prophecy that He clothed in the parable of the wicked husbandman was fulfilled: "And they caught him (the Son of God), and cast him out of the vineyard, and slew him" (Matthew 21, 39).

This terrible deed filled all the Creations with the deepest suffering. Thousands upon thousands of angel voices lamented at the Throne of God: "The Lamb that was slain!" (Revelation 5, 12).

Even Nature was outraged. Darkness came over Golgotha, and the earth quaked.

The Old Covenant was finally broken, the separation from God completed. In token of this the veil in the Temple before the Holy of Holies was rent in twain by luminous hands. Thereby the Ark of the Covenant was also exposed to the glances of all, because it no longer fulfilled its original meaning and purpose as the place of anchorage for the connection with God. Decades later this Temple, which was to be an abode of God, was demolished, just as men in their blind hatred had destroyed the Covenant with God.

Ever since the happening on Golgotha, the World Judgment for the whole of humanity has taken its course, and is now nearing its climax and its end.

In the course of His Mission on earth, Jesus recognized more and more clearly that due to human failure the Old Covenant could no longer be upheld, and that one day a New Covenant would have to be made in order to give yet a last opportunity to those, who were prepared to draw nearer to God in true humility.

It was out of this knowledge that shortly before His physical death He spoke these words: "For this is my blood of the new testament ("covenant" in the German translation), which is shed for many for the remission of sins" (Matthew 26, 28). With His blood that He shed on the Cross He confirmed the Truth of the Word He had brought. *Only following His Word* brings the possibility of redemption from all sins and thereby forgiveness for many.

Thus for over two thousand years He prepared for men with His Word the way to the New Covenant, of which man as a creature dependent on his Creator stands in need; without which there is no longer any connection with God, after it had been disrupted through the crucifixion.

The New Covenant, however, is made by the Son of Man, Whom Jesus Himself proclaimed. He called Him also the Spirit of Truth, the Holy Ghost, the Comforter.

What Jesus, looking ahead, then said about the Son of Man is now being fulfilled in our time.

Even as God revealed Himself in the Old Testament as the God of Justice, in the New Testament as the God of Love, so His last Message from the Grail swings in Justice, Love *and* Purity. For Justice, Love and Purity are one, because in them lies Divine Perfection!

In the clear, severe Light of Divine Purity, the great purification of the whole Creation, including the earth, from all the dirt and evil heaped up by mankind over thousands of years, is being carried out In the World Judgment. Every day we experience more and more clearly that a Creation-Purification planned on so vast a scale does not proceed quietly and gently. The purifying rays that are penetrating Creation grip everything, without exception. Everything must show its true face, even if it has hitherto known how to hide for hundreds and thousands of years: it will come to light in order to perish, if it has been wrong, or it will be strengthened, if it has been active in the right way.

The individual human being is also subject to this purification, and must free himself from all the dross of impure volition.

Purity is also the condition for the New Covenant with God, which requires of men pure loyalty. For out of Purity in the Divine grows loyalty in the human spiritual. What is done in genuine loyalty is pure! It places man in the position to recognize the Will of God in the Words *and* Works revealed by Him, and by a free decision to adapt the human volition to this Will.

Only then can man belong to God, and serve Him in humility with his entire being. But with this he has also brought about the condition necessary for acceptance in the New Covenant. In the radiance of his loyalty he will finally be allowed to enter the long and ardently desired Heavenly Paradise, which will be opened to him through the New Covenant.

190

At a time of deepest psychic Darkness, when countless human beings will have nothing more to do with God, when even numberless Christians say that God is dead, that God withdraws from humanity; when paradoxically there is already talk of a Christian atheism, God reveals Himself more powerfully than ever through His Word. That this Word is contained in a Message from the Grail is the great New that is approaching humanity, of which they have hitherto heard only in myths and legends. This new knowledge is part of the New Covenant with God, after the dissolution of the Old Covenant through the happening on Golgotha.

Israel, the once-chosen people, who at one time were to become "the heart of the nations," no longer exists as *such*.

As Jesus then foresaw, so has it come to pass: "Therefore say I unto you, the kingdom of God shall be taken from you and given to a nation bringing forth the fruits thereof" (Matthew 21, 43). The seeds of these fruits are now planted. A new chosen people is growing up, which will consist of individual human beings chosen by God.

Through their deeds these Chosen ones are to be an example to the nations of a real life in the New Covenant with God, which the Son of Man blesses with the Power from the Holy Grail, Which really exists at the highest point in the Primordial Spiritual Realm. For the Grail too is a Creation of God.

14. THE THIRD REICH (KINGDOM)

The greatest circulatory movement in Subsequent Creation, which lies below the human Paradise, the spiritual home of man, is the gigantic cycle of the Universes whose enormous size and extent are beyond our power of imagination.

There are seven Universes, which in the Revelation of John (1, 11) are designated by name as communities in Asia. Yet the Revelation refers not to earthly communities but to gigantic world-systems, which complete in themselves, pursue their mighty courses in the material world of Subsequent Creation, called Asia in the Revelation.*

The earth belongs to the Universe Ephesus with its enormous solar systems, sun families, star clusters, clouds of gas and dust.

The cycle of our Universe takes many millions of years, and it is only through revelations given from a spiritual standpoint that we learn how far it has advanced, and where we are in the cosmos at the present time. An earthly comprehending is no longer possible here.

But we are able to observe at least a short section of another cycle, which for our understanding is still very great, in order to gain some idea of the vastness of the possibilities of development that lie nearest to us.

We know that the earth revolves around its axis. From this result day and night. Moreover, in 365 days it also revolves around the sun; this brings about the seasons of spring, summer, autumn and winter.

But there is yet a third movement carried out by our planet, and which is caused by the power of attraction of the moon — its axis revolves like that of a top. This movement (precession), which takes place very slowly, causes a constant shifting of the vernal point. The vernal point is the point of intersection of the earth's equator-plane, extended into the cosmos, with the plane of the ecliptic, the apparent orbit of the sun, on which lies the Zodiac with its twelve signs. This is the position of the sun on March 21st each year.

In 25,920 earth-years the vernal point of the sun moves like the hand of a clock through the 360 degrees of the Zodiac. These roughly 26,000 years are called the Platonic Year, or the Great Year. One month of this Great Year would extend over 2,160 earth-years, which corresponds with one age.

---

* See: "Meeting-Point Earth" in Part I.

But even the Great Year denotes perhaps only a World-minute, or even only World-seconds, if we compare it with that Cosmic Clock, which according to Divine Laws determines the length of time for the cycle of a Universe.

The Zodiac is no invention or fantasy of the human brain. It is a fixed, living unit of spheres of radiation or fields of force, which have formed in accordance with the Laws of Creation. The ancient peoples, who were still closely connected with Nature, had the ability to see the working "beyond" in the cosmos. Thus they also learned of the existence of the physically invisible astral Zodiac and its effects.

According to ancient knowledge, the Zodiac consists of twelve fields of force, commencing with 0° Aries, the vernal starting-point of the sun's orbit. Each force field was given a sign, for which names of animals were mainly used. In this connection it should be noted that the invisible *force fields of the Zodiac* are not to be confused with the visible *constellations* of the same name.

Among the animal names are also those of the Four Animals mentioned in the Revelation of John — a Lion, a Bull, a Ram and an Eagle, which are on the steps of the Throne of God (Revelation 4, 6-8). The force field today designated as "Scorpio" was originally named "Eagle," a change already made in ancient times.

The calling of the cosmic force fields by the names of the Four Divine Animals is certainly not without significance. For every force field has a kind of radiation peculiar to it, which in each case for about 2,000 years exercises a furthering and up-building influence on the earth and its inhabitants, depending on which force field the earth inclines towards as a result of its gyratory movement. It is as though the position of the earth at a particular time works like a directional aerial capable of increasingly absorbing radiations from a certain direction, the direction being indicated by the vernal point of the sun.

Actually our whole Universe is a wonderfully ordered radiation-system, in which the tiny earth is significantly placed as focal point of manifold cosmic forces and influences.

It is by no means, as was formerly assumed, without any connections at all in an empty, dead cosmos, but on the contrary it floats in a colorful net of radiations, to which man with his halo of radiations is also closely connected.

The discovery of the atom, this smallest building-stone of the material Creation, makes it easier for us to understand the new, magnificent radiation-picture of the cosmos, because every atomic nucleus emits rays. Hence all unions of atoms, be they things of the earth, the human body or the suns, stars and planets, must also have the most manifold radiations.

Scientific research comes ever nearer to the knowledge of the radiations working in the cosmos. Thus the invisible radiation-belt surrounding the earth has been discovered, as it has also been found that our solar world forms a huge electromagnetic force field that is subject to the Law of Gravity.

Through its radiations the entire cosmos helps to form for humanity the stages of development on which step by step, over long periods of time, they must reach the degree of spiritual maturity that the Creator has ordained for the time of the World Judgment. A great many varying aspects and a wealth of development possibilities are contained therein.

It is just the gyratory motion of the earth producing the ages, which in the course of this development, owing to its long duration, causes extensive changes and effects in Nature and in the life of men, that are stronger by far than those that can be brought about by the two short rhythms of day and night and of the seasons.

Thus each of the cosmic ages receives its special character through the type of radiation-field prevailing at the time; this character also finds expression in the symbolism of the peoples and the cultures of mankind.

The change from one age to the next, thus from one field of radiation to the next, makes itself particularly noticeable.

In our century we are experiencing such a change or transition, from the sphere of radiation called "Pisces" to the sphere of radiation named "Aquarius."

But what has never yet happened in this connection is now taking place for the first time: This time the change of the ages coincides with the great Cosmic Turning Point, which is an outcome of the End Time in the great cycle of our Universe. With this Turning Point there appear what to the earth are new radiations, whose origin is still unknown to mankind. They are producing strong tensions in the cosmos and in the earth, the precursors of which are atmospheric disturbances, climatic changes, underground explosions, more violent earthquakes and volcanic eruptions.

We stand in the midst of this Turning Point, which at the same time brings the World Judgment or the Final Judgment. Any efforts towards reviving old, dead forms in this time are futile. Whatever does not swing in the equilibrium of the Divine Laws fades away *quite visibly*, as if it had never been.

"Everything must become new" is the indelible characteristic of this unique Turning Point, which ends a great past epoch of Creation, and at the same time heralds the beginning of a new period that is to bring the Millennium of Peace, the Golden Age, *if*

194

mankind will recognize and seize the last opportunity to make up for what has been missed and neglected in the spiritual development.

This time is also indicated by a prophecy of the Middle Ages, according to which a Third Kingdom was supposed to be coming. After the Age of the Father and the Son, a similar one of the Holy Spirit was to follow, to be exact the Third Kingdom, which ushers in a completely new way of life.

The idea of the Third Kingdom goes back to the Abbot Joachim of Fiore (Floris), who lived from approximately 1130 to 1202. He was a native of Calabria in Southern Italy. Through an inner enlightenment he came to the recognition of the Three Ages, which are linked with the Divine Trinity.

The Age of the Father was to begin with Abraham and last until just before the birth of Christ. Then came the Age of the Son of God Jesus. This was followed by the Age of the Holy Spirit, which brings the fulfillment of the words of the Revelation of John: "And I saw another angel fly in the midst of heaven, having the everlasting gospel to preach unto them that dwell on the earth, and to every nation, and kindred, and tongue, and people, Saying with a loud voice, Fear God and give glory to him, for the hour of his judgment is come: and worship him that made heaven, and earth, and the sea, and the fountains of waters!" (14, 6 and 7).

Joachim of Fiore also saw the fulfillment of the words of Paul: "But when that which is perfect is come, then that which is in part shall be done away" (I Corinthians 13, 10) during the Age of the Holy Spirit.

His doctrine of the Three Ages was something out of the ordinary for that time. It aroused enthusiasm and a great soaring hope among the people of the Middle Ages, who were afflicted by continual wars.

But it also caused unrest and strife. Last but not least, it met with displeasure from the Church, for it was not free from a heretical way of thinking. Thus, for example, the Abbot supported the view that the renewal of the World would have to proceed not from some institution, but solely from the spirit. His teaching centered not on the return of Christ, but on the Third Kingdom, whose early dawn he proclaimed.

In the course of centuries his teaching of the Third Kingdom was subject to some modifications. Finally in past decades the words "Third Kingdom" ("Drittes Reich" in German) occupied a special place in Germany; however only for political reasons, because of the sequence of the forms of government, thus without any inner relation to the Third Kingdom of the Holy Spirit proclaimed by Fiore.

But in reality it embraces a deeper meaning, because the teaching dovetails into the great World-Happening. Thus the Age of the Father is equivalent to the Age of Aries, which comprises approximately the first two pre-Christian millennia.

The preceding Age of the powerful Earth sign Taurus brought the climax of their culture to some great peoples of the earth. Yet through cultivation of the earthly intellect the knowledge of God had receded into the background. The wise among earthmen had connection only with the leaders of the elements. Thus they worshipped the sun and its animistic guardian like a god, and the Animal of the then prevailing magnetic force-field Bull was sacred to them.

The subsequent Age of Aries was the time of the great helps from the Light for the human-spiritual developing in the Material World of Subsequent Creation. At that time the Will of God inclined towards the spiritually furthest-developed people of the Jews. Moses was their mediator and leader. It was through him that mankind received the Ten Commandments of God, which are still absolutely valid today.

After Moses, came the Prophets, who called on the people to turn back and be obedient to God.

During this period further Forerunners of the Light were incarnated among other peoples, in order to lead them also another step upwards to the recognition of God. They were Buddha in India, Zoroaster in Iran and Lao-Tse in China.

Then followed the Age of the Son of God, which was associated with the Sign of Pisces. Divine Love incarnated on the then already darkened earth, in order at the last moment to stay the ever more rapidly downward-sliding human beings, and to throw them a lifeline in the Divine Word. For Jesus did not come to earth to let Himself be murdered. He wished to bring the Word of Truth. Only the Word could give them redemption. The result was deeply shaming for men. The darkness of soul that held the majority in its embrace did not allow them to recognize and put the Word into deed, so that it was accusingly said: "And the light shineth in darkness; and the darkness comprehended it not" (John 1, 5).

Once more during this time a Forerunner was sent to earth: Mohammed proclaimed his doctrine, which he based on the Truth brought by Jesus, to the Arab people. He tried to establish the true Realm of God on earth.

At the end of the present Piscean Age we realize on looking back how many helps the Light has ever again given during the past four thousand years alone, so that men would keep to the right path.

But during these same millennia, experiences also showed that most men closed themselves to the helping blessings from the Light, and even opposed the Truth with hostility. It is an enormous tragedy in the history of mankind that with the death of their Truth-Bringers and Prophets, decline always set in instead of the expected ascent, bringing almost all effort to naught, and burdening mankind with heavy guilt.

With this recognition we stand at the beginning of the Age of the Holy Spirit, which seen from the cosmic point of view corresponds to the Aquarian Age. But men do not even know Who is this Holy Spirit.

In sacred works of art the Holy Spirit is quite rightly depicted as a Person. Like Jesus He is a Personality, and like Him of Divine Origin.

The Jews already knew the designation "Holy Spirit" before the time of Christ. In the Book of Wisdom (9, 17) it says: "And thy counsel who hath known, except thou give wisdom, and send thy Holy Spirit from above?" In the Book of Sirach (1, 8-10) is written: "There is one who is wise, greatly to be feared, sitting upon his throne. The Lord himself created wisdom; he saw her and apportioned her, he poured her out upon all his works. She dwells with all flesh according to his gift; and he supplied her to those who love him."

Here the Holy Spirit is described as acting Personality, Who "saw her and apportioned her."

Isaiah proclaimed the Holy Spirit as "Servant" of God: "Behold my servant, whom I uphold; mine elect, in whom my soul delighteth; I have put my spirit upon him: he shall bring forth Judgment (Justice) to the Gentiles (men)" (Isaiah 42, 1). Later we also read: "The Lord God, *and* his Spirit, hath sent me" (Isaiah 48, 16). In the Creation-story, the Spirit of God works by the side of God during the Creation (Genesis 1, 2).

In the Revelation, John describes the Holy Spirit as "him, which is to come" (1, 4). He mediates the Grace "from him, which is and which was, and which is to come . . . and from Jesus Christ, Quite obviously he's speaking of two Persons, Him "which is to come *and* Jesus! God Himself does not come into Creation, because it would have to perish in the enormous Power of His Divinity. But already before the beginning of Creation He severed a Part of Himself, as happened later with Jesus: the Holy Spirit. In the Proverbs of Solomon, where the Holy Spirit is called 'Wisdom,' this is said of It: "The Lord possessed me in the beginning of his way, before his works of old. I was set up from everlasting, from the beginning, or ever the earth was" (Proverbs 8, 22 and 23).

Creation, which has come into being through the Holy Spirit, is also maintained by Him in that He sends His Power into Creation at regular intervals, as happened at that

Pentecost when the disciples were permitted to receive the promised Power from On High.

This is also the deep symbolic meaning of the sign of the approaching Aquarian Age, whose Uranian force field now begins to unfold its radiations in the firmament. It represents a male figure, who pours water from a vessel.

This corresponds to a process that takes place in the highest heights of the spiritual Primordial Creation. There is the Grail Castle with the Holy Grail, the Fountain of Life, the connecting-point between the Creator and His Creation. From thence, since the *dawn of Creation*, the Holy Spirit allows the "Water of Life," the spiritual Power, to stream into Creation, at the appointed time each year, for its continuous maintenance and renewal.

After the great purification, which takes place through the World Judgment, men will again be able to receive this Power consciously, and to use it for the joy and blessing of all creatures.

Thus the New Age draws near with mighty changes and upheavals, decreed in accordance with the Laws of Creation, promised by the Prophets of the Old Testament and proclaimed through the Revelation of John.

There are many signs by which to recognize this unique Turning Point of the ages. It introduces a new epoch on earth, in which man will not continue to rule, but the Holy Spirit alone.

He is the Son of Man promised by Jesus, the Will of God in Person, the Comforter, the Spirit of Truth, Who preaches the "everlasting gospel" mentioned in the Revelation of John (14, 6), of which Jesus had already said: "And this gospel of the kingdom shall be preached in all the world for a witness unto all nations; and then shall the end come" (Matthew 24, 14): the end of the Old and the beginning of the New Age.

That will then be the era of the *real* Third Reich (Kingdom), whose coming into being on earth has hitherto been prevented through men's estrangement from God and His Laws.

Part III

WHAT LIES BEHIND IT ...!

Behind everything stands the Will of God, moving and sustaining!

On this side, in the gross matter of this earth, we see everywhere only the ramifications, the *final* effects of this Eternal Will, Which finds expression in His immutable Laws.

For the human spirit it is now particularly stimulating and gladdening to be able to investigate and divine the *deeper meaning* of outward happenings and events; for what is real lies beyond earthly comprehension, and can be grasped only with the spiritual faculties.

This shall be attempted here. At the same time may the reader recognize one thing or another that cannot be fathomed with mere earthly knowledge, and yet represents the reality.

1. THE STARS AND FATE

We have heard at various times of returning evil or good currents of fate, and it may be asked in what way do they come back to their originator, and when does this happen. For here as everywhere some order must prevail which is firmly established in the plan of Creation, and which admits of no arbitrariness. Are these currents of fate controlled, and who takes part in it?

To understand these processes let us begin with the atom. The driving energy in atoms arises through minute spirit-motes which are equipped with a spiritual though *graded* power. From distant heights they stream unceasingly to us, into the Gross Material World, where they give rise to the formation of a great number of atomic species.

They are the same spirit-particles which also accumulate into heavenly bodies. Our sun is one such immense concentration of them, and in its emanation, or differently expressed, in the electro-magnetic waves which it sends out and which we call sunlight, these spirit-particles in turn are contained. This solves the enigma of what in the true sense of the word is the life-giving power of the sun's rays, without which life on earth would be impossible.

But not only the sun, everything else also sends out rays, or better said mingled radiations resulting from the various combinations of atoms among themselves. Thus the earth, the stars, rocks and plants have their specific radiations, likewise the bodies of men and animals. Natural science is only now beginning to grasp these radiations in their initial stages.

All these radiations together result in a widely-ramified, colorful radiation-network, which in turn is linked with other radiations coming from out of the Universe.

In the midst of this vast radiation-network stands the human spirit of the earth with his wreath of radiations, which forms the antenna for the reception of radiations from out of the Universe.

What is decisive for him is how he exercises his free will during his earth-life, what radiations he draws to himself from out of the Universe, and above all how he makes use of the spiritual power continually streaming through Creation. This power is neither good nor bad, but neutral. Only by using it is man able to form his "works," through the volition of his inner perception. He needs the spiritual power as stimulus for the forming of good and bad works, which make up his *fate* (karma), and with which he remains linked until they are redeemed. Man is not capable of creating anything himself; he is only able to form by uniting already-existing individual forms. In this connection it should be noted that these works, just like everything else, send out rays and are active. They are forms which, in union with homogeneous species, give rise to incisive effects.

The activity of these works is very clearly expressed in the language through "activity-words" (verbs), for example as when a thought strikes us, hatred is nurtured in our heart or courage rises, when we take fright, arouse fear, or when envy gnaws at our heart, when we are consumed with worry, or tormented by some craving.

These are no empty phrases, but actual, even if invisible, processes, which are expressed through word-forms.

If now our fateful works emit radiations, and the stars also radiate, then it becomes clear that stars and fate are connected through radiations.

The radiations of the stars form channels in which the reactions corresponding to the nature of the radiations are guided collectively to the originator when according to the Laws of Creation they are due. "For only when it is ripe does the fruit of Fate fall" (Schiller). Evil currents of fate find their way to unfavorable radiations, and good currents of fate to favorable radiations.

If there is no homogeneous fate the channels run empty, bringing neither good nor evil. But in spite of this they still exercise an influence in that, for example, empty unfavorable channels can interrupt good reactions, and vice versa. Through the ever-changing reciprocal radiation of the stars, the most diverse effects are thus produced.

After these explanations, the real meaning of an astrological prediction is now no longer hard to understand. In so far as this is possible with the stars available for calculation today, it can of course be stated when bad or good reactions are possible, when for instance Saturn moving in the sky forms a "bad" radiation-aspect to the position of Mars in the birth-horoscope; but this is still not enough for a fully detailed interpretation. In addition, it must be determined whether any karma is actually passing through the ascertained channels. Thus the one interpreting would at the same time have to be a clairvoyant, or at least work in association with a clairvoyant, to be able to discern the fine currents of fate or the empty state of the channels.

In this connection however it should be observed that in our time the reactions, which for the most part are of an evil nature, are running at full speed, and that therefore the predictions have a considerably greater likelihood of being fulfilled. This is connected with the Cosmic Turning-Point and the Final Judgment, during which through certain radiations an acceleration is called forth in all spheres of life which crowds all redemptions closely together with regard to time, through which striking accumulations of all kinds of fateful events come about. This implies at the same time an accumulation of "hits" based only on *calculations* concerning the future, without knowing whether there are threads of fate for them.

But now in addition to all the predictions comes something else of importance: how does man receive these? In most cases he is disturbed by unfavorable predictions, his confidence, his trust, are impaired, so that even if the stellar channels are running empty, out of fear of what is coming a fulfillment is forcibly brought about which otherwise would not be there.

In the case of favorable predictions, vigilance may slacken in careless expectation of something good, which is equally harmful. Finally there is the danger of being fettered, of an inner constraint if the predictions form the basis of every single action. The inner perception is dulled, and eventually man becomes a slave of his destiny.

Therefore he should know how to assess astrological predictions aright, and on no account should he accustom himself to or make himself dependent upon them, because they are incomplete, and can always be given only in the form of what is *possible*.

Instead he should rely on the inner perception of his spirit, look to the future with calm confidence, and content himself with knowing what the stars have to do with fate: Their radiations serve to let returning effects of fate flow to him in a more concentrated form at those times which are appointed for it according to the Laws of Creation. That is to say he does indeed have the free win for decision, nevertheless he must leave the *consequences* of his decision and the *moment for the return of the consequences* to the Laws of God. He has no influence over these.

Certainly a birth-horoscope accurately calculated also gives indications for the *present time* with reference to environmental relations (upbringing, occupation, relationships with other people, liability to illness, etc.). But to form a judgment on this requires, in addition to the earthly circumstances, the psychic condition and the ethereal environment of the one born, with all the as yet unsevered good and bad threads of fate.

Thus here too the stellar calculation reveals only the possibility of a many-sided interpretation, and it is extremely difficult to discover what is real about it.

Nevertheless a limited use of the horoscope is possible. For it is conceivable that one called for it, who engages in psychic counseling, uses a person's birth-horoscope as a guide-line, in order to recognize abilities, personal disposition and possible karmaic effects in it. Together with the information from the person concerned, these can then be supplemented by the following: handwriting, the lines of the hand, shape of the head and other aids, in order to determine approximately how far the possibilities indicated in the horoscope have been realized at the time of counseling. —

Even though the stars have yet other effects, they are in everything still only participants in the great order-plan of Creation. Man as its *originator* always rig remains the master of his fate.

The activity of the stars thus described gives us the important recognition of *why* they can neither influence the free will of man nor exercise compulsion over him.

On the contrary, the supposed influence emanates from man himself, who in his free choice supplies the "material of fate" which the stars only return to him in the same kind, though many times increased, just as with a seed-grain multiple fruits grow for the sower.

However severe the reactions may often be, man is always in a position to protect himself against returning evil through a timely inward change for the good.

If nevertheless it one day strikes him with full force, then he should not "quarrel with fate", and above all he should not let himself be incited to commit or allow himself to be carried away by further misdeeds. Otherwise he makes his position worse and "jumps from the frying-pan into the fire", as the saying goes.

He should then remember the words of Jesus in the parable: "But I tell you, Resist not him that is evil" (Matthew 5, 39 — Lutheran Bible). If by this we understand the evil that comes back on man, then these words mean that man acts aright when he stands up to his evil fate courageously, and with trust in Divine Justice taking up the struggle with it and living through the consequences of what he has done wrong. There are always breathing-spaces in the course of it. The stars also ensure this by periodically interrupting evil reactions with favorable radiations.

The man thus oppressed and afflicted is thereby forced to awaken spiritually, and eventually emerges strengthened from the struggle with "the power of destiny". Actually in so doing he has conquered himself, because he has overcome his faults and weaknesses. In the consequences of his deeds and thoughts he has recognized his deserved and just fate.

Let us see to it, however, that in future we do only what is good and refrain from evil, so that only good is left to the reactions of the stars. Then a kind fate will fall to our lot, which allows our spiritual development to take place harmoniously, until one day a planetary hour, thus an auspicious, fateful hour is allotted to us here on earth, in which we may recognize the Eternal Truth!

2. THE VISITING OF SINS UNTO THE THIRD
AND FOURTH GENERATION

The Law of Seed and Harvest, Cause and Effect, which can also be called the Law of Reciprocal Action, is a *uniform* Law for the whole of Creation, applying equally to human actions and thoughts, and determining the course of fate.

To this also pertain happenings which are designated as *chance*, with the implication of arbitrariness and blind sway.

In reality, however, they are the effects of lawful processes, which are often strange and inexplicable, because man is no longer in a position to survey and recognize the invisible connections in them.

By viewing his fate intellectually he advances no further. Extra-earthly realms are involved here, which are not accessible to the earthly intellect.

How often we say in regard to fateful events: It was an unfortunate or fortunate accident, chance willed it so, it was brought about by a series of accidents, or it was a game of chance. But the game was known, it went according to incorruptible rules, determined by the Laws of Creation.

In accordance with the same Laws, many human souls must again return to earth to make good, to redeem the sins which they once committed on earth. For earthly beginning stipulates earthly ending in accordance with the Law of the Cycle, by which the ring must close at the place where it was begun. "Thus all guilt avenges itself on earth" (Goethe), according to which the Biblical expression "to avenge" means nothing other than the working out of the Law of Sowing and Reaping.

The same Law is expressed by the Biblical words: "The iniquity of the fathers is visited upon the children unto the third and fourth generation" (Exodus 20, 5).

The visiting does not refer to heredity. What is inherited is only purely physical. We see it for example with drug addicts and drunkards, whose children then suffer from physical defects.

But there is no spiritual heredity. Therefore the visiting refers *only* to the *karmaic reactions* of a wrong which, for instance, parents commit against their children. Its effect goes on from generation to generation, until in one generation a halt is called to the necessary atonement through better recognition, and it is possible for the originator to begin with the redemption of his karma.

One such sin is when parents instill into their children that life does not continue after death, that everything is then ended. This gives rise to very far-reaching, adverse effects, especially if the offspring retain this false view, and pass it on to the grandchildren. These effects continue until in one generation the right recognition of an after-life arises, and the originator is only then able gradually to sever himself from his guilt.

The present-day conditions of moral decline in particular are rooted to a considerable extent with young and old in the fatal view that man lives only once on earth. Hence earth-life is senselessly enjoyed without consideration for one's fellow-men, and with total disregard of the responsibility placed upon man by God. Escape into narcotics and drugs, into illness and suicide, is to some extent connected with this.

At the same time no thought is given to the consequences of the reaction, and yet they take effect, here on earth or there in the beyond, regardless of human volition and thinking, which rarely accords with the Laws of Creation.

3. THE KINGDOM WITHIN US

This expression is often used. People also say: the Kingdom of Heaven or the Kingdom of God within us.

As to the real meaning of these words there are only vague ideas, which leave open the main questions: In what way is the Kingdom of God within man? Has it always been within us? Or does it only enter into man later, perhaps through the Word of God?

The "Kingdom within us" is closely linked with the Law of the Cycle, which can be easily observed in Nature.

The human spirit also is subject to this Law, which means that each one must return to its origin, just as the blood ever again flows back to the heart.

But where does the origin of the human spirit lie?

In the Spiritual Realm, which we call the Paradise of the human spirits, or "the Kingdom of Heaven"; there is his origin, his true home, the Kingdom of God.

Far above the Spiritual Realm is the Divine Sphere, and God Himself in His Unsubstantiality, eternally unapproachable and incomprehensible to the human spirits.

Hence the human spirit cannot bear within it anything Divine, because its lies much *lower* in the *Spiritual* Realm.

It lives there as an unconscious spirit seed-grain, which is released (expelled) from Paradise, and plunges into the material substance of the World that lies below. Here the spirit awakens to full consciousness, and in natural development returns to Paradise as conscious of itself, as the "prodigal son" who has found his way back to his homeland.

The core of man, thus what constitutes the essential part of man, his spirit, is of such a kind as exists in the Spiritual Realm.

Through this he is himself a part of the Spiritual Realm, a part which he as earthman bears within him and which is eternal, whereas all the coverings which envelop the human spirit are transient.

When Jesus was asked by the Pharisees "when the kingdom of God should come" He answered them: "The kingdom of God cometh not with observation: Neither shall they say, Lo here! or, lo there! for, behold, the kingdom of God is within you" (Luke 17, 20 and 21).

In the last Wittenberg edition of the Bible of 1545, published during Luther's lifetime it says, "the kingdom of God is within you."

In a 1916 edition of the Bible the same words are still to be found. Later, however, Luther's translation was changed to, "the kingdom of God is in your midst."

The reason given for this by various sources was inaccuracy in the translation of the original text, and the objection that the Kingdom of God could not have been within the Pharisees because they had opposed Jesus.

Nevertheless we have seen that this is so, because spirit, and with it a part of the Kingdom of God, is in *every* human being. Except that through evil thoughts and actions this "inner kingdom" has been completely buried in some, and in others it is less strong.

But then all is not done with the "Kingdom of Heaven within us." We must earnestly strive, indeed strive with unflinching diligence, really to maintain the link with the native Luminous Fields.

We are helped to achieve this by the spiritual power that comes from the same spiritual origin and streams through Creation.

The spirit within us, like the physical body, needs its nourishment so that it can grow into the necessary consciousness which alone makes it a complete human spirit. Just as the physical body is unable to do without water, so does the spirit need the "Water of Life," spiritual power.

It has surely been noticed already by everyone, when a strong inner shock, whether of deep sorrow or great joy, loosened the dense coverings surrounding the spirit. He then sensed for some blissful moments the nearness of this power, of which he hardly becomes conscious in everyday life.

With the help of this spiritual power, and with the gifts and abilities originally vested in him, man *would* have been in a position to let a Paradise-like condition arise on earth!

Instead of this he is suffering today from an extreme *self-estrangement*. He has estranged himself from his self, his spirit, by allowing the awareness that he has a spiritual core within him to be extinguished.

Only through a *constant* good volition shall we be able to reawaken this consciousness. Therefore let us listen within, let us hearken to the inner voice, and heed every gentle urging of the spirit towards what is beautiful and noble, every sorrow over lost spiritual values, every silent reproach of having done little or nothing yet at all to unfold to full blossom the gifts bestowed by the Creator.

When often in the midst of all darkness and all affliction, we are seized by homesickness for bygone beautiful things, for happy hours formerly experienced, for a tender, deeply spiritual mood, as may perhaps have been the case at a Christmas festival, we usually describe this today by the word: *nostalgia!*

But let us just for once examine closely with the inner perception whether behind it there is not hidden the unquenchable longing of the suppressed spirit that strives away from the earth to the Eternal Fields of the Kingdom of God, of which we bear within us the smallest part!

With the awakening of this inner longing we draw ever more luminous rays from the Universe, which gradually loosen and eventually altogether dissolve the self-created dark covering, so that the spirit on earth can again shine forth radiantly, as once it did in the springtime of mankind!

4. THE I IN THE LANGUAGE

The sojourn of man on earth and in the beyond assists his development from an unconscious spirit-germ to a conscious ego, to a personality conscious of itself, with free will and the responsibility arising out of it.

That is the state man should strive for as soon as he has left Paradise, the spiritual Realm, as an unconscious spirit-germ. In the throes of experiences, and through all kinds of influences assailing him, he must fight for his full spiritual maturity on his Journey through the material substances of the World.

With the attainment of this goal he has completed his cycle through the World, and then returns to Paradise as a fully-conscious personality.

The development to a human spirit conscious of itself is naturally to be found in the evolution of languages. For the spirit of man also forms the language.* The more he unfolds his natural consciousness, the more is this expressed in the language, above all in the introduction and use of the word "I."

Hence it follows that, for instance, in the languages of ancient times the "I" is still little used as a single word. It is completely lacking in the verbs, and is expressed solely in their endings. Only later, with increasing development towards self-consciousness, did the "I," among some peoples, emerge, as it were, from its obscurity within the verbs, and was placed in front of them.

We observe the development of the human spirit to personal ego-consciousness, comprising millions of years, as a recapitulation concentrated into the childhood of present-day man. At the same time we notice that neither does the child yet use the word I, but to begin with employs its first name or a variation of it. Only later does it begin to make use of the word I, as the spirit gradually awakens to consciousness of itself.

If man reflects for once on the actual goal of his development, he will see that his ego has not remained alone. As a result of his wrong development the word "mania" has been added, as an expression of his inner condition as it manifests today, his desire for importance, and his intoxication with power.

Therefore it will not be easy for him to break free from the *egomania* prevalent today, in order to re-discover the interrupted path of natural development to the perfecting of his personality.

---

* See: "Spirit and Language" in Part II.

This involves above all the recognition that his sojourn in the earthly Gross Material World is only a *path*, and not the goal itself. Everything on earth is only a means to the end of spiritual development, to the completion of the cycle whose beginning *and* end lie in Paradise, the home of the human spirit, from which it has issued as a spirit-germ in order to return there as a complete human spirit.

5. ADAPTATION, BUT HOW?

A vital requirement, which Nature strictly observes, is with a few exceptions no longer known to man: *natural adaptation*! He has become incapable of mastering any longer that adaptation which furthers and ennobles his spirit.

The concept of "adaptation" has become grossly distorted, especially in the realm of human association. Whether it is a question of wrong adaptations to harmful customs in marriage and family, or of a more or less enforced adaptation to unnatural social systems.

In the realms of Nature a correct adaptation is taken for granted. Every animal, every flower, every tree adapts to the environment in which it lives — to the zone, the climate, the rays of the earth and the stars. Whether this occurs in the arctic region, in great heat, in water or in the air, everywhere we find a perfect adaptation to the natural conditions.

This automatic adaptation is only one of the many-sided effects of the *Law of Spiritual Movement!*

Man alone closes himself voluntarily to this all-animating, spirit-refreshing movement, which would also spur him on to a healthy adaptation everywhere. His earthly intellect indeed runs at high speed, but his spirit has become too lazy to open itself consciously to the spiritual power-current that moves Creation, and to make use of it in a furthering and up-building way.

Otherwise things would look different on earth today. Harmony and peace would spread, and joyful activity be found everywhere.

Already the Ten Commandments contain in reality enough suggestions for a genuine adaptation, the compliance with which brings only happiness and joy. Especially when it is recognized that to the concept of adaptation in human life there also belongs this: not to harm one's neighbor through some desire or other!

The man of today finds himself in a grave adaptation-crisis, because he is the only creature who for thousands of years has neglected to carry out that adaptation which alone really allows him to become a fully-conscious personality: *the unconditional adaptation of his spirit to the Laws of Creation!* These also include the Laws of Nature, without which research, for instance, can do nothing if it wishes to be successful. For making use of the forces of the earth, water, air and fire means nothing other than adapting oneself to the lawfulness expressed in them.

But unfortunately, in this field natural adaptation often becomes a curse, if the results of research and discoveries are misused to the affliction and destruction of men and animals, and to the pollution of the environment.

Anyone, who now wishes to begin to concern himself with the Laws of Creation, such as the Law of Movement, the Law of the Cycle, the Law of Balance between Giving and Taking, the Law of Sowing and Reaping (the Law of Reciprocal Action), the Law of the Attraction of Homogeneous Species, and the Law of Gravity will gradually open for himself the way to an adaptation to the Will of God. For something other than the Will of God cannot be expressed in the Laws, which are His Work. And all these Laws apply not only to the realm of Nature but also to *human* life.

If man cannot or can no longer come to terms with the Old Testament ideas of God, if he is striving to form for himself a new concept of God, then he should attempt at last to begin with Creation and its Laws. He will always find in them an *imperishable* quantity (constant), an all-embracing, *uniform* whole, which offers him a firm support and does not let him waver so easily.

It can be said that Creation and its Laws make him familiar with the Language of God.

In this way man is able to master his life reliably, and to unfold his personality. There opens up to him an entirely new world-picture, in which he rediscovers himself as a creature who gets to know and to understand his origin, his goal and his task, like a revelation.

Finally he reaches that stage of development at which he recognizes and *acknowledges* the Will of his God and therewith also God Himself, Who is un- approachably enthroned outside His Creation, and has woven into His Work only His Will in the form of the Laws of Creation.

This is the highest stage of adaptation to which man can attain: *the adaptation of his entire life to the Will of God, to His Laws and His Commandments.*

Then gradually he will also adapt the institutions of state and society, and all other realms, to the inflexible Laws of Creation. And such a right adaptation can bring nothing but peace, joy and ascent!

6. NO TIME FOR SPIRITUAL THINGS!

How little time indeed has man for any spiritual happening, although he himself, his real ego, his spirit, is a part of this happening, simply through the very fact that he originates in the Spiritual Realm. There is his Paradisal home, which he has left in the urge and longing to become conscious.

Even on earth a man who emigrates to another country does not forget his homeland, he at least thinks back to it now and then, if he is not even overcome by homesickness for the land of his earthly origin.

But he no longer knows anything of his spiritual home, which lies above in Paradise. Not even a divining of it arises within him. And yet the spirit, filled with repressed longing, is always waiting for the dark walls built around it by human guilt to be torn down, so that his gaze may become free towards the Light.

Man always has time enough for earthly things and earthly customs, but there is no time to spare for spiritual investigating and seeking, although it is actually so essential for his ascent out of this world of perishable matter, which indeed is only meant for him temporarily as a place of learning, of investigating and of development.

Man should indeed produce earthly goods and enjoy them with pleasure, but he must not place the acquisition of earthly possessions *above* spiritual gain, which alone mediates eternal values to him.

Only *these* values which he is able to acquire through genuine inner experiencing give him strong support in the beyond, firm confidence, and genuine trust in God. But the earthly values which he has acquired with the help of his intellect remain behind after death and pass away like the brain which produces the intellect.

It is just the intellect that so often stifles the rising longing of the spirit, pushing aside fruitful recognitions and experiences, declaring that it has no time for them.

May the human being in the pressure of earthly activity swing himself upwards more and more to devote sufficient time to the spiritual. It will bring the spirit multiple gain, here as well as over there in the other world, which no earthly wealth however great can outweigh.

Whether the search for the spiritual relates for example to the question of the origin of the human spirit, its task in Creation, life after death, the spiritual power by which it lives and exists, or whether it concerns its free will, its responsibility, its fate and its repeated earth-lives.

No time for spiritual things! This can only be a lazy excuse of the intellect, because by its nature it is in no position whatever to grasp spiritual things. Its field is the earthly.

The spirit, however, which is eternal, does not know this excuse. It always has time for spiritual things, as soon as and as long as it goes on striving to keep awake its longing for the Luminous Heights!

7. THE GREAT TRANSFORMATION

There are two main kinds of life in the whole of Creation: unconscious and conscious life.

Only through *experiencing* can the unconscious state be transformed into a conscious one. So is it also with the human spirit.

When it leaves its point of origin, men's Paradise, it is a spirit-germ which as yet has no consciousness of its own, and solely under the *urge* of becoming conscious sinks down into the Worlds of Matter in order first of all as a spirit-germ to experience *consciousness of its existence.*

The further development from consciousness of existence to *being conscious of oneself,* with the rising degrees of becoming conscious of oneself, is a long journey, with many re-embodiments (reincarnations) in *human bodies.*

For this the stage of consciousness of existence as transition is of course absolutely necessary, but the spirit-germ may remain there only a certain time if it does not wish to lag behind in its development, and thus in a state similar to that still to be found among some savage tribes.

The full maturity of a human spirit is equivalent to consciousness of oneself, the basis of which is *self-recognition,* that the core of man is spiritual and that his true home lies in the Spiritual Realm.

The completion of this last great stage of development should have been reached today by all human beings sojourning in the World of Matter, because the time for this is fulfilled, according to the Laws of Creation.

At the same time, with the full maturity that can grow only out of experiencing, men would have come into possession of the true knowledge that lies only in the cognizance, without gaps, of the Laws woven into Creation by God.

On these Laws of God, or Laws of Creation, rests the order of Creation, and out of them flows all Creation-Happening. To them also belong the Laws of Nature, which are indeed partly known to science but without the latter's having recognized their origin or "original foundation," because it confines itself solely to what can be proved by the intellect.

That one cannot today speak of either a full maturity of the human spirits or a knowledge of the Laws of God is shown by the immaturity and ignorance of human beings in all that pertains to spiritual development.

218

With regard to their development, mankind are still between the stage of consciousness of existence and that of consciousness of oneself; in which connection it is to be noted that the animal also has a consciousness, but can never become conscious of itself, because it is of an entirely different species from that of the human spirit.

Now what is the cause of this sad standstill and retrogression in the development of mankind? *Lack of experiencing* because only experiencing can form the bridge from the unconscious to the conscious.

Experiencing is possible for the spirit-germ only in the Worlds of Matter of Subsequent Creation, to which the earth also belongs. When it comes in contact here with the coarser and coarsest influences, there is the possibility for it to awaken out of the sleep of the unconscious, and to develop to the highest maturity.

With its *free will*, which is anchored in the spiritual species, the spirit-germ is able to choose *those* experiences which it needs in order to mature.

Yet one or several experiences at certain intervals do not suffice. The spirit must gather and assimilate many experiences and lessons in unbroken succession, until it has reached the maturity-level of the highest consciousness, of being conscious of itself, in the World of Matter.

This highest level of maturity then opens for it the gate to the Spiritual Realm, to Paradise. There it is able to perfect itself ever more in its task of being a link between the Spiritual Realm and the Worlds of Matter of *Subsequent Creation* lying below it.

It may then continue to participate in the weaving of Creation, in a furthering, up-building and ennobling way, because during its Journey through the Worlds of Matter it became thoroughly acquainted with its sphere of work, and could gather enough experiences for its activity.

In being permitted to participate in this way lies the meaning of its existence!

Earthman must not make the mistake of applying to the Creation-Happening the *joint decision-making* striven for or demanded in the purely earthly-social realm.

In the *whole* of Creation it is exclusively the *Will of God* manifesting in the Laws of Creation Which *decides*. The human spirit, despite the fact that through its spiritual nature it is lord, so to speak, in *Subsequent Creation*, can as His creature only participate in that which God has already decided, *but not take part in the decision*. These are two entirely different concepts.

For it is unthinkable that man as a *creature* should decide jointly with his *Creator*, thus take part in determining what has to be done.

On earth also joint decision-making is out of place, because by virtue of his free will every human being is *himself responsible* for what he has to decide. Thus he likewise decides his fate.

If a man intrudes upon the personal environment or sphere or work of another, and wishes to make joint decisions there, he is transgressing against the decisions of the Creator, in which it is firmly established that *personal responsibility* must neither be *shifted* onto other people nor *shared* with others! Disappointments, discord and strife are the result when he does not observe this.

The expression "*joint* decision-making" does not fit into the harmonious swinging of Creation, including the earthly plane. Here, out of a wrong volition, whether due to error, misunderstanding or striving for power, man has coined a *new* expression which narrows and distorts the concept of deciding.

We obtain the right concept if we use the words *participation* and *co-operation* instead of "joint decision-making."

But then there are still other transgressions by man against the decisions of the Creator. An especially grave one was that of the *over-cultivation of the intellect.**

It is the intellect which, through wrong use, does not permit the human spirit to experience *that* which it needs for the recognition of full consciousness, because man put his intellect, which according to Divine Ordinance should be only the *instrument* of the spirit, in the place of his spirit.

The intellect arises in the frontal brain, and is active only for as long as the earthly body is animated by the spirit.

In its liking-to-know-better, the intellect does not allow living happenings to reach the spirit at all, or only weakened and distorted. Thus it prevents the undimmed advance of visible and invisible impressions and influences to the spirit.

Through the predominance of the intellect, with its paralyzing and enervating pondering, man has narrowly limited his possibilities of experiencing.

He thereby closes himself to the luminous currents which he absolutely needs on earth, because these help him in the first place to be continually experiencing and vigilant.

What is happening at the present time, however, is meant to assist him in a way that is capable of violently rousing human beings of a good volition, whereby the way

---

* See: "Spirit, Logic and Intellect" in Part II.

becomes free for a pure, unimpaired experiencing, which consciously makes full use of the supra-earthly radiation-forces, and will not as hitherto let them pass it by.

In these power-currents permeating Creation, without which there is no life, lie both help and salvation for the human spirit.

Thus even at the last moment it is given the opportunity to complete the *great transformation from an unconscious spirit-germ to a personality conscious of itself,* which it has hitherto postponed.

In his earthly garb man is unable to appreciate the magnitude and the spiritual value of this transformation. Only when he has laid aside the heavy earthly cloak, and gradually ascends to higher, more luminous fields, will there come to him a divining of what he has gained with God's gift of a conscious life.

Then his development in Gross Matter has come to an end. But in the Spiritual Realm, in Paradise, it continues steadily, without end, in ever-increasing activity and glowing, in the supreme joy of *being permitted to serve eternally* in the Luminous Kingdom of the Creator!

8. MORE UNDERSTANDING FOR ONE'S NEIGHBOR

How vital is the harmonious relationship of man to man emerges even from the Ten Commandments alone, which Moses once was permitted to mediate to men.

Many centuries later, words were again spoken on earth with the aim of making behavior towards one's neighbors simple and natural, thus pointing the way to Luminous Heights.

"Love thy neighbor as thyself!" said the commandment of the Son of God Jesus, when He saw how envy and self-seeking had overgrown the garden of love of the soul beyond all recognition.

But however much He exerted Himself to shape man's path in the World of Matter through respect and understanding love towards his fellow-creatures into a path of continuous, undimmed happiness leading only through flowering gardens filled with glorious beauty, to the same extent has man closed himself to these exhortations and counsels, and simply disregarded them.

Hardly one earthman still stands *beside* the other. Distrust, envy and hatred have created gulfs which can scarcely be bridged any more, and the concept of the neighbor, as it swings in the God-willed working of Creation, has long since lost its true value and its true meaning.

There was once a time when men were still what we call balanced. They knew the Law of Balance, were living witnesses to the fact that they were allowed to take from the Table of the Lord, from the gifts which God through His Creation graciously permits to be offered to human beings, only as much as they themselves needed. Through this not one of their fellow-men was harmed and taken advantage of, not one was caused suffering through selfish desires. It was a uniformly- radiating streaming of human activity, which was moved in regular pulsation by the Law of Balance in giving and taking.

Today man in relation to his Creator is only one who takes, or rather one who demands, ruthlessly seizing everything he can lay hands on in his selfishness, without showing even the slightest gratitude as a minute gift in return. In addition to this men no longer open themselves to the animating streams from above, but willingly absorb the influences of the Darkness, and pass them on in various ways.

And over all the darkness of human egomania stand in golden radiance the words: "Love thy neighbor as thyself!" Pure and clear, these words float above mankind. Yet only rarely does a light, delicate ray grope its way to them out of the depths, seeking connection and pleading for strength to overcome the individual's own ego, for a just understanding of his fellow-man, who like him is seeking for the Truth.

Man however must concern himself with his neighbor, must learn to respect and understand him as a part of the same spiritual species, as a fellow-creature who has the same path and the same goal: the Spiritual Home, Paradise.

To this end observation of his fellow-men can be very useful to him. Simply because in them he can discover, and in recognizing reflect upon the faults which human nature out of its free volition, thus because of its own guilt, has nurtured outside Paradise in the World of Matter. In view of the ego-stressed character of most men, however, there is always the danger that the observing is not done objectively, and usually becomes a personal comparing, with the result that the one making the comparison imagines himself to be above the faults discovered in the other. According to the words of Jesus, he then certainly sees the mote, the lesser fault, in his fellowman, whereas he does not notice the beam, the same but greater fault, in himself.

On the other hand, impartial, objective observation requires nothing more than for once leaving the ego-stressed standpoint and trying to put oneself in the place of the "object," in this case of the fellow-man, *entering with one's soul into* his thoughts and actions, and not carpingly and critically probing or dissecting with the earthly intellect.

In this connection it may prove a useful hint for the recognition and understanding of the merits and faults, that men have distorted just what is meant to distinguish them. If for instance a man was meant to stand out through *courage*, then with a wrong volition he will pervert it to *lack of courage* and *cowardice*. *Grace* becomes *vanity*, *humility* changes to *arrogance*, *kindness* to *harshness*, and a deep *inner* and thought-life turns into one of excessive *feeling* and *superficiality*. Above all, those qualities and those abilities are distorted through which a human being should be exemplary; and in the distortion every good quality has a definite fault as its opposite. Thus grace and charm change to vanity, and not perhaps to cowardice, which manifests as the opposite of courage.

All these opposites were forcibly brought about through the guilt of the human spirits. They could never have arisen if the human spirits had not forsaken the right path to the Light. Only the evil volition of men thus created, in opposition to the Light, the Darkness which embraces all faults and weaknesses.

If now in the course of these reflections the question arises in our soul: "What then have I distorted that was meant to make me into a serviceable and useful building-stone in the mighty structure of Creation?," then in this first step towards reflection the beginning of the road to self-recognition has been found. To him who treads it will soon be shown the night understanding of his fellow-man, who like himself bears within him the longing for the Luminous Heights, for the Spiritual Home.

The sooner this longing for the Light unfolds to full greatness and strength through the harmonious working together of all good human spirits, the sooner will a reflection of Paradisal beauty then arise on the hitherto so misused earth.

9. WHAT IS HAPPINESS?

In world literature there are a considerable number of writings and books in which an attempt is made to show men the way to happiness. On picking up such promising books and trying to delve into their contents, it can be noted in the great majority of cases that by happiness is meant only a very ordinary earthly advantage in social and material respects.

Above all people strive to achieve a position which, apart from satisfying the need for prominence, brings with it earthly riches. They have thereby attained their goal on the way to happiness, which in this case leads only as far as the earthly senses and feelings are able to perceive it.

It is understandable and commendable if a person wishes to work his way upwards, if he strives to establish a sound material foundation for his earthly existence. But in achieving this goal he still has by no means attained to happiness, that real and true happiness which has its beginning only in grasping and experiencing spiritual events, and yet at the same time permits life on earth to be fully and wholly enjoyed, indeed which alone makes it possible to savor earthly pleasures in pure joy to the full.

In Creation the development always takes place from above downwards. Hence "earthly happiness" too is only a result of the supra-earthly inner perceiving of happiness that can be consciously experienced already on earth.

But it cannot be attained either through intellectual training or by *auto-suggestion*.

For it is wrong to believe that the power to influence lies in man himself, that he is in a position to cure himself of illnesses by his own power, and to be himself the architect of his own happiness. True, each man is the architect of his happiness. But from whence does he draw the material to build with?

The idea of auto-suggestion is in opposition to God, Who alone is the Power from Whose Radiation Creation came to being, and with it also man. But after in it has come into being the creature "man" can actually continue to exist only through the Power coming forth from God. With this recognition nothing remains of any auto-suggestion arising from one's own power! On the contrary, man is in every respect dependent on the Spiritual Power streaming into Creation from God; he must submit to it, otherwise it will turn against him and bring about his downfall.

And this spiritual power is the material that man needs to build his happiness.

He can consciously establish connection with it at any time. The key to this is an inner perception filled with longing to let himself be completely permeated by this power, to surrender to it with wide-opened soul, unreservedly, without any selfish desires whatever. Then it flows into him in the simplest way, with no need for a great effort. Not for anything in the world would man ever again be without this conscious receiving of the power, when once he has recognized that only this being linked with it is his supreme happiness, wherever he may find himself in the measureless expanses of Creation.

Surely everyone has already met with this power, when the soul is awakened by some strong experience, whether it be a deep sorrow or great joy. Then for some moments it senses the nearness of this all-animating power, of which it is not conscious in everyday life.

Where this inner perception still lies slumbering beneath a thin covering, it can be awakened and furthered; where it has already awakened man can strengthen it and let it glow even more through regular attunement in prayer to the Power coming from God.

There are two kinds of prayer: First the prayer which instantaneously arises out of an upwelling inner perception, and only then can be clothed in words; and then the prayer in which words are first arranged and then, reacting on the spirit, release the inner perception, thereby giving the prayer that direction which is willed by the words. Hence there are, to put it briefly, prayers without words and prayers with words. The former are of greater value, for in them the spirit can unfold freely and without constraint and is not tied to words, which can be formed and received only with the help of the earthbound intellect, thereby making a certain limitation of the inner perception unavoidable.

Nevertheless, during their sojourn in the World of Matter the human spirits cannot do without the prayer that is clothed in words, because just here the spirit needs the most varied impressions for higher development, among which the prayer formed in words ranks as one of the first. It is therefore not immaterial what words are used in such prayers and how they are arranged, for words are something living and motivating in the working of Creation. As man uses them, arranges them into sentences, as he pronounces them, so does he also form with them a part of his fate for himself!

Therefore the more the words of a prayer resound in the innermost being of man, the greater also is the possibility thereby — and without undue effort or auto-suggestion, thus in a natural way — of rousing the inner perception, which as an attribute of the spirit is significant for man's fate in a very special way.

Abd-ru-shin, Author of the Work "In the Light of Truth," The Grail Message, has among other things given men two prayers* which fulfil everything in this regard. In their simple and thus so effective way they speak directly to the soul. They are a strong aid in the evoking and growth of that longing which is necessary for the complete and gapless connection with the helping and furthering Rays from the Power of God.

How light it must become around a human spirit, how liberated it will feel when it surrenders completely to the words given to us as morning prayer:

"Thine am I, Lord! To Thee alone in gratitude I dedicate my life; O graciously accept this my volition and grant me the help of Thy Power this day! Amen."

For him who absorbs these words within, who receives them with a live spirit, the day's work will be blessed from early morning till late at night. They will constantly resound in him like a gentle exhortation or a quiet, serene happiness. There is a sacred power surging and weaving in these words, and whoever absorbs the words with his spirit also absorbs the power.

He will not always immediately succeed in obtaining connection through this prayer, because it depends on the depth of the inner perception with which it is experienced. But however weak that may be, through constant awakening it will eventually become so strong and victorious that it will open the way for the blissful experiencing of the wonderful Power from the Creator's Fountain of Life. Then even the weakest person can unfold to full strength within a short time, if he does not weaken in regular inward perception of the words of this morning prayer.

As in the morning and during the day, so also in the evening the same power is available for connection with man, if he longs for it. He is given help for this by the evening prayer:

"O Lord, Who art enthroned above all the Worlds, I beseech Thee: let me rest in Thy Grace this night! Amen."

Sleep will have an invigorating, refreshing and calming effect on a human being who takes over the experience of this prayer with him into another world, a dream world, which however is not a dream one at all, but only appears as such because it cannot be perceived with the earthly senses. We therefore refer to it as transcendental, and every human spirit can cross its threshold when the earthly brain is put to rest through sleep, and thus remains disconnected.

The evening prayer is to help towards this. During sleep the human spirit can come in contact still much more closely and lastingly with various power-currents, and even receive spiritual warnings, or also sudden solutions to certain questions and problems. In reality the natural rest at night is like this: Only the earthly brain, the intellect, sleeps; the spirit however is awake, and blissfully yields to the strengthening influences, provided no excessive intellectual activity makes itself felt disturbingly and obstructively across and beyond the threshold of sleep. But the possibility of preventing this is given by the deep inner perceiving of the evening prayer.

Such prayers lead man to the refreshing Spring of Living Water, which need only be tapped in order to drink from it, and then to regain health in soul and body, indeed completely so. The awakening human spirit, even the poorest and weakest, can receive strength from these prayers to work its way upwards, spiritually and in an earthly sense, to a height never yet known, where it will find that for which all true seekers have already yearned for a long time: "supreme happiness" — which is equivalent to fulfillment of the vow:

"Thine am I, Lord! To Thee alone in gratitude I dedicate my life! Amen."

10. HEAVENLY MELODY

An inconceivably long time ago, a great train of bright little flames went forth from their Eternal Home, where a delicate breath of spring had only just awakened them out of a deep sleep. Many a luminous hand was raised in blessing, as though in a last greeting, and loving, kindly glances followed after them.

The bells of Paradise were ringing as they departed, and even at the last moment they caught this silver-clear tone, and cherished it deep in their young hearts.

Then the little points, whirling merrily, sank into the world-embracing depths.

—

The time came when these delicate little flames had blossomed forth in purity into human spirits, and in the blossoming there mingled a faint note from far, far-away lands, which touched the strings of their hearts like gentle hands, awakening that tone which had sounded so beautiful to them as they departed, and which they had quietly received into their innermost being.

Then they were seized by a vehement urge; for they knew the sweet sound of home, and soon their strings resounded more fully, and their song grew into a melody filled with longing.

That was the time when planet earth still revolved in luminous orbits, and when fresh heavenly dew fell on it each day.

Then came a day when that longing-filled ringing became fainter, weaker. Discords were heard. At first here and there, and then they filled the Universe. Alarmingly the Jubilation of the voices faded, soon the great chorus had fallen silent. No echo could be heard any longer in the Dome of Heaven. The holy singing of earthmen had died away. —

Man had voluntarily created for himself a very effective trap. Following the urge for development, he descended from Paradise into the material substance of Subsequent Creation, but he forgot his origin and was caught in the World of Matter. Thus he could no longer make anything of the urging and exhorting within his heart.

In place of the longing, the yearning for Truth and Eternal Life, the greater part of mankind put the craving for earthly things, the desire for pleasures of the lowest kind. When the Heavenly did for once knock warningly under a dense cover, they sought to drown it in the earthly.

One frenzy after another seized the human spirit. Had some poison paralyzed it that it could so forget the song of its Spiritual Home? Was it no longer able to recall that wondrous sound, which so strangely makes the heart tremble in secret joy?

When people far from their earthly homeland meet with others of their countrymen, the joy of seeing each other again is often endless, and they are proud of their earthly country. But do they then no longer know that they call yet another Homeland their own, one much more beautiful, much more flourishing? Why do they never speak of *this*, their original Horne, Paradise, why do they not rejoice together over it when they meet down here on the earth-plane during their long journey through the Worlds?

Has the sublime song of Heaven then grown so completely silent in the hearts of men? Does not its melody after all still secretly sing and ring, where seeking men on their long journey truly long for it?

The yearning that slumbers in the core of the soul is only veiled. Does man not mark how the unquenched longing is constantly knocking and exhorting, when he sets out on his travels, when he wishes to journey through the lands, across the seas, when he climbs the mountain peaks, or when inexplicable restlessness comes over him in the hurly-burly of everyday life?

If he bursts these coverings with the purity of true yearning, then he is instantly connected with the eternal power of the spirit. On the path of this connection happiness quietly comes to him, a new great hope dawns in his heart.

He who can constantly keep the connection here on earth has succeeded in mastering life, he is gripped by the great love which is always anxious that his fellow-man should also find the impetus upwards to the Blessed Fields.

But he who seeks the true yearning seeks also atonement, the liberation of himself from all the guilt of past earth-lives. He therewith obliterates the traces of wrong paths which he had followed, and achieves already on earth a high degree of spiritual consciousness.

Thus man will then be firmly anchored in earth-life, and yet able to draw from the full Fount of Heaven. And the more he draws, the more alive becomes that healthy idealism which, within natural limitations, always creates lasting spiritual values, thus building a golden ladder upon which his spirit may finally enter Paradise.

What a miracle will then take place! Unconscious little spirit-sparks went forth from Paradise, and they will return as personalities conscious of themselves; they had already been in the Kingdom of God before, and yet they can see and experience it only after they have allowed their longing for the complete understanding of the Laws of Creation to mature far from home, after there is bestowed upon them, with the attainment of full consciousness, at the same time the knowledge that they are allowed to exist eternally.

Do you hear how an invisible hand glides over the golden strings of the Heavenly Harp, and how more and more loudly it rings and sings the pure, sublime melody, so that the sound may awaken the longing of your spirit, and blessed recollections rise up from the depths? Once more you can so fan your yearning with it that it may burst into flame, scorching everything base that holds you down, and luminous rays may strike your soul.

Then after a long, long time the gates of the Blessed Lands from which you once, slumbering, took the first step will be opened again. You will return on that path by which *those* human spirits may come who did not forget that bell-clear Heavenly Song, and let its last note, which they caught even as they were departing, resound in a jubilant chord.

Therefore make room within yourselves for the true longing, and free your- selves from all petty considerations. May what is great and pure be your wish and goal eternally!

11. THE SECRET OF GRAVITY

The problem of gravity has indeed always been a fascinating and mysterious one, and the search for a solution is still of importance also for the present time. In the forefront of this search is the wish for the neutralization of gravity.

Isaac Newton (1642-1727) went into the problem of gravity very deeply. It is said that he was prompted to do so by an apple falling from a tree. The idea came to him that, like the earth, all bodies might have an attracting quality. He expressed this in his Law of Gravity (Gravitation). In this law the effects were indeed understood and mathematically established, but the question of the *nature* of gravity remained open.

The force with which an object is attracted by the earth is assumed to be that of gravity. As a result of this force all bodies fall in the direction of the earth's center. If their fall is impeded by some obstruction, they exert a pressure on the latter which is described as weight.

If we wish to fathom the nature of gravity, we must look for a new way, which however cannot be followed "from below upwards." After only a short distance this would necessitate a halt at the earthly gross material boundary.

The direction of research must lead from above downwards. In this direction there is only one possible solution. All forces and force-fields manifesting in the World of Matter (i.e. in Subsequent Creation) and constantly renewing themselves have their origin in *one* power alone: *spiritual power*, with its various *gradations*. It is the *root* of all forms of energy!

Now the origin of this one power must not be sought on earth and in its surroundings, but outside of Subsequent Creation, the Material World. This calls for a step upwards, over and beyond the earthly boundary, in order to come to reality, which also offers the solution to the coming about of gravity.

In any progressive research, realms that lie outside the known five senses must be included today in order to advance. Indeed we are unconsciously doing this already. For the discovery and application of physical laws is nothing but the acknowledgement of that invisible power which gives rise to these laws.

Therefore it should not be too difficult to envisage a power that comes from heights which are lighter and more luminous than Subsequent Creation.

These Luminous Heights are in the Spiritual Realm which lies above Subsequent Creation, and at whose lowest boundary is to be found men's Paradise.

The currents emanating from a power-center in the Spiritual Realm force their way over the boundary of the Spiritual Realm, and flow through the parts of Creation lying below it.

To avoid erroneous conceptions, it should be pointed out that these spiritual currents *are not God Himself*, perhaps in the sense of pantheism, but they come only out of the *Radiation* of God. That is an important difference.

Now as soon as these currents have been forced across the boundary of their origin they have, through the magnetic attraction-power peculiar to them, an attracting effect on their alien, non-spiritual surroundings.

On all the animistic, ethereal and gross material planes lying below the Spiritual Realm, these currents on their way downwards attract small particles of these planes from the *loose* substance existing on each one and envelop themselves with them, whereby the radiation changes each time. In the course of this the initially uniform currents divide into innumerable tiny spirit-motes or spirit-particles. In addition the loose substance attracted from the particular plane is simultaneously compressed, which in turn causes it to become heavier and sink further.

We observe the same lawful happening in a different form in the earthly, when the loose substance of mist condenses on bare copper cables under high voltage, or when in the purification of gases the loose particles of dust contained in them are attracted to the high-voltage field of electrodes, thereby forming a denser substance.

Finally the spirit-motes, equipped with several coverings, pass from the Ethereal World, the beyond, into the Gross Material, and here give rise to the formation of elementary particles. The atoms made up of these combine into numerous molecules, and thus constitute the *material substance* of this world, which through the spirit-motes in reality contains spiritual power, thus "energy." But mark well, this spiritual power is but the lowest gradation of the spiritual, and therefore a species different from the human spiritual, which among other things has a greater power of attraction.

In this attracting, compressing and sinking is expressed what we call the Law of Gravity, which manifests in the same way throughout all Subsequent Creation. It is called Subsequent Creation because it took form subsequent to the Spiritual Creation. It is a coarse reflection thereof.

Expressed differently, this means: The distancing of the enveloped spirit-particles from the spiritual power-center in the Spiritual Realm brings about the beginning of the Law of Gravity. In this connection the extent of the distance depends on the heaviness of the enveloped spirit-particles. The heavier they are, the further they must distance themselves from the magnetic power-center of the Spiritual Realm, with which they always remain connected by way of radiation, whatever the distance.

In accordance with the Law of Gravity, on its journey from Paradise to the earth, man's spirit-germ must envelop itself with the respective loose species of the intermediate planes through which it passes, right down to the earthly gross material body as the outermost of the coverings. The finer coverings form the soul, with the human spirit as core. Without these coverings as transitions it would not be in a position to enter the earth-plane and to live and work there.

From all this it emerges that the spiritual, as soon as it is freed from its coverings, must return to the Spiritual Realm, which is not subject to the heaviness known to us. Just as the human spirit is able to enter into Paradise only when it has severed the last of its alien coverings. —

Through the attraction of the power streaming from the Ethereal World into the Gross Material World arises the condition which we designate as gravity, in that the power compresses finely-distributed particles of gross material substance into matter, which sinks because of the heaviness thus produced.

But likewise all the particles of substance that lie between the World of Gross Matter and that of Fine Matter are borne along by the power streaming at a uniform rate as it penetrates into the World of Gross Matter, and presses them downwards in the direction of the earth.

Accordingly the idea that the earth as a very large mass must have an attracting influence on smaller masses is only *one* possibility. But it could equally well be that in reality the *streaming-in of the radiation-power from the cosmos*, and with it the pressing towards one another of the separate masses through this power- current, *is the cause of gravitation!* This obviously effects the pressing downwards of matter in the direction of the earth.

Thus also a pendulum would not necessarily be drawn downwards through the attraction-power of the earth, but through the pressure of rays coming from above.

In 1959 the suggestion was made at the International Congress on Satellites and Rockets that the definition of the concept of gravitation (gravity) should be altered, to the effect that no longer should the attraction-power of the earth but rather the *repulsion-power* of the cosmos be accepted as the cause of gravitation. This opinion already comes nearer to the explanation given here.

Nor must we forget that the power described was in existence even *before* the earth came into being. Consequently the earth has only issued from this power and therefore cannot be the origin of this power but only its product, upon which the superior power continues to stream and exert pressure.

In the years 1912 and 1913 the decrease in the supposed radioactive radiation of the earth at increasing heights was to be measured by means of rising balloons. In the course of this, people were astonished to find a very intense *increase* in the radiations instead of the expected *decrease*. These radiations, however, did not come from the earth but out of the cosmos! Thus *ultra-radiation* was discovered, a cosmic *radiation* not known until then, with a very high power of penetration.

This cosmic radiation is constant, that is permanent and unchanging. In it occur particles with extraordinarily strong *energies*, which can reach any place whatsoever on the surface of the earth from all directions!

Is it not then obvious that, in this energy-invested cosmic radiation which penetrates into the earth's atmosphere from the depths of the Universe, we suspect ramifications of the currents of enveloped spirit-particles?

It is they which form the elementary particles whose core is energy, thus spiritual power, which presumably in the disintegration of radium manifests in the gamma rays as electro-magnetic radiation.* Only this energy, together with the animistic forces of Nature, animates and moves gross material substance, which in itself is without life!

In this cosmic radiation could also be found the key to the opening up of new energies!

Man never has the power or the strength to neutralize the whole power of gravity working in Subsequent Creation. On the other hand, it will at some time later be possible for him, through the wise use of the Creation-Laws, to bring about a weightlessness on earth in *limited* cases.

In so doing he will logically follow the reverse way, and will have to loosen and refine the previously dense, united particles of substance. An indication of what direction the search could take in this is given us by the obvious application of the example of a hot-air balloon. Here the molecules of air are heated, and thereby driven apart. The heated air is not as heavy as the atmosphere outside, and thus allows the balloon to rise. This sinks back to the earth when the same density, or rather heaviness, as that of the outside air is reached again inside through cooling off. For density and heaviness have a causal connection.

---

* See: "The Secret of Atomic (Nuclear) Energy" in Part I.

Certainly the peoples of ancient, bygone cultures had more knowledge of cosmic forces than we have today. Ancient traditions tell of the neutralization of gravity in men and objects. In the case of large constructions it is said to have been possible to move the heaviest stones into place without effort. In this connection we recall, for example, the stone blocks of the pyramids, or the massive squared stones of the Inca buildings, weighing up to 200 tons. Although there are enough theories about the building methods of those days, it has still to this day remained completely unexplained just how the stone blocks were moved and fitted together.

In the book *Lao-Tse*, one of the book-series of Grail Foundation Press, we find the following sentence in the description of the building of the Temple: "Precious stones from distant quarries were brought along with the aid of animistic helpers."

In the volume *Ephesus* of the same book-series it says: "While the women were engaged in preparing the meal and tending the animals, the men fetched trees from the forests to build their dwellings, hauling them along with the powers of giants. Hjalfdar knew how to summon and make use of special forces, so that the building of their dwellings advanced rapidly."

In Atlantis, too, the nature-beings helped with heavy work through their colossal powers ("Atlantis," *Past Eras Awaken*, Vol. II).

What kind of powers could these have been, which long, long ago were *consciously* used to transport heavy stones and timber, and in other heavy work? Apart from mechanical aids, one involuntarily thinks in this connection of the neutralization of gravity, or rather of a counteraction to gravity through the use of certain forces of Nature. To accept this is by no means so far-fetched today, in this age of atoms and radiations.

There is a direct reference to gravity in the book *From Past Millennia*, in a prophecy thousands of years old, which points to the present time and the near future. There it says: "Age-old wisdom which, foreseeing, sang of this time is becoming truth. Only now does man grasp the treasures of the earth, and how to apply them to bring blessing. He is learning anew to control the powers of the Universe. - Man discovers afresh the eternal Laws of Nature. Through wise instruction he is learning to neutralize the gravity of bodies. To what is perfect he gives new forms, everything strives upwards."

Some attempts to neutralize the mysterious power of gravity have also been made in more recent times. By evoking a certain vibration, by producing anti-gravitational fields and screening devices, through a metal alloy which renders the invisible cosmic radiations ineffective in a certain direction, or by electro-gravitation. There is also mention of laser beams, which could be used to neutralize gravity.

In the end all attempts to neutralize gravity on earth are probably based on effecting certain structural changes in the elementary particles of the atoms.

Already in 1927 Abd-ru-shin, Author of The Grail Message, *In the Light of Truth*, explained in the journal "Der Ruf" ("The Call"), numbers 5, 6 and 7, the coming-into-being and effect of the spiritual power-currents which give rise to gravity. His explanations were published again later in the book *Fragenbeantwortungen* (1953, Vomperberg/Tyrol and Stuttgart; published in English as *Questions and Answers* in 1972).

On the basis of this revolutionary Grail Knowledge there arises a totally different concept of the cause and effect of the mysterious power of gravity, a concept which has been rendered here in broad outline to provide a *stimulus*.

Progressive science and research can accordingly proceed from entirely different assumptions, resulting from the *Law of Gravity* in relation to the no less important Creation-Laws of *Reciprocal Action* (Cause and Effect) and of the *Attraction of Homogeneous Species*.

Undreamed-of progress can be made with these new recognitions *when the time is right!*

12. WHAT IS TIME?

With Creation there also came into existence space and time. Nothing in it is spaceless and timeless. Therefore in the whole of Creation there is a concept of space and time. For Creation is a work, and as such limited. To this work belongs inseparably that time in which spaces have formed.

Whereas Creation came into being only progressively, that is by stages in Creation-planes, the Divine Kingdom lying above it has always been there, because it is inseparably connected with God, the Prime Source of all life. But God is from eternity to eternity, without beginning and without end.

The concept of the Eternity of God is inconceivable to the human spirit. But the Work of God, Creation, which issued from His Radiation with the Words "Let there be Light", can be grasped by the spirit of man, and therefore also the concept of space and time pertaining to Creation.

Creation comprises the *Spiritual Realms*, in the lowest of which the human spirit has its origin, and the Creation formed in the image of the Spiritual Realm, *Subsequent Creation*. To this belong the divisions of the *Ethereal World*, which we call the beyond, and of the *World of Gross Matter*, to which our earth belongs.

A faint inner urge causes the unconscious human spirit-germs to leave the Spiritual Realm, so that in lower-lying planes or Worlds of Matter they will achieve consciousness of themselves in the struggle for existence, namely through the foreign influences assailing them.

Even though there is one concept of space and time for the whole of Creation, it nevertheless forms differently on each plane of Creation, according to the nature of the plane. At the same time the concept of space and time becomes narrower with the increasing distance from the Spiritual Realm, through the ever-increasing density of the region concerned. Linked with this is the ever-decreasing ability to absorb experiences.

This is the reason why there is no absolute, that is no independent concept of space and time in the whole of Creation. Space and time cannot exist by themselves alone, they must always stand in relation to things which are in space, as for example the stars in the universe.

This is also expressed in Albert Einstein's general theory of relativity. It explains, for instance, that everything in the universe is interdependent; there is nothing absolute in it, everything has a relation, that is a connection with everything else.

From this we can further deduce that in the final analysis the whole of Creation is dependent on the Creator Himself.

The concept of time thus depends in each case on the individual planes of Creation, and man must inwardly perceive it in different ways according to the plane on which he sojourns, or with which plane he as an earthman is linked.

On earth for instance, because of the density of his brain, man needs the longest period of time to receive and live through a number of impressions. In the beyond the period of time for this is already significantly shorter because here the brain, from which thinking and intellect develop, no longer exists, and only direct experiencing in the inner perception of the spirit is still decisive.

Therefore the human spirit experiences the ethereal time-concepts of the beyond differently from the earthly gross material ones. This difference is shown also in mediumistic messages. As a result of the accentuated over-development of the day-brain (large brain) for thousands of years, it is rarely possible to apply ethereal, supra-earthly conceptions of time to the earthly in such a way that, for example, in the case of predictions the earthly time of fulfillment can be accurately specified.

We experience the difference in time also in dreams, when during sleep the connection between soul (the spirit with its finer coverings) and physical body is loosened. Then a whole lifetime can unroll before our inner eyes in seconds or minutes.

In the Spiritual Realm itself the experiencing in a single earth-day is then as great as on earth in a thousand years.

On this ratio is based also the statement of time in the Revelation of John, which was given from a high spiritual standpoint. The earthly periods of time are expressed in "spiritual" days. When it says: "three days and an half" (11, 11), this means approximately 3,500 earth-years. This is the length of time between the earth-life of Moses and the present Cosmic Turning-Point. In the German Lutheran version the same earthly time is rendered in another passage of the Revelation by the description: "a time, and two times, and half a time" (12, 14).

But man has lost the knowledge of these eternal things. In place of the inner perception, which alone is able to maintain the connection with the origin of the human spirit, he put the all-questioning intellect.

He therewith suppressed the true inner perceiving of time which he brought with him from his spiritual homeland. The real concept of time was pushed aside, because it cannot be grasped intellectually.

Through this also the many philosophical teachings, which in spite of all their sagacity are not in a position to recognize the ultimate meaning of time, because it is of a spiritual nature, have hitherto proved unavailing.

Unconsciously modern man indicates the loss of the true time-concept when he says "he has no time." By this he demonstrates not only the earthly lack of time, but also the want of a higher understanding of time.

The *natural* narrowing-down of the concept of time, which results from the distancing from the Spiritual Realm, must not mislead man into covering the spiritual time-concept with earthly time-concepts.

We do indeed need the concept of time bound to the earthly as an aid for the passing of events, for progress and order on earth, but over and above this transient arrangement of time into years, months, weeks and hours, we must not forget the imperishable value of "time" which can be grasped only with the inner perception of the spirit.

How small in comparison is the perceptive faculty of the intellect, which belongs to the earthly brain! It is no longer capable of grasping even the happening in the millions of years of the earth's development. This is possible for the spirit alone.

When the spirit really bestirs itself we sense very well that there is yet another concept of time than the earthly one.

We can also say that time appears to us according to how we move inwardly. In this connection the ability and strength of receiving and experiencing, which depend on the maturity of the spirit, form the measure for the passing of our time.

How often have we already experienced in our earth-life that the days were much too short and time seemed to fly past. On the other hand there is also stand-still and retrogression if a wrong volition of the intellect will not allow the soul to soar upwards.

This phenomenon of different perceptions of time has been under investigation for some time. In the course of this it was established that man also has an "inner clock," "soul clock" which often does not agree with the earthly clock.

It is known, for example, that with the young the inner perception of time is extended, whereas with older people there is the prevailing inner sensation that time is moving ever faster. Or let us think of the different experiencing of time on our holidays, when the first days pass more slowly, those in the middle normally, and the last ones much too quickly.

Speed also, the relationship between distance and time, gives rise to different inner sensations of time. According to Einstein time is not something absolute. To measure it a standpoint, a reference system, is always needed. This can be a railway train traveling at a *constant* speed, in which we are sitting. A train traveling alongside us gives the impression that it is standing still. But if the other train is traveling more slowly, we have the impression that our train is traveling faster. If, however, the other train travels faster, then we think we are going more slowly. Thus three different impressions during a *constant* speed of our train!

Not only has man an inner or rather a biological clock. It is also to be found in Nature; but there it is moved by other currents of power. It determines for example the exact beginning of the flights of migratory birds in autumn from northern to southern latitudes.

Sometimes the precision of the biological clock becomes disastrous, as in the case of a species of wild geese whose habitat is in the steppes of Western Siberia. Owing to some kind of environmental influences they have shifted their fixed quarters further south. Their inner clock, however, has not reacted to this change of place. With unfailing precision it drives the geese at the same time as always to set out for their winter quarters, which lie 3,500 kilometers away in India.

But it happens too early, because in the more southerly region the geese start their molting season later, and are not yet in a condition to fly when the great migratory excitement seizes them and it is time for departure.

What do the geese do now? At the time appointed by the biological clock, they set out *on foot* in vast numbers. Thus in about ten days they travel approximately 150 km, until they reach a lake on which they can recuperate. Meanwhile their feathers have grown so far that only now can the normal flight proceed over the remaining distance. During their march on foot they suffer great losses through exhaustion and beasts of prey. —

But let us return to the explanation of the original concept of time. Man has lost it, and this loss is particularly marked in the inversion of standpoints. Earthman regards himself as the static point, in that he lets time pass him by. He speaks of times which change, and he believes that time moves on.

However, if time has existed from the beginning of Creation, if the human spirit issues from the eternal time and can return thither again, then it is not possible for time to move past him.

Reality shows an entirely different picture, which compels us to change our thinking: Time stands still! However we, the human beings, hurry towards it, move within it. For time is unchangeable and intransient. Only the forms change, just as the spirit of man always remains the same, whereas the forms of his physical body change continually.

Just as in general the entire Subsequent Creation is subject to an unceasing "dying and coming into existence", and only the Laws that bring this about are eternally the same!

Gottfried Keller divined the reality when he said in his poem, "*Time standeth still*":

Time moves not, it standeth still,
We pass on through it.

This verse, which could never be properly explained, will now be better understood by us. And another verse in the same poem strikes us:

A drop of morning dew sparkles
In a ray of sunlight;
A day can be a pearl
And a century nothing.

This could be a comparison between the experiencing in higher planes in the time of one earth-day, which is like a pearl, and the experiencing on earth during a century. —

Time is closely linked with spiritual Light-Power which, coming from the highest starting-point of the Primordial Spiritual Realm, fills all the spiritual parts of Creation lying below it, and thence radiates into the World of Matter, into Subsequent Creation, as well.

Thus also outside its spiritual homeland, Paradise, the human spirit moves in this Power, which in time is eternal. He swims in it, so to speak, becomes more or less strongly conscious of it, depending on the degree of his ability to receive impressions and experiences, and draws from this Power the eternal values it holds in readiness. He is even able *already on earth* to find the experience of Truth in this Power, because it comes from the Truth.

True time therefore is also eternally the same in the past, present and future, because it rests in the Spiritual Power which streams to us out of Eternity, and knows no earthly limitations.

In earthly life, on the other hand, past, present and future are perceived separately in the context of time and space, and only a fraction of the wealth of spiritual happening in these three sections of time can be experienced by earthmen. This is due to their dense material covering, which brings with it narrowness of comprehension.

The spiritual power indelibly records every experience and happening in the great Book of Creation, and preserves it. Nothing of it is lost, and it is possible to make proclamations from it at any time.

242

We find the best examples of this in the works *From Past Millennia* and in *Past Eras Awaken*, as well as in the accounts of the Forerunners (Grail Foundation Press).

In all these books it is clearly and distinctly stated how the blessed spirit of the seer opens itself to the Power in order to draw from its records and collections for the past, present and future, and to reproduce from them in words that which the Light allows to be given to mankind at the time of the fulfillments. —

In conclusion, let us once more be reminded that we, the pilgrims through the deep vale of the World of Matter, are not those at rest whom time passes by like landscapes at the window of a railway train, but *on the contrary those who are in motion.*

The way through the World of Matter of Subsequent Creation was not granted to us so that we should cling to earthly things and make them our idols, but for the sake of recognition. On this journey we are meant to grow and mature in spirit, so that this can one day leave the dense sphere of the World of Matter in order to hasten fully conscious in the Ray of the Luminous Power towards the Spiritual Realm, where space and time eternally form a complete whole in the Living Power of the Creator.

13. GARDEN GNOMES

If our eyes were suddenly opened to enable us to see into the inner working of Nature, we should be lost in amazement and wonder.

Everywhere we should discover the forces active in Nature to be living beings, who take part eagerly and conscientiously in the coming into being and passing away in the vast realms of Nature.

All these small and great nature-beings, whom we may also call the small and great animistic beings*, have human forms, because, apart from their animistic core as basic species, they have within them a little of that which man bears within him as the core: the spiritual, which stipulates the human form.

If we could look more closely, we should also finally discover the original of the garden gnome of which approximate images, more or less well produced, adorn many gardens.

This glimpse behind the curtain of the beyond is of course possible only for such human beings as have the gift for it, thus who are clairvoyant. It is they who at some time or other have drawn the figures of the dwarfs or gnomes, and passed them on.

The little nature-beings, to whom the elves, as well as the nixies, salamanders, sylphs and so on belong, had already been active on earth long before man set foot on it for the first time. Without their participation there would be no mountains, meadows, rivers, lakes and seas.

The whole of Nature is animated by these faithful servants of God, who carry out His Will and Commandments most accurately in all things.

Since they swing selflessly in the Will of God they can neither be malicious nor do wrong. Only men have imputed such things to them.

All over the earth, from ancient and also more recent times, there are many traditions about the nature-beings. They are mentioned in the Bible, for example in the Gospel of Mark (4, 35-41), where it says: "And Jesus arose, and rebuked the wind, and said unto the sea, Peace, be still. And the wind ceased, and there was a great calm."

This simple, Biblical description expresses nothing other than that Jesus spoke to those nature-beings who are active in the elements of air and water.

---

* You can read about the great animistic beings, also called "gods" and "goddesses", in the essay "The Virtues" in Part II.

Of Paracelsus, the famous physician and student of Nature in the Middle Ages, tradition has it that even as a boy he was able to see the little nature-beings at work in the lead mine at Kärnten. His father attended the miners there as a doctor.

The gnomes shared with him much knowledge of their activity, explaining the mysterious forces in flowers, metals and minerals, and how they are to be used for health and for the healing of illnesses. Later Paracelsus published a pamphlet on his experience with the water, earth, fire and air beings.

The people of former times saw and heard these beings much more than is the case today. It was a blessed working together, a joyful giving and receiving in helping and supporting love.

But for a long time now, with a few exceptions, men have through their ever-increasing materialistic attitude lost the connection with the helpers in the beyond. They were finally banished by them to the realm of fairy tales and fables.

Their real forms were rendered ever less true to nature, and the already-existing knowledge of their activity became superficial and merged in fantastic stories, which hardly correspond any longer to reality.

Last but not least, during certain times the knowledge of the nature-beings was forcibly suppressed as heresy.

Nevertheless the nature-beings still exist even today, in full activity. They direct and guide, tend and protect, foster and nourish, form and unite. On the astral plane they create wonderful prototypes and models for the gross matter of this earth.

Or they take part in the great flights of migratory birds, which contain so much that is mysterious to men, in which sun, stars and magnetic fields are indeed outwardly important; but behind it stand the animistic servants, controlling and helping.

They warn also of coming natural events, to which warnings animals are particularly sensitive. This, however, has nothing to do with either instinct or the sixth sense, but the animals simply see the nature-beings and recognize their warnings, because owing to their related species they are more receptive to them than men.

Animals then pass on the warnings to men through conspicuous behavior, by which the lives of many have already been saved in this way.

In the Book of Numbers (22, 21-35) such a vision is described very expressively. The ass on which the Prophet Balaam was riding suddenly saw before it a higher being, an angel of the Lord holding a naked sword in his hand, and refused to go any further.

At first Balaam did not see the angel and struck the resisting ass three times, until his eyes were opened. Then he could also see the angel, and recognize that he himself was on the point of doing something wrong.

In their activity the nature-beings work with rays, which they bind, combine, lead towards and direct away from, and which so to speak are their instruments. Thus the little master-builders are also active in the coming into being of matter from atoms.

It will be a blessed and peaceful time when men are again able to take up the connection with the small and great beings of Nature. Clairvoyance is not absolutely necessary for this. It is enough if the human spirits through constant, genuine effort awaken in themselves the faculty of divining, and in their *inner perception* try to draw near to these beings.

Trust and a pure heart are what is needed for this. He who only wants to satisfy his curiosity or stimulate his imagination will find no connection.

But the servants of God still mourn over the human spirits who like to know everything better, whose arrogance and derision have already had to become silent in connection with many other intangible things, when that which previously could not be seen was in the meantime suddenly made visible through instruments that had been refined.

Certainly there are still people today who are able to see the nature-beings. But for the most part they remain silent about it, and keep their experiences to themselves, unless for once they meet people who are open for it, to whom their knowledge is of spiritual benefit. –

According to these explanations it is surely not so far-fetched to regard the "garden gnomes" as symbols of the actually-existing little nature-beings, who also help human beings in manifold ways. But should the plaster gnomes be an inducement to concern ourselves more closely with the lovable living beings, then even they would fulfil a task not hitherto intended for them.

For it is remarkable how the use of these artificial garden gnomes has become so widespread in many countries. Perhaps this is also an indication of the fact that the beings of Nature are still quite strongly anchored in popular belief. But with an earnest volition, out of belief can one day grow again a knowledge of the realm of Nature in its full vitality.

For Nature is nothing other than the natural unfolding of the activity of the animistic servants. But for man Nature with all its animistic working is an indispensable step in his spiritual development on earth. The more he is linked with Nature, the sooner is he able to begin his spiritual ascent.

14. THE DISEASE OF CANCER

This terrible disease is rightly referred to as the "scourge of humanity." It is becoming ever more widespread, and up to the present time it still has not been possible to bring it under control.

Millions of people are stricken with it. Tens of thousands of scientists and medical men are striving to discover the cause of this disease. Millions are spent on cancer research every year. Experiments are constantly carried out in laboratories in order to find a solution.

However many cancer-agents there are, surely all must have something in common, which allows the healthy cell to become a cancerous cell.

Therefore the *fundamental* process must be sought. In doing so, we must include those beyond-earthly spheres which we are in a position to grasp only with the inner perception of our spirit.

First of all let us consider the cells of which the human body is composed.

At the beginning of the embryonic development there are no differing cells. Only during the development of the growing child's body do the cells differentiate from one another and form the individual organs of the body.

Now how do the cells come to unite into different organs? What forces regulate them in such a way that out of them are formed, for instance, the heart, the brain, the liver, the lymphatic system? Who provides the information for this?

Forces of nature that have taken on form, which we can also call nature-beings, are at work here. On the astral plane, which lies nearest to the World of Gross Matter, to the earthly, they create the astral body as a model, as a prototype, after which the child's body is only *subsequently* formed.

In this astral body, which is of finer matter, the whole design of the body, after which the corresponding cells then unite into organs and so on, must therefore be pre-formed or "programmed" by way of radiation. The astral body or the astral cloak is an important connecting-link between spirit, soul and body during the whole of earth-life. With physical death it disintegrates.

There is a good indication of the existence of the astral body: the *phantom-pains* which occur in a limb that no longer exists!

Why? Because the astral body, which has the form of the physical body, is not damaged when a limb is severed. It retains the limb severed from the physical body! Hence the pains in the missing physical limb, which really make themselves felt on the still existing astral limb, hitherto described as phantom because it is not visible to the physical eye. Phantom-pains cannot be without foundation but must have a body, where *they* can be *locally* felt.

Until now the often unbearable phantom-pains could mostly be treated only for a limited time with pain-killing drugs. But of late good results are being achieved with acupuncture, originating in China, which is applied to sound limbs. Through this phantom-pains can often be absent for months.

But let us return to the cells. It has been stated earlier that the whole physical structure is pre-formed by the nature-beings on the astral plane. This also includes the building-stones of the individual organs, the body cells with all their components.

Many of these components have been investigated by science. These include for instance the nucleus, and the protoplasm surrounding the nucleus. In the nucleus are to be found the chromosomes, in which the genetic information or "heritage" is stored. All processes in the cell, which include above all the important cellular respiration, are regulated from within the nucleus.

Now there are yet other components of the cell, which are not visible to the physical eye. To these belong for instance minute spirit-particles, which stream from spiritual power-centers lying far above the Paradise of men right down to us, into the World of Gross Matter, where they give rise to the formation of elementary particles and atoms.

They are of course also to be found in the cell molecules, which are composed of atoms, and they have contact with the spiritual radiation of the human spirit incarnated in the physical body. For this reason they deserve special attention in the investigation into the cause of cancer.

Today the radiation of the human spirit is greatly weakened and dimmed through the predominantly materialistic attitude of earthmen, which is directed to this world. Therefore the radiation is hardly able any longer to exert an animating influence on the functions of the cells and organs, in order to achieve a "radiant health."

If we now imagine that to this generally weakened spiritual radiation there is further added a physical damage caused by long-lasting irritation of cells through toxins, then the structure of the cell molecules will be so altered that the regulation of the cells is greatly impeded. They can no longer receive the right information. This results in faulty regulation, and the oxygen supply gradually fails. As a consequence the cells begin to ferment, and together with substances of the nutrient fluid form an unrestrainedly increasing growth: the *cancerous tumor* as the *final* stage of a prolonged spiritual and physical disturbance.

The degeneration and unbridled growth of the affected cells also permeates even the surrounding healthy parts of the body. At the same time there is in addition the danger of parts of the cancer reaching distant areas of the body with the lymphatic or bloodstream, and giving rise to similar cancerous formations (metastases) there.

But the prolonged irritation of the cells through toxins calls for reference to one physical organ which should be given special attention in the investigation of cancer: *the liver!*

It is a miraculous work in itself. Its task is so many-sided that it can be described as an extraordinary organ. Apart from its activity as the most important detoxification-center, it helps in multifarious ways with metabolism, among other things.

Therefore its disorder always affects the *whole* body profoundly. On the other hand the liver is capable of regenerating its own damaged cells, and even of rebuilding missing cells.

With normal activity everything is carefully converted, sifted and filtered in the liver. In the course of this toxins are broken down, made harmless and secreted. Hence the liver needs a constant good blood circulation. A healthy liver ensures pure blood.

If, however, it becomes diseased, it is no longer in a position to break down the various toxins sufficiently; these will penetrate into the circulation, causing chronic conditions of irritation in the cell-tissue, and so create the soil for cancer.

Consequently with preventive measures and with cancerous diseases the toxins forming in the body in the process of metabolism, and the toxic substances entering it from outside must not be overlooked, in connection with which above all the kind of nutrition and the metabolism play an important part, the more so if through heredity there is already a tendency towards cancer. But also environmental factors which have a direct cancer-evoking influence from outside on the cells, as for example chemical substances and foreign rays (X-rays, radioactivity, earth-rays), have to be taken into account.

According to present-day knowledge the resistance-potential of the body cells to cancer is limited. Therefore efforts are being made to discover ways and means of stimulating the body to render cancer harmless, rather than nourishing it.

But here again it should be remembered that the liver is the most important organ in *cancer-resistance!*

Already in 1929 Abd-ru-shin, Author of The Grail Message, *In the Light of Truth,* wrote in the journal "Der Ruf" ("The Call"), publication for all progressive knowledge, number 13, under the "Medical Section," Cancer Research:

"Any cancerous growth is conditioned by the incapacity and insufficient activity of the liver! This must be borne in mind. A healthy liver with a really normal activity does not permit any kind of cancer to develop. Therefore among young people a correspondingly sensible way of living should already be strictly observed. Even among those already ill, the emphasis should be placed mainly on that! With the recovery of the liver the power of the illness is broken, no matter where it is located."

This text was again published in 1953 in the book *Fragenbeantwortungen* (Grail Foundation Press - English edition - "Questions and Answers". 1972). In a lecture given by Abd-ru-shin in 1935, which was published in German in 1950 and in English in 1959 (Vol. III of The Grail Message, *The Destroyed Bridge*) he mentions once again the importance of the liver:

"Quite apart from the smokers themselves, having to breathe in such tobacco smoke hampers the normal development of many an organ in infants and children, especially the necessary firmness and strengthening of the liver, which is particularly important for every person, because when functioning in the right and healthy manner it can prevent the establishment of a cancerous center as the surest and best means of resistance to this plague."

Meantime this recognition has spread further. Thus Dr. A. Vogel, Teuffen, Switzerland, writes in his book *Der kleine Doktor* (*The Little Doctor*, 1973 Edition, published privately):

"The liver is the most important barrier in the fight against cancer. As long as this miraculous laboratory is functioning well, a cancerous degeneration of the cells cannot take place. Since the liver thereby occupies a key position in the fight against cancer, we should seek to maintain it for ourselves as an efficient barrier because, as has been stated before, cancer will then be given no opportunity to develop. "

In his book *Die Leber als Regulator der Gesundheit* (*The Liver as Regulator of Health* 1975, A. Vogel, Teuffen, Switzerland), Dr. Vogel mentions the following in the chapter on "Cancer and the Liver":

"On one of my trips to America I had a discussion with one of the best-known cancer researchers, who on the basis of his many years of experience confirmed to me that no cancer patient had yet been brought to his clinic who did not have a disturbed functioning of the liver and pancreas. Since other cancer researchers have also expressed similar views about these connections, it can in fact be said: no cancer without a malfunctioning of the liver and pancreas.

Dr. H. Anemueller, in his book *Gesundheit durch sinnvolle Ernibrung und Diat* (*Health through Sensible Nutrition and Diet*, 1963, Paracelsus Publishing Co.), explains:

"It should be borne in mind that in every case of cancer the liver is damaged, and its performance greatly impaired. For this reason alone the food-intake must be Limited. The restoration of a normal liver function is one of the most important objectives of the dietetic treatment of cancer."

The English researcher Caspar Blond, M.D., wrote in the medical journal *Hippocrates* (Vol. 11, 1956) to this effect:

"Cancer is the result of a chronically progressive liver-insufficiency. There is no doubt that food poisons play a part in this." (Liver-insufficiency means an inadequate working capacity of the liver.)

The importance of the liver is also shown by its significance in the interrelations between spirit, soul and body. It is more subject than other digestive glands to the influence of the frame of mind. Not for nothing are there such (German) popular sayings as: "A louse has run over his liver," when someone is irritable or annoyed, or "anger gnawed at his liver", thus damaging his health. And one who is extremely irate "spews venom and bile," which is produced by the liver. Even the Babylonians had a greeting: "May your liver become smooth!" This meant: "Do not be angry, moderate your anger."

The word hypochondriac (a sufferer from morbid depression) is related to "hypochondrium," by which is meant the area under the arch of the ribs, thus the region of the liver, which points to the fact that this disease is associated with the liver.

Not for nothing has the word *liver* an identity of sound with *life*!

But the majority of men have more and more distanced themselves from real life and thus also from Nature. Man is no longer linked with Nature!

Therefore he must again become alive in spirit, and a necessary step towards this is *Nature*! Liberation from the hitherto-existing unnatural way of life lies in observing the Laws of Nature. —

But man should give more consideration to his physical body right from the earliest years, and not only when pain makes itself felt. He should earn the foundation for a natural way of living in future, and above all practice a *wise moderation*. This refers for example to *right nutrition, breathing, movement, personal hygiene and balance between work and rest*. For after all the physical body is the most important instrument which the Creator has entrusted to us for our *spiritual* development, the goal of which is not the earth, but the Paradise of the human spirits that lies far above it.

But more than anything man must not forget Nature when he is ill, and must remember the old Biblical word which still applies today: "God hath created medicines out of the earth, And let not a discerning man reject them" (Sirach 38, 4). The whole of Nature, with its manifold healing powers, gives him the best helps and remedies for health and disease — even for the disease of cancer.

However, the remedies alone are not enough. In all illnesses it is necessary for the spirit of man himself to *help with* his recovery, in order to ensure a permanent cure. If he merely lets the remedies do their work, the recovery will not last long, since the cause of it has not been removed. In the final analysis the cause lies with the human spirit, with its *free will*, with which he *himself creates* his environment as well as *his diseases*, regardless of whether this happens only in this earth-life, or whether dim threads of fate from earlier lives cause diseases hidden in his physical heritage to manifest.

But just as man creates the diseases for himself, so is he likewise in a position to do away with them by giving up his materialistic attitude, and humbly directing his gaze upwards, to Luminous Heights.

Only from thence come strengthening radiations which allow his spirit to glow. In its once more pure and powerful radiation his sick body can then recover its health, supported by the healing gifts of Nature.

But if it is already too late for an effective cure, it is a comfort and a help to know that *only the earthly cloak* can be diseased, never the spirit, which with its finer coverings forms the soul.

Also the sick person can so purify his spirit that at his earthly death, freed from the burden of the diseased physical body, he may joyfully rise upwards into those Blessed Fields which, far from earthly pain and earthly suffering, exist in the Light of Divine Grace!

15. THE BLOOD AS IDENTITY CARD

At the beginning of the 20th century the four blood groups A, B, AB and O were discovered. Since then many details concerning the blood and its composition have become known to science. These include also the discovery of further blood group systems, and the establishing of blood formulas for racial groups, families and individuals.

According to the most recent research, connections are also revealed between blood groups and diseases. Thus one group is less susceptible to certain diseases than another. In plagues the one blood group is likewise less at risk, while it is harder for the other group to overcome them.

Scientists are said to be even now certain that with further refinement of the differences they will be in a position in the foreseeable future to determine a personal blood formula for every human being, so that it can be proven that one day there will hardly be two persons whose formulas correspond in every detail.

This has led to the observation that the individual composition of a person's blood could be used on an identity card, because this composition is clearly adjusted to the person of the holder.

The assumption that every human being must have his own blood formula, which reflects only his particular nature, is right.

It is based on a process that has hitherto remained unrecognized, and which was made known only by Abd-ru-shin in his Grail Message, in the lecture "The Mystery of the Blood."

With his explanation, *the spirit forms the human blood,* he gave a completely new, fundamental recognition.

That it is the spirit that forms the blood is shown by the fact that the blood exists only while the spirit is present in the body. Only with the entry of the spirit into the developing child's body about the middle of pregnancy does the blood form in the small body and begin to circulate.

When the spirit leaves the body at earthly death, thus when earthman "gives up the ghost", the blood is no longer there either. The arteries are empty of blood. The blood has lost its form, and only congealed residues of blood are still in the veins.

Now since every spirit — with its finer coverings called soul — has its *free will* from its origin, the spiritual development is different with each human being. No two persons are alike in this. Every human being develops and uses his abilities and qualities in a way differing from that of his fellow-man. Therefore to place men on the same level and make them equal is contrary to the Laws of Creation.

Hence every spirit also forms its blood in a different composition, in the way peculiar to itself, so that if an exact analysis should one day be possible, the personal blood formulas will never be identical, just as in the case of finger-prints.

Therefore it is understandable that at all times more has been suspected in the blood than only the fulfillment of physical functions. There was always a divining of the interrelations between spirit and blood, and many sayings and expressions indicate how closely connected the blood is with the spirit.

Thus, for example, for something to "pass into one's flesh and blood" (German) means to have assured mastery of something, to absorb something completely, it becomes second nature, as it were. This includes not only comprehending with the "fleshly" brain, but also grasping with the spirit, which is figuratively indicated by the blood.

The reaction of spiritual expressions instantly affects the blood, when it drains from the face with agitation, when horror makes it curdle, when someone turns crimson with shame, or when a person's "blood runs cold," thus when he is very afraid.

All these confirm the recognition that the spirit forms the blood.

The further investigation of the blood and the knowledge of its real purpose have undreamed-of consequences for a future healthy development of the human spirit on earth.

16. MECHANISMS OF EVIL

At all times there have been people who were able to see and read thoughts. But if thoughts can be seen, then they must represent something, and have content and form. However these forms are of finer matter than the coarse earthly. They can therefore be perceived only by those human beings whose inner eye is opened for it, thus who are clairvoyant.

Similarly the helpers in the beyond can read our thoughts, and make use of this possibility to help us, to give us advice and to appeal to our conscience. In special cases they can even employ the radiations of pure thought-channels, to work through these right into the coarse earthly.

One need not be clairvoyant, however, to be convinced of the reality of thoughts. There are still other indications of their existence: the transference of thoughts from one person to another without giving utterance to the thoughts. We read about it from time to time, or have experienced for ourselves how thoughts which we direct at a particular person, which are "intended" for him, are picked up by him, as it afterwards turned out. In this connection distance plays no part; just as little does the fact that the people may be inside houses at the time of these transferences. Thoughts are simply lighter and finer than gross matter, and therefore are able to penetrate walls in the same way as radio-waves.

For a long time now man has been in a position to measure thought-waves. Another proof that they have substance, the radiations of which can be determined by means of the finest instruments.

Real thoughts are glowed through by the inner perception of the spirit. Otherwise they are cold and feeble.

They arise through the activity of the frontal brain (large brain). From the thoughts in turn is formed intellect. As the brain belongs to the earthly, is part of the perishable body, it likewise ceases to exist at death. Accordingly it is no longer possible for man to think and to use his intellect in the beyond. In their place appear other means of communication.

For this reason the intellect is only able to grasp earthly things. Anything that goes beyond this is no longer "understood" by it. One is simply at one's wits' end, the understanding comes to an end, or it is beyond the intellect, as soon as it is a question of extra-sensory, extra-earthly things, which come into the sphere of spiritual comprehension only.

However perishable the brain, the thoughts generated by it nevertheless continue to exist because, as they are formed, radiations of a finer nature are received, which permit the thoughts to outlive the death of the gross material body.

In this way they also belong to the works which follow man at his death (Revelation 14, 13). In the beyond they await the departed soul, and hold it fast in gloomy lowlands if the thoughts were of an evil nature, or in the case of good thoughts they form a path for a gladdening progress into lighter regions.

In his book *Heavenly Thoughts* Karl May, who knew or divined more than his narratives allow one to realize, says on this subject: "Every man is the creator of his own world. His deeds are the solid, his words the fluid, his thoughts the imponderable (weightless) components of this world. He not only makes it for himself for here, but will not be able to renounce it in that life either."

Recently thoughts and their transference (telepathy) have become the subject of exhaustive scientific research. But as is usual today, the results are mostly not used for constructive purposes.

So, for example, people are eagerly exploring the extent to which telepathy as so-called mental radio would be practicable in wars, in espionage, in politics; and they are already considering how the thoughts of enemies in war can be confused, and how it may be possible for thought-transference to be prevented or distorted through jamming-stations.

But this is not yet enough. The abuse goes further. Through the concentrated influence on human brains, they wish forcibly to exercise a total thought-power on larger groups of people.

It is not possible, however, to break down a person's moral barrier through the evil volition of others, nor even through telepathic encroachments upon his private life, against the will of the person concerned. With firm confidence in spiritual help anyone can summon enough will-power to ward off evil thoughts, and not allow them to take effect in his personal sphere.

Of what use is all this research if people neglect above all to learn details about the nature and effect of thoughts, with a view to a spiritual upward striving and to a healthy earthly up-building.

We can no longer remain indifferent spectators of a happening which each day brings new, evil surprises, but are now forced to concern ourselves seriously with problems which lie outside our sensory perceptions, that is to say, in the spiritual sphere, because ultimately our *spiritual survival* also depends on it.

The view was recently expressed that crimes could possibly be prevented if, through basic research, adequate information were obtained about the mechanisms which at regular intervals drive human beings to the collective crime of genocide.

These mechanisms, or rather collective actions, are rooted in part it the dark thought-centers, of which there are as many as the crimes man is able to devise. But there are also thought-centers of peace and pure love.

In accordance with the Law of the Attraction of Homogeneous Species, similar thoughts unite in centers. These in turn are connected with homogeneous spheres of Darkness and of Light.

All those involved in them are linked with these concentrations of evil or of good by threads, and receive via this line of connection an ever new supply, which allows evil as well as good to grow within them. And some day the moment comes when one or several persons, or whole masses, will transform for example an evil which at first was embodied only in thought-forms, into deeds somewhere on earth, and in this way perpetrate a *collective crime*. There are no earthly barriers in this. All of them, in whatever country they may be, are connected with one another through a *real collective guilt*.

Thus it happens that we hear of crimes of a similar nature perpetrated in the in most diverse parts of the earth. "It is in the air," as the popular saying goes. Something unpleasant or disastrous is impending. But to this "air" also belong the thought-forms with their radiations, which press towards realization, and wherever there are weak or dark places the fruits of evil volition manifest on earth.

Such cases are now brought to our attention nearly every day. Let us for instance only consider the new types of crimes. First there is a "precedent," an isolated case, which then as a chain reaction is followed by others.

Of the "thought-sinners" only the wrongdoers whose deeds are physically visible can be caught and convicted. The remaining "accomplices" stay at large because their complicity is invisible.

All, however, *without exception*, are subject to the Laws of Creation, which in their incorruptibility provide for a just reaction; but also for the severance of the dark threads of fate, if the readiness for it exists in the originator through a continuing good volition and conduct.

In contrast to the foregoing statements, a collective crime pictured according to earthly interpretation, which places the burden of the criminal deeds of individual members on the community (nation, family), cannot be substantiated either legally or morally.

For on earth, where the homogeneous species are not separated, participants and non-participants, the guilty and the innocent, find themselves intermingled in a community.

If therefore a collective guilt is thrown upon a community, those not involved are also implicated and morally degraded (discriminated against).

From all the explanations it is already evident that thoughts *cannot be free*. On the contrary, we must often pay even a very heavy penalty for them. In ancient times there was a saying: "No one is punished for his thoughts." Later this was changed to the proverb: "Thoughts are free."

If a man allows bad thoughts to arise within him, they are not free, thus not free from punishment. According to the simple Law, "What a man sows he must reap," these thoughts return many times over to their originator as evil fate, which was put into the world by himself. Man has at all times full responsibility for what he thinks and does.

How important it is then also *to be alert in thought*, and to examine what "goes through one's head." Above all, reflection on the world of thoughts should increasingly prompt us to awaken and cultivate within us the concept of the pure and noble, so that we shall not one day have to reproach ourselves with being involved through frivolous thoughts in the evil deeds of others, which deep in our hearts we detest and condemn.

If we bestow as much purity as possible on our thoughts, we thereby further the thought-centers of good, and help to eliminate the "thought-garbage" that devastatingly contributes to the environmental pollution in the beyond and on this side, and thus gradually to close down the "mechanisms of evil" to which the dark thought-centers also belong. They must then wither and dry up, because they no longer receive any supply. Therein also lies ultimately the prevention of all crime.

17. THE GRACE OF GOD

Although the Law of Reciprocal Action (Seed and Harvest) is strict and inexorable like all the Laws in Creation, yet the Grace of God has also been woven into it. Only this gives man the *possibility at all* of being able to redeem a transgression against a Divine Law or Commandment, thus an offense, a sin, as soon as he has recognized his wrong volition in the experiencing, and in steadfast striving turns inwardly to the good. That is a Grace of God which many people endeavor in vain to understand, perhaps also because they think that they must deny the re-embodiments of the human spirit which in many cases are necessary for redemption, thus deny the possibility of repeated earth-lives granted to the human spirits by God.

And yet this Grace of God — in contrast to the Luciferian principle of merciless temptation and seduction of the human spirits to sin — is unutterably vast and great to human understanding. Without this Grace of redemption, man would never be in a position to free himself from the burden of his sins. He would have to carry it around with him eternally.

The question of whether Divine Grace is given unconditionally, or whether it is dependent on the fulfillment of the Divine Commandments, is answered by the Law of Balance between giving and receiving, to which Jesus referred with His words, "It is more blessed to give than to receive" (Acts 20, 35).

Something must be given by the human spirit as balance, as counter-value for the Grace: *trust in God* and His Will, which is closely bound up *with the observance of His Laws and Commandments*. Trust is the basis for the help of God, for His "Forgiving Grace".

The concept of Grace must therefore not be taken *one-sidedly*. Forgiveness is not possible through faith alone, if faith is not followed by the good deed.

Thus man also experiences the extraordinary Grace of God in the *pre-redemption* of his evil karma, if he honestly strives to give purity to his inner perceptions and thoughts, and to adjust his doing and thinking to the Laws of Creation. In time he thereby creates for himself an increasingly pure ethereal environment, which must eventually have a definite effect on all that is earthly.

He gradually loosens his dark fetters, imbues his surroundings with refreshing, up-building spiritual currents, thereby effecting the mitigation or disintegration of returning karmaically-stipulated dark currents by the lighter radiation. Finally the redemption continues to take place only symbolically, in which "chance" may "play a part" through strange guidance and Providence; or situations arise of which we might perhaps say that it could have had a worse ending. With that a feeling of inner relief spreads, as though something menacing, something dangerous had brushed against or passed by us.

With this also we experience one of the many manifestations of Grace which the Creator has bestowed upon us in His Laws.

It is a further Grace that the human spirit is permitted to dwell in this wonderful Creation, in order with a free volition to mature in it to a fully conscious personality. This can take place in complete harmony and joy. For sorrow and pain are not necessary for it. These are brought in by man alone. They are not willed by God!

How often we beg that God's great Grace may be upon us. But have we even once considered wherein God's Grace lies?

18. THE ETERNAL COUNSEL OF GOD

Anything that befalls man in the way of hardship is very often called fate, and looked upon as a higher power which determines his life.

But in reality it is men themselves who shape their fate or karma, which depending on their free decisions is either good or bad, exactly in accordance with the Law that he who has sown it must reap the seed many times over, even if it be only in later earth-lives. Every moment man gives cause for fateful consequences in the future, and every moment he stands in the reactions of previous decisions from the present and from past earth-lives.

Thus men living on earth today must also be answerable to themselves for what they willed and thought in former earth-lives. In this connection it matters not whether the volition was general or directed at definite other human beings. This should exhort us to act with caution, and heighten our sense of responsibility, so that in the future, whether on earth or in the beyond, evil reactions that darken and make our lives painful will no longer be possible.

Therefore let everyone who is struck by more or less severe "blows of fate" remember above all that *he* is the originator, and not some other person.

Perhaps at one time he has done something evil to a fellow human being, who had to suffer from it *innocently*. To the innocent sufferer the Laws of Creation always bring a compensation in some form or other, provided he forgives the wrong-doer. But to the guilty one dark threads of karma become attached at the very moment of the deed, which unfailingly return to him as the fruits of his volition. This is then the "punishment" which he inflicts upon himself. In reality it is the just balance of his evil volition, the real "compulsion to atonement."

From this point of view the doctrine of *predestination* must be considered differently from hitherto. According to this it is believed that the decree of God, firmly-established from eternity, determines who among men is admitted to eternal bliss and who is doomed to eternal damnation. This gives the impression that *from the outset* a definite number of human beings are allowed to attain to eternal salvation, and another definite number are eternally lost.

Against this stands the free will of decision bestowed on men by God, which implies that it lies solely with man himself whether he wishes to strive upwards or -downwards.

The executors of his decisions are then the Laws of Creation which, in carrying out his free will, let him attain to Luminous Heights or to dark depths.

What Karl May says in his book *Heavenly Thoughts* points also in this direction:

"Do not smile about it, for it is true. Your thoughts, words and works are recorded in the 'Book of Life' by none other than yourself."

Thus the decision for eternal life or for eternal death lies not with God but only with man. He himself bears the responsibility for his deeds and thoughts, which lead him upwards or downwards. Through His Laws God only allows the decisions of men to be carried out.

Only in this is revealed to human beings the *Eternal Counsel of God* (Psalm 33, 11), which from the inception of Creation is expressed in His immutable Laws, and which is closely linked with the *Omniscience of God* that cannot be separated from Justice and Love.

19. THE TRUMPETS OF THE WORLD JUDGMENT

Through the Fall of Man, through the turning away from God, humanity have contributed much, very much, to intensifying *for themselves* the World Judgment, which is now heading towards its climax.

Not without reason is a *suicidal program* by mankind being spoken and written about today, a sinister, gruesome program, the obstinate execution of which brings ominously near the danger of total self-destruction.

In this program the earth plays a special role. Exploited, devastated and besmirched through wanton deeds and thoughts, it moves through space; the earth, once made over to men to hold in trust for their responsible use and spiritual maturing, as a starting-point from which, as on a heavenly ladder, they could have entered directly into Paradise.

The forces of Nature bestowed treasures and fruits of this earth in full measure on the individual peoples, to make natural use of and to heed them as a protection and support for their spiritual progress.

But they were meant and indeed had to pass on their surplus, in strict obedience to the Law of Balance between giving and receiving.

However the gifts of Nature, which through a stimulating and invigorating exchange should have contributed to peace and harmonious working, are very often unscrupulously misused to the injury, suppression and destruction of fellow human beings.

The great comprehensive Law of Creation, to maintain always a just balance in giving as well as in receiving, in every respect and in all spheres of life, has already for a long time simply been heeded no more.

Is it not then an inevitable consequence that through the guilt of men the world is falling to pieces, plunging out of balance, which now in the World Judgment must be forcibly restored through the Will of God?

There are many signs by which men on earth can recognize this unique World Judgment.

Certainly they ponder over these, but they apply to every event only the yardstick of their intellect, and not that of their inner perception. In so doing, however, they never measure themselves! Now they must experience that their keenest intellectual acumen cannot make up for the emptiness of their souls, and that striving only for earthly things must not be regarded as the highest goal.

There is no continuing development for man in this, because the spirit within him urges towards higher things. He must *awaken* the noble abilities slumbering within him, so that he is able consciously to fulfil his task in Creation: to be a connecting link between the World of Matter and his homeland, the Spiritual Realm, in that already down here and later from above he has a furthering, up-building and ennobling influence upon this world. Therein lies the *meaning of life*, which is also decisive for the future Kingdom of Peace.

A Kingdom of Peace that is founded by the Divine Will requires human beings who have recognized the meaning of life. Only they are able to bear within them and to spread abroad true peace.

But where are such human beings to be found today and what must yet come to pass in terms of suffering before they are ripe for the new Kingdom of Peace that is to be established on earth after the World Judgment!

As yet the earth is still heavily weighed down by the oppressive burden which mankind have forced upon it over thousands of years through their evil deeds and volition.

Indeed how very tiny is this earth in the enormous expanses of the Universe, and how great the Grace of God which is granted to it at this Turning-Point! For it is chosen to be a point of anchorage for the Radiations of the Light.

Soon there will also glow for it in the end-time of the World Judgment the dawn of a future in purity and beauty, with a humanity who have humbly and gratefully recognized the Will of their Lord and God, and who live in accordance with it.

Before this, however, humanity must patiently endure the purifying waves of the World Judgment in order to wash their souls clean in them and to become new in themselves.

Many indeed know of the coming of this World Judgment but they are still awaiting the *trumpet-blasts* which are to herald it.

Let those who thus wait follow attentively just for once the news from the countries of the earth. Each day brings reports of political disturbances, economic distress, famine, of outrages and dreadful misery; plagues and drought afflict mankind, the earth quakes and destroys whole cities within seconds, deadly hurricanes rage along, volcanoes belch forth devastating fire, rivers overflow their banks, tearing away homesteads, cattle and men.

Are these not trumpet-blasts for the Judgment, when here today and there tomorrow the waves of terror and dread roll over mankind, to shake them violently awake even at the last moment? What is sinister and new in this is the abundance of events never before experienced, the speed with which they follow one another.

But who allows himself to be touched by them, unless they directly affect him personally?

And yet even as one "not actually involved" he could in certain circumstances greatly mitigate his burden of fate, which will one day also strike him in the World Judgment.

For if he does not close himself to other people's distress and suffering, and exerts himself to experience and inwardly perceive it with them, then something begins to flower within him which will envelop him like a protective mantle: *compassion*, which selflessly seeks to help all human beings who still bear within them a spark of longing for the Light!

In the midst of all the confusion he will then receive the help of God in the same measure as he opens himself to the Light, and will thus be able to give comfort and confident hope to many wounded souls!

20. "WHICH IS TO COME" (Rev. 1,4)

At the beginning of his Revelation John conveys Grace "from him, which is, and which was, and *which is to come ... and* from Jesus Christ." These are quite obviously two Persons Who are spoken of. "Which is to come" and Jesus!

God Himself will not descend into Creation, because it would have to perish in the enormous Power of His Divinity. But He can sever a Part of Himself and send it into Creation, as happened with Jesus. In exactly the same way God severed yet another Part of Himself, the Son of Man, Whom Jesus promised at the time of His earthly existence and Whose Name Isaiah proclaimed in his prophecy: Imanuel! (Matthew 25, 31; Isaiah 7, 14).

He is the Creator and Upholder of the whole of Creation, He is the Word through Which all things are made, and of Whom it was proclaimed: "In the beginning was the Word, and the Word was with God, and the Word was God" (John 1, 1). It was *He* to Whom John referred when he spoke of Him Which is to come: Imanuel, the Son of Man!

The entire Creation came into being in the Radiation of the Son of Man. And with it also the human spirits. Later, in Subsequent Creation (the World of Matter), many of them of their own volition pursued wrong courses, withdrawing ever further from God. To free them from their confusion and entanglement for they themselves were no longer able to do so God in His great Love severed from Himself a second Part, and allowed it to "become flesh": Jesus of Nazareth.

The Son of Man could not yet come at that time because He was being prepared for His Mission ordained for a later period. But mankind, who had become engulfed in Darkness, needed immediate help. It was a Divine Act of Emergency, and when Jesus saw how little His Word was heeded and observed, or in Biblical words, when He perceived that "the darkness comprehended him not" (John 1, 5), He promised the coming of the Son of Man, Who "would guide them into all truth" (John 16, 13).

Thus in the Divine Kingdom Imanuel is the First-born and Jesus the Second-born Son of God. But in the World of Matter, on earth, Jesus was "the first begotten of the dead" (Revelation 1, 5), for He incarnated there first in order to help men, who were as though dead spiritually, whereas Imanuel followed Him only later, as the Judge appointed by God in the Final Judgment.

His judicial activity is described exactly in the Revelation. Through John He sends His judgments to the seven World-Churches, also to our World-Church Ephesus, after closely examining them, for "all the churches shall know that I am he which searcheth the reins and hearts" (Revelation 2, 23). Here the rein, the organ of purification, stands for purity, and the heart for the inner perception of the spirit. The human spirit is searched as to how, in the course of his development, he has used his inner perception. What is decisive in the Judgment is the purity of his inner perceptions, thoughts and deeds.

All the dreadful ethereal forms of sin which men have put into the World through their wrong deeds and thoughts, including the great city of Babylon and the beasts, will be destroyed in the great Final Judgment through the Radiation-Power of the Son of Man.

He also vanquishes the "dragon" (Lucifer), chaining him for a thousand years, so that men can help undisturbed with the up-building of the Millennium on earth (Revelation 20, 1-3).

His Word is as a "sharp two-edged sword," by which the "nations" must judge themselves (Revelation 1, 16; 19, 15).

The concept for the word "nations" (Revelation 19, 15; 20, 3; 21, 24), like much else in the Revelation, must not be taken in the earthly sense. It is intended as a concept of Creation for those human spirits who are still in the development-stage in the Material World (Subsequent Creation) below Paradise, whereas the word "Jews" in the Revelation describes all those human spirits who have attained to a higher development and are already matured spiritually. Only thus is the utterance to be understood: "and I know the blasphemy of them which say they are Jews (that is, spiritually mature human beings), and are not" (Revelation 2, 9; 3, 9).

At the end of the Revelation the Son of Man says: "And, behold, I come quickly; and my reward is with me, to give every man according as his work shall be" (22, 12). Those words clearly indicate that man himself must receive the corresponding reward for his good and bad deeds. This is based on the personal ability of the human spirit, which he cannot throw upon anyone else, also not upon Jesus. "The Lamb of God, which beareth* the sin of the world" (John 1, 29), does not mean that Jesus has taken or will take away their sins from men. Such an easy taking-away of sins is opposed to all the Laws of Creation. On the contrary. it is meant to express that it can be seen from the wound-marks of Jesus what sin men have committed against Him in having "slain Him like a Lamb" without guilt (Revelation 5, 12).

---

* Lutheran Bible

Hence men cannot cast their sins upon Jesus (Isaiah 53, 6), but in virtue of their own responsibility they themselves must bear their burden of guilt; or, as we also read in the Revelation: Men must themselves wash their robes (souls) and make them white (7, 14). Only the Word of God can help them in this. If they strive to observe it, their souls will become pure, and they will be able to pass in the Judgment.

But then they will also recognize the Son of Man proclaimed by Jesus, Who already had His being before the beginning of Creation. "I am Alpha and Omega, the beginning and the end, the first and the last," says the Son of Man of Himself (Revelation 22, 13). The beginning, because through Him Creation came into being, and the end, because He would remain as the Last if His Creation should ever cease to exist.

He is likewise the Spirit of God, Who is also called the "Holy Spirit." With the Words "Let there be light" (Genesis 1, 3) His Radiation surged across the boundary of the Divine Kingdom into the Universe that was void of Light, and from this Radiation there was formed in the beginning the First Creation, Primordial Creation. With this Happening the Holy Spirit did not become merged in His Creation. Hence in the account of Creation, which is to be understood spiritually, it is clearly stated: "And the Spirit of God moved *upon* the face of the waters (Creations)" (Genesis 1, 2).

To make it possible for Creation to remain in existence forever, and to prevent Imanuel from being drawn back by the mighty Radiation-Power of God, a small Part of Him was incarnated in Primordial Creation, and thus most closely linked with that kind of species in which humanity have their origin. Thus He became the Son sent by God to men, the *Son of Man*, the link from God to mankind, *the Eternal Mediator*.

But the Part put forth into Primordial Creation is "Parsifal," King of the Holy Grail, Who is in the Grail Castle, and linked with the Son of Man lmanuel in the Divine Kingdom by an unbreakable bond of radiation. These are two Personalities, Imanuel — Parsifal, but they are one in their working. For example, in the Revelation the Angel who comes down from Heaven (20, 1-3) and binds the dragon (Lucifer) is synonymous with Parsifal.

Now it is also clear why the Son of Man Imanuel must be called the "Outborn Son," whereas Jesus, Who has again become one with the Father, is the Inborn Son. He is King in the Divine Kingdom, whereas lmanuel is King of the whole of Creation.

Most closely bound up with the Son of Man is the happening of the Sealing. 144,000 human spirits were "sealed in their foreheads" (Revelation 7, 3) in the Spiritual Realm. They were to bear on their foreheads the Sign of God, the equal-armed Cross, the Sign of the Truth, after vowing loyally to serve God and His two Sons, namely "Him which sitteth upon the throne" (Imanuel) and "the Lamb" (Jesus) (Revelation 7, 10), and to help the Son of Man in the up-building of the new Kingdom of God.

The twelve tribes mentioned signify that those sealed were chosen from the twelve different groups of mankind. Each of these groups has a special homogeneity rooted in the spiritual talents and virtues (Revelation 7, 4-8).

As the Up-builder of Creation, the Son of Man sustains and renews it. The Source of renewal and sustenance is the Holy Grail, the "fountain of the water of life" (Revelation 21, 6), which is in the Grail Castle, the "temple of God" (Revelation 11, 19; 15, 5).

The Grail, a Chalice, contains the Eternal Power which through the Son of Man is poured out into Creation once a year.

Man must gradually make himself familiar with the thought that not only on earth are all things formed, but also beyond the earth in the supra-earthly regions, though from finer, lighter species of Creation. Indeed the earth is only the coarsest image of the already existing supra-earthly prototypes, which are far more perfect and beautiful than the forms visible to us. Thus later on, in the new era of peace, there shall one day be built on earth an image of the supra-earthly Grail Castle.

This Grail Castle stands, in fact, at the highest place in Primordial Spiritual Creation, far above the Paradise of men. It is the only point of connection between God and His Creation; it could also be said that it is an intersection point of radiations, a transformation-center for the Radiation-Power which comes from the Divine Kingdom above it, and is passed on through *the Son of Man, the Creative Will of God*, into the lower-lying Creation.

The human spirit, too, fives from this pure Power, but unfortunately has for the greater part applied it wrongly, and misused it for base purposes.

Just as the heart allows the blood to pulsate through the body, so the Spiritual Power streams out of the Grail through Creation at regular intervals. The pulse-beat of the heart is a reflection of this mighty pulse-beat of Eternal Life, because everything that takes place "above" is repeated "below," in many variations.

In the Revelation John describes many events relating to the Grail. His spiritual eye beheld mighty happenings, which he was allowed to mediate and pass on to mankind. In Jesus' day the time had not yet come for men to be able to grasp the Knowledge of the Grail, but now the stage has been reached in the development of mankind where the Knowledge of Creation also includes the Knowledge of the Grail.

This Knowledge will give the spiritual character to the new era which is now dawning with the Cosmic Turning-Point, because then the human spirit Will be able consciously and gratefully to receive the spiritual Power, the Water of Life, streaming from out of the Grail, for the blessing and joy of all creatures in Creation.

Therefore the words at the end of the Revelation are full of promise: "And let him that is athirst come. And whosoever will, let him take the water of life freely" (22, 17). To him who uses this Power aright the Gate to Paradise will open, and he will be permitted to receive the crown of life (Revelation 2, 10), the gift of being allowed to live eternally.

Whereas at that time the words of John, who as John the Baptist on earth "bore record of the word of God, and of the testimony of Jesus Christ" (Revelation 1, 2) "Grace be unto you from him which is to come,' it should today read: "Grace from Him Who has come." For meanwhile the great promise of the coming of a second Son of God into Creation has been fulfilled. As in those days Jesus, the Son of God, brought the Word, so today is it proclaimed by the Son of Man, Imanuel. For both are Sons of God, and one in God!

21. "BUT WHEN THE SON OF MAN COMETH…"

1

The handing down of spoken words is a difficult problem, especially when spiritual values are to be conveyed. How easily gaps of memory occur in the course of transmission, and how much people are inclined to fill these gaps with ideas corresponding to their own way of thinking and their own views, so that the original meaning of what was said is often entirely lost.

Unfortunately the words of Jesus as recorded in the New Testament are no exception here, still less so since they were not collected and written down until decades after His physical death. The authors based their writings on oral transmission or written notes, with which they also interwove their own views.

As regards the sayings of Jesus, we are dealing not with intellectually-bound earthly explanations but with spiritual explanations and teachings which comprise the entire knowledge of Creation and which were partly misunderstood right from the beginning, and were then also passed on as such. For Jesus Himself said that in some things He had not been understood by His hearers, indeed not even by His disciples. In the very transmission of what was not understood, an alteration of what Jesus really said is inevitable.

Everyone knows that even after a short time he cannot exactly reproduce something he has heard, and if there were several listeners each one would describe it differently. This was already the same in past millennia, and even spiritual inspiration could never quite eliminate it in the case of the disciples and the authors of the Gospels, although their intentions were of the best.

That this problem of transmission also troubles theological circles, and not only at the present time, is shown in the explanations of D. Johannes Weiss, Professor of Divinity, in his essay, "The Three Older Gospels" (1907). In this he assumes that the Gospel of Mark was written approximately 40 years after Jesus' life on earth. He then continues:

"But the period of 40 years is nevertheless long enough to justify the anxious doubt as to whether in fact a reliable recollection of the events, and above all of the sayings of the Lord, still existed. Or had lack of understanding and deliberate intention, fanciful misrepresentation and fiction already accomplished their work of distortion and destruction, before the Evangelists undertook to protect the treasure from further decay and mutilation? Closing one's eyes to this doubt does not help, nor does the naive assertion that this was not the case, or the pious belief that God would not have permitted such damage to the teachings of Jesus, so necessary for us. Only thorough historical investigation and criticism will avail."

After giving examples from the Gospels to show how Jesus' sayings were changed and modified, Professor Weiss, in another passage of the same essay, expresses the following view:

"Considering these instances of misunderstanding and reshaping, we may well be overcome with painful regret that Jesus' words were not written down and passed on to us by His own hand, as is the case with Paul and so many other personalities who have led us to God. And we must earnestly ask: Were not many widely-diffused rays of His Light lost, because the mirror which was to hold them was too small and too dull? It can be safely assumed that some aspects of His Being have remained unknown to us because there was no observer who could have understood them. Many words would be lost because they did not call forth a response in the souls of these people. The selection preserved for us would be influenced by their narrow range of ideas, and certainly many a word was originally given a greater and deeper meaning than we read into it today."

So in connection with certain passages of the New Testament, the question as to what were the actual words of Jesus is really justified, and we must beware of asserting with regard to such doubtful texts that Jesus spoke in that way! In many matters Jesus did not speak as is explained and taught on the basis of false traditions. Take an example from Luke 14, 26: "If any man come to me, and hate not his father, and mother, and wife, and children, and brethren, and sisters, yea, and his own life also, he cannot be my disciple."

Jesus, Who is "Divine Love," would never have made discipleship dependent upon "hating" one's closest relations. In doing so He would have been inviting sin. And this immediately shows the absurdity of these transmitted words which Jesus is said to have uttered. He would have asked that too close personal ties should be avoided and that one's ego should not be placed in the foreground, so that His disciples might dedicate themselves without burden or restraint to the lofty task.

Equally inaccurate is the transmission about the Son of Man, with which we shall deal here in detail. At the end of His earthly activity Jesus gave His disciples the promise concerning the coming of the Son of Man. By the Son of Man He meant not Himself but another Person. The disciples did not understand this, and believed that Jesus Himself was the Son of Man, an assumption which was certainly understandable and excusable at the time, because they were living in imminent expectation of the Final Judgment and the return of Jesus.

Nevertheless — hardly had Jesus uttered what to mankind is the most significant prophecy — than the foundation was already laid for a very fateful error, which was passed on and finally incorporated in the Gospels. Hence they contain a number of incorrect or at least obscure phrases about the concept of the Son of Man, which Jesus in His simple and clear manner of expression would never have used.

2.

Clearly Jesus proclaims the coming of a second Envoy from God: "Nevertheless I tell you the truth; It is expedient for you that I go away: for if I go not away, the Comforter will not come unto you; but if I depart, I will send him unto you. And when he is come, he will reprove the world of sin, and of righteousness, and of judgment. . ." (John 16, 7-8).

"I have yet many things to say unto you, but ye cannot bear them now. Howbeit when he, the Spirit of truth, is come, he will guide you into all truth: for he shall not speak of himself..."

"He shall glorify me: for he shall receive of mine, and shall shew it unto you. All things that the Father hath are mine: therefore said I, that he shall take of mine, and shall shew it unto you" (John 16, 12-15).

"But the Comforter, which is the Holy Ghost, whom the Father will send in my name, he shall teach you all things, and bring all things to your remembrance, whatsoever I have said unto you" (John 14, 20).

"Whosoever therefore shall be ashamed of me and of my words..., of him also shall the Son of man be ashamed, when he cometh in the glory of his Father with the holy angels" (Mark 8, 38). Just this last sentence is at once rendered unintelligible through the wrong assumption that Jesus and the Son of Man are one and the same Person.

All these words of Jesus refer to another Person, and not to the *impersonal* Power which Jesus had also promised His disciples: "And, behold, I send the promise of my Father upon you: but tarry ye in the city of Jerusalem, until ye be endued with power from on high" (Luke 24, 49).

This promise referred to the outpouring of Power through the Holy Spirit, an event which has been repeated every year at a definite time ever since the inception of Creation, for its maintenance. In those days the disciples experienced the fulfillment of this event at Whitsuntide, after being inwardly prepared for it through the grievous experience occasioned by the sudden and violent death of their Lord.

The activities which in His promise Jesus associates with the other Person, such "to guide into all truth," "to preach," "to teach," "to bring to remembrance what Jesus has said," can only be carried out by a *person*, and therefore they necessitate a personal fulfillment.

In the explanatory notes on the New Testament, published by Otto v. Gerlach , Professor of Divinity and Court Chaplain (Berlin 1863), it is stated: "These words 'He shall not speak of himself' make sense only in regard to a person, not to an impersonal power or manifestation of God." In addition there is special reference to the importance of this great teaching of the Holy Scriptures regarding the Personality of the Holy Spirit, which was not nearly enough appreciated.

By the designations "Spirit of Truth," "Comforter" and "Holy Ghost" Jesus meant the Son of Man, Who will come to continue His Mission.

Not the least of His Works, by virtue of His High Office — for He comes from God will be to set right the errors in the transmissions and interpretations of Christ's words.

3.

And the Son of Man it is Who brings the World Judgment to men, because He is Justice. Whereas Jesus, Who works in Love, emphasized that He had not come to judge (John 12, 47). The judgeship was laid by God upon "Justice" in person, upon the Holy Spirit! His activity is manifested in the immutable Laws of Creation, and a transgression of these Laws is a sin against the Holy Spirit, which cannot be forgiven and must be expiated. Hence the words of the Bible, that sins against God and the Son of God can be forgiven, but not blasphemy against the Holy Ghost (Matthew 12, 31-32; Mark 3, 29).

How many earnest Christians have pondered in vain over the sense of these words, and have been oppressed by them, because they did not know the real meaning of the Holy Spirit. His Work lies in the adamantine and incorruptible Laws pulsating through Creation. To these also belongs the Law of Sowing and Reaping, which acts uniformly in the earthly as well as in the extra-earthly.

In the sense of this Law the thoughts, inner perception, conduct and actions of man are just as much seed as that which is placed in the earth, a spiritual seed which the one who has sown it must himself reap. No one else can gather the harvest of this seed for him, whether it be good or evil. Nor can Jesus do so, for He cannot change or evade the Laws of Creation, because He, as the Son of God, is just as subject to the Laws of His Father as are the creatures. For He stated explicitly that He would fulfil the Laws of His Father, and not destroy them (Matthew 5, 17).

Hence a man cannot forgive his neighbor the sins against the Holy Spirit. On the other hand, he has the power and also the right to forgive a wrong inflicted on him personally, and thus to prevent at the outset an evil reaction for the wrong-doer. It is in *this* sense that the words of Jesus: "Whose soever sins ye remit, they are remitted unto them..." (John 20, 23), should be understood.

Thus a man who, for instance, inflicts sorrow or harm on a fellow-man through his propensity for evil, can be pardoned immediately by the person in question, but only by him. In this way no evil threads of fate can develop out of this personal harm inflicted. The sinful propensity, however, which the wrongdoer bears within himself, and which was the motive for this deed, cannot be forgiven him by anyone. He must personally detach himself from it through true repentance, which is equivalent to a complete inner change for the good. If in the future he then heeds and obeys the Laws of the Holy Spirit instead of opposing them, the Grace of God which rests in these Laws will always be with him!

For the same reason Jesus was certainly able to pardon the abuses inflicted on Him personally, but was not in a position to prevent the grievous fate brought upon mankind through their rejection of His Mission and His Message from running its course, and from having to be resolved now in the World Judgment.

4.

The question of when the World Judgment will come is already answered for all those who look about them with open eyes.

We are standing in the midst of the great final reckoning of the Judgment Day or the Last Judgment. Daily we experience in ever-increasing intensity and frequency its effects, that is the consequences of the evil seed we have scattered in the world for thousands of years. The very frequency of events is a special feature of the World Judgment. It is the consequence of an undreamed-of, tremendous acceleration of everything that exists and is caused by the Divine Power which the Son of Man brings unchanged into Creation for the Judgment.

We need only for once contemplate the events which already for decades have brought mankind in ever-increasing measure unrest, horror, despair, distress and death, in order to recognize that an invisible power must stand behind them.

Whether it be the ever more violent dissensions, the schism, mutual distrust, wars, riots, the atomic arms race, political entanglements, economic difficulties, the unbelievable fate of individuals and masses, crimes, scandals and crises, or new diseases and epidemics, the natural catastrophes, as well as the unusual atmospheric conditions and temperatures over the whole earth.

Atomic power cannot cause the frequency and the unusual character of these happenings, but only the Divine Power anchored in Creation, against which the entire atomic power used by men, as well as man himself, is as nothing!

The attempt to control the swelling tide of chaos, or even to arrest it, is therefore doomed to failure. Man is simply flattened by the spiritual and earthly events, and is often confronted overnight by totally new situations and facts, with which he can cope only with the help of God.

Had men not long since forsaken their way to God, there need not be this terrible Judgment, in which everyone must receive his self-earned punishment for the sins he has nurtured in many earth-lives. For Jesus did not take all the sins of the world upon Himself through His death on the cross, which men regard as a necessary propitiatory sacrifice. The sins are still there, and come upon us like a gigantic burden in the World Judgment, which is carried out before our eyes, and which will strike every man at his time exactly according to the Law. "For whatsoever a man soweth, that shall he also reap" (Galatians 6, 7). This applies to all men, irrespective of their creed . . . .

5.

But let us once more return to the past and search out further words and sentences referring to the Son of Man, to His activity, His Mission and His coming. Perhaps such a retrospective view will bring a better understanding of the present.

In the Old Testament it is particularly Daniel and Isaiah who prophesy about the Son of Man. Isaiah calls Him by the name that God has given Him: "Imanuel!" (Isaiah 7, 14). This name has not been recognized in its true significance until now because men, without examination, generally adopted the view of the Evangelist Matthew that Jesus was Imanuel. This is one of those cases in which the Evangelist, in combining traditions, added his own erroneous view, naturally without evil intent. This error does not appear in the other Gospels.

Thus Matthew reports: "And she shall bring forth a son, and thou shalt call his name Jesus... " (Matthew 1, 21), and subsequently likewise applies the prophecy of Isaiah (Isaiah 7, 14) ". .. and shall call his name Imanuel... " (Matthew 1, 23) to the birth of the Son of God. This in spite of the fact that the two names are quite different, and that Jesus never called Himself Imanuel, nor was He ever so called; moreover He was never addressed by the name Son of Man.

In his wider vision Isaiah gives a noteworthy sign for the time of Imanuel: "Take counsel together, and it shall come to nought; speak the word, and it shall not stand: for God is with us" (Isaiah 8, 10). (Matthew 1, 23: "Emmanuel, which being interpreted is, God with us").

These words purport that the Son of Man is Executive Justice, Whose eternal and immutable Laws pulsate through Creation. Anything men do that is not in the sense of these Laws cannot last and must perish. But henceforth this will take place with uncanny acceleration, brought about through the Divine Power which the Son of Man brings unchanged to Creation for the Judgment. "For God is with us!" And wrong actions can no longer as before be concealed for a time, but must within a short time reveal themselves as such, visible to all. The increase in conferences which have come to nought, the empty promises, the perplexity, are signs of a wrong "counseling" and "speaking the word," and are part of the indications concerning the fulfillment of the prophecy.

A further sign of this is the appearance of the many false prophets (Matthew 24, 11). They are given this name because they promise to the seeking and erring human souls something which only the Son of Man has the power to grant! When they are there, the true Prophet will also step forth!

It is to Him that Paul also refers in the words: "For we know in part, and we prophesy in part. But when that which is perfect is come, then that Which is in part shall be done away" (I Corinthians 13, 9-10). Only God is perfect, and His two Sons Jesus and Imanuel, Who both as a Part of God are eternally one with Him, and remain separate only in Their activity. For the Son of Man, Imanuel, also comes from God, as Jesus clearly states John 16, 7-15), and is therefore according to earthly concepts a Son of God.

When Paul spoke these words, the disciples' Pentecostal experience was already past, so that his words cannot be referred to that event, as has been done.

An unknown prophet, whose prophecies are to be found in the Book of Enoch, also received deep insight into the spiritual happening and into the future of Imanuel, the Son of Man. We learn from this book that the Son of Man was already in being before the existence of Creation, and that He was at first hidden and only revealed to the chosen ones. But let us read the relevant passages from the prophecy itself:

"And I asked the angel who went with me and showed me all the hidden things, concerning that Son of Man, who He was, and whence He was and why He went with the Head of Days? And he answered and said unto me: 'This is the Son of Man who hath righteousness, with whom dwelleth righteousness, and who revealeth all the treasures of that which is hidden'" (Enoch 46, 2-3).

"And in that place I saw the fountain of righteousness which was inexhaustible; and around it were many fountains of wisdom; and all the thirsty drank of them and were filled with wisdom, and their dwellings were with the righteous and holy and elect. And at that hour that Son of Man was named in the presence of the Lord of Spirits, and His name before the Head of Days. Yea, before the sun and the signs were created, before the stars of the heaven were made, His name was named before the Lord of Spirits. He shall be a staff to the righteous whereon to stay themselves and not fall. And he shall be the light of the Gentiles, and the hope of those who are troubled of heart" (Enoch 48, 1-4).

"And the kings and the mighty and all who possess the earth shall bless and glorify and extol him who rules over all, who was hidden. For from the beginning the Son of Man was hidden, and the Most High preserved him in the presence of His might, and revealed him to the elect" (Enoch 62, 6-7).

"And there was great joy amongst them, and they blessed and glorified and extolled..., because the name of that Son of Man had been revealed unto them. And he sat on the throne of his glory, and the sum of judgment was given unto the Son of Man, and he caused the sinners to pass away and be destroyed from off the face of the earth, and those who have led the world astray" (Enoch 69, 26-27).

Presumably the Book of Enoch, which is not contained in our Bible, has been fully preserved only in the Ethiopian translation, after the Hebrew or Aramaic original was lost. Already at an early date the Book of Enoch was received into the Old Testament Canon of the Abyssinian Church. Thus in the seventeenth century it came to Europe as the Ethiopian Book of Enoch, as distinct from other, but only incomplete translations. It belongs to the so-called apocryphal (secret) writings, which according to Luther "cannot be considered equal to the Holy Scriptures, and yet are useful and good to read."

The tidings conveyed in the Book of Enoch, that the Son of Man was known by name even before the existence of Creation, are found again in the Proverbs of Solomon. There the Son of Man, Who is called by the name "Wisdom," says: "The Lord possessed me in the beginning of his way, before his works of old. I was set up from everlasting, from the beginning, or ever the earth was" (Proverbs 8, 22 and 23).

We learn further from these Proverbs of the nature of the task assigned by God to the Son of Man. We learn that He was "by him, as one brought up with him" (Proverbs 8, 22-3 1). His "Work," however, is Creation!

Finally the Son of Man says: "For who so findeth me findeth life, and shall obtain favor of the Lord. But he that sinneth against me wrongeth his own soul: all they that hate me love death" (Proverbs 8, 35-36). The words "that sinneth against me" are equivalent to the sin against the Holy Spirit, which has already been explained.

6.

These references are of course not exhaustive. Many another prophecy apart from the Bible refers to the coming of a great helper for humanity. The holy tidings of this were not given only to the Jewish people, although for the Jews in particular they have an especially fateful meaning.

For in those days most of them, in their expectation of the Messiah, rejected Jesus as the Son of God, although at that time they bore within them the greatest potentiality for spiritual understanding, and had therefore been singled out as the chosen people for the incarnation of the Envoy of God. For them, too, the last opportunity to redeem the guilt of their former failure has come if they recognize the Son of Man, Imanuel, as the Messiah foretold by their prophets, and so longingly awaited for thousands of years!

The Son of Man could not yet come at that time. He was in the midst of His extensive preparation for His great Mission, a preparation lasting thousands of years according to human conceptions. This however was not intended until the time of the Cosmic Turning-Point, which is taking place at the present time in accordance with the unalterable Laws of Development, and is simultaneously connected with the World Judgment.

In the meantime men would have sunk into night and darkness as a result of their volition being constantly turned away from the Light. As speedy help was imperative, God the Father in His inconceivable Love sent Jesus to be incarnated in the Gross Material World, to reestablish directly the connection with God, which mankind had long since severed — this for the sake of the few who still carried within them a spark of longing for the Light. It was a Divine Act of Emergency, which resulted in Jesus' coming to earth without great preparations, and after completing His Mission, although remaining personal, He again had to return wholly to the Father as the Inborn Son (John 16, 28), and as Ruler in the Divine Kingdom; for "His Kingdom is not of this world" (John 18, 36). The Kingdom of the Son of Man, on the other hand, is the entire Creation, including the World of Matter. From the beginning He was firmly linked with His Work as the "Upbuilder" of Creation, so that He remains "Outborn" as the Eternal Mediator between God and mankind "... that he may abide with you forever" (John 14, 16).

For this reason He bears the name "Son of Man," not perhaps because He was to be born of earthman. This could not be the case, for the simple reason that His earthly birth was not originally intended. According to prophecy the Son of Man was to have appeared for the Judgment "coming in a cloud," that is, outside the earthly sphere. The change in this was a further great Deed of Love on the part of the Creator, occasioned by men's continual failure.

Already by the end of the earthly activity of Jesus it was apparent that mankind would not recognize His Mission. This did not consist in coming to earth to permit Himself to be murdered, but in bringing the Truth, the Word of God, so that in the Word of Truth men could find and tread the way to the forgiveness of sins and redemption.

And so it could be foreseen that the great majority of men would not follow the way shown to them, and would persist in their spiritual indolence. Their final doom could then no longer be arrested; for the few who were striving upwards had not the strength to prevent the fall into the abyss.

Hence the Son of Man could only completely help, and save man and the earth from total destruction, by bringing them His Message personally. Only thus was He in a position to reach spiritually those earthmen who were still of good will, and through the Word of God, which He brought in earthly form, to throw out to them in their desperate straits a sure lifeline from their immediate proximity.

7.

That this stupendous event has already taken place on earth without being recognized by the majority of Christians, can be attributed in part to the faulty transmission of the concept of the Son of Man, hardly noticed until now, and to the fact that human ideas and expectations are so little in harmony with Divine fulfillments.

Thus, in exact accordance with the prophecy of Jesus, the appearance of the Son of Man took place at an hour when men were not thinking about it (Matthew 24, 44)! Outwardly a man among men, recognized only by a small number of seekers, the Son of Man dwelt on earth in Abd-ru-shin, and left it again after a lengthy path of suffering, abuse and disappointments.

In the Grail Message "In the Light of Truth" He brought to human spirits in this world and the beyond the new Knowledge of Creation. In this the Teaching of Christ is fully and completely confirmed and presented as it actually is, free from all faulty transmissions, and free from all human additions.

At the same time the Grail Message is the evidence which reveals the Son of Man as Envoy of God. For the earnest seeker it is written therein: "He should examine the words within himself and let them come to life without heeding the speaker. Otherwise he derives no benefit from them."

To human beings, and especially to adherents of the Christian faiths, it is so completely strange that the Son of Man now brings a Grail Message and calls Himself Abd-ru-shin, that most of them refuse to concern themselves with it. And once more the words of Jesus sound in our ear: "Nevertheless, when the Son of man cometh, shall He find faith on the earth?" (Luke 18, 8).

They justify their rejection by saying that Jesus never spoke of the Grail. But they do not recollect His words: "I have yet many things to say unto you, but ye cannot bear them now. Howbeit when he, the Spirit of truth, is come, he will guide you into all truth" (John 16, 12-13).

To this Truth belongs the knowledge of the Grail, whose actual existence is confirmed and explained in the Grail Message. The Holy Grail is a Vessel in the Grail Castle in the highest Spiritual Realm, in Primordial Creation, at the border to the Divine Kingdom. From this Vessel, in eternal rhythm from the beginning of Creation, through the mediation of the Son of Man, the Holy Spirit, the streams of Living Water flow into Creation for its sustenance and continuance. "I am Alpha and Omega, the beginning and the end. I will give unto him that is athirst of the fountain of the water of life freely," so reads the promise of the Son of Man in the Revelation of John (21, 6). The "fountain of the water of life", however, is the Holy Grail!

Already from time to time in the course of thousands of years tidings of the existence of the Grail in the Spiritual Realm have come to earth, but they have been rendered all too earthly by the human intellect, so that the true source remained unclear and clouded, and the genuine longing for the exalted and pure that lies in the Grail could not arise in the souls of men.

Unfamiliar as this new knowledge may appear at first to seeking man, he cannot avoid occupying himself with it; because the time is simply ripe for it.

The Cosmic Turning-Point, with its cataclysmic and irresistible events, has already begun. And with every great turning-point, which is always related to Creation's state of maturity at the time, there is also linked an extension of the Knowledge of Creation. At the present Turning-Point the new Knowledge has been personally revealed by the Son of Man, Imanuel, in fulfillment of the Words of the Son of God, Jesus: "When, however, the Son of Man cometh..."!

With this Turning-Point the promise of Jesus, which He gave at that time in regard to His own coming as a consolation to His people "... I will come again..." (John 14, 3), also became a reality. His presence in Creation at the time of the Last Judgment, through a process of radiation closely connected with the Son of Man, Imanuel, is the fulfillment of His return! This process, however, will always remain incomprehensible to the human spirit!

The Message of the Son of Man is now the last Divine Revelation for mankind, which closes a long evolution of the human spirit-germ into a spirit that has become conscious of itself, and initiates a new great epoch in the Light of Truth, beginning with the long and ardently desired Millennium, which all those who are pure in heart may enter.

Let the human spirit bow in humility before the infinite Wisdom and Goodness of its Lord and God!

Part IV

A GATE OPENS

1. VIGILANCE

Another earth-year has drawn to a close, a year which is equal to the revolution of the earth around the sun, but which in comparison to the immense revolution of the world-parts represents perhaps only a minute or a second of the cosmic clock.

And yet in the twentieth century now coming to an end, this year has also been one of the most important and significant ever experienced by mankind. For it was a year of the Cosmic Turning-Point, a year of the Final Judgment, one that has once again brought rich experiences and recognitions to anyone who with open eyes and open heart has interested himself in events in his own sphere of life and in the world around him.

Various kinds of thoughts move us at the end of a year that has passed, and the beginning of a new one.

And not least is it concern that fills our thoughts, and evokes in us unrest, anxiety and cares with regard to earthly matters.

But this is not the concern that is meant here. It ought to be negligible in comparison with that concern which is directed at *spiritual* advancement and willing obedience to the Commandments and Laws of God.

Only this aim can be the basis of genuine concern, which is far removed from the concept of those cares that are related only to money and property, as well as to physical well-being, cares which today oppress mankind and often torment them to the point of despair.

And yet man is capable of destroying at a blow the tangle of gray earthly cares, if just for a matter of seconds concern for his spiritual development were to lend him that vigilance which instantly finds a way out of dull despair to the height of an existence worthy of man, without tormenting cares about everyday needs, without the constricting pressure which the tie with material substance exerts on the spirit of man.

Only he who is *spiritually concerned* is also spiritually vigilant! A man who is vigilant in spirit does not allow himself to be too much weighed down by earthly cares, or even dominated by them.

Spiritual concern has nothing oppressive about it, but is free of all the distorted concepts with which earthmen have debased the true meaning of the word "concern."

Because they no longer know concern for spiritual well-being, their intellect has put in its place as a travesty the brooding concern over material things which, grown to gigantic size through homogeneous currents, constricts men and holds them captive like high, dismal walls.

For the human spirit dwelling in the Worlds of Matter of Subsequent Creation, there is the ever-present danger of spiritual indolence. Therefore it is necessary for him to be vigilant, and to remain vigilant, to a greater extent away from his spiritual home.

But external influences and impressions alone are not enough to keep him inwardly vigilant, to stimulate him, or eventually to rouse him from the onset of his spiritual slumber. There must also be the concern from within, to be willing to receive spiritual influences aright and turn them to good account, with the object of remaining constantly vigilant.

A man who closes himself to these processes is not concerned about advancing spiritually, because just for this he needs spiritual power as urgently as daily nourishment for his body on earth.

Such a human being then is not vigilant over absorbing and assimilating within him only good impressions, but in his indolence surrenders to bad currents which make him discontented and sullen, if they do not even fill him with envy and hatred.

Against this there is only one protection: constant vigilance of the spirit!

Where there is vigilance, where faithful spiritual watch is kept, be it in the higher and highest spheres or down here on earth, there also is the highest degree of aliveness, there lives the concern for further development and swinging solely in the Will of God, never evading it, or disregarding it by even the slightest thought.

Where true vigilance reigns there is joyful activity, happy fulfillment, constant readiness to do the good deed at any moment, wherever it may be, readiness to fight against the Darkness, and the unconditional applying of one's whole personality to the Light!

This is helped by that concern which leads to alertness, which does not allow the spirit to become lax and to fall asleep — the true concern! Perhaps Wilhelm Raabe meant this kind of concern when he wrote: "Nor had I realized until now that concern is one of the best things in and about the world."

In a public opinion poll the question was asked: "What do you regard as the most important problem of the present time, and what conclusions do you draw from it for your personal existence now and in the immediate future?"

The most important problem of the present time is undoubtedly the *problem of voluntary spiritual indolence*, linked with physical comfort!

Psychologists today are already speaking openly of the decline in spiritual abilities, of an "inflation" that concerns not the economy but the *psyche*. The comfort which has arisen through over-cultivated prosperity and perfected mechanization was one of the great dangers to the spiritual development of man.

But what follows from this for the present and future is accordingly the genuine concern for the *awakening of the spirit* out of its dangerous twilight-sleep.

2. KNOW THYSELF!

True recognition sees things as they have been ordained by the Creator from the very beginning; it is neither subject to fluctuations and delusions nor dependent on the intellect, which indeed is useful as an instrument for the spirit on earth, but is never able to raise itself above that.

Through learning and observing the intellect can acquire "cognitions," broaden them and make use of them for earthly activities, but it can never attain to a spiritual "recognition," because in the nature of things this is not possible for it.

This is reserved for the spirit alone, which through recognitions in the course of its journey on earth creates for itself values that remain in existence even after its earthly death, and open up for it the way of return to the Eternal Home.

Thus the recognition, the ability truly to recognize, is a characteristic of the spirit, which always remains alive if the good volition is there, no matter where the spirit may be on its paths through the vastness of Subsequent Creation.

But how does a human spirit come to recognition; what motivates it meaningfully and in accordance with the Laws of Creation to recognize something with its spirit?

True recognition is preceded by an *experience* that has been called forth through some shock or other of a serious or a joyful kind.

Only when an impression is so strong that it is able to strike the spirit is there the cause for an experience, for which the upward-striving spirit is ready at any time, since after all it originates in a part of Creation where continuous experiencing is the condition for being allowed to exist eternally.

That is why the spirit which is in the process of development positively hungers for opportunities of true experiencing, in order to attain as quickly as possible to that degree of inner susceptibility equivalent to the one prevailing in Paradise.

The spirit finds these opportunities everywhere in Creation through the Law of Attraction of Homogeneous Species, which quickly lets it experience what it desires.

It is a Grace of the Creator that the human spirit-germ, whose home is in the Realm of joyful Activity and Perpetual Experiencing, is yet able far from its home to come to *that* experiencing which makes it a conscious human being of full value, although in the beginning it is only an unconscious precipitation of a spiritual species which was the last to separate from the *Radiation* of God.

Only the coarser radiations of Subsequent Creation, of the World, which spreads out below the Eternal Paradise of man, the adapting to the various coverings of the World of Matter, are the means and ways to a shaking and loosening of the at first still unconscious spirit-germ, bringing it the awareness of its surroundings and of its self.

The process of development from the unconscious spirit-germ to the human spirit conscious of itself remains a miracle of Divine Grace, the more so when we consider that it is actually only this shaking and loosening through Creation- species alien to the spirit that bring about an awakening, and lead it to a gladdening activity and working in Creation as long as the good volition remains.

But with this awakening also comes that experiencing which can be the foundation for true recognition.

In order to achieve this, man must not forget one thing: *himself!* Self-knowledge was demanded even in the days of ancient Greece. The temple of Apollo at Delphi bore the inscription: "Know thyself!" That means strive to recognize your own nature, your origin, your abilities, but also your faults and weaknesses.

Do not forget yourself amid all the wonderful things in Creation that draw attention to themselves, the wealth of events that crowd in on you daily, offering opportunity for the most diverse observations and experiences.

Man certainly needs the courage to be prepared to make unpleasant discoveries in the contemplation of himself; nor should he disregard his so-called "endearing" weaknesses.

Yet at the same time he must not fall into unhealthy pondering, but must set to work in a natural and objective way.

Above all he should recognize that like all creatures he is dependent on his Creator, and does not enjoy any special privileges. As a product of Creation he is of course also subject to the Laws of Creation, without distinction, without the slightest deviation.

That provides the right standpoint for a contemplation of his environment which is of benefit to the spirit, and makes it possible without bias and prejudice to recognize in his fellow-man also a creature striving upwards, who like himself needs to be considered and respected.

Although all human spirits have the same origin in the Spiritual Realm, Paradise, nevertheless owing to their free will they differ from one another through their varying spiritual development and maturity. They are free in their choice of decision, alone responsible for their thoughts and actions, and therefore cannot cast their guilt on others, nor on the Son of God!

These are some important recognitions on the path to self-knowledge. They are the basis for moral ascent, the prerequisite for higher spiritual development.

At the beginning of the "Know thyself" is the recognition of one's own faults and weaknesses, the severance of evil threads of fate. That demands a constant, earnest volition, because at the same time one basic evil has to be overcome: vanity, which does not so easily allow itself to be thrust aside, and often induces self-delusion.

Self-knowledge is the first step to improvement. If the improvement towards what is good continues, it will not be long before one virtue which is important for the man of today gains entry into his soul: humility! And to the humble God gives the help of His Power at all times!

3. SELF-CONTROL

Unpredictable and wavering today is the human spirit dwelling in the World of Matter, Subsequent Creation, who according to the Will of the Creator should know only a constant joyful working and upward striving.

Clear and pure as are the paths of the human spirit in the supra-earthly luminous fields, so are they tangled and dark in the earthly sphere.

Even though the Love of the Creator had intended also here on earth a paradise which in the Radiance of His Eternal Grace was to have become a second home for the human beings sojourning in Subsequent Creation for their development, until their spirit was mature for the Paradise in the Spiritual Realm, the Realm of Eternal Joyful Activity.

All happening in the whole of Creation is clear and simple; even the human spirit is able within its limitations to grasp it, if this happening does not go above spirit and beyond its origin, the Paradise of man.

But the man of today narrow-mindedly closes himself to higher recognitions. He has bound himself too firmly to material substance.

Now however the time has suddenly come when he must sever himself from it if he wishes to end the unhappy state of affairs, and unconditionally open himself anew to the power flowing from Luminous Heights. All circumstances and events are clearly urging towards this step.

To sever means here nothing other than to regard the earthly, which belongs to material substance, from a higher viewpoint, to stand above it at all times, in other words to master material substance.

Only the spirit of man is able, by virtue of its origin, to occupy this higher plane. It alone has the necessary perspective, and understands the connections in the weaving of Creation. To help man in his earthly working he has been given the *earthly* intellect as an *instrument*. Strictly speaking, the intellect also belongs to material substance, because it is composed of the thoughts arising in the perishable frontal brain; for all material substance is perishable.

Now in order to be in a position to win back the lost firm ground in his life-sphere, man must not forget *self-control* as an important help. It has to do with the spirit, and is closely linked with consciousness of oneself. Once he becomes conscious that his ego, his core, is *spirit*, this recognition will make self-control very much easier for him.

It brings with it in a natural way the control of the body. As well as the intellect, the instincts, which in conjunction with the intellect produce the feelings also belong to the body. Out of the working together of intellect and feeling arises the imagination. The temperaments have also to be fitted in here, because they are dependent on the radiation of the blood, which in turn produces a corresponding effect in the brain. They all belong to material substance.

A self-controlled person sees to it that he keeps his thoughts, and with them his intellect, constantly under the control of his spirit; thereby he curbs his instincts and temperament, and keeps feeling and imagination within their natural bounds.

Rightly directed, the instincts of the body, which manifest in feeling, are beneficial and helpful to man. But as soon as he loses control over them, and unrestraint breaks forth, he becomes a plaything of his feelings, which make him unpredictable and moody, and finally do not allow him to shrink from evil deeds. Uncontrolled, they become a source of the worst kinds of passion.

J. G. Fichte rightly said: "The root of all morality is self-control." For the opposite, letting oneself go, has already caused much suffering, has fostered many a propensity for what is bad, which made much trouble for the originator and his surroundings, and could only be overcome with the greatest effort. How often has the necessary consideration for one's fellow-men already been grossly disregarded through lack of self-control and culture.

In the final analysis, it is also lack of self-control, together with weakness of will and irresponsible letting oneself go associated with it, which, among other things, opens the way to drug addiction. However diverse may be the motives for it: curiosity, loneliness, boredom, demoralization, elimination of conflict or the wish to deaden the senses for some reason or other.

The toxic chemicals affect the brain through the blood. Just imagine what confusion these toxic substances cause in the sensitive circuitry of the brain-cells, and how the already generally weakened small brain, which establishes the connection with the solar plexus and the soul, is further exposed to paralyzing influences.

Prolonged use of hashish, for example, leads to reduced efficiency of the brain, interference with the memory and impaired reactions. In a series of examinations of younger drug addicts, changes in the brain were diagnosed such as are usually found only in cases of arteriosclerosis with old age.

The often-quoted "extra-sensory" effects of drugs are purely earthly-material in nature. But as already mentioned, the physical body with its nerves and large brain, both of which play a decisive part in the coming-into-being of thoughts, intellect, feeling and imagination, belong to material substance, thus to the earthly. Although finer than the physical body, they nevertheless still belong to material substance.

Without exception the dream images, the ecstasy of color and the so-called feeling of happiness of the drug addicts move solely within the sphere of influence of this finer gross material substance. In reality the thoughts, the feeling and the imagination become very much confused, which in turn gives rise to great errors and delusions.

Just the "elevated mood" that sometimes manifests at the beginning is very deceptive, because it conjures up something unreal. The reversal sets in quickly enough, and severe depressions, if not even illness and early death, are the evil consequences of drug addiction.

Once again man commits an act of self-destruction. In this instance through self-administered poison.

All this could be avoided if he would rouse himself to exercise self-control. Life on earth offers enough opportunities for this at all times, whether in dealing with people generally, at home or at school, in eating and drinking, or even during the hours of rest. This however requires a serious, constant effort.

Success finally shows itself in the harmony between spirit and body, which for example is expressed in the lightness and beauty of the movements. Only on the basis of this harmony can man develop in the right way at all.

To become a human being who, through the maturity of his spirit, knows how to control himself in an exemplary way in all situations, is a high goal.

4. BELIEF, KNOWLEDGE, CONVICTION

Although Jesus Christ was born among the Jews, the Chosen people at that time, and had His sphere of activity there, yet the Word of Truth He proclaimed was meant not only for the Jewish people but for the whole of mankind. This is quite clearly expressed in His call to His disciples to go forth into the whole world, and bring the Word of Truth to the souls longing for it.

Thus the words of Jesus were transmitted to posterity and became the foundation of Christianity, which stipulates the highest demands and the greatest activity for the human spirit, if it is to be a true and God-willed Christianity.

Only he who receives aright the Word proclaimed by Christ and assimilates it within him, bringing it to life so that it also becomes deed outwardly, deserves to be called a Christian. For it is not the denomination that makes the Christian, but the Word of Christ when wholly fulfilled by man.

What alone counts before the Laws of the All-Highest is how man stands inwardly, whatever he may be in his earthly garb. For example, the worth of a human being in Creation has very little to do with his earthly occupation, With the way in which he earns his living, but is closely connected with what is called "nobility of heart" and "tactfulness." A manual worker of noble heart is of greater value before God than a king who is lacking in this respect!

Indeed it is this inner culture that first makes man a human being, and enables him to recognize in the words of the Son of God what just he needs for his spiritual ascent.

From the initially childlike pure belief that Jesus demanded in accordance with the power of comprehension of the people in those days, the inner conviction could then have gradually arisen in the further development, through a knowing experiencing of the Laws and Commandments of God.

This is how it *should* have been. But for a long time now the once valid foundation for this has been lacking: the childlike belief born out of simplicity and naturalness.

For meantime the majority of men have so trained their intellectual thinking, so keenly sharpened their instruments for thinking, that the simple belief has been ever more repressed, and finally lost altogether.

Therefore in place of this belief must now come that conviction which can only be gained from the *true* knowledge, through inflexible weighing and examining.

By this is to be understood not merely intellectual judging, which is unable to cross the boundary of the earthly; but over and above this must come into action the intuitive perception, which is called forth by the working of the spirit, and which alone is able to divine and grasp all that is "transcendental."

True knowledge is *spiritual* knowledge, which embraces the knowledge of God and His Laws, and their effects in the visible and invisible Creation.

He who wishes to gain knowledge about the mysteries of life must adjust himself to the Will of God in His Laws, and carry them out.

Now since the Creator is Eternal Perfection, and hence also His Will, Which is anchored in the Laws of Creation, any knowledge which man acquires on the basis of the Laws of Creation will also be right.

Wherever it is applied it will release harmony, allowing neither gaps nor doubts to arise, because it has a natural healthy soil on which it can flower and thrive gloriously, even in the possession of earthly mankind.

A man who bears within him spiritual knowledge, the knowledge of the wonderful Laws of God in Creation, to which the Laws of Nature also belong, the knowledge of their absolute incorruptibility and strict Justice, of the love and grace that work hidden within them, of guilt and atonement, which these Laws mediate to men — such a man will find it impossible to hide this knowledge from the outside world; he must live it himself, and be an example to his fellow-men.

Such a man can spread around him only peace and up-building thoughts, contentment and happy confidence, the striving for joyful compliance with the Will of God; he will be a faithful helper and a furthering influence in every respect to his neighbor as well as to his people.

If we consider the knowledge of present-day humanity from this point of view, not much is left of the true knowledge. But in its place man has created a knowledge *of his own*, which he formed according to *his* will, without at the same time taking into account the *Will of God*. Today we are experiencing with absolute clarity the collapse of this human self-knowledge.

However for the seriously seeking human being there is nothing left but to make his own the Knowledge of Creation that is once more offered to him as true Knowledge from out of the Light of Truth, so that he can attain to that level of maturity which he must now occupy at the great Cosmic Turning-Point.

Where once man's childlike simple belief bore within it an undefined longing for the pure and sublime, which helped him on to spiritual maturing, today the new Knowledge of Creation must awaken the spirit and enable it to mature in humility, until it has found its innermost conviction.

In this conviction lies the true worship of God, which manifests in the human spirit's observing and obeying the Laws of God, not only with his volition, thoughts and words, not only at certain times and hours, but unceasingly also through the deed.

5. CONTENT AND FORM

If man wishes to become clear about the weaving and working of the Laws of God in Creation, about growing and maturing, coming-into-being and passing-away, then he must also know what concepts are embraced by the expressions "content and form," what significance they have for his development.

The honest striving after Truth shows him the way here, so that with inner alertness and attentive, objective observation of his environment he will find the bridge to a higher knowledge, which will gradually reveal to him all the glories of Creation in a clearness that gives him infinite happiness, and finally causes him to rejoice at the wonderful Wisdom of the Creator which is expressed even in what is most minute and insignificant.

Just in observing the visible forms around him man can attain to the most profound reflections, which reveal to him processes and happenings that were previously hidden from his sight, but which are now laid bare with complete clarity, filling him ever again with marveling joy and reverence.

Even the very knowledge that all pictorial forms of Subsequent Creation, the World of Matter to which Nature also belongs, have in the higher and highest Spheres models, prototypes, far more beautiful still, should induce the seeking spirit to examine more keenly and attentively all that he sees around him, in order to obtain from it valuable stimulus for reflection.

In the whole of Creation, beginning with Primordial Creation below the boundary of the Divine Realm, down to the densest material substance of Subsequent Creation, there is nothing unformed, because everywhere there is movement and through it life. Life generates heat, brings about forming.

The concept commonly used on earth of the "dead mass" which is animated and formed through a content is not valid in those regions of Creation where there is still intrinsic heat. There the expressions content and form merge into a single concept, because the form bears intrinsic heat within it, and does not have to be first animated by a force.

Only the World of Matter, in itself immobile, makes it necessary to separate the concept content-and-form into an animating content and a form of material substance that is to be animated. For the World of Matter, as the last and coarsest precipitation of the Divine *Radiation*, can no longer generate its own heat; therefore something more has to be added, which heats, animates, binds and forms it: the content. This content consists of animistic and spiritual force, splitting-off from the creatively-forming Power of God.

So is it also on earth, which is part of the World of Gross Matter. No creature is in a position to form anything without the co-operation of these forces as the driving-power, either consciously or unconsciously, and all that has already become form has arisen out of the splitting-off from the Divine Power. The human spirit is just as dependent on the use of these forces; it is part of its task to use them formatively, but only for those forms in which beauty is purely expressed.

The animistic creatures, which are also active in Nature, fulfil this task continually in the highest joy of sacred permission to serve, because in their volition they are bound to the Will of God; whereas with the human spirit, who is endowed with free will, there is the possibility that in engendering forms it will *of itself* intermingle evil volition, which will result in malformations that bring discord and confusion, disaster and destruction.

Such malformations can be observed with man himself, because he has the ability to exercise a formative influence not only on his environment and beyond, but also on himself and his body-coverings.

Therefore a malevolent person will also be recognized outwardly. Just think of the facial expression, of the eyes as the mirror of the soul. Psychic weaknesses and faults eventually make themselves felt in corresponding parts of the body and organs or their functions.

If we could cast a glance into the extraterrestrial planes, we would see that also the fate (karma) of man is formed in a multiplicity which at first seems like confusion, but on closer inspection allows a strict order, in accordance with the Law of Attraction of Homogeneous Species, to be recognized. They are the forms of the intuitive perceptions, thoughts, words and outward deeds.

All these activities are called forth through the volition of the human spirit, in that it exerts a pressure which determines the nature of the forms.

Thus it forms its fate, its path of life. Through a continuous good volition the threads of its intuitive perception can grow upwards right to the Luminous Heights, to be anchored there. In this way it creates for itself a "Jacob's ladder," which finally leads it up to Paradise.

Conversely, through a constant evil volition it is able to create a path leading in the opposite direction to the darkest depths, which are called "Hell." Hell consists of forms which have been produced by men hostile to the Light, through the wrong use of spiritual power.

When it is said: "... and then he (the Son of Man) shall reward every man according to his works" (Matthew 16,27) or "their works do follow them" (Rev. 14,13) or "Behold, I (the World Judge) come quickly; and my reward is with me, to give every man according as his works shall be" (Rev. 22,12), then by "works" is meant all that earthman has formed for himself in his free power of decision. They are the physically visible deeds as well as the physically invisible thoughts and intuitive perceptions, which come to the fore especially when the human soul is severed from its earthly body through death. In the beyond it then finds again all these works in good or evil forms, exactly corresponding to the nature of its volition.

With the ability to form, the human spirit is given a great power, but with it also an immense responsibility with far-reaching consequences; because the whole of Subsequent Creation, which embraces all the Worlds of Matter, belongs to its sphere of activity.

Thus for example it was possible for the darkness formed by men gradually to grow so heavy as to force the earth from its originally luminous course into regions of Darkness.

A human spirit can only dissolve the evil forms connected with it in this way when it deprives them of the content, the nourishing power, by giving up the wrong volition that created those particular forms. They will then wither away.

Therefore it is far better for man not to burden himself first with dark works, but to keep on striving to give beauty and purity to his thoughts, words and deeds.

Not for nothing has the Creator placed man amid the glorious Nature of this world; he is meant to learn from it, and gather experiences that will let him mature.

He will then recognize that in the World of Matter there is a perpetual coming-into-being and passing-away, growing and maturing, in which he participates according to his nature. It could also be said: the content remains, only the forms change; just as the human spirit, which always remains the same, at each incarnation assumes a different form for its earthly body-covering.

It is a blessed resolve when we strive to make evil volition no longer the content of the forms to be shaped by us.

Only through a living, radiant content of all forms engendered by him will man finally be uplifted far above space and time of the Worlds of Matter, into Fields of Bliss.

6. GENERATIVE POWER

Generative power arises at a certain stage of physical maturity; though still of a gross material nature, it is of its finest consistency.

With the setting-in of generative power man casts off his childhood, he is no longer a child and becomes an adult.

Therewith he is spiritually fully responsible for his thoughts and actions, in which connection spiritual is not to be confused with intellectual.

The earthly laws adapt to this development, and declare the young person to be of age, which in Western countries is mostly between the ages of 18 and 21.

Generative power, which marks an important turning-point in earth-life, is able to mediate to the human spirit a wonderful upswinging to what is noble and if the time for it is used aright. For the precious maturing in this power is pure, 1 to be gained step by step, until the spirit, having attained its full vigor, is in a position to make its influence fully felt in the World of Matter.

Therewith it is also able to master the physical instincts, and to keep them within natural bounds. To this also belongs the control of earthly desire and enjoyment, which must begin even with the first thoughts, if these should urge to wrong actions that are harmful to our fellow-men.

Here the intuitive sense of physical shame, which awakens simultaneously with the generative power, comes to the aid of the spirit. Although today, as a result of the great spiritual decline of mankind, it is brushed aside as something outdated and backward, before long it will be able to take its rightful place again, through bitter recognition of wrong thinking and doing.

In reality it is a gift of God, which swings in purity. Without the sense of shame, genuine grace in a woman is not to be thought of, nor is the full unfolding of womanly abilities possible.

The deeper reason for the generative power lies in the *transformation* of the blood which is brought about through the *urging of the soul*, with the spirit as its core, and through the *maturing of the body*. This transformation requires a change in the *radiation* of the blood, and it is precisely this radiation which, as the last bridge in the earthly, helps the spirit to fully conscious activity in the World of Matter.

Presumably it is that glandular system particularly concerned with the blood-radiation that passes the finest active substances, the hormones, directly into the blood through its glands, thus for example the pituitary gland (hypophysis), the pineal gland, the thyroid gland, the pancreas, the adrenal glands, the sex glands!

Of these the pituitary gland is set above all others. It secretes many hormones, by which it controls and influences other glands.

At the beginning of physical maturity the urging of the soul probably affects this gland first, so that it will pass on impulses to the sex glands, which now begin to produce sex hormones. These hormones would then seem to contribute to the forming of the generative power by assisting with the transformation of the blood-radiation!

Certainly with the generative power there also sets in the sexual instinct as a consequence of this power. But the generative power remains *independent* of it! It knows no age-limit, and still exists even when the sexual instinct has ceased. Hence we must distinguish clearly between generative power and sexual instinct, which has to do with propagation, and is subordinate to this power and must be controlled by it!

The glandular system is of vital importance to the physical and spiritual development. For indeed it is responsible for the harmonious running of the inner functions of the organism, and even the slightest disturbances and alterations in it can create serious disorders in hormonal activity, by which the blood and the spirit are also affected.

This sensitivity of the glands would also seem to make itself felt in many an evil karmaic reaction!

Perhaps there is a connection here with the happening of the present World Judgment described in the Revelation of John:

"... and there was a noisome and grievous sore* upon the men which had the mark of the beast, and upon them which worshipped his image" (Rev. 16,2).

By which the glands and the blood are marked as points of attack for evil volition all over the world!

Now perhaps we can appreciate how important it is to keep our body in good health as a treasure entrusted to us by God, to enable it to have the right blood-composition at all ages.

Here reference should be made above all to a *natural, moderate diet*. For especially the knowledge of the right choice of food and drink will become one of the strongest helps for the human body.

---

* "gland" in German.

Then man's intuitive perception will again be so refined that through the choice of diet he is able to bring about the favorable blood-composition suited to him at any one time. Sometimes the declining of dishes hitherto customary, and the wish for other food, is a part of this.

But as well as solid and liquid nourishment, we must not forget the third kind of "food-intake": the art of breathing!

To one called for it, there opens up a vast field for favorably changing wrong blood-compositions through *individual*, natural kinds of diet, which indeed influence the glands as well. These absorb the valuable nutrients offered, and use them to build up the mysteriously-working hormones which in turn contribute to "radiant health", thus to a healthy blood-radiation.

All this wonderful co-operation is expressed quite simply: "Food and drink keep body and soul together!"

It will be a blessed time when, in the not-too-distant future, the senseless bloodshed caused over thousands of years by the evil volition of men comes to an end, and in place of it begins a "bloodless renewal" of the human race, through the great knowledge of the true significance of the blood, without whose proper radiation the human spirit is unable to accomplish a fully conscious earthly working, and the spiritual ascent connected with it!

7. ALL GOOD COMES FROM ABOVE

Surely many a one already has reflected on this oft-used proverb and in so doing probably asked himself how such a "coming" takes place.

If we want to tune in to a certain station on the radio, we need the right wavelength for it. Often the pushing of a button is enough to obtain the desired station.

As it is below, however, so is it also "above"!

There are for instance "transmitting stations" in Creation which lie far above the stars. They are points that transmit luminous rays of the most diverse kinds, far finer and more delicate than radio-waves, which cannot be seen either and yet are effective.

The Love of the Creator has placed these radiation-points in His Creation to help and strengthen man during his journey through the deep vale of the World of Matter.

With man, it is "pushing the inner button" that effects a connection with these helping and furthering rays. It is activated by psychic vibrations, which in turn are released by a strong wish, a prayer, or longing for the pure and beautiful.

All this brings about a loosening of the soul, which then admits the fine currents corresponding to the longing.

But for this connection-seeking a really good volition is first needed. For "he who desires good, should first be good" (Goethe, Faust 11).

Last but not least, we are also helped to this end by the new Knowledge of Creation which is given to us in the Grail Message. This Knowledge causes all that is wrong and rigid in the faith hitherto practiced to fall away, so that that Truth which prepares the way for a firm, undeviating conviction of the spirit rises resplendent before us, and penetrates to our innermost soul.

Thus the human spirit is able to draw to himself all good in the form of these luminous, delicate radiations - the good he needs for his spiritual upward-striving. He is borne ever further upwards, until one day he is allowed to leave the World of Matter forever. Then he has so strongly realized and experienced in his thoughts and actions *all the good coming from above* as to enable him to begin his ascent to those Fields that are called the Blessed.

8. WHERE DOES EVIL COME FROM?

This is a question on which many already have reflected without finding the right solution. There is for instance the view that the fallen archangel Lucifer is the source of all evil, that he is responsible for it, because it is inconceivable that God should have created a monster with the name "man" which for thousands of years has been spreading wickedness, malice, baseness and cruelty in the world.

And there is another question: If through His death on the cross Jesus Christ the Son of God reconciled sinful mankind with God, why have they not improved in any way since then? On the contrary, evil in all its degrees has increased more and more since the time of Christ. People even speak of a "blood-stained history of Christendom"!

In this connection let us consider the following: God created the human spirit with a *free will*, which stipulates personal responsibility.

In the beginning every human spirit was pure. He made use of the neutral spiritual power, "the water of life" (Rev. 21,6-22,17) streaming through Creation, solely for good thoughts and deeds. It was only in the course of his long development in the World of Matter (Subsequent Creation) that as a result of his self-will and vanity he turned more and more to the material, and closed himself to higher influences. Therewith he laid the foundation for all evil.

From then onwards he used the spiritual power to produce evil forms of intuitive perception. In the finer material regions these united, in accordance with the Law of Attraction of Homogeneous Species, into huge centers, to which also belongs Hell, which is nothing other than the product of men who misuse the spiritual power to that end.

In this spiritual decline of mankind, Lucifer the fallen archangel plays the part of enticer and tempter.

He came from the Divine Realm. His self-will brought about his downfall. Instead of lovingly tending the human race, as was meant to be his task, he introduced the wrong principle of merciless temptation, and thereby exposed to destruction all that is weak.

However, it is the fault of men if they succumb to this principle voluntarily. By nature they are spiritually strong enough, and also have numerous helps from Luminous Heights, which assist them to defend themselves successfully against dark influences.

Where then does evil come from? *From man alone!* He puts it into the world, no one else!

God, Purity Himself, could never have created such monsters as have now populated the earth for a long time. He so created all human spirits that they were pure in the beginning. Only later did they darken and defile their pure spirit-core *themselves, of their own accord*. Thereby many made themselves instruments of the Darkness.

It is as the transmitted words of Jesus declare: "That which cometh out of the man, that defileth the man. For from within, out of the heart of men, proceed evil thoughts..." (Mark 7, 20-21). And now there is one great question: Did Christ, through His death on the cross, really reconcile this depraved mankind with God? To this there can be only one answer: A mankind who for the most part, even before the death of Christ, and afterwards still much more so, have been putting evil into the world right up to the present time, thus doing the very opposite of what Christ in His sermons and parables demanded from them, could not expect to be reconciled with God, and still less could they hope that through His death Christ took upon Himself all the sins of men! How indeed should it be possible for someone to take the sins of another upon himself when, in fact, the *suffering* arising out of these sins affects only *the sinner himself*, whereby it is obvious that *the sinner* must reap what he has sown, and no one else, not even Christ!

9. NIRVANA

The word Nirvana comes from Sanskrit, an ancient Indian language, and means blowing away, a flame expiring. One school of Buddhist thought regards Nirvana as the final goal of human life after death, that is in the sense of a disappearance of the spirit, a complete dissolution of the personal being.

A concept which does not fit in with the reality of the whole Creation-Happening. No doubt wishful thinking gave rise to the belief in a Nirvana, in order to proceed to a state of complete rest in the beyond, released from all earthly troubles and burdens.

Here one cannot help thinking of the expression "eternal rest" commonly used in the West, which is supposed to fall to the lot of the deceased.

These are concepts that are opposed to the Laws of Creation. Thus on the contrary, throughout Creation the Law of Movement demands constant movement of oneself, which on earth must lie in a healthy alternation between times of work and of rest, without any exaggeration in either!

But hand in hand with earthly work must also go *spiritual* activity, so that on passing over earthman will take with him good "works," which are imperishable, and will help him on his way upwards. For at physical death he must leave his earthly treasures behind, because they are of a different nature from the consistency of the regions beyond.

By works is meant here his deeds, thoughts and intuitive perceptions, which he puts into the world during his earth-life; whether good or evil, they are kept for him even after his death.

Far is the way for the human spirit, varied its experiencing, and often must it be born again into human bodies, until with a constant good volition it attains to that maturity and lightness which release it from the confines of the earth, and allow it to rise higher towards the final goal, which can only lie in the spiritual.

For the core of man is living spirit, hence the goal too must be filled with life. But this he will find only in the Spiritual Realm, the Paradise of man.

Therewith he fulfils the Law of the Cycle, which ordains that everything must return to the place where it began. With man, however, the starting-point is Paradise, which he left long, long ago as an unconscious spirit-germ, and to which he can return at his highest maturity as a spirit become personal.

There is no question here of dissolution nor of eternal rest. For the Paradise of man is the Realm of Eternal joyful Activity, in full consciousness of oneself.

If a *dissolution* can be spoken of in this connection at all, it refers to the *cloaks* or *coverings* of the *human spirit*, also called "garments," "raiment," "robes" in the Bible (Rev. 3,4-5/7,14). On its path of development through Creation these coverings are placed around it as a protection and an "instrument" in the various spheres which it traverses on its downward journey, right to the last covering, the gross material earthly body.

Now when the human spirit that has become conscious of itself is returning on its path to Paradise, as it strives upwards to its spiritual home all the coverings placed around it must dissolve one after the other in the respective spheres.

This dissolution is a special Grace of God, for unless the material and animistic coverings are laid aside there is no ascent, and no entrance into the Spiritual Realm!

Not until the last tiny particle of the last covering of a different species has fallen away does Paradise open to the human spirit, and in its human form it may pass through the gate to the Spiritual Realm. Only there is it safe in the Eternal Glory of the Light!

But if it deviates from the right path, if it gets lost in the World of Matter and caught in it, it will suffer dissolution along with the disintegration of the World of Matter, which sets in at a definite time. In the course of this it will lose the hard-won consciousness of itself, or ego-consciousness, and through its own guilt will then have been actually effaced from the Book of Life. This effacing is also called in Revelations (20,6 and 12) the "second" death (see also Proverbs 10,7 and Sirach 31,5).

Buddha, who was carefully prepared for his earthly mission in a luminous realm in the beyond, did not give men the doctrine of Nirvana. He knew that the Laws of Creation do not permit of such an impossibility.

Anyone who reads present-day descriptions of experiences and events in the close proximity of death, which report on life in the beyond and the people dwelling there, does not have the impression of eternal rest or even of final dissolution at all!

10. NATURE IS ALWAYS RIGHT

These words are contained in a conversation of Goethe with Eckermann (13. 2. 1829): "... but Nature will not stand any nonsense. She is always true, always earnest, always strict. She is always right. The mistakes and errors are always those of man. Nature spurns the inadequate, and only to the open-minded, the true and pure does she yield, and reveal her secrets to him."

In this utterance lies the deep meaning of Divine Truth. Nature with its Laws is part of the Laws of Creation, which God has woven into Creation as unchangeable, thus always remaining the same. The Will of God is expressed in these Laws. And since God is the Truth, it is also contained in His Will, hence in His Laws.

Thus Nature is always right, she always does what is right, because she is a part of Divine Truth!

11. INCARNATION IN PAST, PRESENT AND FUTURE

The Knowledge of Creation includes the doctrine of *incarnation*, which precedes birth. Without incarnation a human soul cannot come to earth. Incarnation takes place in the middle of pregnancy. Then the human soul waiting in the beyond enters the growing child's body. About that time the first movements of the child become noticeable, because the little body is "ensouled," provided with a soul.

Thus the human soul already exists before birth, which means that all of us have already lived on earth before, not only once but several times, and therefore have died the same number of times, thus experienced death and dying.*

For good reasons, the recollection of these former lives is generally denied us, although every day we unconsciously apply many of the experiences gathered in previous earth-lives.

In reality re-embodiments (reincarnations) signify *development* for the human spirit until it is in a position to leave the constraint of the earth, in order finally to attain to that maturity which opens the gate to Paradise for it. That is the essential thing with these repeated earth-lives. If it is possible at the same time for man to sever evil threads of karma from previous earth-lives, then this is a special Grace of God which He grants to His creatures within His Laws of Creation.

Incarnation can always be only into a human body, not into some animal or other. Under the Creation-Law of Attraction of Homogeneous Species this is impossible, because only "birds of a feather flock together," thus attract only homogeneous species, in this case the human spiritual.

Only once, at the beginning of the evolutionary history of the human race, did the human souls have to incarnate in animal bodies. But these were the most highly developed animals, which were especially prepared for it. Soon after that they became extinct. They resembled the present-day anthropoid apes.

That was inconceivably long ago, at the start of the coming-into-being of man on earth. Then *noble* animals had to serve temporarily as a transition, because as yet there were no *human mothers* on earth. Here the striving towards a *longlasting further development* on both sides provided the connection.

The incarnated human spirit was thus enabled to unfold further in the gross material

---

* Compare the essay "Incarnation and Rebirth" in Part I.

earthly world, and at the same time to raise and advance the latter through its spiritual influence.

At all times there have been receptive human beings who believed in re-embodiment, who were convinced of it.

The doctrine of incarnation is deeply anchored in the spiritual knowledge of the East. In the Christian religions it has been neglected or altogether suppressed.

But the knowledge of previous lives and re-embodiments advances irresistibly, and the spiritual horizon, too narrow until now, widens ever more to magnificent recognitions. A new spirit pervades the whole world, supporting and furthering any honest quest for the Truth.

That to the disciples, for example, a previous life with reincarnation was not strange, is indicated by their question about the man who was born blind, when they asked Jesus: "Master, who did sin, this man, or his parents, that he was born blind?" (John 9,1 and 2).

What is essential for our considerations is the *phrasing of the question*, and this question gives expression to the belief in a former life, irrespective of how it is answered!

This is just as decisive for the further question to Jesus (Matthew 16,14) and to John the Baptist (John 1,21), respectively, whether he was the reincarnation of the Prophet Elijah. The answer of Jesus has been transmitted obscurely (Matthew 11,14; 17,10-12). John the Baptist replied: "I am not" (John 1,21).

At the announcement of the birth of John the Baptist (Luke 1,17) we read: "And he (John the Baptist) shall go before him (Jesus) in the spirit and power of Elijah." This was no doubt to indicate that John the Baptist was not Elijah, but that he was chosen to work in the Power of God and in the spirit of Elijah, thus according to his intentions.

Elijah, the "man of God", who as Prophet of Israel lived in the 9th century B.C. under King Ahab, fought against the cult of Baal and supported the worship of God (Jahwe) alone. His earth-life has been richly embellished by men. Accordingly, he is supposed not to have died, but to have been carried up to Heaven with his earthly body in a chariot of fire (2 Kings 2,11). This fanciful story is today wrongly interpreted also as meaning that Elijah went up in a spaceship!

According to an account in the Bible his earthly body was never found. Hence it is assumed in various quarters that it was altogether impossible for him to be re-embodied at the time of Jesus, because at that time he had been carried off with his earthly body, and consequently could not have incarnated into a second earthly body!

This false conclusion is not valid, simply because according to the Laws of Nature an earthly body perishes at earthly death, and only the spirit with its finer coverings arises. If a discarded earthly covering is not found, this is no proof that it was carried off or that it arose with the spirit. This applies to the earthly body of Elijah as it does to the earthly covering of Jesus, which has not been found to this day.

Here further mention should be made of the LORD's words which were mediated to Jeremiah, and which likewise point to a prenatal existence: "Before I formed thee in the belly I knew thee; and before thou camest forth out of the womb I sanctified thee, and I ordained thee a prophet unto the nations" (Jeremiah 1,5). But let us now concern ourselves with incarnations in the present time.

Therewith it should be noted that the human souls who today incarnate in human bodies are old souls, who have been on earth several times before, with more or less strong ties, faults and weaknesses. Only the new earthly bodies are *childlike* in each case. Man himself is by no means a *clean slate* at birth!

This on the one hand is the explanation of "child prodigies," who even as children accomplish exceptional things which they could not have acquired in their short earth-life. On the other hand, it also explains the often hard lot of children born into bitter poverty and distress, or burdened with a hereditary disease.

Many see in this a great flaw in the Creation-Happening, an injustice, and therefore they murmur against God, not reflecting that it is just these souls who bring with them a heavy, self-incurred fate.

Even God cannot intervene here, in order perhaps to prevent all the sad happenings to which men themselves give rise. He cannot annul His own Laws, which through His Creative Will He once wove, adamantine and unalterable, into Creation. For God is perfect, and there-fore also His Will and the Laws of Creation arising from it, which formed and sustain our World. But what is perfect does not change, cannot change. Therefore God will not arbitrarily ordain that wheat shall suddenly grow from a grain of oats, or a good fate arise overnight from evil human deeds! Otherwise there would be no justice either. But all this does not mean that to those struck by blows of fate we should not extend *compassion*, which always comes from the heart, and therefore also reaches such human beings as are inwardly open to it.

Neither has God allowed all the sufferings on earth, nor does it testify to the futility of earthly existence. But it is a living proof of the extent to which man misuses his free will, and brings all hardship upon himself of his own accord.

Equally little is it God's Will that for decades already the earth has been over-popu-lated by human beings who swarm on to the earth in large numbers from the regions of Darkness, and incarnate here.

That is an *arbitrary* transgression committed by men against the order of Creation, according to which only those human beings may live on earth who have not allowed the longing for the Light in their soul to die away, and who as *guests* in Creation are prepared to keep the Commandments and Laws of God.

Whereas about the middle fifties of the last century the earth still had a population of one thousand million people, today it has more than four thousand million, a population increase with which no other epoch of the earth's history can even remotely compare.

Basest instincts, unrestrained yielding to sexual desires, and a lowest-ever morality offer the dark souls those homogeneous, dim vibrations which enable them to incarnate, and which in this way contribute immeasurably to the increase of mankind on earth.

How such an increase takes place through the attraction of homogeneous species is shown by the statistics of only a single case. They refer to the descendants of a woman drunkard, thief and vagrant who lived at the beginning of last century.

Her descendants increased in number to 834 persons, of whom the lives of 709 could be investigated with the help of the authorities.

Thus the following facts emerged: Of the 709 investigated, 106 were born illegitimately, 142 were beggars, 64 paupers, 181 prostitutes, 76 were convicted of crimes, and of these 7 were sentenced for murder. Estimates were made of what this family cost the state: In 75 years it amounted to 5 million marks in subsidies, prison costs, etc.!

Today the invasion of the earth by dark creatures has reached terrifying proportions. It contributes to a great extent to all disastrous happenings, and not only increases the social misery, but makes itself felt in all fields, bringing at the very least great disquiet and insoluble problems. Under these also fall crimes already committed by children and adolescents. They even commit murder and excel in cruelty.

Blessed therefore be the time, no longer too far off, when the radiations of the World Judgment, now in full working, will check the influx of dark hordes to the earth, and only those souls will still be admitted for incarnation who, filled with the longing of their spirit for the noble and beautiful, find homogeneous parents on earth. –

Just as naturally as the human soul departs from the earthly body through death, so does it also enter upon earthly existence through incarnation.

Once the knowledge of incarnation is universally taught in schools of the future, mankind will have taken a great step forward in their spiritual development.

12. "THIS GENERATION SHALL NOT PASS…

How are we to understand the Biblical words "This generation shall not pass, till all these things be fulfilled" (Matthew 24,34)?

These words were spoken by Jesus at the end of His great oration about the future, relating to the Last Judgment. In many cases they were interpreted by people then living to mean that their generation would experience the end. They believed that Jesus was thinking of the fulfillment of this End-Time, and the coming of the Kingdom of God, not in the distant future but close at hand.

This, however, would not agree with the following words: "But of that day and hour knoweth no man, no, not the angels of heaven,* but my Father only" (Matthew 24,36). Accordingly, the final outworking of the Last Judgment in connection with other similar utterances is rather to be expected in a then still distant future.

Today this Biblical passage is also interpreted as meaning that the Jewish race has remained intact, that it has not perished.

But Jesus gave a deeper meaning to His words. He wanted to express by them that all human souls incarnated in the Jewish people during His lifetime who had not accepted His Teaching, or had even reviled, mocked and personally persecuted Him, would be incarnated again on earth today at the time of the Last Judgment in order to *have* to make their final decision for or against the Message of God.

But for this it is not necessary for all Jews of that time to be incarnated among the present Jewish people. This is connected with spiritual development, for which earthly-religious boundaries are by no means decisive with regard to reincarnations.

An example of such a reincarnation is Theresa of Konnersreuth, who once reviled Jesus on the cross, and must bear His wound-marks as stigmata in her reincarnations until she recognizes the grave sin she committed at that time.**

Through His words above, Jesus referred indirectly to the fact of reincarnations.

---

* In the Lutheran version is added "nor the Son."

** See also the essay "In thine own Bosom lies thy Destiny" in Part 1.

13. THE RADIATION OF MAN

Man leaves the human Paradise, the Spiritual Realm, as an unconscious spirit-germ in order to become conscious, to develop into a fully-conscious personality in the course of his journeying through the planes of Creation that lie below Paradise.

After his departure from Paradise, his "being expelled," a covering is placed around the spirit-germ in the first plane of a different species, "to cover its nakedness." So it goes on. In each plane through which it passes on its way downwards to the earth, it receives a further covering from the homogeneous substance of these planes.

When it arrives at the earthly gross material boundary it already wears coverings from the animistic and ethereal planes, and in this state is called "soul", with the spirit as its core. Through its coverings it is connected with those planes in which it has sojourned.

This process of covering could perhaps be compared to some extent with a man on earth who journeys from the hot zone in the South to the cold zone in the North. The further north he goes, the more numerous or the thicker become the coverings which he has to place around his naked body to protect himself against external influences, and to retain his ability to move about.

It is no different in the great World-Happening either. Proceeding downwards from the Spiritual Realm, the cooling-off becomes ever greater and the covering denser.

Now before man can become fully active on earth, he requires as a final covering a cloak of a material homogeneous to the substance of the earth – the physical body.

We can picture the various coverings as skins placed one inside another, as in an onion.

Today, through the knowledge of the atom, we are in a better position to conceive that the coverings from the various planes of Creation between the Spiritual Realm and the earthly sphere, which the human spirit dwelling on earth carries with it, send out rays, as also does the core of these coverings – the human spirit. Now there are even instruments which demonstrate that man has radiations, which are continually changing.

In earthman the radiations of the finer coverings, together with the radiations of the physical body, form a combination which results in a colorful wreath of radiations, called by some aura and by others od, the "fluid" that surrounds man. With this radiation-wreath he determines the strength of the waves for the vibrations which he absorbs out of the cosmic radiation-system.

The combination of radiations must always be harmonious, so that the spirit of man can develop fully in the World of Matter.

The concept of a human aura, or radiation, is thousands of years old, and clairvoyants of all times have been able to see it.

It is also expressed in the language, when for instance someone says: "His whole being radiates peace and serenity."

The human radiation is communicated to objects which man carries about with him, and to his writings, as well as to photographs, something which is in fact well-known and made use of in various fields.

In illness the radiation changes. Mediumistic people are able to recognize in the radiation-wreath that hidden seat of disease which has given rise to the physically visible disease in the first place.

The knowledge of the radiation of earthman is part of the image of man which will be decisive for the New Age.

In many cases of a judgment, the aura will indicate the real condition of the soul to one who looks deeper. Here no deception is possible.

Finally, this radiation is also decisive for the World Judgment. For in it a man's works, that is his thoughts, intuitive perceptions and deeds, find expression.

14. THE ASTRAL BODY

How does the human spirit sojourning in the beyond come into an earthly body? By incarnating midway through pregnancy into the developing body of a child.

But this is not possible directly, unless through special forces a model, the so-called "astral body," is *first* shaped of a finer material substance, only after which does the gross material body then form.

Only through the astral body can the soul work on the earthly body, but then it still needs also the *radiation* of the blood as the last bridge to full activity on earth.

If gross matter is classified as coarse, medium and fine gross matter, then the astral body belongs to medium gross matter.

There are some things that point to the existence of the astral body. Acupuncture for example.

This is a Chinese method that has been used for thousands of years in the diagnosis and cure of diseases through the insertion of fine needles in certain parts of the body.

The most important points in acupuncture lie along the so-called meridians, a definite number of which run vertically through the body. This makes it possible to treat pains and diseases from points that lie further away from the seat of the disease. Thus for instance heart and circulatory troubles can be influenced from a point on the left little finger. What is essential is that the points lie on those meridians which are related to the parts of the body or organs concerned, whether it affects the meridian for the stomach, intestines, gall-bladder, or for the heart, lungs, spleen, liver and kidneys.

Now it could be imagined that it is the *astral body* through which these meridians with their networks run like energy-paths. What nerve-paths are for the physical body would then for the astral body signify the fixed meridians, which naturally have a connection with the nerves.

They must be of finer consistency than the physical body, because they are not to be found in the tissues of a corpse. At physical death, not only the physical body but also the astral body disintegrates with the meridians.

Thus there is no anatomical proof that these meridians exist; and we can only imagine that they were at one time detected by persons who could see "deeper," thus who had mediumistic gifts.

But yet another indication of the existence of the astral body can be given.

This body fills out, as it were, the whole physical body; it corresponds to it in shape, because the earthly body was actually formed on the astral model.

Now if a limb is severed from the earthly body, the astral body is not affected, and the meridians continue to run through the astral part of the missing member. This indicates that the astral body is less dependent on the earthly body than vice versa.

It has already been pointed out elsewhere that pains which are still felt where a gross material limb has been removed have their origin in the astral part. These so-called phantom-pains can be successfully treated through acupuncture from a distant point in the body.

As the astral body is forming, good and evil radiations, karmaically caused by the human spirit through the exercise of its free will, are connected to it with the help of the stars.

Thus the fundamental disposition or the astral ground-plan which is decisive for the future earthly existence of the newly-born person, is formed. It corresponds exactly to the state of his soul at the time of his coming to earth, with all the still-existing good and bad threads of fate. This is expressed, among other things, in the person's name, in the lines of the hand, the shape of the head, the handwriting, and not least in the birth-horoscope as "radiation-picture," in so far as the stars concerned are known.

Often threads of fate which cause a physical defect, or at least the tendency to it, are woven into the astral body.

For man cannot escape his fate. He has to accept it, because in some previous earth-life *he himself* has put it into the world, or has given it the forms which must then develop automatically through the working of the Laws of Creation, and which he brings with him to earth at his birth, just as he takes them over with him again at his death, be they old or newly added forms.

Hence there can be no question of fatalism in the sense of blind belief in a preordained fate imposed by some power or other.

Perhaps it is in this sense that the following words of the poet are to be understood:

"As on the day that gave thee to the world
 Faced were the planets by the sun's salute,
 Thenceforward didst thou ever more increase,
 Under the law by which thou didst set out.
 So must thou be, thou canst not flee thy self,

318

Thus spake aforetime sibyls, prophets thus;
And no time and no power can e'er destroy
The moulded form that, living, doth evolve."

(J. W. v. Goethe in "Urworte orphisch")

The newly-born has ample opportunity later as an adult to change for good or evil the disposition which he brought with him at birth, because the free will remains with him as the property of his spiritual nature. This enables him, through a really good volition, to sever himself from all evil fate (karma).

15. MAN AND HIS NAME

The name which earthman bears during his earth-life is of exactly the same significance as the position of the stars at his birth.

Even in ancient times people said, "nomen est omen," the name is the fate.

Thus the nature and essence of the bearer are also expressed in man's earthly name; he actually is what his name says. The name swings in the rhythm of his psychic state at the time.

Goethe writes of this in his work "Dichtung und Wahrheit", Part 2: "A man's proper name is not perhaps like a cloak that merely hangs about him and can be tugged and pulled if need be, but a perfectly-fitting garment which indeed is completely attached to him like the skin itself, that cannot be scraped or flayed off without injuring the man himself."

From the meaning of the individual letters of a name, their position in relation to one another, a person Called for this purpose is able to make important statements, be it about the gifts and qualities, faults and weaknesses, tendency to illness and professional talents, or about his attitude to the world around him, etc. But this high art of interpretation is reserved for a later time.

To the earthly name belong the surname and one or more forenames. The surname is established from the very start. But only a part of the nature of the name-bearer is described by it. The other part is expressed in the forenames which are given at birth.

From then onwards the earthly name is protected by law, and may only be officially changed for very good reasons.

In addition, it must be particularly stressed that the choice of forenames is by no means dependent on chance.

Whatever may be the motives which determine the choice of name, be it from family tradition, admiration and reverence for historical personalities, artists and poets, or from an attempt to find forenames that sound well with the surname, it will always turn out that the chosen forenames correspond to the nature of the incarnated soul. For this process always takes place from within outwards, even though it seems to be an outward act.

In accordance with the lawful outworking, Parents cannot do other than choose forenames appropriate to their children's psychic state, which they already bring with them into their earth-life.

Now just as a person has voluntarily acquired his present earthly name in his previous earth-life through his intuitive perceptions, thoughts and deeds, so is he already in his present life weaving the good or bad threads of fate for his future name, which in his next incarnation will lead him, in accordance with the Law of Attraction of Homogeneous Species, to those parents who are of a like nature with him and therefore bear the name appropriate to him.

Hence it follows that a change of name can take place only at the beginning of a new earth-life, apart from a few exceptions as for instance changing the forename after a physical sex-change.

Essentially the forenames are meant to indicate *more* the talent and abilities, and the surnames *more* the karmaic connections determined by fate.

If at marriage the wife assumes the husband's surname, her maiden name will be a part of her nature, and through the Law of Attraction of Homogeneous species will also act as a contributing factor in regard to incarnations.

This can be outwardly denoted by joining the surname of the wife to that of the husband to form a compound name, which is certainly done in some countries, perhaps out of the recognition that the wife does not give up her personal identity when she marries.

It is no different if, conversely, the husband on marrying assumes the surname of his wife where this is permitted by earthly law.

Even though the knowledge of the actual significance of the name has been lost, still the name has always had a special influence and value in the cults of almost all peoples and eras.

Thus the inner value of the name is also concealed in popular sayings such as: "A good name is a rich heritage" or "the greatest blessing, which alone prospers, is the good name at all times." In Shakespeare's "Othello" we read: "Good name in man and woman ... is the immediate jewel of their souls."

But even if man has woven an evil fate for himself in his name, and is born with a more or less "burdened" earth-name, he need not despair. At any moment he can begin with an inner change for the better; very soon the dark tapestry of fate will become interwoven with luminous threads, and his name too will begin to vibrate in a different, a lighter rhythm.

While surnames generally last for several generations, the forenames that go with them are subject to a shorter succession.

Thus there will always be forenames which are "top favorites" for a time, until they are replaced by other favored first names.

With them the character, abilities and modes of behavior of the human spirits incarnated at a particular time also change.

All this is the expression of progressive development in the sense of the Laws of Creation, and not least, these changes correspond to the "spirit of the age," to the constantly changing stellar radiations at specific times, which are very significant for human development. These natural processes and transitions should also be taken into account in regard to problems between the generations.

Moreover, man should always be aware that his earthly name can be a help and a support to him.

16. THE PICTORIAL IN CREATION

Everything in Creation is formed, and what is formed manifests in a picture. Only God is outside His Creation, and therefore not to be comprehended in a human picture. At most, man may visualize "the Eye of God", as it is mentioned in Psalm 33, verse 18.

Now when it is said, "God created man in his own image" (Genesis 1,27), this referred not to man on earth, but to the first *Spiritual* Creation, the Primordial Creation with the first spiritual Primordial Beings. *These* are the images of God, and only after these prototypes did the human form of the subsequently-created Spiritual Realms take shape, among them also earthman.

Thus the whole Creation presents itself in a picture. We can really only experience it pictorially. Even when it is described in words, a picture of it simultaneously arises in the spirit. To absorb pictorially with the intuitive perception of the spirit means living experience.

Therefore the word "picture" has a special meaning in our language. We are in the picture, we get an exact picture if we have a clear idea of something, or we put someone in the picture; on the other hand we form a wrong picture of something if we are not able to visualize it clearly in order to form a right concept of it.

To form a concept we need a picture, and this in turn is called forth by the word; color and sound are also involved.

If for example we describe an object as a "table," a definite picture arises which awakens the concept of the table; to this belong its shape, color, material, function. Each one however will see the table differently: round, square or rectangular, colored, iron, wooden, etc., but the *basic picture* "table" always remains the same.

While man on earth needs the words of his language in order to form concepts, these fall away in the ethereal substance of the beyond. For with physical death the large or frontal brain, which produces the thoughts, the intellect and the words, also perishes. Thus beyond the earthly realms there are no longer any spoken words but only pictures, which have to form the concepts. They help men to communicate with one another. Through their nature it can be recognized immediately what the spirit wishes to communicate to those around.

Something similar is also reported by persons who after physical death have been "on the other side" for a short time, and have come back into their earthly bodies. According to that they heard neither voices nor other sounds in the region beyond. They seem rather to have directly picked up the "thoughts" of the spirit-beings around them. Although communication was not in the mother-tongue of those concerned, the sense of what had been "said" was clear and distinct, and it was not easy to translate this kind of communication into earthly language.

In the gross material earthly, on the other hand, man first has to impress his spiritual volition on the back brain, which under this pressure forms pictures that are condensed and reshaped by the large brain into writing, speech and deed.

Conversely, the impressions of outward happenings are passed on through the large brain via the small brain, which in turn transmits them to the spirit in pictures. The more vividly man seeks to visualize pictorially what his five gross material senses convey to him from without, the stronger and more lasting the impression, which can be brought forth from the subconscious at any time through some outward or inward cause, and made accessible to the day-consciousness.

As mediator between spirit, soul and body, the small brain has a part in the subconscious. It is of finer consistency than the coarser large brain, can retain experiences in pictures and intuitive perception, and at any time pass them on as memory to the day-consciousness, which arises in the large brain.

Thus memory is retained in the small brain, also called intuitive brain, because it alone is able to receive and assimilate manifestations of the spirit. In the English language this connection can still be recognized in the expression "by heart," which means "from memory." Thus if man wishes to say something from memory, he must bring it out from the heart. Originally the heart meant the solar plexus, the point where the spirit maintains connection with the physical body through the small and large brain.

How good a memory is depends on the extent to which it is possible to absorb impressions and experiences in the subconscious of the small brain, and then according to need to recall them again undistorted into the day-consciousness. That depends largely on the harmonious co-operation between the large brain (intellectual brain) and the small brain (intuitive brain).

Today a considerable disparity prevails in this co-operation. For a long time man has neglected his intuitive brain and allowed it to become stunted, while one-sidedly over-cultivating his intellectual brain. The consequences manifest in the often faulty and distorted transmission of impressions through the large brain, and in the weak or hazy absorption by the small brain.

Through this the impressions remain on the "surface," they do not go deep, and this gives rise to the concept "superficial." Comparing this with a photographic plate, these processes result in an *under-exposure*, which is equivalent to an image that is too weak, or lacking, because of too slight penetrability of the large brain or weakened activity of the small brain.

We have something similar with forgetfulness. People overcome it by each time vividly imagining what is to be retained for a shorter or longer period as memory.

On the other hand there is the possibility of an *over-exposure*. The pictures formed by the small brain are then so strong and lasting that they move and control man's soul for some time, and under certain circumstances cause hallucination. Such pictorial impressions are called forth, for example, through fright, terror, fear, or sudden violent invasions of a person's life, when at the same time the shaping of corresponding forms in finer material substance takes place with increased speed and intensity. Such forms reciprocally receive a supply of power from already-existing concentrations of the same kind, and for a time prevent the too strongly absorbed picture from fading and being obliterated.

Television brings with it a special kind of "over-exposure." Quite apart from the fact that the radiation of television sets is harmful to the brain of children and young people – as has been scientifically proved – the effect of the picture can also hamper the development of the personality. There may well be an excess of pictorial impressions here which can simply no longer be assimilated, and which cause other necessary functions like speaking and thinking to be retarded, or even bring about psychic damage.

This is all the more serious because children are only able to learn word-language gradually, and at first are completely dependent on the pictorial, above all on *examples*. Therefore they must be taught pictorial comprehension carefully and without overdoing it. But for adults too the absorbing in pictures, pictorial visualization, is of importance for spiritual advancement.

Christ knew that, and hence often spoke to people in pictorial parables in order thereby to appeal directly to their souls, and to make the spiritual happening in Creation clear to them, thus showing the simple way to the Truth.

Unfortunately the content of His parables has been frequently misunderstood, right up to the present time.

For instance, let us consider the words that Christ spoke to the rich young man "... take up the cross!" (Mark 10,21). Here many people visualize Christ's cross of suffering, and as usual form the concept that a readiness to suffer is linked with the taking up of the cross, above all for those who are prepared to follow Christ. With this meaning the concept has been absorbed into the vocabulary: "God has laid a heavy cross (burden, sorrow) on me."

In reality Christ wished to express something quite different by His words. He came out of the Divine Truth, and the symbol of Truth is the Cross with *equal* arms, which was already well-known long before Christ's life on earth. What Christ wished to say with His words was. To take up the Cross daily means to live at all times according to the Truth, to absorb within us the Truth He proclaimed.

God does not wish men to suffer, nor need they if they obey His Laws, which contain the Truth.

With the "entrusted pounds," which men are to make the most of (Luke 19, 11-28), Christ was referring to the noble and pure abilities which man is to awaken and develop. Through negligence and indolence these will not come to flower, but are "buried."

Or let us consider the picture of the wise and foolish virgins (Matthew 25, 1-12) which refers to the End-Time, the Last Judgment. The bridegroom is the Son of Man proclaimed by Christ (e.g. Mark 8,38). He comes by night, thus at a time when He will not be recognized by most men. One part of mankind (five foolish virgins) will pass by the Truth proclaimed by Him, because their spirit is not aglow; it has gone to sleep. The other part of mankind (the five wise virgins) will recognize Him and receive His Divine Word, because they were able to kindle their spirit in good time with their longing for the Light. With the purity of their faith they are permitted to take part in the marriage of the bridegroom, that is, in the New Covenant which the Son of Man makes with mankind, through which the gate to Paradise is opened for them.

When Christ spoke of the mote and the beam (Matthew 7,3), He was comparing with these pictures the great and small faults and weaknesses of man. If he is irritated by faults which he detects in his fellow-men, he himself bears within him these *same* faults to a far greater extent. In this parable the same type of fault is exemplified in the same material of beam and mote: that is in the wood.

An excellent example of a picture-language in the beyond is the Revelation of John, which John the Baptist was permitted to receive in high spiritual planes that lie far above the earthly regions, and to pass on to men on earth. Let us read just verse 2, chapter 16, which deals with the first of the seven plagues in the World Judgment: "And the first (angel) went, and poured out his vial upon the earth; and there fell a noisome and grievous sore upon the men which had the mark of the beast, and upon them which worshipped his image."

This plague particularly affects the physical body of man. What here was revealed in pictures about two thousand years ago in the Spiritual Realm will be fulfilled at the present time on the earthly plane as unknown and mysterious diseases, which above all poison the blood and glands, and spread swiftly and devastatingly over the earth like a plague.

People who bear the mark on them will be struck by it; a mark peculiar to those people who acknowledge only the "beast," namely their over-cultivated earthly intellect, while on the other hand they completely suppress their spirit. The image they worship is crass materialism. They are no longer able to keep alive within them enough longing for the Light to connect them with the helping and strengthening rays of the World Judgment. Instead they will be struck full force by the plagues released through the increased Light-pressure, which they draw to themselves because, by suppressing their spirit, they commit a great sin against the Holy Spirit, thus against the Laws of God.

After these few examples of an expressive picture-language from past eras, mention should also be made of those pictures which are produced in the large brain in connection with physical feeling, and described as "imagination." They are without spiritual power, affect only the originator, and do not radiate upon the environment like intuitive pictures.

The ones that stir and drive are always those pictures which are produced by the spiritual volition, whether they have arisen through inward or outward impressions. Through them the man with a continuing good volition gradually creates for himself a rich inner life with inestimable values, because the pictures and forms that have thus arisen find connection with homogeneous centers in Creation from which undreamed-of help and strengthening is retroactively bestowed, so that everyday life too is permeated with furthering radiations, for the blessing of Creation and his fellow-men dwelling in it.

The pictures formed during earthly existence through experiencing endure after earthly death, and follow man as his works when he leaves the earth. If they swing in purity they can form strong anchorages on his path to Luminous Heights. Nothing of the living intuitive pictures is lost. They are "stored" as though in a computer in the great "world-memory," and unwind as in a film before the spiritual eyes when man "recalls" them, or when they are shown to him by the spiritual guidance, even if they came into being thousands of years ago!*

It happens more and more frequently that people who as the result of an accident or an illness have found themselves on the threshold of death, and returned to their physical bodies, have experienced such "films." In the beyond they were shown a playback, in rapid succession, of pictures from their past earth-life, often in full detail, or else only with the heights and depths. Usually associated with this review were counsels, instructions and admonitions, which proved very useful and beneficial for their further earth-life.

In this way many of these people form a noteworthy bridge between the earthly and the beyond. They bring with them valuable experiences which, while certainly intended in the first place for them personally, nonetheless also contain general recognitions, even if it be only the one that "with death all is not over."

Lastly, through this the connection with "the other side" is made ever closer, and the recognition furthered that this side and the beyond form one *whole*. The separation has been introduced only by man.

---

* See Book-series of the Grail Message Foundation

17. COLOR AND TONE

How important colors are for us appears in the manifold expressions in our language. For instance, if we speak ill or enthusiastically of something we describe it in the darkest or brightest colors; or an account is colored because it does not correspond entirely with reality. As soon as we admit our conviction, we show our colors; and if we want to stress a point and present it more vividly we simply give it more color.

But in personal life also color is of importance, even in the choice of colors for our surroundings and our clothing, according to personal taste.

Nature mediates to us a right experiencing of colors. What joy we derive from a rainbow with its natural colors: red, orange, yellow, green, blue, indigo and violet. Already in ancient times it was regarded as a symbol of the Covenant between God and men (Genesis 9,13), and in the Revelation of John a rainbow appears around the throne of the Son of Man (4,3).

All the colors that are combined in the rainbow are found individually again in manifold ways in the Nature around us, be it the green of the meadows, forests and oceans, the blue of the sky, the golden yellow of the sun or the red of sunset and dawn, the violet of twilight and the colorful sparkling of the stars, not to speak of the many colors of animals, flowers, fruits and stones. Goethe recognized the great value of the colors and their powers, as is clearly evident from his theory of colors.

Colors radiate, and have definite wavelengths. They bring us benefits of many kinds if we use them rightly. A few comments should be made here about the effect of the most important colors and their connections.

Red, which has the longest wave-length, has a stimulating, rousing effect, it awakens enthusiasm, courage, resolution, energy, aggressiveness and adventurousness. Fire and the pulsating blood are red.

Yellow radiates warmth, gives confidence, optimism, cheerfulness and freedom from care. "Yellow-toned" people have sunny natures.

Nature offers us green in rich abundance. With "Mother Green" we recover from the bustle of everyday life. How calming and strengthening it is when our eyes rest on green meadows, for "color-vision" also influences the mind. Green symbolizes hope, growth, ripening, the not yet complete that still gives hope of fulfillment!

Blue is a cool color, and has a calming effect on man. Good results are achieved when abnormally agitated people are put in blue rooms.

The cold ice-blue of winter is more indicative of what is contracting, hardening, inward-turning, while the light blue of the sky mediates faithfulness and constancy.

Violet is connected with man's relationship to God. Trustful faith in God, veneration of God and respect for His Laws are a part of it. Violet is the color of ceremony, of dignity, and finally the expression of highest wisdom and recognition.

Orange gives warmth, cheers, and fills one with the joy of life.

Of course there is also a close relationship between color and temperament.

Colors play an important part in healing therapies. Here diseased parts of the body are irradiated with colored light. In this connection red has a stimulating effect; it expands the vessels, stimulates the circulation and increases the red blood corpuscles. Yellow warms, animates and strengthens. Green is related to the organs of digestion, including the liver and gall-bladder. "To turn yellow with jealousy and green with envy" indicates diseases of the greenish gall-bladder and the liver (yellow skin color). Blue allays pain, calms overwrought nerves, helps to contract and tightens the connective tissue. It is also said to have a favorable effect on the lymphatic system.

A completely different method from color-radiation in cases of physical diseases is the direct action of color on the blood-radiation. Here colored stones, which must always be *individually* composed, are brought into contact for a longer period with the blood-circulation at specific points of the body. The blood-radiation is so altered through the colored stones that it is able to absorb radiations from the Universe, which gradually provide spirit and body with new upbuilding and refreshing powers.

But only later will it be possible for called ones to practice this kind of healing, when human beings have adjusted themselves to the Will of God, thus to His Laws, and are once more close to Nature.

Even the ancient Egyptians in their healing art used the colors of precious stones, with which they treated diseased parts until the balance was restored in the disturbed aura of the person. For this the healers had to be clairvoyant and able to see delicate radiations, or at least to have a very refined intuitive faculty.

And still today there are persons so gifted. They are able at once to recognize points of disease, or rather a wrong vibration in the finer astral covering of man. – In India the healing power of precious stones has been used again in more recent times.

When we come now to speak further of the relation between color and tone, we must know that beyond the earthly realms *color and tone are one*. There colors sound and tones have colors, and the higher we go into Luminous Spheres, the more sharply do tone and color stand out.

Only to earthman do color and tone appear to be separate, because only in this way is he able to perceive them through his dense body-covering. But the memory of the unity of color and tone in the extraterrestrial regions still exists in the human language in words like "tone-color" and "color-tone", or when we give a lighter or darker "tone" to a picture.

There are however specially sensitive persons who even here on earth are able to experience color and tone as a whole. For example, when the note C sounds on an instrument they see a ruby-red color, for according to the order of Creation the seven colors of the rainbow correspond to seven keynotes; hence to each color belongs a definite tone. These people who have a refined intuitive faculty experience musical pieces as a glorious play of colors, rather like illuminated dancing water fountains.

Therefore if we consider that beyond the gross material world color and tone cannot be separated from each other, we perceive the whole of Creation as one mighty symphony of colors, in fullest harmony.

All colors issue from the Divine Primordial Power, and permeate Creation as glorious, sounding color-radiations, right down to the World of Matter, where they manifest in Nature and give testimony of this wonderful happening.

With his colorful radiations earthman makes manifold connection with the color-rays of the Cosmos, and is thus in a position to weave himself a many-colored carpet of fate, with the most beautiful and purest colors, if at the same time he scrupulously observes and follows the self-acting Laws of Creation!

18. THE MYSTERIOUS NUMBER 666
IN THE REVELATION OF JOHN

A picture which has always been the subject of close consideration and interpretation is the "beast with two horns," above all because of its connection with the mysterious number 666.

"And I beheld another beast coming up out of the earth; and he had two horns like a lamb, and he spake as a dragon" (13,11).

"Here is wisdom. Let him that hath understanding count the number of the beast; for it is the number of a man; and his number is Six hundred threescore and six" (13,18).

All human interpretations have been fruitless until now, whether individuals, or religious and earthly powers of different centuries, were taken to be the beast.

For the beast with two horns (= 2 words) stands for the *world-embracing* concept *The Sin!* But the name of the man who has the same number as the beast called *The Sin* is *John the Baptist!* The number 666 is explicitly given as the key to it.

Like any other number, the number 666 also bears within it the sharpest contrasts. Thus with the number 666 there is on the one hand the sin in the service of the Darkness, the cause of all evil, the adversary of God; it is the sin which rules the world, entices to evil, and ever again persuades to the worship of the first beast (13, 1), which embodies the "absolute dominion of the earthbound intellect."

On the other side stands John the Baptist, the high and pure spirit, the faithful and humble servant of the Light, the blessed mediator of Divine Revelation; as a powerful warrior against the sin, his name swings in the same number.

Only a wise Providence which is anchored in the Omniscience of God could express in picture-language almost two thousand years ago what today in the German language called for it is fulfilled "literally," that is, in the words "The Sin" and "John the Baptist." This prediction is based on no arbitrary act. It could be given only within the Laws of Creation in regard to the wrong path of fate which mankind, in their free volition, had chosen at the time of the Revelation.

At the appointed time, the same wise Providence gave to men called for it the key to the solution of the mystery of the number 666, which is to be found in the Laws of Numbers swinging in Creation.

But how did a connection come about between the Laws of Numbers and the German language chosen for the solution? For this purpose the Laws of Numbers had to receive earthly coverings into which they could be anchored: the letters.

In a long development, words were formed from the letters until, through moving the individual letters to and fro in the use of the language, the right words swinging in the Law of Numbers had been formed. Among other things, the so-called sound-shifts (c. 250 B. C. and c. 660 A. D.) give eloquent proof of this.

The whole language-development was always directed by a wise guidance which proceeded through influencing the spirit of men, the "inner voice."

Man's ability to form words lies in his spirit as a special gift of the Creator. Naturally this applies to all languages, not only to German! Even in the Creation-story it is mentioned that man made use of this gracious gift of forming words, and gave the beasts a name (Genesis 2, 19-20).

A faint reflection of the Living Word of God, out of Which Creation arose, still lies in the human word. Therefore the human word is also living, and has a releasing effect, for good or bad, according to how man uses it in his freedom of will. Even though the releases still lie close to the earthly, with wrong use of the language they can nevertheless have devastating consequences, and bring about the downfall of whole peoples.

Rudolf G. Binding (1867-1938) describes very well the vitality of the language:

"The language is the infallible, complete picture of the character of every people, automatically containing all its traits; the true face of its inner being and the voice of its heart. No other expression of its being is so complete and so much its own. In the language, indeed even in the individual word, the spirit and the nature of the nation come to light; they enter the space of history, enter the space of the world and the stars. Richness and poverty of their soul, strength and weakness of their being, depth and height of their flight, sincerity and simplicity of their feelings, greatness and nobility of their mind, breadth and narrowness of their humanity: for each they are born anew in every word that springs from the soul of their people. Today as in the past – into all future as ever" (Of the Power of the German Word as Expression of the Nation).

But let us return to the German language. As this approached its completion, there were also, at the appointed time, Called ones who, responding to the gentle prompting of their luminous guidance, began to investigate the numbers and their Laws.

Thus they discovered the Laws of Numbers, through which the mystery of the number 666 could be revealed. To publish the Laws of Numbers here would be going too far, and is reserved for a later time. Only the result of the calculations shall be mentioned, because it may be of interest.

Thus not without reason was the German language in particular carefully prepared over a long time. Many Chosen ones had taken part in this. Martin Luther, whose language-creation was briefly dealt with in Part 1, was only one of them. But he was very important, because he set a landmark in the development of the German language, and because he so translated the Revelation of John into the new German language that this translation could serve as the foundation for the later opening of the Seven Seals, in accordance with the Laws of Numbers. Thus, for example, Luther rightly translated the *number of a man*, as opposed to other translations which say *a human number*. This can apply to many human beings, whereas "the number of a man" refers to one particular number, namely that of John the Baptist.

The present Cosmic Turning-Point, which brings with it the World Judgment, is a time of Divine Fulfillments, and one of these Fulfillments is the unveiling of the Revelation of John, the opening of the Seven Seals; the mysterious number 666 is also part of this.

The accordance of this number with the words "The Sin" and "John the Baptist" confirms the rightness of the linguistic development, as well as the right fitting of the Laws of Numbers into the language. Often enough have human lack of understanding and liking-to-know-better disturbed this development, or sought to impede it.

All the more should the Germans in particular strive to recognize what high Grace lies in the fact that their language is chosen as the instrument of great fulfillments. It is like a precious stone, meticulously cut, which must be protected and is not to be sullied or altered in its structure, as unfortunately happens or is attempted ever again.

How closely "Germany" ("Deutschland") is linked with the immense World-Happening is shown by the translation of this word according to the Laws of Numbers. It swings in the number 666! That means power! And how has power especially been abused and sinned with in Germany, instead of being used to create a God-willed Kingdom of Peace.

Thus is unveiled for us the mystery of the number 666 in Chapter 13 of the Revelation of John, who is called "the Baptist." Who else could it be but this high Called one, who was allowed to baptize Jesus, the Son of God, on earth!

Through the "matter-of-fact" numbers we experience how wonderful are the Laws which the Will of God has placed in His Creation, and how after thousands of years the great, loving guidance brings to fulfillment everything ordained by the Omniscience of God.

In the sphere of numbers this can be understood even with the intellect, for "Let him that hath understanding count the number of the beast: for it is the number of a man; and his number is Six hundred threescore and six" (13,18).

19. DIVINE MIRACLES AND HUMAN MIRACLES

The miracles of Jesus came about neither through interventions in the order of Nature nor through annulment of the Laws of Nature!

In His miracles Jesus had to keep strictly to the Laws of Creation or the Laws of Nature, which in their immutability allow of neither exceptions nor arbitrary acts. Thereby He fulfilled the Laws of His Father.

When Jesus raised the dead He could do so only as long as the connection, the so-called silver cord*, between the physical body and the soul still existed. This was the case with the raising of the daughter of Jairus. Hence the words of Jesus: "Weep not; she is not dead, but sleepeth," and later the statement: "and her spirit came again."

At the same time we recognize that body and spirit are of two different species! The spirit, the eternal – with its finer cloaks called soul – which lives on after death, and the earthly body, the transient, which disintegrates when the spirit leaves it.

Only Jesus in His Divine Power could recall the soul into its earthly body, and as a human spirit it had to obey the Divine Will.

The process was exactly the same with the raising from the dead of Lazarus and the young man of Nain.

In the case of possession, the alien spirit also had to obey the Divine Will, and leave its victim. When the spirit of earthman is indolent or weak, it is possible for a spirit in the beyond to take possession of his physical body in order to work on earth through his brain.

The "casting out" of such an "unclean" spirit is described in the Bible, Mark 1, 23-26.

The miraculous healings of Jesus took place in accordance with the same Laws of Nature. Therefore in each case the physical organs to be healed had to be still functioning to such a degree that through the increased pressure of the healing power the fine cells of the body-parts affected could be stimulated into healthy activity again, enabling the body to regain its full health.

In addition, the supplicant had always to be filled with trusting faith, and open himself humbly to the healing power.

---

* See: "The Silver Cord" in Part 1.

336

The words of Jesus: "According to your faith be it unto you!" point to the Law of Balance between Giving and Taking.

Giving oneself in all humility and simplicity prepares the way for the *taking*, the receiving of gracious help. Where this condition was lacking the healing power could not be absorbed.

Even at the present time miraculous healings are possible! It happens that here and there a human spirit endowed with grace is given special power, with which he accomplishes miraculous healings, thus the healing of diseases hitherto regarded as incurable.

But this power bestowed is *not Divine!* It cannot be measured or compared with the Divine Power in its original state in which Jesus worked, and which far exceeded what is humanly possible!

The human spirit, which has within it nothing of the Divine but only *of the spirit*, has at its disposal only the powers in Creation, thus outwith the Divine, which in comparison with the Divine Power have a greatly reduced working potential.

One of these Creation-powers is magnetism, an animistic force of Nature which Called ones have been using for a long time now, for the blessing of mankind.

All these genuine healing-powers, however, are given only to those who, being Called for the purpose, receive and pass them on in purity and humility.

But there are also other ways that lead to wonderful recoveries of diseased bodies.

Let us mention those miracles that take place at springs or other places. They are connected with genuine "heavenly visions," relating not to Mary of Nazareth, but to the spiritual radiation-picture of the Queen of Heaven, Who has Her Origin in the Divine Realm*.

With trusting faith, and prayers intuitively perceived in purity, the way to this spiritual radiation sometimes opens for supplicants, making them receptive to wondrous healings and dispensations.

Unfortunately there is always the danger that through wrong ideas and foolish behavior men will cloud and disturb such high and pure connections.

May these explanations lead to the recognition that all healing and strengthening powers always come from *without*, thus they are *not within us*, and can only be *received!*

There is much talk of miraculous hearings through hypnosis. Yet the process is anything but a miracle. In reality it has to do with an invasion of the personal sphere, which

---

* See: "The Queen of Heaven" in Part 11.

brings about a binding of the spirit, and therewith a forcible elimination of the free will!

Its place is taken by the alien will of the hypnotist, who imposes his will upon the one hypnotized, thereby making him dependent on himself.

Hence through this alien intervention only a temporary *artificial* healing is brought about, which in certain cases has to be maintained through repeated hypnosis, until one day the treated illness or addiction appears again, as itself or in some other form.

In any case, the will of the one hypnotized is thereby weakened, and valuable time lost for him in which, through the very experiencing of his illness, he would have been in the position to mature spiritually by it!

Moreover, it is possible that during the time in question he has missed valuable opportunities of *genuine* healing, which he himself could have brought about voluntarily through personal effort of will.

Therefore it is not easy for man to free himself from this hypnotic binding, because to do so he must set to work with all the strength of his spirit.

Most people have hardly any idea of how dangerous the application of hypnosis is, because they do not know its final effect in the beyond. For as stated, it binds the spirit, and the free will is thereby suppressed, regardless of whether the one treated has consented or not. Even with consent he is unable to eliminate the working of the Laws of Creation, because hypnosis is opposed to these Laws and thus is a sin against the spirit, which has grave consequences for all who practice it! —

Let us now look also at the other happenings around Jesus which have been handed down as "miracles."

While out on Lake Genneserat, Jesus calmed the turbulent waters: "And he arose and rebuked the wind, and said unto the sea, Peace, be still! And the wind ceased, and there was a great calm" (Mark 4, 39). Actually Jesus was speaking to those nature beings, the servants of God, who are active in the elements of air and water, thus a quite natural happening.

They belong to the same nature beings as are mentioned in Psalm 104 "...who walketh upon the wings of the wind. who maketh his angels spirits: his ministers a flaming fire."

The so-called miracle of the feeding was no miracle, but a parable. Through men's imagination it became a rumor, which like many another wrong was later recorded in the Biblical traditions.

Jesus meant not earthly but spiritual food, the Word of God. He said of Himself: "I am the bread of life" (John 6, 35).

Men absorb but little of the Bread of Life, the spiritual power; most of it they allow to pass by, heedlessly scattering it like crumbs, which alone would suffice to give spiritual food to thousands of human beings, indeed to many more still.

Jesus was not in a position to create suddenly from a few loaves and fishes a quantity of food for thousands of people. According to the Laws of Creation that was impossible.

In accordance with these Laws, it was equally impracticable for Him to turn, for example, stones into bread, to let His gross material earthly body fall from the pinnacle unharmed, or to come down from the cross. Even as the Son of God, Jesus was unable to infringe the Perfection contained in the Laws of His Father, otherwise they would simply not be perfect.

Lucifer well knew this when he approached Jesus with the temptations. He wanted Jesus to forfeit credibility in the eyes of the people, if for instance He had wished to turn stones into bread.

If today it were possible for us to look at a miracle through a slow-motion camera, we should find that the running off of the individual successive processes corresponds without a gap to the working of the Laws of Nature. But it takes place with extraordinary speed and concentrated power, which in the case of the miracles of Jesus far surpassed human ability! As we are unable to survey these processes we describe them as miraculous, as miracles.

We see only the last phase of the miracle, thus the final effect, and draw mainly wrong conclusions in respect of the whole process which to us is unknown.

After these explanations we may unhesitatingly regard the miracle as part of the Christian faith; for this is based on the incorruptible, adamantine Laws of God, which even in all miracles are not annulled but fulfilled.

In reality the whole of Creation is one single tremendous miracle which we are allowed to experience with open heart every day!

20. THE SEARCH FOR TRUTH

What we are dealing with here is not the sum total of the views and the thinking of any particular social group – known as ideology – but, standing far above that, the longing of the earnest seeker for the Truth.

The wish, deeply sensed intuitively by many, for values which are changeless, to which they can hold fast in their soul with confidence, is nothing other than the search for Eternal Truth.

Only values that are linked with the Truth will give to a moral philosophy a lasting content which is binding for men, and decisive for their spiritual development.

Truth remains ever the same, eternally changeless.

It begins far above the Paradise of man, in distant Heights which remain forever closed to the human spirit.

We recognize it in the Laws of Creation, because these come from God, Who is the Truth! The more we experience and recognize the Laws of Creation, the nearer we come to the Truth.

Man must obey these Laws, adjust himself according to them, if he wishes to be joyful and happy. There is no alternative; otherwise he will suffer harm.

How the Laws of Creation can be applied in solving very controversial problems of the present time shall be shown by some examples in the essays that follow.

Just now we are concerned above all with the Creation-Law of Attraction of Homogeneous Species.

These essays are dealt with from the *spiritual* standpoint, and are intended as a stimulus to reflection on those things which cannot be perceived with our five senses, but only with the intuitive perception of the spirit.

21. THE ENVIRONMENT OF MAN

The theory established decades ago that the environment moulds the man, and hence also his intelligence, or that man is a product of his environment, is again today very much the subject of lively discussion. Some say that man, whether gifted or not, brings everything with him "from the cradle," others that the environment is all, it endows man or it does not endow him; he cannot become better if conditions do not permit it.

To solve these questions we must seek to discover what happens *before birth*, for the moment of earthly birth is not a suitable starting-point for our considerations, since the individual soul does not, as is often assumed, come into being only in the space of time between procreation and birth.

It is already in existence, and may even have had many earth-lives. But how does the soul come into the earthly body? In no other way than through incarnation! Soon after procreation the human soul with the spirit as core, which is awaiting an incarnation in the beyond, stays in the vicinity of the mother-to-be, and enters the child's body about the middle of pregnancy, whereby the incarnation takes place.

But this does not happen arbitrarily, instead it is strictly governed by the *Creation-Law of Attraction of Homogeneous Species*, which runs *uniformly* through the whole of Creation, and has only been investigated and recognized in its smallest part.

The popular saying aptly describes the Law of Attraction of Homogeneous Species with the words. "Birds of a feather flock together."

In Nature its effect can be observed everywhere. Even in the most minute things it manifests in the union of the same atoms or molecules, as for example with the growth of crystals.

The solution of social questions and problems is also based on the Law of Attraction of Homogeneous Species.

The whole social life of earthly mankind takes place under its compulsion. Whether it concerns a union for religious, professional, economic or political reasons. Always people who in some way are suited to each other will come together.

The ancient peoples still divined the effect of this important Law, and obeyed it unconsciously by separating into professional and cultural classes. Within these, on the basis of man's homogeneous species, each one was able to receive the strength which furthered his natural development.

However the division into *upper, middle* and *lower* classes, which emerged as time went on, was *wrong!* It gave rise on the one hand to envy and hatred, on the other to conceit, arrogance and indolence, and as a final result to class-conflict!

But in reality only the *co-operation of all classes* can offer a harmonious development.

For every class that comes naturally into being is *of full value in its nature*, and has abilities and good qualities which the others do not have; it is a necessary link in the whole.

A lasting social peace and ascent is only guaranteed when the individual classes, *standing side by side*, work together with mutual respect and consideration, thereby complementing one another, and thus forming a powerful, complete national whole. –

Essentially with an incarnation the attraction is caused by the *homogeneity* of the approaching soul and that of the parents, or of another person who is often around the expectant mother.

In this connection both good qualities and weaknesses may form points of attraction.

Thus for example it is conceivable that the mutual attraction occurs through the musical abilities of one parent, which appears outwardly like physical heredity. In this environment the soul concerned is able to develop its homogeneous abilities to the full.

On the other hand, there is the possibility of an alcoholic attracting a soul which has yielded to the same addiction. In this case the homogeneous environment allows the incarnated soul to experience its own weaknesses. That may awaken an ever-increasing repugnance, and finally the firm volition no longer to be a slave to drink, or simply not to take it in the first place; yet the opposite too is possible if man does not see reason, and becomes still more enslaved to his addiction.

In addition there may be some karmaic ties involved with a member of the family, which date from a previous earth-life.

Whatever the reasons for an incarnation, it always takes place in absolute justice.

But one very important factor must yet be taken into account: *the free will!* For with it man determines his personal nature, which is decisive for the attraction into the homogeneous environment.

The free will is peculiar to man, it is inseparably linked with his spiritual nature. To many human beings the free will, the spiritual volition, is unknown, because the volition of the intellect, which results from the activity of the brain, masks the free will, which works out of the free intuitive perception of the spirit.

342

Once man in a free decision has allowed the intellectual volition to gain the upper hand, he bears the responsibility for all the consequences arising therefrom, until he recognizes this unnatural condition and once more surrenders the lead to the free will.

It is just the *free will that does not allow a leveling and equalizing*, because through the free will every human being has attained to a *different* state of development for himself. This explains the fact that men are not equal by nature!

Otherwise they would all have to have the same fingerprints, the same handwriting, or the same faces.

But is there not a contradiction here? On the one hand it is stated that like species attract one another, and then again that according to their state of development men are not equal, but different; how then can they mutually attract one another at incarnation through homogeneity?

The contradiction is cleared up when we learn that man is only a part of the great spiritual species of Creation. Only the many spiritual parts, joined together, result in the *complete* species.

Nevertheless man as a *part-species* is capable of producing *complete, self-contained species* in his intuitive- and thought-forms, through development of the abilities and gifts slumbering within him, through the cultivation of faults and weaknesses, of good and evil characteristics.

They all form the basis for attraction. –

Equality of opportunities is also to be considered from the point of view of free will. Only the *offer* of the opportunities is the same for everyone. Each must use them differently according to his personal decision of will, that is, with the resolution which is based upon his spiritual volition.

During childhood, of course, the free will is dormant. It is replaced by the *imitative instinct*, which is present in every creature. During this time the child is prepared for earthly life through upbringing, school and example. At the same time, in accordance with its development, it must be brought into close contact with Nature, the full experiencing of which is a necessary step for the spiritual unfolding that follows later.

This begins with the attainment of adulthood, when the spirit breaks through at the time of physical maturity. Then the free will becomes active again, which is bound up with full responsibility for further development, the preparation for which had rested until then with the parents or educators.

Man is now able to alter the predisposition he has brought with him at birth, according to his free decision for good or bad.

At the same time, once he becomes an adult, he continues according to his nature to form his ethereal environment, which until then was in a state of inactivity, thus which remained intact for him. But this state of inactivity is not absolute, because a child too can redeem threads of fate and form new ones, although not to the same extent as an adult who stands fully conscious in Creation.

We must not interpret the concepts in question too narrowly. Besides the earthly environment, there is yet a finer material one which is invisible, and which consists among other things of good and evil forms of the deeds, the thoughts and the intuitive perception, including the current threads of fate or karma.

This is the primary and therefore stronger environment, according to which the earthly one has to form.

Supposing that through some circumstance or other (a mistake, accident to the parents, death of the mother during childbirth, adoption, etc.) a child is taken even as a baby from a bad environment into which it has been incarnated, and given a place in strange but better conditions, its ethereal environment will not necessarily change as well. Thus it is quite possible that upon the child's attaining adulthood the connection with its unchanged ethereal environment will be revived, and the old bad nature break through, often causing great disappointment to the educators concerned. –

To conclude our reflections, let the following picture once more arise before us:

The human spirit incarnates into those circumstances which are homogeneous to it, because here especially the Creation-Law of Attraction of Homogeneous Species is decisive.

The environment does not form and mould man, *but man forms the environment*, in that his nature attracts other homogeneous kinds or is attracted by these, as with incarnation. Thus he creates for himself that environment in which he lives, with which he associates or "keeps company." Hence the saying: "A man is known by the company he keeps." We could also say: Our environment is our mirror-image!

This environment can support and further the already moulded homogeneity of a human being by giving him what he needs for his continuing development, whether it be freedom from faults and weaknesses, the awakening of dormant abilities, the kind of upbringing, education, tuition, or generally speaking the whole preparation for earth-life that is suited to this environment.

Therefore it is not possible to become the victim of an environment or of circumstances which man has chosen for himself in accordance with his nature.

For the same reason no man can be the product of his environment, when he is attracted at incarnation as an already finished product, or better expressed, as an individual personality, by this homogeneous environment.

In applying the above explanation, we are now in a position to visualize the following:

If more and more human souls of good volition incarnate into a better environment, the good, with its invisible centers in the beyond, will be so furthered and strengthened that the Darkness encircling the earth will be gradually forced back into those regions to which by virtue of its evil nature it belongs, *there* to give full vent to mutual raging.

This of course presupposes that *men on earth must make a beginning* by devoting themselves solely to the good, the pure and the beautiful, thus creating that more luminous environment in which homogeneous human souls are able to incarnate.

Genuine peace and pure joy would then soon spread their blessings for all time on this so neglected earth.

This is indeed a great hope, but in the present time of utter spiritual decline it is only possible for it still to be fulfilled with the Power and Help of God!

22. IS INTELLIGENCE INBORN?

In the essay "The Environment of Man," it was explained that each man moulds his earthly covering differently from his fellow-man. For at incarnation he chooses not only his environment, his parents, but also his earthly covering, and at the same time determines what its nature will be, in which his psychic state, his ethereal environment with all good and bad threads of karma, has a decisive part.

Hence also the differing conditions of the human brain, which in turn are important for the thoughts, the intellect and the intelligence.

The intellect is made up of the thoughts which arise in the frontal brain. If the intellect is trained, thus cultivated, there follows as a measure of the more or less cultivated intellect the *intelligence*, which embraces for example the reasoning, mathematical and linguistic abilities.

But with earthly death the brain passes away, and the intellect and intelligence perish with it. Neither can be taken over into a new incarnation. What remains intact, however, is the human spirit's experience, gathered over long periods of time in learning to use the perishable brain as an instrument, making it subservient to himself.

This benefits the human spirit at every further incarnation, when once more it has to develop intellect and intelligence in the new earthly body, during which process the quality of the intelligence depends on the physical inheritance which the incarnated human spirit has chosen for itself.

Thus with a normal brain it is possible to produce a useful intellect and develop it into a good intelligence, whereas inherited deficiencies in the brain lead to a lesser intellect and a less well-developed or poor intelligence. Just think for example of the children of alcoholics. Yet even in these cases it is possible to eliminate many a deficiency through a favorable change in the blood-composition, or rather in the blood-radiation.

In contrast to the earthly brain, the more or less pronounced *spiritual* abilities can *not* be *inherited*. They are always peculiar to the human spirit concerned. He can give nothing of them to another, and with each incarnation brings them again to earth as his personal spiritual property.

If parents and children have similar spiritual abilities these have not been inherited, but *attracted* through the *same nature*.

346

Detailed scientific investigations have been carried out on the controversial issue of whether intelligence is inborn, or can be acquired by cultivation. The result was predominantly in favor of heredity. At the same time it emerged that differences in intelligence exist not only among individuals but also between peoples and races.

Another investigation concerned identical twins, who were separated at birth, and had grown up in completely different environments. Later they displayed a similar intelligence, indicating a strong hereditary influence.

With reference to intellect and intelligence, the question of what really *is so special about the human brain* is ever again raised. Brain-research has gained deep insights into the structure of the brain and how it works. Detailed comparisons have been made between the animal and the human brain, but in the structure of the brains no fundamental differences have been found that might have explained the special achievements of the human brain.

The above question immediately brings us nearer to the solution, if we regard the brain as that which it is intended to be in accordance with the order of Creation: as an *instrument*, which serves man as well as animal to move and find their way about on earth.

Accordingly, the difference lies not so much in the brains as in the *invisible core*, which animates the body and makes use of the instrument.

With the animal it is the animistic animal soul, with man it is the spirit, which brings forth the highest achievements from the brain and hence is able to accomplish incomparably more with it than any other living being.

Thus human spirit and animal soul are two fundamentally different species of Creation. If we now speak of the *human soul*, this means the spirit with its finer coverings, which it still bears after laying aside the earthly covering.

Therefore the *special factor* does *not* lie in the *instrument "brain,"* but with those beings who make use of and operate it. However, only man, by virtue of his spirit, is able to make complete use of it.

Yet here too no man is like another. As already explained, this lies in the quality of his brain, which he brings with him as part of his physical inheritance into that environment which he chooses for himself.

Therefore the *social background*, the environment, is *not in a position to make* the differently endowed brains *equal*, or to *cultivate equal intellects*. How the individual person develops his intellect from the fundamental disposition peculiar only to himself is left to his free will alone. Yet the environment can help him in this, and support and further his individual disposition.

But an over-cultivation of the intellect, which arises in the *frontal brain* (large brain), results in a stunting of the soul, as can be seen all over the world today. Thereby the *small brain*, which is an important mediator between the large brain and the soul, is suppressed.

If *in the future* we wish to develop healthy methods of upbringing and progressive educational systems for our children, including a natural schooling of the brains, we must consider the concepts of "environment" and "intelligence" also from the *spiritual* point of view, and give them the place which according to the order of Creation is their due.

When the time is right a form will certainly be created which will further the intellectual maturity in a way that is right according to the Laws in Creation.

Here too there must be no equalizing, but individual furthering in accordance with the saying: *"To each his own!"*

Then there will be no more looking down on another because he shows only poor or moderate intelligence.

In the first place, this outward symptom of deficiency may be balanced by a richer inner life, which is far more valuable, and besides, an upright person will always respect in another his particular state of development at the time, and help him with his further development and upward-striving.

For in this respect no man is like another, and this very *inequality* calls for *mutual regard* among all men of good will, irrespective of their social background and the quality of their intelligence!

23. FREE FROM CONSTRAINT

These words are used when it is to be specially emphasized in a document that the resolution expressed in it was made voluntarily, thus without constraint and uninfluenced.

The opposite then is the free will which is curbed or altogether suppressed by compulsion. That manifests in many ways.

There is forced labor, compulsory education, coercive measures, family constraint, social constraint; people bemoan the force of circumstances, of customs, of habits, or they find themselves hard pressed, and finally bow to the force of tradition.

The individual human being too imposes many a constraint upon himself. He suffers from compulsive brooding, from compulsive movements and compulsive actions.

And who does not know obsessive ideas, psychic and mental processes which again and again crowd in on one, and often cannot be dispelled in spite of one's knowing better, in spite of their absurdity.

Nothing good is contained in all these expressions, because as with so much else man has debased and distorted the concept "constraint."

In reality, *natural constraint* has existed from the very beginning, as a result of the effects in accordance with the Laws of Creation.

However, as man limited his spirit more and more, giving the upper hand to his intellect which is directed solely towards earthly things, he no longer understood the natural constraint which is borne by the warmth of the spirit.

Against it he set the cold, perverted constraint of the intellect, based on feelings of power, threat, extortion and violence.

For thousands of years now men have exercised such a constraint on their fellow-men in the most diverse forms.

Thus one part of mankind always sought to hinder or completely suppress the other in its God-willed development towards spiritual maturity, and to dispute his upward-striving fellow-man's right to his own personality, his own thinking and volition.

Just let us think, for example, of the various forms of slavery, of serfdom, of the inquisition.

Let us recall the tenet of the ecclesiastical territorial system laid down in the Religious Peace of Augsburg in 1555. "He who rules the land determines also the religion" (Cuius regio, eius religio). Subjects who refused to accept the sovereign's religion could be forced to leave the country. Here too a gross transgression of the free spiritual development of the person was demonstrated.

All this has been increasing right up to the present time. Of course in many things the form was changed, but the basic evil remains: an absolute striving after power, together with deliberate suppression of the spiritual and earthly development of one's fellow-man for personal advantage, by making use of all manner of constraints.

In this connection, however, one thing must be home in mind, which lays itself like a heavy burden on those who exercise the wrong constraint, namely the responsibility!

He who compels a person to do something *which is not in accord with the Laws of Creation*, be it through a deed, sufferance or omission, burdens himself with guilt, and must bear the responsibility for what the person concerned thinks and does under the constraint imposed. This begins with the restriction of the outward freedom of action, and increases to the binding of the spirit by force through hypnosis.

But just hypnosis, which is practiced today to an ever greater extent, is regarded by many as harmless. The opposite is the case!

Even consent by the person treated with hypnosis does not absolve the practitioner from the responsibility, because according to the Creation-order free will and responsibility cannot be separated.

During hypnosis, however, the spirit is bound and its free will paralyzed. Consequently the responsibility is logically transferred to the one who induced this binding of the spirit. Responsibility cannot be demanded of a bound, unfree spirit. Hence for everything which the person treated with hypnosis does or fails to do, the responsibility lies solely with the person who practices the hypnosis. –

Thus the unnatural constraint proceeding from the intellect is opposed by the natural constraint of the Laws of Creation, which cannot be overlooked in its effect.

Let us assume that a farmer wishes to sow wheat. He knows exactly that if he wishes to reap wheat as the fruit he may not use rye for it. Thus the Laws of Nature, which after all are only a part of the Laws of Creation, compel him to sow wheat. Accordingly he stands under their constraint and must obey them strictly, submit to them, in order to receive a multiple of *homogeneous* grains for a particular seed-grain.

Then surely it is no longer a great step to the recognition that man too stands under the unalterable constraint of the Laws of Creation, and that he must expect only evil as the reaction for his evil thoughts and deeds, and for good deeds only good. As he sows, so will he always receive as harvest only the *same kind*, whether planting seeds, or thoughts and intuitive perceptions "sown" into finer material substance. Through the incorruptibility of the Laws of Creation, mistakes are impossible.

Now many think that the Law of Sowing and Reaping, also called the Law of Reciprocal Action, applies only to the *earthly* sowing; it could still be surveyed, because the sower knows of his sowing!

However, the Laws of God are not so one-sided that they take effect only on one part of Creation. Like all other Laws of Creation, the Law of Reciprocal Action holds good for the *whole* of Creation, for this side and the beyond, thus also for processes not visible on earth, which include the forming of thoughts and intuitive perceptions. Man must receive the harvest of the seed planted by him, at the moment which inevitably comes about from the working of the Laws of Creation.

He is certainly free in the choice of his decisions, owing to the free will peculiar to his spiritual nature, but the consequences arising from them are in turn subject to the constraint of the Laws of Creation.

Nevertheless man is able to feel free from their constraint as soon as he goes *with* them; just as he does not feel the current of a river if he does not resist it, but swims with it.

That happens only if he obeys these Laws aright and lives with them, if he earnestly strives to recognize the Will of God working in the Laws, and translates it into deed in everyday life in his thoughts, words and actions.

We must therefore distinguish between the natural constraint borne by the Laws of Creation swinging in Divine Love, and the cold, wrong constraint of Luciferian character, with the hall-marks of threat, extortion, oppression and violence.

Man cannot do without natural constraint, he needs it for the unfolding of his spiritual powers; without it he would slacken and become indolent, whether it be the constraint directly wielded by the Laws of Creation, or that exercised by men in the sense of strict and just love! This holds good even for the upbringing of children from birth onwards through the careful application of an outward constraint.

To become free of all wrong constraint is therefore a demand which the Will of God now makes on men, so that their spiritual ascent can begin unhindered.

24. TECHNOLOGY AND CULTURE

Technology, together with civilization, is a product of the earthly intellect, and hence subject to the mark of transience.

Technology is good for the human spirit, and useful in facilitating its earthly path, which it has to tread for the purpose of its spiritual development.

Culture is produced by the *spirit*, and only the works of the *spirit* are lasting.

The more mature the spirit, the more perfect its cultural activity, as it strives to recognize the Laws of God, as well as to achieve and maintain connection with the spiritual currents and prototypes in Creation. Through the recognitions thus gained it furthers and ennobles the earth-life in all its spheres, whether in respect of religious endeavors, style of life, language, social life or art, literature and the law.

Therefore technology must never be raised to the position of ruler. It must be subordinate to the human spirit as the bearer of all culture.

Present-day technology, with its undoubted great development, lacks the spiritual background to prevent its misuse. It has slipped from the control of the spirit. We see the consequences of this in the way technology is used, above all the great inventions: for the destruction and suicide of mankind!

25. MAN, THE AGGRESSIVE CREATURE

The words "aggressive" and "aggression" are very much the subject of discussion at present. They do not have a good ring about them. For they are always associated somehow with malevolent thoughts and actions.

In the search for motives behind man's aggressive behavior there is no agreement. Above all, the question discussed is whether there is a social basis for it or a biological one, that is, whether it is inborn.

Once the cause has been found, then all else can be readily deduced from it.

Inconceivably long ago, man in his spiritual beginnings took over as earthly body the end-form of an animal species which afterwards became extinct. These animals resembled today's anthropoid apes*.

Very gradually, over many earth-lives, man has adapted the animal bodies to human behavior. But at a very early stage he made a grave mistake, out of which arose the hereditary sin. Growing conceited and beginning to strain after power, he attached too great an importance to a physical organ that was meant to be an instrument, and cultivated it out of all natural proportion.

This refers to the large or frontal brain, and the intellect emanating from it, which with the continuous growth of the brain became too powerful, finally suppressing the spirit of man, instead of serving it as an *instrument* as had been intended.

Herein lies the root of *all* evil, the *inherited* sin, in which the *tendency* to an over-developed brain is ever again inherited, and with it the danger of fostering new sins.

Here too lies the *biological* cause of *man's aggressive behavior*, which has nothing to do with an inborn "primeval instinct," and is as old as the hereditary sin. Its ineffaceable traces can be pursued through thousands of years in world-history.

This wrong behavior manifests according to the *degree of over-cultivation* of the brain, and the resulting suppression and limitation of the spirit, in quarrel-someness, hostile behavior to the point of ruthlessness, arbitrariness, use of force, destructiveness, maliciousness and brutality.

Even the very wars waged over thousands of years are irrefutable proof of this; be they religious wars, wars of succession, dynastic wars, civil wars, wars of conquest, and whatever other kinds there may be.

---

* See the essay "The Origin of Man and the Human Races" in Part 1.

This shows clearly enough how little mankind have concerned themselves with their God-given task of building a paradise on earth after the Heavenly prototype!

According to an estimate in 1950, in 3,875 years there have been only 323 years of peace, but 8,250 peace treaties!

All down the ages it has been one continual fluctuation, *one* triumph of injustice following another, then again reciprocally bringing defeat and decline in their wake; because never yet, through war between men or between tribes, peoples and nations, has a truly *just* settlement been brought about that would have produced *true balance* between the warring powers.

War and conflict, as men have waged and still wage them, are always solely the expression of spiritual power turned aside into the Darkness by the dominating intellect, which results in nothing but crime and destruction.

Men no longer know the common struggle *for* the Justice of God, the struggle for *spiritual* recognitions, for obedience to the *Laws of God*. For this they must first grow to maturity again.

But then all the more stubbornly do they fight for earthly influence and power, for earthly possessions, and their willful lust for rulership. But the cause of it lies only in their unnaturally enlarged intellect, which according to the original decree was to be exclusively for *earthly* understanding, as an instrument of the spirit.

If today people speak of the impotence of aggression-research, if they cannot find the source that feeds human aggression, then they should occupy themselves intensively with the maldevelopment of the large brain, for which however not Nature but man himself must be held responsible.

Even the bad environmental influences which man creates for himself, as well as the over-taxing of the brains of young people in upbringing and education, have a disastrous effect on this development. Whether the young are aggressive at all, or to what extent they can become so, depends also on how the brains are trained.

The human *spirit* itself is *not* by nature *aggressive*. Its spiritual nature knows only *up-building and peaceful activity!*

But that does not mean that the love of peace should degenerate into a comfortable and cowardly unwillingness to fight.

Peaceful working demands of earthman the strongest activity, combined with the greatest vigilance in the spiritual and the earthly respect, in order to recognize approaching evil of any kind *in time* and to fight against it in thought and deed. To this in the earthly sphere belong *defense-training*, and the readiness in an emergency to protect and defend one's native land against invading enemies with prudence and courage.

Aggressiveness will not be removed from the world through anti-authoritarian measures, as is taught today, for instance through "free," that is unrestrained indulgence of the sexual instinct, but through *awakening the spirit*, which alone is in a position to bring about a balance, to ennoble the body and its instincts, and so create a pure atmosphere of peace!

26. THE MAJORITY DECIDES

The majority decides, but not only with regard to elections and voting in the earthly realm. In the great Creation-Happening also it determines the way which mankind have to follow in their spiritual development, whether it be good or bad, leading into the Darkness or towards Luminous Heights.

But then it is unfortunately a sad fact that for thousands of years now the majority of mankind have chosen the way into the depth, and in their spiritual decline are drawing ever nearer to the abyss.

They would also drag with them the minority who are seriously striving for the good, if at the last moment God did not separate the evil from the good forever.

We are now in this time of the great sifting and purification carried out by the World-Judge. During this time every human spirit must reap what it itself has sown, whether it be good or bad works (Matthew 25,32 and Rev. 22,12).

Jesus prophesied about this End-Time. His words concerning it have been handed down to us by the Evangelists. Likewise John in his Revelation described the time of the great World Judgment, and the Cosmic Turning-Point which belongs to it.

For a long time man has allowed his intellect, which emanates from the perishable brain, to rule instead of his spirit. Through this he has been caught in the earthly-material, and separated himself from God.

But now, amid great upheavals and changes, the time of absolute dominion of the intellect is coming to an end. Regarded as a whole it has been an oppressive time, because for thousands of years mankind had to follow *that* way which was determined by the majority: the way into the Darkness, the road of hopelessness, of force, of oppression, of degradation.

This dark, lost majority, which has poisoned the whole life of men, will cease to exist in the World Judgment, as is proclaimed in the Revelation of John!

Then is the way clear for those human beings who are striving towards the Light. In the coming thousand-year Kingdom of Peace on earth God grants them the opportunity to continue and complete their spiritual ascent unhindered at last!

During these upheavals and changes the stars in their positions relative to one another play a decisive part. With their radiations they prepare the ways into the earthly, and loosen the soil for the new spiritual seed!

356

27. THE FUTURE KINGDOM OF PEACE

Even though we are to live in the present, we do at times give some thought to the future. Anyone for once rather depressed by the ever-worsening state of confusion on earth asks himself what shape the future will take. Is it still possible at all to emerge from these sad conditions of the present time? True, people speak of a Kingdom of Peace that is to come one day, but what will it be like in such a Kingdom?

There is a promising future for all men who still retain within them a spark of longing for the Light; it is based on the no longer distant earthly Kingdom of Peace of a thousand years, whether men are to experience this in their present earthly garb, in a later reincarnation, or from the beyond.

In this Kingdom of Peace, or Kingdom of God, it is a question of adjusting the earthly laws, as indeed the whole of earth-life, to the Laws of God in Creation, thus to the Laws of Creation, to which the Laws of Nature also belong. Until now that has not been the case, as is proved by the depressing state of affairs.

In the new Kingdom of God, man will indeed retain his free will but under the heightened radiation-pressure he can no longer use it for evil thoughts and actions without at the same time suffering instant harm. That is to say, the reciprocal action sets in at once and he must immediately reap what he has sown, whereas hitherto there have often been long time-lapses between spiritual seed and harvest.

Therefore man as crown of Creation, or more precisely as ruler in the Material World of Subsequent Creation, has to learn again to recognize and to obey the Laws of his God.

Hence he must investigate them thoroughly in order to find in them the Will of God, to Which he must adjust his whole earth-life, be it legislation, jurisdiction, art, education, science, public health or commerce, industry, technology, finance or military affairs.

The resultant understanding of the Creation-Knowledge will be taught above all in the schools, so that already children can grow up in this Knowledge, and become conscious of the fact that they are only *creatures,* who must submit to the Will of the Creator.

In the new Kingdom man must also make a fundamental change in his social order, subjugating it to the order of Creation. This means that a division of earthmen into definite homogeneous groups will take place, as was customary with ancient peoples. There were castes of priests, doctors, warriors, artists, merchants, craftsmen and so on.

In those days men still had some idea of the *Creation-Law of Attraction of Homogeneous Species* applicable here, which has remained alive in the popular saying "Birds of a feather flock together." At the same time this is an example of how earth-life is to be adjusted to the Laws of Creation.

Therefore each will live in the environment that corresponds with his nature, where he is at home among his kind, and is able to continue his harmonious development in joint swinging.*

All this in turn requires a healthy leadership, which means that there must be personalities who have genuine qualities of leadership, to which belong above all a sense of justice and exemplary conduct.

It is a fundamental requirement in Creation that some should lead others. As long as there is development, there must be leaders, who in each case are on a higher step, thus who have greater experience than those to be led, and who carry out their task with outstanding ability. They will always be chosen and appointed from a place above them, which also is only a link in that chain of guidance which reaches from the earth up into the highest spiritual heights.

Thus later too, each people will again receive the leader chosen from "Above," that is from the Spiritual, under whose leadership it can develop beauty and its own culture to the highest flowering.

Now if those to be led choose their leader themselves, as is common practice for example with the democratic party-systems, this does not accord with the Laws of Creation and is of great disadvantage to the earthly and spiritual development of men. A glimpse into these systems, with their continual dissensions and their perpetual party squabbles and strife, shows this clearly enough!

On the other hand it can be understood that the democratic form of government more or less represents an inevitable development, after all kinds of rulers with undivided sovereignty had so misused their power over thousands of years that belief in the just discharge of such a high office was lost. Often too the expression "by the grace of God" was merely a formality, when these very words should really have been a pledge to pay special heed to the Laws of God!

However, the foundations of the new forms of government will no longer be the laws and systems devised by men but the Laws of God. They must be recognized and adhered

---

* See also "A Glimpse into the Future" in Part 1.

358

to by individuals, by the family and by governments, thus in private and public life.

Once the *spiritual* welfare in human development is of paramount importance, the class-conflict will also cease, because each one is in the place which through his birth he has chosen for himself, in which he is able to develop psychically and in the earthly sense to an individual personality.

In this connection a very important new way of thinking arises, which will also give a new meaning to the expressions connected with the word "social": that classes which form *naturally* stand *not below and above one another* but *side by side*, in joint working for a true humanity.

For all men who are united in these classes or castes, however varied they may be in their earthly level of education, have a common origin and hence also a *common goal*: The *Paradise of man* in the Realm of the Eternal Spiritual!

And in the coming Kingdom of Peace the goal is to spread a reflection of the Heavenly Paradise on earth. It is to become a Kingdom of True Peace, which can only arise if in future men live strictly in accordance with the Divine Laws in Creation, which they will then have recognized.

All this may still be regarded now as an impossible happening; but it is good and beneficial to begin already to occupy oneself with it in thought. For thoughts too have an effect, and open ways into the new time, which under the effect of new Cosmic radiations is powerfully announcing itself!

28. TEACHERS OF MANKIND

The earth is a great school for the human spirits. Here they have to develop to that stage of consciousness which is decisive for admittance to Paradise, and is to be designated the stage of consciousness of oneself.

This development comprises long periods of time, and cannot be completed in *one* earth-life.

The human spirit must return to the earth a number of times, and incarnate in human bodies, until it has reached the degree of spiritual maturity and the inner purity which brings with it a final turning-away from the sway of the earth, and a continuing ascent into Luminous Heights.

In a school there are teachers who educate, further and guide the pupils to the next higher level in the school.

In the same way, for earthmen in the great school of humanity there were teachers who were meant to show them the way to the Truth as the final goal.

Truth is eternal and unchangeable, it remains ever the same, and is recognizable to us in the Laws of Creation, including the Laws of Nature, which are equally unchangeable. The recognition of these adamantine Laws leads without deviation to God, because His Will is expressed in them, because through them we learn what God wills. To investigate and to obey this Will is the highest task of man. If we adjust ourselves to the Will we fare well, and become joyful and happy

All this was known to the teachers of mankind like Moses and the Prophets, Zoroaster, Lao-Tse, Buddha and Mohammed, whom God sent to the different peoples on earth. They were lovingly and carefully prepared for it in Luminous Realms.

In faithful fulfillment of their task, they sought to guide the people of their races, according to the prevailing degree of soul-maturity, step by step towards the Light, to teach them how they must live in accordance with the Laws of God, so that at the end of the earthly school the spiritual striving of the peoples could have been united into one *single acknowledgement of Divine Truth.*

All of these, and others besides, were Forerunners of the Truth, for the Truth-Bringer Who is promised for the time of the present great Cosmic Turning-Point. Even the Son of God, Jesus, referred to this Truth-Bringer, Who brings after Him the World Judgment.

For even the school of humanity on earth comes to an end one day; there is a leaving-examination for the human spirit, who must prove that he has developed aright the abilities which God bestowed upon him.

We are now in this time of the great spiritual examination, and the examination-results are shattering, as the abundance of ever-accumulating hopeless events all over the earth clearly shows!

What has become of the former teachings of God? Hardly anything still remains of their original content; it has been adulterated, distorted and misused. Only isolated grains of truth are still to be found among confusing, rigid dogmas. Even the Message of the Son of God has been misunderstood, and wrongly interpreted in many respects.

Just let a picture arise before us in spirit:

We behold the Temple of Truth, the Grail Temple with the equal-armed Grail Cross on the Dome, surrounded by smaller side-temples with the corresponding symbols on their domes. They embody the spiritual teachings of past millennia, as for example the teachings of Zoroaster, Lao-Tse, Buddha, Mohammed, of Judaism and of Christianity.

The symbols of some teachings have been preserved up to the present time.

Thus the lotus-flower for Buddhism. In its loveliness and purity the opening flower points men to the striving for purity and to firm connection with the stream of life, just as the lotus-flower is naturally rooted in the bed of the flowing water.

For Islam the sacred symbol is the crescent moon.

Mohammed had a vision: he beheld a gracious supra-earthly picture, the Queen of Heaven (not the mother of Jesus) standing on a crescent moon.

Thus he found the symbol of Islam, linked with the obligation to honor women at all times and to support them in their high task, which they have to fulfil in the service of the Most High. They stand under the protection of the Queen of Heaven, Who is the ideal for all womanhood in Creation!

Judaism has the Star of David as the sacred symbol of belief. It consists of two triangles, one inside the other; one with its apex upwards, the other with its apex downwards. The two triangles are to symbolize the inseparable connection between the visible and the invisible world.

For Christianity, however, Christ's cross of suffering will be transformed into the Sword of Justice in the Judgment, through the lengthening of the lower arm of the Grail Cross!

All teachings were pure in their origin. Had men kept them pure, had they not in the course of thousands of years distorted them according to their ideas or used them for selfish ends, these individual temples would today be only *transit temples* to the *one Temple of the Truth!*

But as it was, all the paths which the Divine teachings pointed out came to an end in the temple of the particular religion. They do not lead on to the Temple of Truth, because through their own guilt men keep the gates to the thoroughfares closed! –

Today the religions which have arisen out of these teachings actually appear often full of contradictions, and even conflicting in their creeds. Moreover, for a long time now people of different faiths have been fighting each other, so that a *uniform striving for the Truth* and its recognition cannot be spoken of!

It is not enough for the *one* God to be acknowledged by all; the Truth which God has anchored in His Laws of Creation must also be recognized. That demands an earnest striving for recognition of these Laws, an objective examination of one's own dogmas in accordance with these Laws, and finally the courage to make the necessary corrections!

All this is now being brought about through the radiations of the Cosmic Turning-Point, so that the ring of the great evolution of mankind can close for Light-seeking men in the recognition of Divine Truth.

In the same way as the Light-Happening of this Cosmic Turning-Point has already caused the teachings then willed by God to come into being once more, undistorted, in word and script, just as they were once given to men by their teachers.

From past millennia and past eras, picture follows upon picture of spiritual and earthly happening, once more the paths are shown which were to have led *through* the individual temples, to unite in the Dome of Light at the time of the Cosmic Turning-Point!

ALPHABETICAL INDEX

GLOSSARY

Explanation
I = The World, as it could be!
II = Knowledge for the World of Tomorrow!
III = What lies behind it ...!
IV = A Gate Opens
The figure following the Roman numeral shows the number of the lecture.

The author Herbert Vollmann has drawn his knowledge from the Work:

IN THE LIGHT OF TRUTH: THE GRAIL MESSAGE
by
ABD-RU-SHIN

The *Grail Message* is a special book which clearly answers the unsolved problems of human existence. The vast knowledge mediated in its pages leads the earnestly-seeking reader — who weighs and examines objectively — out of all the chaos of the present-day confusion and distortion, to clear recognitions.

This book commands attention by its forceful language, by the clarity of its thoughts and by the setting right of distorted concepts, unmistakably and sometimes severely but irrefutably explained.

The Laws in which the entire Creation came into being and exists are plainly set forth and man's responsibility before God and his fellow-men is revealed and explained. The reader who opens himself to these recognitions will experience the indestructible inner security of his own personality restored.

Leather edition, three volumes combined
ISBN 3-87860-150-6
5.5" x 7.75"
1,061 pages

Linen edition, three volumes combined
ISBN 1-57461-006-6
5.5" x 8.5"
1,062 pages

Paper edition, three volume boxed set
ISBN 1-57461-003-1
6" x 9"
1,079 pages

Paper edition, Volume I only
ISBN 1-57461-000-7
6" x 9"
210 pages

Original edition: German
Translations available in:
Arabic, Czech, Dutch, English, Estonian, French, Hungarian,
Italian, Mandarin Chinese, Portuguese, Rumanian,
Russian, Slovak, Spanish

For more information about this work, visit www.GrailMessage.com

Other Titles from Grail Foundation Press

THE TEN COMMANDMENTS OF GOD & THE LORD'S PRAYER
by Abd-ru-shin

*

LAO-TSE
Life & Work of the Forerunner in China

*

BUDDHA
Life & Work of the Forerunner in India

*

ZOROASTER
Life & Work of the Forerunner in Persia

*

EPHESUS
Life & Work of the Forerunner Hjalfdar in Prehistoric Times

*

PAST ERAS AWAKEN, VOLUME I
from the lives of Krishna, Nahome, & Cassandra, Mary of Magdala

*

PAST ERAS AWAKEN, VOLUME II
from the lives and times of Atlantis, the Incas, John the Baptist & Jesus

*

PAST ERAS AWAKEN, VOLUME III
*from the lives and times of Ancient Egypt, Lucifer, Nemare, Amenophis, Nefertiti,
Tut-ench-amon, Jesus & the Apostles*

*

FROM PAST MILLENNIA
from the lives of Moses, The life of Abd-ru-shin on Earth, Mary & The life of Jesus on Earth

*

The Life-Cycle Trilogy by Dr. Richard Steinpach:

WHY WAS I BORN? BRIDGING BIRTH & JUSTICE

HOW CAN GOD ALLOW SUCH THINGS?

WHY WE LIVE AFTER DEATH?

*

*Available through the book trade
Or directly from the Publisher*

*Grail Foundation Press
P.O. Box 45
Gambier, Ohio 43022
Tel: 1-800-427-9217, e-mail: info@gfp.com
www.GrailMessage.com*

For more information, contact:

AMERICA:
GRAIL MOVEMENT OF AMERICA
2081 Partridge Lane
Binghamton, New York 13903 USA
Tel: ++1.607.765.6981, Fax: ++1.734.468.4220
e-mail: info@gfp.com

AUSTRALIA:
GRAIL MOVEMENT IN AUSTRALIA
Kalorama Chalet, 9 Falls Road, Kalorama
Vic. 3766, Australia
Tel: ++61.3.9728.1185, Fax: ++ 61.3.9728.1173
e-mail: hugo@imagineering.net.au

CANADA:
GRAIL MOVEMENT IN CANADA
La Pineraie, Lac Simon
Chénéville, Prov. Québec, JOV IEO Canada
Tel: ++1.819.428.7001, Fax: ++1.819.428.2642
e-mail: fdgc@sympatico.ca

GREAT BRITAIN:
GRAIL MESSAGE FOUNDATION
P.O. Box 5181
Milton Keynes, MK2 3ZG, Great Britain
Tel: ++44.1908.274256, Fax: ++44.1908.647821
e-mail: gralgb@aol.com

NEW ZEALAND:
GRAIL MOVEMENT IN NEW ZEALAND
P.O. Box 32-006, Devonport
Auckland 9, New Zealand
Tel: ++64.4450014, Fax: ++64.9.4451707
e-mail: v.b.brown.1@xtra.co.nz

NIGERIA:
GRAIL MOVEMENT IN NIGERIA
1/11 Commercial Avenue, Yaba-Lagos
e-mail: suun@infoweb.abs.net

THAILAND:
MR. ULF LAUTERBACH
169/2 Moo 10, Bna Pa, Kaeng Khoi,
18110 Saraburi, Thailand
Tel: ++66.36.244.898, Fax: ++66.36.244.675
e-mail: grail_th@hotmail.com

GERMANY:
STIFTUNG GRALSBOTSCHAFT
Schuckertstrasse 8, 71254 Ditzingen, Germany
Tel: ++07156.5096, Fax: ++07156.18663
e-mail: info@gral.de

Or visit us on the web: www.GrailMessage.com